The Image of God

THE IMAGE OF GOD

Gender Models
in Judaeo-Christian Tradition

Edited by
Kari Elisabeth Børresen

Fortress Press
Minneapolis

THE IMAGE OF GOD
Gender Models in Judaeo-Christian Tradition

First Fortress Press edition, 1995.
First published under the title *Image of God and Gender Models in Judaeo-Christian Tradition* by Solum Forlag in 1991.

Interior design: The HK Scriptorium, Inc.
Cover design: Brad Norr
Cover art: *Eve's Apple*, Bronze Sculpture, © 1994 Edwina Sandys

Library of Congress Cataloging-in-Publication Data

Image of God and gender models in Judaeo-Christian Tradition
    The image of God : gender models in Judaeo-Christian tradition / edited by Kari Elisabeth Børresen.
        p.   cm.
    Originally published: The image of God and gender models in Judaeo-Christian tradition. Oslo : Solum Forlag, 1991.
    Includes bibliographical references.
    ISBN 0-8006-2951-5 (alk. paper)
    1. Image of God—Biblical teaching.   2. Image of God—History of doctrines.   3. Sex—Religious aspects.   4. Woman (Theology)
    I. Børresen, Kari Elisabeth.
    BS652.I43   1995
    233'.5—dc20   95-24827
                                                                        CIP

Manufactured in the U.S.A.   AF 1-2951
99   98   97   96   95   1   2   3   4   5   6   7   8   9

Publisher's Note

The text of the book published in Norway by Solum Verlag
has been taken over with a few additions and corrections of
typographical errors only. Because of the diverse origins of the
contributors, inconsistencies remain. Our aim was to make this
important content available to readers at the lowest possible
cost.

Fortress Press

Contents

1
INTRODUCTION: *IMAGO DEI* AS INCULTURATED DOCTRINE

∽ Kari Elisabeth Børresen

The purpose of this international, interdisciplinary, and interdenominational collection of articles on image of God and gender models is to illustrate the *gradual* inclusion of women in *fully* human God-likeness, as realized by interpretation of Scripture through Christian tradition.

The idea of *imago Dei* is fundamental in theological anthropology, being a primary example of interaction between the concept of God and the definition of humanity. Nevertheless, the Judaeo-Christian doctrine of God-likeness has hitherto only sporadically been analyzed with explicit reference to male and female gender. Using human genderedness as the main analytical category, in the sense of combined biologically given and socio-culturally shaped female and male existence, this volume therefore presents pioneering research.

Traditional Christian gender models are here traced from late antiquity, through the Middle Ages, and to the Reformation. These major elements of historical theology are covered in the present collection: Genesis creation texts, early Jewish religion, Pauline letters, early Christian mainstream and fringe material, patristic, early medieval and scholastic authors, Luther and Calvin. A concluding essay pursues the formation of Christian God-language into this century, focusing on its significance for feminist hermeneutics.

Phyllis A. Bird (Methodist) treats God-likeness and sexual distinction in Genesis 1–2. She makes clear that "male and female he created them" in Gen. 1:27b is linked to the fertility blessing that follows in Gen. 1:28 and not to the preceding image text of Gen. 1:26-27a. "Male and female" refers to the bisexuality that humans share with animals and is consequently unrelated to God's image.

From the history-of-religion perspective Anders Hultgård (Lutheran) explores the androcentric impact of the first man, Adam, representing collec-

1

tive humanity. He finds that in early Jewish sources women are implicitly regarded as not being God-like. The presupposed and basic incompatibility of Godhead and femaleness is manifested in sacrificial worship. Here women are segregated and placed with children and proselytes. Even the animal victims are predominantly male.

Lone Fatum (Lutheran) presents a thorough analysis of Pauline texts, in particular 1 Cor. 11:7 and Gal. 3:28, from a feminist perspective. She demonstrates that Paul's androcentric dualism is counterproductive. Affirming that men exclusively share *imago Dei* in the creational order, Paul defines women's redemptive equivalence in terms of *estrangement* from female inferiority: either they must strive for perfect manhood in Christ or they must become asexual.

These stratagems of including women in a religious framework where womanhood is either absent or alien are further surveyed in both central and marginal Christian sources. Giulia Sfameni Gasparro (Catholic) clarifies how various encratite concepts of original human perfection as being all-male or presexual consider femaleness or sexual differentiation *as cause of* or *resulting* from the first sin. She shows that the correlated split between spiritual God-likeness and gendered corporality remained fundamental in so-called orthodox doctrine, as exemplified by the leading Greek church father, Gregory of Nyssa.

Kari Vogt (Catholic) analyzes the redemptive transformation of women into Christ-like perfect manhood, a theme found more frequently in Christian than in Gnostic texts. She notes that the metaphor of becoming male is applied also by women, e.g., the Desert Mother Amma Sarra.

From the third century onward, women's salvational God-likeness is *backdated* to creation, by connecting the sexual distinction of Gen. 1:27b to the preceding image text of Gen. 1:26-27a. Kari Elisabeth Børresen (Catholic) outlines this innovative exegesis, which was initiated by Clement of Alexandria and elaborated by the leading Latin church father, Augustine. Galatians 3:28 is here invoked in the sense of sexless *imago Dei*, attributable to women *in spite of* creational gender hierarchy. Augustine neutralized 1 Cor. 11:7 by allegorical interpretation, depicting asexual God-likeness in andromorphic disguise. On the contrary, Antiochene exegesis and Ambrosiaster explicitly invoke Paul in order to *exclude* women from being created in God's image, a privilege defined as male dominion or men's imitation of divine priority. Børresen demonstrates that this corroboration of women's subordinate status survives in early medieval exegesis, by being falsely attributed to Ambrose and Augustine and as a result being incorporated in canon law. When scholastic anthropology repeats Augustine's gender-free *imago Dei*, the pseudo-Augustinian idea of male precedence remains influential and is used in arguments against women's ordination to the priesthood.

Reformation doctrine does not modify the norm of creational gender hierarchy in church and society. Jane Dempsey Douglass (Presbyterian) surveys women's God-likeness as interpreted by Luther and Calvin. She notes that Luther postulates Eve's equality in paradise but invokes her punishment in Gen. 3:16 to strengthen female subjection as ordained by God. Calvin resolves the contradiction between inclusive exegesis of Gen. 1:26-27b and literal affirming of 1 Cor. 11:7 by restricting Paul's judgment of women's secondary status to the realm of human governance.

In her hermeneutical note, Phyllis Bird states that the indisputably man-centered perspective of the creation accounts does not hinder a subsequent inclusive understanding of human God-likeness. From the viewpoint of the present she locates Genesis 1-2 within an ongoing conversation of canonical, postcanonical, and contemporary partners. The ensuing gradual *humanization* of *imago Dei* is precisely displayed by this collective volume and is recapitulated up to our time by Rosemary Radford Ruether (Catholic). The patristic invention of women's creational God-likeness, affirmed by means of asexual privilege in andromorphic disguise, is in the twentieth century followed by another *innovative* exegesis: both women and men are now considered God-like *qua* male or female persons. Fully human status in terms of complete religious capability is no longer reserved for exemplary theomorphic men or spiritually God-like women.

With Ruether I find it important to emphasize the resulting *incoherence* between this new holistic *imago Dei*, where the previous male or genderless definitions are relinquished, and the still-prevailing manlike or metasexual God-language. In Greek Orthodox and Roman Catholic doctrine and symbolism, this enduring incompatibility between Godhead and femaleness is most clearly upheld in christology and ecclesiology. Surviving from the early thought of *imago Dei* as exclusively male, traditional typology transposes God-willed gender hierarchy from creation to the redemptive order. In nuptial imagery God-like Adam prefigures Christ, who as new Adam and divine Redeemer is incarnated in perfect manhood. The ancillary role of *non*-theomorphic Eve is here reenacted by the church or Mary as new Eve, representing dependent and consequently womanlike humanity. It is essential to keep in mind that this theological gender play remains the basic doctrinal hindrance for women's ordination to the priesthood in the non-Protestant majority of Christendom.

When present theological anthropology defines female human beings as fully God-like, such accommodation to post-patriarchal culture in western

Europe and North America builds on the previous patristic insertion of women in creational *imago Dei.*[1] I consider this theological inculturation to be part of the continuous revelatory interplay between God and humanity, acted out in shifting historical contexts. The reforming cardinal of the Renaissance, Nicolaus Cusanus, perceived the temporal unfolding (*explicatio*) of God's eternal enfolding (*complicatio*) in terms of incarnated revelation, centered in Christ and realized in a manner understandable for human beings (*humano modo*).[2] From a feminist standpoint, this human mode is problematic in the sense of having been based on *men's* experience of God and therefore having been formulated in male-gendered God-language. The few female writings that have survived in Christian tradition were largely controlled, selected, and transmitted by clerical authority.[3]

In my opinion, a fruitful and healthy theology, *sana doctrina,* must be inspired by the Roman Catholic understanding of the coherence between Scripture and tradition as parts of an ongoing revelation. Centered in Christ, this concept of *revelatio continua* must be enriched by the Greek Orthodox belief in the Holy Spirit as acting through human history. Both visions presuppose holistic anthropology in the sense that creation is not totally alienated from God in consequence of the fall, and that redemption is fulfilled by divine and human interaction. The Greek church fathers' doctrine of Christ's incarnated and resurrected humanity as the prerequisite for redemptional human wholeness (*theosis*) is of exemplary value for feminist God-language. Stripped of its connotations of perfect manhood or sexless excellence, this patristic anthropology can serve to bridge the persistent gulf between Godhead and womanhood, conforming to the present holistic definition of human God-likeness. When both women and men are understood to be theomorphic, God can be described by both male and female metaphors. Only when verbalized in terms of both women's and men's equivalent gendered experience does theology become a fully human discourse.

Notes

1. Kari Elisabeth Børresen, "In defence of Augustine: how *femina* is *homo.*" In *Collectanea Augustiniana,* edited by B. Bruning, M. Lamberigts, J. Van Houtem, Mélanges T. J. van Bavel (Louvain, 1990) 411–28.
2. Kari Elisabeth Børresen, *Nicolaus Cusanus's dialoge* De pace fidei: *Om trosfreden* (Oslo, 1983).
3. Kari Elisabeth Børresen, "Women's Studies of the Christian Tradition." In *Contemporary Philosophy,* edited by G. Fløistad and R. Klibansky, A new survey 6. Philosophy and Science in the Middle Ages, part 2. (Dordrecht-Boston-London, 1990) 901–1001.

2
SEXUAL DIFFERENTIATION
AND DIVINE IMAGE
IN THE GENESIS CREATION TEXTS[1]

∾ Phyllis A. Bird

Traditional interpretation of Genesis 1–3 combined elements of two creation accounts (1:1–2:4a and 2:4b–3:24) to articulate a view of human origins, human nature, and the relationship of the sexes which ignored the distinct language, dynamics and intention of the two sources. Modern biblical scholarship has re-exposed, and sharpened, the long-noted tension between the juxtaposed accounts, linking the two versions to larger literary complexes within the Pentateuch.[2] By giving attention to the stylistic and theological differences between the two accounts and identifying them with different historico-religious settings and purposes, modern critical scholarship has opened the way to a re-union of the texts, as sources for theological anthropology, that honors and preserves the peculiar contributions of each.

In this article primary attention is directed to the Priestly (P) account in Gen 1:1–2:4a, which introduces the distinctive notion of the divine image in human creation. The Yahwistic (J) account in Gen 2:4b–3:24 is given summary analysis for its contrasting and complementary view of sexual differentiation and its notion of a distortion of the original relationship of the sexes.

The critical question addressed to the Priestly account concerns the relationship of sexual distinction to the divine image. The answer to that question requires attention to the structure of the larger account and to the meaning and function of the two parallel statements (27a and 27b) within it. My argument, briefly stated, is as follows. Gen 1:27 may not be isolated, or interpreted in relation to vs. 26 alone, but must be understood within the unit constituted by vss. 26–28. Within that unit, vss. 27–28 form an expanded parallel to vs. 26 in which 27b is a plus, dependent upon and preparatory to the *following* statement in vs. 28 and dictated by the juxtaposition in vss. 27–28 of the themes of divine likeness and sexual reproduction. The specification of human sexual distinction and its position in the text are determined by the sequence of themes within the account and by the overall structure of announcement and execution report within the chapter. The result of my analysis is to dissociate the word of sexual distinction, sp. sexuality, from the idea of the divine image—and from the theme of dominion—and to associate it with the more general theme of fertility or sustainability of the created order, which runs through the entire Priestly narrative of creation.[3]

The Priestly Account of Creation:
Overall Structure and Themes[4]

The Priestly account of creation is an exceedingly compressed account, marked by a repetitive structure of announcement and execution report ("Wortbericht" and "Tatbericht"). But it is also comprehensive in its intention and design, attempting to identify, locate and describe in their essential features all of the primary elements and orders of creation. The author has chosen his terms with care, from names to descriptive statements. As Gerhard von Rad has rightly emphasized, only what is essential is here; nothing is accidental or included merely because it stood in the received tradition (1961:45). Though bound in significant measure to the items, order and conception of process found in older creation accounts of the ancient Near East and circulating in Israelite tradition, the Priestly author has selected from the tradition and shaped it to carry his own message. And though the history of the Priestly composition is itself complex, the final design and wording is governed by a unified conception and purpose and the account set as the lead statement in a larger historico-theological work. Thus every assertion and every formulation in this highly compact and selective account warrants careful attention and questioning with regard to its origin and meaning.

Because descriptive statements are so limited in P's account, the two that amplify the report of *adam*'s creation are immediately striking:

(27aβ) *běṣelem ʾělōhîm bārāʾ ʾōtô*
(27b)   *zākār ûněqēbâ bārāʾ ʾōtām*

(27aβ) in the image of God he created him;
(27b)   male and female he created them.

The parallel construction invites the question of how the two clauses are related. But other questions impose as well. Why does 27aβ repeat the content of 27aα? What is the relationship of vs. 27 to vss. 26 and 28? And why of all that might be said about *adam* does the author choose to emphasize the bi-sexual nature of the species, using language employed elsewhere by P to characterize the animal orders but omitted from their description in Genesis 1? The answer to all of these questions lies in an analysis of the structure of vss. 26–28 as a whole and of the place and function of these verses within the overall structure of Gen 1:1–2:4a and the larger Priestly work.[5]

The primary concerns of the Priestly creation account are two: (1) to emphasize the dependence of all of creation on God—made explicit in the framing structure that marks each stage of creation: "God said . . . and it was so," and (2) to describe the order established within creation—as an order determined by God, from the beginning. Secondary or subordinate concerns are evident in emphasis on the permanence, or maintenance, of the created cosmos and its orders, and in anticipation of the history that will be played out within it, a history centering upon *adam* and initiated in the final, climactic word of creation and blessing.

> (26) *wayyōʾmer ʾĕlōhîm*
>   *naʿăśeh ʾādām bĕṣalmēnû kidmûtēnû*
>   *wĕyirdû bidgat hayyām ûbĕʿôp haššāmayim*
>   *ûbabbĕhēmâ ûbĕkol-hāʾāreṣ*
>   *ûbĕkol-hāremeś hārōmeś ʿal-hāʾāreṣ*
> (27) *wayyibrāʾ ʾĕlōhîm ʾet-hāʾādām bĕṣalmô*
>   *bĕṣelem ʾĕlōhîm bārāʾ ʾōtô*
>   *zākār ûnĕqēbâ bārāʾ ʾōtām*
> (28) *wayĕbārek ʾōtām ʾĕlōhîm*
>   *wayyōʾmer lāhem ʾĕlōhîm*
>   *pĕrû ûrĕbû ûmilʾû ʾet-hāʾāreṣ wĕkibšūhā*
>   *ûrĕdû bidgat hayyām ûbĕʿôp haššāmayim*
>   *ûbĕkol-ḥayyâ hārōmeśet ʿal-hāʾāreṣ*[6]

(26) And God said:
> "Let us make *adam* in our image, according to our likeness,
> and let them have dominion over the fish of the sea
> and the birds of the air,
> and the cattle and all the earth
> and everything that creeps upon the earth."

(27) And God created *adam* in his image,
> in the image of God he created him;
> male and female he created them.

(28) And God blessed them,
and God said to them:
"Be fruitful and multiply and fill the earth and subdue it,
and have dominion over the fish of the sea and
the birds of the air,
and every living creature that creeps upon the earth."

Image and Dominion

The order described in Genesis 1 is progressive, structured as a two-fold movement oriented toward the earth and culminating in *adam* (Anderson 1977:154-59). The crowning species in this account is defined, uniquely, in terms of a dual relationship or identity, a relationship to God and to co-inhabitants of earth. Humanity, according to this statement, is created "like God"[7] and with dominion over other creatures. The two statements of vs. 26 must be understood in conjunction; in P's construction they belong to a single thought complex. Nature or design in creation is related to function and status, or position: the firmament is to divide the waters, the luminaries are to give light (and in their specific identity as planets, to mark time and seasons, etc.), and humankind is to rule over the realm of creatures.[8] The presupposition and prerequisite for this rule is the divine stamp which sets this creature apart from all the rest, identifying *adam* as God's own special representative, not simply by designation (command), but by design (nature or constitution)—i.e., as a representation of God.[9] The notion of the divine image serves here to validate and explain the special status and role of *adam* among the creatures.

The adverbial modifier *bĕṣelem-*, further qualified by *kidmût-* in vs. 26 describes a correspondence of being, a resemblance—not a relationship nor an identity, even partial identity.[10] And it is a resemblance described in terms of form, not of character or substance (Humbert 1940; Koehler 1948).[11] *Ṣelem* as a metaphor for likeness is concrete, formal, holistic—and "empty," lacking specific content, and thus an ideal term for P, who employs it with changing connotations in changing contexts (cf. 5:1, 3 and 9:6). Here, in its primary and initial use, its content or implications must be spelled out, and that is the contribution of *wĕyirdû* ("let them have dominion"). The *ṣelem* *ʾĕlōhîm* in Genesis 1 is, accordingly, a royal designation, the precondition or requisite for rule.[12]

While the expression of Genesis 1 is unique, drawing upon the language of Mesopotamian (-Canaanite) royal theology in its employment of the term *ṣelem*, the idea of the royal status of *adam* is not. It is prominent in Psalm 8, where the language of coronation is combined with the language of dominion to describe the distinctive status and role of humanity in creation. Thus *selem:* "image" and *RDH:* "to have dominion" must be understood as belonging to a single complex of ideas and describing a sequence of thought which parallels exactly the two-fold statement of Psalm 8.

The Unique Creature

The special interest of God in this culminating act of creation and ordering is registered at a grammatical and lexical level by a shift in the word of announcement from intransitive verbal forms or verbs of generation to an active-transitive verb, and from third person to first person speech. The verb *ʿāśâ:* "make," which has heretofore been used only in the execution reports, to emphasize the divine activity, is now taken up into the announcement itself. The becoming of *adam* is inconceivable apart from God's own direct action and involvement; the willing of this creation requires divine commitment.

The structure of the final word also differs from that of the words that describe the other orders of living things. For them no purpose or function is announced or reported. And each order is referred to an already existing element of earth (land and water) as its locus and proximate source. In contrast, *adam* is assigned a function or task by the very word of announcement, a task defined in relation to the other creatures and to the earth, which is its habitat but not its source. Humanity is also distinguished from other orders of life by its direct and unmediated dependence upon God. For *adam*, habitat is neither source of life nor source of identity.

The Wortbericht emphasizes the exalted, isolated position of *adam* within the created order, as one uniquely identified with God and charged by God with dominion over the creatures. Yet the full account insists that *adam* is also creature, sharing both habitat and constitution with the other orders of animal life. The creation of humankind stands in the overall structure of the Priestly creation account as an amplification and specification of the creation of the land animals, and the two acts of creation together comprise a single day's work. This classification of *adam* with the other creatures of earth has required an adjustment in the account of the sixth day's work, for the formula of blessing which speaks of the filling of earth (parallel to the filling of the seas in vs. 22) cannot be addressed to two orders occupying the same space. The expected blessing of the land animals has accordingly given way to the blessing of *adam*, the supreme land creature (Schmidt 1973:147; Westermann 1974:196).

The combination of events on the sixth day suggests that *adam* is to be understood as a special type or species of earth creature. In contrast to *adam*, all other life is described in broad classes, with subclasses or species (*mîn*) recognized but not named.[13] Thus grasses and fruiting plants represent the primary classes of vegetation, each with its myriad individual species, while "fish," fowl, cattle and creepers describe comparable classes of animal life. *Adam*, however, is an individual, at once species and order, a creature among creatures yet apart from them and above them.

Sexual Distinction and Blessing

The word that most clearly located *adam* among the creatures is the blessing of vs. 28 and the specification that immediately precedes and prepares for it: *zākār ûnĕqēbâ bārāʾ ʾōtām:* "male and female he created them." But the theme articulated in these coordinated clauses reaches beyond the world of creatures addressed by the word of blessing to include all life. For P, there is a corollary to the idea that all of creation is derived from God and dependent upon God. It is the idea of the permanence and immutability of the created orders. For living things, with their observable cycles of life, permanence must be conceived in dynamic terms, as a process of replenishment or reproduction. Thus for each order of living thing explicit attention is given to the means by which it is to be perpetuated. That is the meaning of the cumbersome and seemingly unnecessary specification that both classes of vegetation were created bearing seeds—i.e., equipped to reproduce their kind (Maag 1955:39). And that is the meaning of the blessing that imparts to all creatures the power of reproduction: "be fruitful and multiply and fill the earth/ waters."[14]

Adam is creature, who with all other created life is given the power of reproduction through the word-act of creation, receiving it in the identical words of blessing addressed first to the creatures of sea and sky (vs. 22). It is in relation to this statement that the specification, "male and female he created them," must be understood. The word of sexual differentiation anticipates the blessing and prepares for it. And it is an essential word, not because of any prehistory which related a separate creation of man and woman, but because of the structure of the Priestly account and the order of its essential themes. Sexual constitution is the presupposition of the blessing of increase, which in the case of the other creatures is simply assumed. In the case of *adam*, however, it cannot be assumed, but must be specially articulated— because of the statement that immediately precedes it.

The word about *adam* is two-fold in both Wortbericht and Tatbericht; it identifies humanity by nature or constitution and by position or function. And the primary word about the nature of *adam*, and sole word of the Wortbericht, is that this one is like God, created in resemblance to God as an image or representation. This audacious statement of identification and correspondence, however qualified by terms of approximation, offers no ground for assuming sexual distinction as a characteristic of *adam*, but appears rather to exclude it, for God (*ʾĕlōhîm*) is the defining term in the statement. The idea that God might possess any form of sexuality, or any differentiation analogous to it, would have been for P an utterly foreign and repugnant notion. For this author/editor, above all others in the Pentateuch, guards the distance between God and humanity, avoiding anthropomorphic description and employing specialized terminology (e.g., *bārāʾ*) to distinguish divine activity from analogous human action.[15] Consequently, the word that identifies *adam* by reference to divine likeness must be supplemented or qualified before the blessing of fertility can be pronounced; for the word of blessing assumes but does not bestow the means of reproduction.

The required word of qualification and specification is introduced in vs. 27b. *Unlike* God, but *like* the other creatures, *adam* is characterized by sexual differentiation.[16] The parallel clauses of vs. 27aβb form a bridging couplet between the primary and emphasized statement concerning the divine likeness, introduced in the Wortbericht (26) and repeated as the lead sentence of the Tatbericht (27aα), and the pronouncement of the blessing of fertility (vs. 28)—a new theme found only in the Tatbericht. It recapitulates the word about the image, in an emphatic yet qualifying manner, and adds to it the word of sexual distinction:

> *běṣelem ʾĕlōhîm bārāʾ ʾōtô*
> *zākār ûněqēbâ bārāʾ ʾōtām*[17]

The two parallel cola contain two essential and distinct statements about the nature of humanity: *adam* is created *like* (i.e., resembling) God, but *as* creature—and hence male and female.[18] The parallelism of the two cola is progressive, not synonymous. The second statement adds to the first; it does not explicate it.[19]

Expansion and Conflation in the Tatbericht

The position of the specification of humanity's bi-sexual nature is dictated by the larger narrative structure of the chapter and by the themes it must incorporate. Here, following the pattern of the preceding acts or episodes, the Wortbericht conveys the essential content of the word about the order (viz., created according to divine likeness and given dominion), and the Tatbericht repeats it. And here, as in the parallel account of the sixth act of creation, the Tatbericht is expanded by a word of blessing, introducing the sub-theme of sustainability alongside the primary theme of order. But in vss. 27–28 the introduction of the word of blessing, with its clarifying prefatory note, has broken the connection between image and dominion articulated in vs. 26. In the expanded execution report, the word that conveys dominion is joined directly to the preceding words of blessing, creating an extended series of imperatives, all apparently governed by the rubric of blessing (*wayĕbārek ʾōtām* [vs. 28])—and all apparently conditioned by the dual qualification of bi-sexual nature and divine resemblance. Such a reading of vss. 27–28, however, which treats the series of words addressed to *adam* as homogeneous and relates both statements of nature (God-like and bi-sexual) to the whole series without discrimination, ignores the interpretive clues contained in the Wortbericht and in the parallel construction of vs. 22. Fertility and dominion belong to two separate themes or concerns: one, the theme of nature with its sub-theme of sustainability (fertility), the other, the theme of order with its interest in position and function. The word of sexual distinction pertains only to the first—and has relevance or consequence in P's theology only for the first.

There is no message of shared dominion here, no word about the distribution of roles, responsibility and authority between the sexes, no word of sexual equality. What is described is a task for the species (*kibšūhā*) and the position of the species in relation to the other orders of creatures (*rĕdū*).[20] The social metaphors to which the key verbs point are male, derived from male experience and models, the dominant social models of patriarchal society. For P, as for J, the representative and determining image of the species was certainly male, as 5:1–3, 9:1, and the genealogies which structure the continuing account make clear.[21] Though the Priestly writer speaks of the species, he thinks of the male, just as the author of Psalm 8. But maleness is not an essential or defining characteristic. Against such reduction or confusion of attributes the word of bi-sexual creation stands as guard by its progressive parallelism to the word of God-like creation and its common referent, *adam*. What distinguishes the species (viz. the divine image) distinguishes every individual and sub-class thereof – here specifically the two genders.[22]

In our analysis the meaning and function of the statement, "male and female he created them," is considerably more limited than is commonly assumed. It says nothing about the image which relates *adam* to God nor about God as the referent of the image. Nor does it qualify *adam*'s dominion over the creatures or subjugation of the earth. It relates only to the blessing of fertility, making explicit its necessary presupposition. It is not concerned with sexual roles, the status or relationship of the sexes to one another, or marriage. It describes the biological pair, not the psycho-social pair; male and female, not man and woman or husband and wife. The specification is not dictated by tradition, but is P's own formulation, dependent upon his overarching theme of the sustainability (fertility) of the created order. It does not presuppose an original androgyne (the progressive specification of attributes is logical, not temporal), but a bi-sexual order of creatures as the crown of creation. And it is to this order that all of the statements of task and position refer.

The priestly author is concerned in his account of origins with the orders of nature, not culture; he offers no reflection on the social consequences or correlates of his view of the human order. In marked contrast is the Yahwist's account (2:4b–3:24), which focuses attention on the tension between nature and culture, or the disparity between the created ("original" or intended) order and the historically experienced order – precisely as this tension is exhibited in the relationship of male and female.

Sexual Distinction in the Yahwistic Account[23]

The Yahwistic account of creation differs from the Priestly account, to which it is joined, in language, structure, theology, and mood. Its many signs of original independence require that it be understood on its own terms before being interpreted in conjunction with the preceding account.[24] While the layers and seams of earlier tradition are more obvious in J's composition than in P's, the present form of the text requires that chapters 2 and 3 be treated as a unit, composed of two interlocking episodes.[25] In the Yahwist's account, creation and "fall"[26] together tell the story of the conditions under which human life is lived. Although history begins outside the garden, the garden is the site of the estrangement which manifests itself in history. The seeds of destruction have already been sown when the journey of our ancestors begins. Thus J's account of origins is a two-part drama, which includes divine-human interaction in its essential statement.

This essay does not permit full or adequate consideration of the dynamics and intention of the Yahwist's composition. Attention must therefore be limited to those features of the account that have significance for understanding the meaning of sexual differentiation within it. Of fundamental importance is the literary form and structure of the narrative. In the Yahwist's account, story and the storyteller's art replace the liturgical cadences and technical terminology of priestly declaration. Circular movement marks the narrative structure, in contrast to the linear progression of Genesis 1, and dramatic action/interaction describes states and relationships. Time has no meaning here and sequence of action no ontological significance. The first and final acts of creation together describe a single action; the creation of humankind is not complete until the woman stands beside the man, manifesting that essential aspect of humanity hidden or latent in the first exemplar. Only when the pair appear together on the stage does the divine-human interaction begin and the consequential action of the story. Similarly, in the account of the "fall," neither sequence of actions nor preferred motives is of consequence. The woman is not judged until the man has also eaten; and both are understood to have acted in full knowledge of the prohibition and its consequences.[27] Thus "order of creation" and "order in the fall" are notions foreign to the Yahwist's conception and composition.

How then does the Yahwist understand the relationship of the sexes and what is the meaning of his uniquely bifurcated account of human creation?[28] The essential plot of the Yahwist's narrative may be summarized as follows. Yahweh God forms "the human" (*hā'ādām*) as the first of the creatures, earth creature par excellence, by origin and vocation.[29] Presented as an individual (*hā'ādām*, with the article, in contrast to P's collective *'ādām*, without the article [cf. Lussier 1956 and Barthelemy 1981]) and envisioned as a male (specifically, a peasant farmer), the name by which he is designated betrays his true identity – and the problem of his singularity. For although he bears the appellation of the species, he does not fully represent it. The personification is defective in its limitation to the male alone. The remainder of the chapter describes in dramatic action the overcoming of that defect and the resolution of the tension latent in the initial presentation.[30]

The narrative is androcentric in form and perspective. It is told from the man's point of view and describes the man's need for a companion and helper. The resolution of the problem is accordingly signaled by the man's response, in his recognition that the one who confronts him is truly like him, not merely in appearance, but in substance – "of the same bone and flesh" (2:23). This climactic word of recognition, emphasizing the identity and equality of the two (now designated by the alliterative social terms, *'îš:* man and *'iššâ:* woman),[31] gains significance and impact from the tension-heightening action that precedes it. There Yahweh forms from the earth all of the animal species in a trial-and-error attempt to produce a suitable companion for the man. It is only with the woman, however, that the man's need is finally met, for unlike the animals, the woman is not a separate order of creation, but shares fully the nature of *adam*. The dramatic requirement of creating two from one, which arises from the initial presentation of a single representative of the species, leads to the ingenious solution of extracting a rib from the human-presented-as-a-man and "building" a woman − a solution that recognizes the woman as one substance with the man, yet unique.

The Yahwist's account gives special emphasis to the bi-sexual nature of the human species in order to stress the relationship between the sexes, here presented in psycho-social rather than biological terms. And although the help which the woman is meant to give to the man is undoubtedly help in procreation, the account in Genesis 2 subordinates function to passion. The attraction of the sexes is the author's primary interest, the sexual drive whose consummation is conceived as a re-union.

Genesis 2, like Genesis 1, contains no statement of dominance or subordination in the relationship of the sexes, but its narratively constructed emphasis on the equality of the two is the foundation and prelude to its negation in Genesis 3. There we encounter an explicit statement of the woman's subordination to the man—not, however, as representing the order of creation but rather as a sign of its sinful perversion. The Yahwist sees the disobedience of the man and woman to the divine command as the root sin that disturbs the original harmony of creation, and he sees the consequences of that sin in the painful and alienated existence which he knew to be the human lot. The estrangement introduced into the divine-human relationship works itself out in every other relationship (von Rad 1961:148–49). Estrangement from God manifests itself for the man in estrangement from the earth out of which he was created and on which he depends for his work, estrangement experienced as pain in his labor; and the estrangement from God manifests itself for the woman in estrangement from the man from whom she was created and on whom she depends for her work, estrangement experienced in the pain of her labor, childbirth.[32]

But there is a further dimension of this pain of estrangement, which breaks the symmetry of suffering, and that is the destruction of companionship between the man and the woman. For the relationship of companionship, established in the creation and exhibited in the mutual drive of the sexes toward each other (*he* will leave father and mother, his own flesh and bone, to cleave to her [2:24], and *her* desire will be for him [3:18]), is broken by the added word of judgment: "he shall rule over her" (3:16). The companion of chap. 2 has become a master. The historical subordination of woman to man is inaugurated – and identified as the paradigm expression of sin and alienation in creation.[33]

Reuniting the Texts: Interpretive Conclusions

The union of the Priestly and Yahwistic accounts of creation as successive episodes in a comprehensive statement of origins requires the canonical interpreter to observe both the order of the component accounts and the tension between them. It also requires attention to new meanings that move beyond the original terms and intentions of the individual accounts as they are brought within a new and larger context of interpretation. That interpretive context must finally include the canon as a whole, in interaction with the multiple and changing contexts of the interpreter. It requires multivalent and multidimensional reading.

To conclude my analysis, I have attempted to spell out briefly some of the primary meanings and inferences suggested by a reading of the combined P-J creation narrative as viewed in a canonical context and addressed by the question of the meaning of sexual distinction in relation to the divine image.

1. The notion of creation in the image of God is the lead and controlling statement of the account, with consequence for all canonical reflection on the nature of humankind and its place within the created order. It refers in this initial and determinative usage to humanity as a whole and may not be limited to any individual or sub-group of the species.

a. This understanding is not qualified by P's subsequent personification of the species in an individual named Adam, who perpetuates the essential created nature of the species by fathering offspring in his image. Adam is presented in 5:1a, 3 as an individual exemplifying the species. That the species *adam* is understood as collective/plural and bi-sexual is evident in the recapitulation of 1:27 in 5:2 and in the explicit referral of the name to the plural object (*wayyiqrā* *'et-šĕmām* *'ādām:* "he called *their* name *adam*"). The Priestly writer's narrowed attention to the male line in history does not thereby limit humanity or the image to the male of the species.

b. The Yahwist's individualizing of *adam* in his story of the first human pair also prohibits collapse of the collective into the singular and consequent reduction of the image to the male. A consistent grammatical distinction is maintained in Genesis 1 and 2 between the noun with the article (*hā'ādām:* the human), used exclusively in chap. 2, and the anarthrous noun (*'ādām:* humankind) employed in chap. 1. Genesis 2 signals by narrative plot as well as grammar that "the human" and humankind are not fully coterminus in the first specimen of the species.

2. The divine image, as a distinguishing attribute of humankind, is not lost or effaced by the disobedience of the pair or by the consequent divine judgment.

3. The content of the image is unspecified and therefore open to new interpretation. Special consideration should be given, however, to its original connection with oversight or rule in the exploration of new meanings. As an expression of relationship to God employed to express a relationship to other creatures, it invites continued reflection on the special privilege and responsibility of humankind within the created order.

a. As an attribute of the species, it requires both male and female for its full representation and for exercise of the responsibility it implies. Thus it demands social arrangements within the human community and ecological arrangements with the rest of creation that maintain the God-like nature of all members of the species and their collective responsibility for oversight of the God-created order.

4. Balance, implying equality, is a central feature of the presentation of male and female in both creation accounts. As a structural feature common to both accounts it demands greater weight in interpretation than the particular, culturally determined metaphors used to describe the nature and task of the primeval pair. In P this balance is expressed through symmetrical construction, in J through dramatic action and interaction. The side-by-side appearance of male and female in P's account of simultaneous creation is matched by J's account of face-to-face encounter climaxed by the man's joyf il acknowledgment of the woman as his long-sought counterpart.

5. P's treatment of sexual differentiation focuses solely on the biological level, but its limited statement contributes an essential element of any biblically informed theology of sexuality. P declares that sex, as differentiation and union, is intended for procreation and is to be understood as a divinely given capacity and power governed by blessing and command. The word that activates the endowment, however, addresses the species, not the individual, and is limited in its application by the setting in which it is spoken, a limitation made explicit in the qualifying amplification, "and fill the earth." It is a word for beginnings, not for all time; the "command" is neither absolute nor universal. It must be repeated and reinterpreted in changing historical/ecological situations.[34]

6. J's account provides an essential complement to P by focusing on the psycho-social meaning of sexuality and its historical manifestations. Compan-

ionship, the sharing of work, mutual attraction and commitment in a bond superceding all other human bonds and attractions – these are the ends for which *adam* was created male and female and these are the signs of intended partnership. For J, sexual differentiation is the ground and precondition of community, which requires the individual to reach beyond the self for fulfillment of basic needs.

a. But the requirement of an other to satisfy the individual's needs opens the way to exploitation, whose tragic consequences J so clearly depicts in the historical relationship of (the) man to (the) woman.

b. The Yahwist's attention to the social and historical dimensions of sexuality requires the canonical interpreter to consider the sociohistorical conditions under which the relationship of the sexes takes place. And the ethical judgment implicit in his account requires corresponding ethical reflection and judgment by the contemporary theologian. Biblical anthropology, as exemplified in the P-J creation account, joins to the question of nature or ontology the question of history and ethics. The movement from ontological speculation to ethical reflection and judgment, exhibited in the present order of the combined texts, thrusts the interpreter forward into the full canon of Scriptures as the arena in which the meaning of human existence as male and female must finally be understood – and prepares the reader to discover that meaning in negative as well as positive experience.

Concluding Hermeneutical Note

In my interpretation I have insisted that the biblical writer's understanding and intentions must be sought and respected by the contemporary exegete. This obligation is not nullified by recognition of multiple authors and stages of composition, though it is made more complex. And it involves no claim to freedom from bias nor demand for agreement with the author. Rather it opens the way for dialogue with the text in which the integrity of the ancient writer is affirmed and guarded. I adopt an historical-critical approach to the biblical texts because I believe that they present themselves, even in the best modern translation, as ancient and foreign compositions, which must be understood in the context of the world in which and for which they were produced.

But I would also insist that the meaning of a text cannot finally be limited to the author's (or editor's) understanding or intention, (1) because the word once written is released from the author's control to acquire new and unintended, or unenvisioned, meanings; (2) because the canon of scripture in which the word is preserved and transmitted qualifies it by setting it in a larger literary and theological context, which brings it into conversation, and conflict, with other texts; and (3) because the church in which the word is read and proclaimed understands it as having present, revelatory meaning. Thus the text is located within a conversation that has both ancient (canonical and post-canonical) and contemporary partners. In my understanding, the revelatory content of the word and its contemporary meaning are apprehended only through this conversation and may not be identified with any particular text or locution nor with the author's imputed intention.[35]

In this volume, which examines the church's conversation with the *imago* text through history, I have focused on its earliest canonical form and setting. Beneath the overload of meaning heaped by tradition on Genesis 1 and its companion text in Genesis 2–3 I have found a more limited and differentiated meaning. And as a Protestant exegete, it is this text behind the tradition that I take as the starting point for my conversation and my search for revelatory meaning.

Genesis 1 invites, and demands, renewed reflection on the meaning of sexual differentiation as a constitutive mark of our humanity and the meaning of God-likeness (image) as the defining attribute of humankind. And it contributes to this constructive task by its silences as well as its assertions. Genesis 1, in contrast to most interpreters, does not link its two fundamental statements about *adam*, but juxtaposes them as parallel holistic assertions, ordering them, however, so that the *imago*-dominion statement is prior and encompassing. Nor does the text establish any hierarchy within the species, either of gender or function; all of its statements pertain to the species as a whole. Thus it may serve as a foundation text for a feminist egalitarian anthropology, since it recognizes no hierarchy of gender in the created order.

This does not make the Priestly writer a feminist, nor deny the patriarchal assumptions that stamp his language and thought. His basic concepts of image, dominion and subjugation are rooted in male metaphors, and he shows no consciousness of tension between the balanced symmetry of his gender proclamation and the disproportionate weight of his masculine descriptive terms. Thus some might find justification in his linguistic images for the traditional interpretation of *imago*-bearing *adam* as male (an interpretation which rests, however, on conflation with Genesis 2). Such an interpretation fails, however, to observe the writer's intention and thereby, I believe, misconstrues his message. Here intention is expressed primarily by the structure of the argument, rather than the culturally captive language that serves as its vehicle. While the Priestly writer's language is indisputably androcentric and patriarchal, patriarchy is not his message in Genesis 1.

Even less is it the message of the Yahwist, who counters the conspicuous androcentrism of his account with explicit narrative qualification: although the woman is taken from the man, he cleaves to her, acknowledging her power over him; and although he is destined to become her master, that domination is presented as the consequence of sin, not as design in creation.

(1987)

Notes

1. This essay is an abbreviated and extended form of my article, "'Male and Female He created Them': Gen 1:27b in the Context of the Priestly Account of Creation," *HTR* 74 (1981) 129–59. That article should be consulted for full argumentation and documentation of the lexical and syntactic issues discussed in relation to Genesis 1.

2. Recent Old Testament scholarship has attempted to move beyond the fragmenting approach of older source- and form-critical interpretation (see, e.g., Clines 1976; Miller 1978; and Childs 1979: 142–45, 148–50). Nevertheless, critical scholars are virtually unanimous in recognizing two originally distinct accounts in Genesis 1 and 2 and in relating them to "Priestly," and "Yahwistic" author-redactors respectively. See commentaries (especially Westermann 1974; von Rad 1961; Speiser 1964; Brueggemann 1982) and Schmidt 1973.

3. This argument, reflecting the understanding of most Old Testament scholars, was originally formulated in opposition to the widely influential treatment of Karl Barth (1958: 183–206), whose view of the relationship between the divine image and the male-female duality is reinforced by Phyllis Trible's treatment (1978: 16–21). See Bird 1981: 131–134.

4. I assume for Gen 1:1–2:4a a unified work by a priestly editor/author active in and during the Babylonian exile, who edited an already existing Israelite creation account (perhaps extant in multiple variants, or supplemented by material from other traditions) to form the opening chapter of a great history of beginnings reaching from creation to the death of Moses and climaxing in the revelation/legislation at Sinai. Whether the author/editor was a single or corporate "individual" is irrelevant to the argument of this essay. The two essential assumptions of my analysis are (1) that the present (final) edition of the material displays a unified overall conception characterized by recognizable stylistic and theological features and forms part of a larger whole displaying similar literary and theological characteristics, and (2) that the present form of the composition in Genesis 1 is the result of a complex history of growth, stages of which are apparent in the received text, but can no longer be isolated or fully reconstructed.

I agree with Werner Schmidt (1973) that the framing structure of *wayyōʾmer ʾĕlōhîm* + *wayĕhî-kēn* and the Wortberichte as a whole belong to the final editor and give evidence of selection, shaping and expansion of older material. I am less certain about the recovery of the underlying tradition or of the relationship of Wortbericht/Announcement to Tatbericht/Execution Report. I retain the terms to refer not to independent literary compositions, or traditions, but to literary features of the final composition. See further Bird 1981: 135 n. 13.

5. I omit from consideration vss. 29–30, which constitute a distinct unit and lack any connection with vs. 27b. See Bird 1981: 136 n. 15.

6. Textual variants are few and of minor significance for our analysis. See Bird 1981: 137 n. 18.

7. The basic meanings of the terms *ṣelem* and *dĕmût* are "representation" and "likeness" (see further below). The prepositions, which are used synonymously, create parallel and synonymous adverbial clauses which describe the manner and end of construction (*adam* is "modeled" on *ʾĕlōhîm* and is consequently a model of *ʾĕlōhîm*). The intention is to describe a resemblance of *adam* to God which distinguishes *adam* from all other creatures – and has consequence for *adam*'s relationship to them. See the classical studies of Humbert 1940 and Koehler 1948; also Horst 1950; Stamm 1956 and 1959; Loretz 1967; Clines 1968; Barr 1968 and 1971; Miller 1972; Snaith 1974; Mettinger 1974; Sawyer 1974.

8. For the understanding of *wĕyirdû* as a purpose or result clause, see, *inter alia*, Schmidt 1973:127 ("damit sie herrschen"); NEB ("to rule"); Snaith 1974: 24; and Westermann 1974: 216.

9. Westermann has correctly emphasized the adverbial character of *bĕṣalmēnû kidmûtēnû* (1974: 214), basing his analysis on the consensus of recent scholarship which rejects the *b*-essentiae interpretation and recognizes the essentially synonymous meaning of the two phrases, whose interchangeable prepositions must have the meaning "according to," "nach" (so LXX [*kata* for both] and Vulgate ["ad" for both]) (201). But although, strictly speaking, it qualifies only the action of God and not the object of that action (Westermann 1974:214), I would argue that the Priestly writer intended to characterize *adam* by this formulation, to specify more closely the essential nature of humanity while avoiding direct description. P intends a comparison between God and *adam*, but he intends it to be indirect. The prepositions guard against identity, even the identity of an image or icon. Strictly speaking, *adam* is not the image of God (so rightly Westermann) nor one possessing the divine image, but only one who is like God in the manner of an image or representation.

Since *bĕṣelem ʾĕlōhîm* describes, indirectly, the nature of *adam*, it characterizes all humankind in all time and not simply the original act, or specimen, of creation. The stamp of divine likeness must therefore be understood to be transmitted not through repeated acts of God but through the process by which the species is perpetuated in its original identity, viz., through procreation (Gen 5:3).

10. On the meaning and relationship of the two terms see Koehler 1948:20–21;

Humbert 1940:163; Sawyer 1974:421. Cf. Miller 1972:299-304; Maag 1955:34. Further, Bird 1981:139 n. 23.

11. *Ṣelem* in P's use is neither the naively literal image assumed by those who fail to recognize the determining metaphor (described below) nor the description of a conversation partner or counterpart. In response to continuing attempts to spell out the content of the image, James Barr has recently argued that the term *ṣelem* was deliberately chosen for its opaque etymology and ambivalent connotations as the best term available in Hebrew to describe a likeness without giving it a particular content (Barr 1971:12-13). Cf. Stamm 1959:19; Horst 1950:267; and critique in Bird 1981:139-40 n. 24.

12. The argument for viewing the expression as a royal motif is spelled out in Bird 1981:140-143, with examples from Mesopotamian texts and discussion of Egyptian parallels. The genius of the formulation in Gen 1:26 may be seen in its use of a common expression and image of Mesopotamian (-Canaanite) royal theology to counter a common image of Mesopotamian (-Canaanite) anthropology, viz., the image of humanity as servant of the gods, the dominant image of Mesopotamian creation myths. The language that describes the king as one who stands in a special relationship to the divine world is chosen by the author of Genesis 1 to describe humanity as a whole, *adam qua adam*, in its essential nature.

13. König 1911; cf. Schmidt 1973:123; Westermann 1974:174-75, The differentiation of plant and animal life into species or types does not find a correspondence in the sexual differentiation of humankind, described in vs. 27 (*contra* Schmidt 1973:107 n. 1).

14. While the immediate intention of this word in its expanded form (including *milʾû*) is surely to describe the filling of an empty earth through the multiplication of original specimen pairs, there may be another intention as well, a polemical one. For P, the power of created life to replenish itself is a power given to each species at its creation and therefore not dependent upon subsequent ·ites or petitions for its effect. The emphatic and repeated word which endows life with the means and the power of propagation undercuts the rationale of the fertility cult — and in yet another manner deposes and annihilates the gods; for the power to create life and to sustain it belongs to God alone, who incorporates the means of perpetuity into the very design and constitution of the universe, and the power to rule earth and its creatures is delegated to *adam*. Thus the gods are denied all power, place and function by this account, whether to create, renew or rule. See further Bird 1981:146-47 ns. 45-46.

15. See Bird 1981:148 n.49.

16. The specifying clause, "male and female he created them," must not be understood as distinguishing humans from other creatures or as giving to human sexual distinction a special meaning. In the economy of the Priestly writer's account it is mentioned here only out of necessity (see below). The same specification, in the same terms, *zākār ûneqēbâ*, is made elsewhere with reference to the animals — and for a similar reason of clarification and emphasis. In the Priestly

account of the flood story, the author wishes to make clear that the "two of every sort" of animals that are to be brought into the ark constitute a minimal pair, capable of reproduction, and thus he specifies, *zākār ûnĕqēbâ yihyû:* "they shall be male and female" (Gen 6:19; cf. 7:9).

The Priestly writer has chosen his terms, as well as their placement, with care. *Zākār* and *nĕqēbâ* are biological terms, not social terms – as *ʾîš* and *ʾiššâ* in 2:22–24. Harmonizing of the creation accounts of Genesis 1 and 2 has affected the translation as well as the interpretation of the terms in 1:27, especially in the German tradition, where the rendering "Mann und Frau" (Westermann 1974:108; Schmidt 1973:127 *inter alia*) or "Mann und Weib" (Gunkel, *Genesis*, 103; Zürich Bible, 1942; "Luther Bible," rev. ed., 1964 *inter alia*) is common.

17. On the prehistory of the text, see Bird 1981:149 n. 51. I regard the couplet in 27a as the work of a single author, more specifically, the final editor, and view the seemingly awkward or redundant *bĕṣelem ʾĕlōhîm* as a deliberate qualification of the preceding *bĕṣalmô*, perhaps employing a phrase from an earlier stage of the tradition. The repetition of *bĕṣelem* with its significant variation in 27aα and β has an important theological purpose. The reflexive singular suffix of 27aα requires that the image be referred directly to God, the sole and single actor, and not to a lower order of divine beings (*contra* Gunkel 1917:98 *inter alia*). It thus "corrects" the impression of a plurality of deities which might be suggested by the plurals of vs. 26. But *bĕṣelem ʾĕlōhîm* qualifies the masculine singular antecedent by repetition of the name, which in its third-person formulation gives both precision and distance to the self-reference. With its ambiguous plural form and its class connotation, *ʾĕlōhîm* serves, as the plurals of vs. 26, to blur the profile of the referent.

18. The shift from collective singular (*ʾōtô* ["him"]) in the first colon to (collective) plural (*ʾōtām* ["them"]) in the second is significant. The author relates the nόtion of the divine image only to an undifferentiated humanity as species or order and thus takes pains to use the singular pronoun in both clauses of vs. 27 employing *ṣelem*, despite the fact that the plural has already been introduced in the verb (*wĕyirdû*) of the preceding verse.

19. *Contra* Barth (1945:219), who sees 27b as a "geradezu definitionsmässige Erklärung der Gottesebenbildlichkeit." Cf. Trible (1978:16–21), who finds in the parallelism of vs. 27a metaphor in which "the image of God" is the tenor and "male and female" the vehicle (p. 17). This interpretation rests on a faulty syntactical analysis which isolates vs. 27 as a unit of speech/thought. The metaphor is the creation of the interpreter. Schmidt, who judged 27b a secondary addition on grounds of vocabulary, style and meter, notes that apart from Gen 1:27 and 5:1–2 the themes of divine image and sexuality are associated nowhere else, either in the OT or in the ancient Near East (Schmidt 1973:146–47). He failed to recognize, however, why the two are juxtaposed here. See further below.

20. On the meaning of these two terms and the relationship of the charge to "sub-

due" (*KBŠ*) the earth to the word giving dominion (*RDH*), see Bird 1981:151–155.

21. When P moves from proto-history (creation) to "history," his view of humankind is limited to the male actor or subject. Thus *adam* becomes Adam and is renewed in Noah and his sons, not Noah and his wife. The blessing of fertility is addressed in 9:1 to the men alone, with no mention of the wives, who as necessary helpers in the task of maintaining the species are explicitly noted in the enumeration of those entering the ark. The pointed reference to the unnamed wives of Noah and of his three sons in 7:7 and 7:13 has the same function there as the specification of "male and female" in 1:27. This theme of reproductive capability also finds expression in the phrase, "other sons *and daughters,*" incorporated into the summarizing statement of each generation of P's otherwise all-male genealogical tables (5:4, 7, 10, 13, 16, 19, 22, 26, 30; 11:11, 13, 15, 17, 19, 21, 23, 25). The history in which P's theological interest lies is a history carried by males and embodied in males. Females come into view only where the issue of biological continuity or reproduction is raised.

22. My argument in summarizing the Priestly writer's view analyzes the intentions and assumptions of the author as inferred from the text in its ancient setting. However, the text itself permits an egalitarian reading, I would argue, despite the fact that it must be viewed as unintended and unforeseen by the ancient author. It not only permits such a reading, it encourages it, by the "emptiness" of its key terms, the structure of its pronouncements, and its restraint from specifying social roles and responsibilities. An egalitarian reading, however, belongs to a new context of interpretation, in answer to a new question beyond the horizon of the ancient author – but no less valid for its novelty. The inability of the Priestly writer to envision, or accept, the argument constructed upon his text does not lessen its force nor render its logic less compelling. See below.

23. The following summary treatment is meant to complement my analysis of the Priestly account without presenting a full analysis of the structure and meaning of the Yahwist's narrative or the history of interpretation. For questions of introduction, see Westermann 1974 and Brueggemann 1982. Recent interest in literary and structural analysis, combined with feminist concern over traditional interpretations of woman's role in the creation and "fall," have led to a sizeable new literature on Genesis 2–3 challenging and complementing older studies. See especially McKenzie 1954; Steck 1970; Walsh 1977; Kutsch 1977; Trible 1978:72–143; Naidoff 1978; Patte 1980; Rosenberg 1981; Hauser 1982; also Bailey 1970; Mettinger 1978; Sandys-Wunsch 1982.

24. Cf. Childs 1979:148–150 for insistence on the controlling force of the canonical union.

25. Westermann 1974:259–67. For fuller analysis of scenes and structure see Trible 1978:72–143; Walsh 1977; Patte 1980; and Rosenberg 1981.

26. The term "fall," as well as the concept, is alien to the text. I employ it only as a

conventional designation. See Westermann 1974:374-380, and Brueggemann 1982:40-44.

27. I am not convinced that the author intended to differentiate the woman's and the man's responses as Trible has done, though her contrasting of the woman's reflective act (she is "intelligent, sensitive, and ingenious" in her disobedience) with the man's "belly-oriented" acquiescence (he is "passive, brutish, and inept") is an effective counter to traditional interpretations of the woman's role in the fall (Trible 1978:113). I would refer the differentiated narrative depiction to customary male and female roles in food preparation and consumption, though a more specific mythic or aetiological tradition may underlie the representation.

28. While the separate creation of man and woman is known elsewhere (though not from the ancient Near East), the Yahwist's account is unique in its theme of the man's need for companionship (possibly an expression of the motif articulated elsewhere in the myth of the androgyne). It is also unique in encompassing the account of animal creation within the account of human creation, subordinating the animal orders to the human order by means of a circular structure comparable in effect to the linear structure of Genesis 1.

29. Formed from the earth (ʾădāmâ) to till the earth (2:5, 7; 3:23). Cf. Naidoff 1978.

30. My summary traces one line through the narrative. However, the multilayered nature of the account requires a multileveled interpretation. At one level, the name and the characterization of the first human must be seen as determined by the tale of the man and the garden with its ʾādām/ʾădāmâ (earthling/earth) aetiology, the tale that provides the framing inclusio for the two chapters. At another level, the name and the depiction of its bearer are to be understood in terms of the class designation *adam* and its incomplete realization or representation in the single specimen. Linked to an aetiology of the sex drive, this understanding presents the species as essentially embodied in (a) man and (a) woman and views wholeness in terms of differentiation and union rather than identity or absorption (cf. Westermann 1974:276-282; Trible 1978:80-81). In the present form of the text, the latter interest dominates the chapter. However, I do not think one can eradicate the male image of *hāʾādām* from this passage as Trible attempts to do (1978:80 and 140, n. 8).

31. See Rosenberg 1981:13-14; McKenzie 1954:559; cf. Walsh 1977:174, n. 32.

32. Reading ʿiṣṣĕbônēk wĕhērōnēk (3:16) as hendiadys with Westermann (1974: 356) and most commentators. I cannot accept Carol Meyers's view that the verse speaks of multiplying the woman's work *and* pregnancies or her elimination of the sense of painful labor from the parallel clause, bĕʿeṣeb tēlĕdî bānîm (Meyers 1983:344-46), though her article makes a valuable contribution to the study of women's roles in ancient Israel. Cf. Miller 1978:48 n. 49 for recognition of the parallelism between the man's and the woman's punishment.

33. The divine word spoken in judgment is neither a curse nor an eternal decree determining the fate of all future generations, but rather the dramatic representation of the consequences of sin as experienced in the generations known to the

author. An aetiological tale of the painful conditions of life is joined by profound theological reflection on the root cause. That the examples chosen (field labor and childbirth) no longer represent the chief sources of pain in the lives of most Westerners today demonstrates their aetiological and historically conditioned character. They must not be absolutized but read as signs of an underlying disorder, whose clearest persisting sign is the continuing alienation of male and female perpetuated by patriarchy. See, *inter alia*, Westermann 1974:355-63 and Trible 1978:116-32.

34. See Bird 1981:152-53 and 157.

35. For a fuller statement of my understanding of the nature and authority of the Bible and the means of seeking and appropriating its message, see my book, *The Bible as the Church's Book* (Bird 1982), especially pp. 67-79 and 94-108.

Works Consulted

Anderson, Bernhard W. (1975): "Human Dominion over Nature." Pp. 27-45 in *Biblical Studies in Contemporary Thought.* Ed. M. Ward. Somerville, MA: Greeno, Hadden, and Co.

Anderson, Bernhard W. (1977): "A Stylistic Study of the Priestly Creation Story." Pp. 91-109 in *Canon and Authority in Old Testament Religion and Theology.* Eds. George W. Coats and Burke O. Long. Philadelphia, PA: Fortress.

Bailey, J. A. (1970): "Initiation and the Primal Woman in Gilgamesh and Genesis 2-3," *JBL* 89:48-56.

Barr, James (1968): "The Image of God in the Book of Genesis – A Study in Terminology," *BJRL* 51:11-26.

Barr, James (1971): "The Image of God in Genesis – Some Linguistic and Historical Considerations." Pp. 5-13 in *Ou-Testamentiese Werkgemeenskap van Suid-Afrika: Proceedings of the 10th Meeting, 1967.*

Barth, Karl (1945): *Die Kirchliche Dogmatik,* III/I. Zollikon-Zürich: Evangelischer Verlag.

Barth, Karl (1958 & 1961): *Church Dogmatics,* III/I (1958) and III/4 (1961). Edinburgh: T. & T. Clark.

Barthélemy, D. (1981): " 'Pour un homme,' 'Pour l'homme' ou 'Pour Adam'? (Gen 2, 20)." Pp. 47-53 in *De la Tôrah au Messie. Mélanges Henri Cazelles.* Eds. Maurice Carrez, Joseph Doré, Pierre Grelot. Paris: Desclée.

Bird, Phyllis A. (1981): " 'Male and Female He Created Them': Gen 1:27b in the Context of the Priestly Account of Creation," *HTR* 74:129-59.

Bird, Phyllis A. (1982): *The Bible as the Church's Book.* Library of Living Faith. Philadelphia, PA: Westminster.

Brueggemann, Walter (1982): *Genesis.* Interpretation. Atlanta, GA: John Knox.

Childs, Brevard S. (1979): *Introduction to the Old Testament as Scripture.* Philadelphia, PA: Fortress.

Clines, D. J. A. (1968): "The Image of God in Man," *Tyndale Bulletin* 19:53-103.

Clines, D. J. A. (1976): "Theme in Genesis 1-11," *CBQ* 38:483-507.

Gunkel, Hermann (1917): *Genesis*. Göttinger Handkommentar zum Alten Testament, 4th ed. Göttingen: Vandenhoeck & Ruprecht.

Hauser, Alan Jon (1982): "Genesis 2-3: The Theme of Intimacy and Alienation." Pp. 20-36 in *Art and Meaning: Rhetoric in Biblical Literature*. JSOT Suppl. Ser. 19. Eds. David J. A. Clines, David M. Gunn, and Alan J. Hauser.

Hornung, Erik (1967): "Der Mensch als 'Bild Gottes' in *Ägypten*." Pp. 123-56 in Oswald Loretz, *Die Gottebenbildlichkeit des Menschen*. Munich: Kösel.

Horst, Friedrich (1950): "Face to Face: The Biblical Doctrine of the Image of God," *Interp* 4:259-70.

Humbert, Paul (1940): *Études sur le récit du paradis et de la chute dans la Gènese*. Neuchâtel: Secrétariat de l'Université.

Koehler, Ludwig (1948): "Die Grundstelle der Imago-Dei-Lehre, Gen 1:26," *ThZ* 4:16-22.

König, Eduard (1911): "Die Bedeutung des hebräischen *mîn*," *ZAW* 31:133-146.

Kutsch, Ernst (1977): "Die Paradieserzählung Gen 2-3 und ihr Verfasser." Pp. 9-24 in *Studien zum Pentateuch. Walter Kornfeld zum 60. Geburtstag*. Ed. Georg Braulik. Vienna: Herder.

Loretz, Oswald (1967): *Die Gottesebenbildlichkeit des Menschen*. Munich: Kösel.

Lussier, Ernest (1956): "ʾADAM in Genesis 1, 1-4, 24," *CBQ* 18:137-39.

Maag, Victor (1955): "Alttestamentliche Anthropogonie in ihrem Verhältnis zur altorientalischen Mythologie," *Asiatische Studien* 9:15-44.

McKenzie, John L. (1954): "The Literary Characteristics of Genesis 2-3," *Theol Stud* 15:541-72.

Mettinger, Tryggve N. D. (1974): "Abbild oder Urbild? 'Imago Dei' in traditionsgeschichtlicher Sicht," *ZAW* 86:403-24.

Mettinger, Tryggve N. D. (1978): "Eva och revbenet − Manligt och kvinnligt i exegetisk belysning," *STK* 54:55-64.

Meyers, Carol L. (1983): "Gender Roles and Genesis 3:16 Revisited," Pp. 337-54 in *The Word of the Lord Shall Go Forth. Essays in Honor of David Noel Freedman*. Eds. Carol L. Meyers and M. O'Connor. Winona Lake, IN: Eisenbrauns.

Miller, J. Maxwell (1972): "In the 'Image' and 'Likeness' of God," *JBL* 91:289-304.

Miller, Patrick D., Jr. (1978): *Genesis I-II: Studies in Structure and Theme*. JSOT Suppl. Ser., 8. Sheffield: University of Sheffield.

Naidoff, Bruce D. (1978): "A Man to Work the Soil: A New Interpretation of Genesis 2-3," *JSOT* 5:2-14.

Otto, Eberhard (1971): "Der Mensch als Geschöpf und Bild Gottes in Ägypten," Pp. 334-48 in *Probleme biblischer Theologie*. Ed. H. W. Wolff. Munich: Kaiser.

Patte, Daniel, ed. (1980): *Semeia* 18. Genesis 2 and 3: Kaleidoscopic Structural Readings.

Rad, Gerhard von (1961): *Genesis. A Commentary*. Old Testament Library. Philadelphia, PA: Westminster.

Reiser, W. (1960): "Die Verwandschaftsformel in Gen 2, 23," *ThZ* 16:1-4.

Rosenberg, Joel W. (1981): "The Garden Story Forward and Backward: The Non-Narrative Dimension of Gen 2-3," *Prooftexts* 1:1-27.

Sandys-Wunsch, John (1982): "Before Adam and Eve – or What the Censor Saw," *SR* 11:23-28.

Sawyer, John F. A. (1974): "The Meaning of *běṣelem ʾělōhîm* ("In the Image of God") in Genesis I-XI," *JTS* 25:418-26.

Scheffczyk, Leo, ed. (1969): *Der Mensch als Bild Gottes*. Darmstadt: Wissenschaftliche Buchgesellschaft.

Schmidt, Karl Ludwig (1969): "Homo imago Dei im Alten und Neuen Testament." Pp. 17-20 in *Der Mensch als Bild Gottes*. Ed. Leo Scheffczyk. Darmstadt: Wissenschaftliche Buchgesellschaft.

Schmidt, Werner (1973): *Die Schöpfungsgeschichte der Priesterschrift*, 3d ed. WMANT 17. Neukirchen-Vluyn: Neukirchen.

Snaith, Norman (1974): "The Image of God," *ExpTim* 86:24.

Speiser, Ephraim A. (1976): *Genesis*. Anchor Bible. New York: Doubleday.

Stamm, Johann Jakob (1956): "Die Imago-Lehre von Karl Barth und die alttestamentliche Wissenschaft." Pp. 84-96 in *Antwort. Festschrift K. Barth*. Ed. E. Wolf *et al.* Zollikon-Zürich: Evangelischer Verlag.

Stamm, Johann Jakob (1959): *Die Gottebenbildlichkeit des Menschen im Alten Testament*. Theologische Studien, 54. Zollikon-Zürich: Evangelischer Verlag.

Steck, Odil Hannes (1970): *Die paradieserzählung: Eine Auslegung von Genesis 2,4b-3,24*. Biblische Studien, 60. Neukirchen-Vluyn: Neukirchen.

Trible, Phyllis (1978): *God and the Rhetoric of Sexuality*. Philadelphia, PA: Fortress.

Walsh, Jerome T. (1977): "Genesis 2:4b-3:24: A Synchronic Approach," *JBL* 96:161-77.

Westermann, Claus (1974): *Genesis*. BKAT, I. Neukirchen-Vluyn: Neukirchen.

Recent Bibliography

Bird, Phyllis (1994): "Genesis 3 in der gegenwärtigen biblischen Forschung," *JBTh* 9.

Jónsson, Gunnlaugur A. (1988): *The Image of God: Genesis 1:26–28 in a Century of Old Testament Research*. Coniectanea Biblica, Old Testament Series 26. Lund: Almqvist & Wiksell International.

Sawyer, John F. A. (1992): "The Image of God, the Wisdom of Serpents and the Knowledge of Good and Evil." Pp. 64-73 in *A Walk in the Garden: Biblical, Iconographical and Literary Images of Eden*. JSOT Suppl. Ser., 136. Eds. Paul Morris and Deborah Sawyer. Sheffield: University of Sheffield.

3

God and Image of Woman
in Early Jewish Religion

∞ Anders Hultgård

Introductory Remarks

Writing an essay on such topics as early Jewish religion and ideas of God from the viewpoint of the history of religions, I feel that some preliminary remarks are needed.

God is one of the most complex and evasive concepts in our modern western civilisation. At the root, there is a Jewish and a Greek component. During more than two millennia of religious, intellectual, and scientific evolution, the concept has received additional meanings and has also been placed in new settings leading to reinterpretations of its traditional content. A fundamental mistake is to equate the modern western concept of "God" with that of the biblical texts as is commonly done in theological and popular literature. This equation which is understandable from the viewpoint of theology and faith, is primarily brought about by using (unconsciously or deliberately) the word God (with a capital letter) when referring to the supreme deity of the Israelite-Jewish communities of the first millennium B.C.E. and the first centuries C.E. Much work done in the field of feminist theology seems to presuppose such an equation. By projecting the modern image of a genderless and sublimated God back into the biblical times, it becomes possible to reinterpret a massively patriarchal body of texts in more "favourable" directions. This appears to me but an attempt to save the Bible as the canon of church and synagogue.

To avoid ambiguity the scholar writing on early Jewish and Christian religions needs a clarification of the term "God." I am not able to present a generally accepted definition, but I can at least clarify my own use of it as a historian of religion.

The words "God" or "the Divine" denote the totality and variety of a given social group's concepts of what the scientific study of religion defines under the categories "deity," "god/goddess," "supreme being," "highest spirit," "higher supernatural being." The religio-historical concept "God" or "the Divine" may thus mean one god only or many deities, as well as intermediate models e.g. a divine couple, one supreme deity surrounded by minor divinities or by other supernatural beings.

God in the religio-historical meaning is, therefore, to be distinguished from a) God in a general sense as a concept of modern western civilization current in theology, philosophy and literature and also in popular use, and b) God as a personal name of the supreme deity of Judaism, Christianity and Islam.

The definition of "early Jewish religion" is intimately bound up with the problem of determining who were Jews in the period concerned.

Territorial and linguistic criteria as well as political ones e.g. citizenship are of little help in defining who is a Jew. A more appropriate definition would be the following: Jews are those groups and individuals who from the Persian period onwards preserve an ethnical and a cultural (including religious) continuity with the Israelite population of pre-exilic Palestine. The religious continuity appears particularly in the worship of the national god YHWH (Yahweh).

Early Jewish religion is thus the religion of Jews (defined as above) living in the Persian, Hellenistic and Roman periods up to the emergence of rabbinical Judaism in the early second century C.E.[1] It should be remembered that early Jewish religion is represented also by the Samaritans and the primitive Christian movement.[2]

Ideally seen, the ultimate goal of the scholar who studies the religious concept of a culture in the remote past, is to elucidate the meaning and function of these concepts to the living humans of that past. In practice, however, as in the case of early Judaism, the scholar is confronted with a source material which has come down to us incompletely, through deliberate selection and by chance.

The groups who were responsible for the shaping and selection of the texts handed down in the Hebrew Bible or Old Testament represented only one form – although an important one – within the wide variety of religious beliefs and practices of early Judaism.[3] These groups, although far from uniform, may conveniently be spoken of as the YHWH-alone movement.[4] It is not until the the first century C.E. that the YHWH-alone movement succeeds in creating a more dominant and normative form of Jewish religion to which there were still many exceptions, however.

The bias inherent in the source material shows itself in another way. The extant documents have been produced by men.[5] In the early Jewish culture women were generally not in the position to create and publish literary works. These emanated from the hands of priests, levites, scribes and sages,[6] officials and merchants, professions from which women either were excluded by law or absent by convention and custom. One may ask, however, whether the image of YHWH would have been much different if articulated by women. Probably not, if still set in the same cultural framework.

The worship of one god is prominent in early Jewish religion, although not exclusive. This supreme god is a male deity with a personal name YHWH known also as YHW. The importance attached to the male character of YHWH certainly varied between the different groups and individuals who articulated ideas of God. In some Jewish circles YHWH may have been thought of as standing above any sexual distinction. Yet to preserve his char-acter as personal god YHWH had to be spoken of in either of the grammatical genders masculine and feminine. The male-centered worldview of the Israelite-Jewish tradition did not leave room for any hesitation in the choice.

YHWH is frequently referred to by a number of other terms such as *hā-ʾĕlōhîm* or *ʾĕlōhîm*, *ʾĕlāh* "the god" or "God" in Hebrew and Aramaic texts corresponding to ὁ θεός or θεός in the Greek sources, *ʾădōnāi* "my Lord" or "the Lord." The corresponding Greek words ὁ κύριος or κύριος usually render the proper name YHWH.

Although these terms and others apply to one and the same deity, they carry nonetheless different connotations. When for example YHWH is called ὁ θεός (or θεός) by Greek-speaking Jews, something of the meaning attached to this concept in the Hellenistic world is being transferred to the Jewish god.[7]

God means, then, in early Judaism primarily YHWH.[8] In order to avoid anachronistic readings of the term "God" in its early Jewish context, I will use the personal name YHWH to denote the supreme deity of the Jews. In quota-tions from the sources, however, the terms of the original text are indicated.

The activity of YHWH in the world was often mediated by forces and manifestations which were thought to preserve a substantial identity with the deity, although they did not represent the person of YHWH himself in his entire and unveiled majesty. Such manifestations are the Glory (*kĕbōd* YHWH), the Messenger (*malak* YHWH), the Name (*šēm* YHWH) and the Spirit (*rūaḥ* YHWH). Particular aspects and qualities of the deity may be personified and appear as more or less independent divine figures, a tendency well known from the history of religions. It was not alien to the Israelite-Jewish religion either as indicated by the figure of Wisdom (*hokmāh*). The supernatural beings known as "angels," "holy ones" or "sons of God" belong also to the divine sphere as independent figures subordinated to the supreme deity YHWH.

How does the image of woman relate to the early Jewish concept of God? This is the main question to which attention will be directed in the present study. An answer will be sought by investigating two different topics within the conceptual world of early Judaism.

The first is the image of woman as reflected in the creation accounts and in didactic texts on the nature of woman. The second is the position of woman and the female in the sacrificial system.

Early Jewish Creation Accounts

With the acceptance of the Pentateuch in the Persian period as the basic religious document of Judaism, the creation texts in Genesis 1:1-2:4a and 2:4b-3:24[9] set the guidelines for nearly all subsequent accounts on the origin of man in early Jewish religion.[10] Being part of the sacred *tōrāh* both Genesis stories were in equal degree considered divine revelation and could not be opposed as conflicting accounts. The various restatements and reinterpretations of Genesis 1:26-27 and 2:7, 15-24 often combine elements from both accounts. Sometimes the one is preferred to the other in the way that only one account becomes focus of the interest.

Most of the early Jewish accounts on the origin of man are short accounts which show no interest in the consequences of sexual distinction at the act of creation. Woman is not explicitly mentioned. The use of general terms for man such as the Hebrew *ʾādām* and the Greek ἄνθρωπος "humankind" shows, however, that the inclusion of woman is presupposed.

The texts in this group are in approximate chronological order: *Qohelet* 7:29; *Wisdom of Ben Sira* 15:14; 17:1; *Book of Jubilees* 6:8; *Rule of the Community* III, 17-18; *Hodayot* I, 15; XIII, 14-15; *Testament of Naphtali* 2:5; *Wisdom of Solomon* 2:23; 9:2; Philo *De Fuga et invent.* 68 and *De Confus. ling.* 179; *Syriac Apocalypse of Baruch* 14:18; *Fourth Book of Ezra* 6:54; 8:44; *Slavonic Enoch* 30:8; 44:1; 65:2; Josephus *Ant.* 1,32.

Some of these texts also state that man was created in the image of YHWH (*Ben Sira* 17:1-10; *Jub.* 6:8; *Test. Napht.* 2:5; *Wisdom of Sol.* 2:23; *4 Ezra* 8:44), but there is no attempt to relate this idea to the distinction of male and female within the human person as in Genesis 1:26–27. On the other hand we find different interpretations of what it means for man to be an image of the deity, which by force of logic would apply to woman as well.

In *Jubilees* 6:8 the prohibition of shedding a man's blood is based upon the YHWH-likeness of man.

According to *Testament of Naphtali* 2:5, the god-likeness of mankind presupposes some sort of constitutional identity between YHWH and man, which forms the basis of the perspicacity and omniscience of the deity:

"There is no pretence and no thought (in man) which the Lord did not know, for he created every man (ἄνθρωπον) in his own image (κατ᾽ εἰκόνα αὐτοῦ)"

In *Wisdom of Solomon* 2:23 it is said that YHWH (ὁ θεός) created man for immortality since he made him in the image of his own character (εἰκόνα τῆς ἰδίας ἰδιότητος)

A peculiar variant of the "image" ideology is found in *Slavonic Enoch* 44. YHWH (*gospodỹ*) created mankind "with his own two hands" as a likeness of "his own face." The consequence is that man appears as a symbol of the deity and

"whoever insults a person's face, insults the face of the Lord, whoever treats a person's face with repugnance, treats the face of the Lord with repugnance."[11]

The terms *ʾādām*, ἄνθρωπος etc. in all of the creation texts mentioned above, are to be interpreted generically. Woman is included, but the androcentric perspective of early Judaism makes it probable that man in these texts is in the first place represented by the male part of the human person. This can be seen in some texts where the generic term "man" (*ʾādām*) clearly means the first man considered as a male individual (*4 Ezra* 7:70 and 6:54). In summarizing Genesis 1:26–27, these passages use a wording which reveals that the first human being is conceived of as a man with the proper name Adam.[12] In other words the account in Genesis 2:7, 15–24 functions as a clue to the understanding of Genesis 1:26–27.

In the accounts which, without mentioning Eve, draw solely upon Genesis 2:7, 15–24, the primordial man is of course Adam who potentially carries the woman in his body (*Sib. Or.* III, 8–9, 24–28, *Similitudes of Enoch* 60:8, *4 Ezra* 7:11, 70 and 116).

The creation accounts dealt with so far have no explicit mention of the woman. They can be said to represent the conventional approach for describing the origin of man. The need is not felt to precise the position of the woman within the primordial couple or in relation to the Divine.

In the cases, therefore, when reference is made to sexual distinction at the creation, either according to the "male and female" formula of Genesis 1:27 or to the "Adam and Eve" myth of Genesis 2:15–24, specific concerns seem to be involved. The texts of this type deserve particular attention because they may reveal fundamental ideas on God and woman inherent to early Judaism but usually not explicitly articulated. These texts stem from different milieus and periods, and reflect different viewpoints and interests.

In the *Book of Tobit* we encounter a diaspora community of Media and northern Mesopotamia in the late Persian or early Hellenistic period.[13] The religious importance of Jerusalem is clearly set out and Jewish ethics and practices are emphasized. The description of the wedding of Tobias and Sarah in chapter 7 provides the immediate background for the reference to the creation of man in chapter 8. Before going to sleep the freshly married couple prays to YHWH for mercy and protection (*Tobit* 8:5–8). The opening doxology praises YHWH as creator of heaven and earth. This is directly followed by a restatement of the Yahwistic account on the creation of man with an allusion to the power of reproduction emphasized in the Priestly account:

"Thou madest Adam (τὸν Ἀδάμ)
and thou madest for him a helper and a support, Eve his wife
and from them both the race of men came into being
and Thou didst speak: 'it is not good for the man to be alone,
let us make him a helper like him'" (8:6).[14]

The elements selected from the Genesis account are those which show the priority of the man and define the role of the woman. That role is seen first from the perspective of the man: woman is made to support her husband. Then also from the viewpoint of humankind: both the man and the woman have been given the task of procreation. These characteristics are typified in Adam and Eve, the primordial couple, and repeated in all subsequent unions of man and woman.

The mention of the creation of Adam and Eve in *Tobit* 8:6 may have a ritual background in the wedding liturgy, that which later came to be known as the *seder birkat niśśūʾîn*, the seven marriage benedictions. The introductory formula of the prayer in *Tobit* 8:5 εὐλογητὸς εἶ ὁ θεός is the usual one in Jewish liturgy and corresponds to that of the marriage benedictions *bārūk ʾattā ʾădōnāi ʾĕlōhēnū . . .*" blessed be Thou Adonai our god." The second and third of these benedictions, attested in the Talmud (*b Ket* 8a), refer to the creation of man. *Tobit* 7:12–14 contains the earliest evidence for the written marriage agreement, the *kĕtūbāh*.[15] The third marriage benediction follows the same line of thought as *Tobit* 8:6. The creation of the man (*hāʾādam*) is mentioned first and it is only with him that the *selem* concept is explicitly connected. Then follows the reference to the creation of the woman: "(blessed be YHWH) who erected for him (sc. Adam) out of himself a building (*binyān*, cf. *wayyiben* of Gen. 2:22) for eternity." The expression "for eternity" is an allusion to the perpetuation of humankind.

If the statement on the creation of man in *Tobit* 8:6 has its original setting in the ritual of marriage, its presentation of woman takes on a particular significance.

The most influential group within the Jewish community of Palestine in the Hellenistic period was no doubt the Zadokite or Aaronite priesthood.[16] They administrated the sacrificial worship at the Jerusalem temple, which was the ideological and spiritual centre of the Jews both in Palestine and in the diaspora. From their ranks the high priest was chosen and they represented the official religion of Judaism. From the early second century B.C.E. a tension appears within the Zadokites between hellenizing circles and nationalistic-religious groups. This tension leads to the Maccabean uprising and is then continued in the split between Hasmoneans-Sadduceans and the Essene movement.

Beside their concern for the cult, the Zadokites had a strong interest in the legal aspects of the torah. This interest is prominent in the *Book of Jubilees* which is best characterized as a "complementary paraphrase" to the Book of Genesis.[17] In the *Jubilees* haggadah serves the overall purpose to lay down halachic rules. The treatment of the creation of man in 2:13–14; 3:1–14 is no exception. The way in which the author of *Jubilees* combines the two creation stories in Genesis is significant. The world history is in *Jubilees* divided into jubilees and weeks and the Priestly creation account is naturally placed in the first week of the first jubilee (*Jub.* 2:1–33). The presentation of *Jubilees* follows rather closely the text of Genesis 1. New is the idea that the angels and the spirits of the phenomena of nature were created on the first day, and the emphasis put on the Sabbath. The creation of man is restated according to Genesis 1:26–28, but without the mention of man as made in the image of YHWH.[18]

The Yahwistic creation story is placed in the second week (*Jub.* 3:1–35) except for the creation of Adam which is stated once again to have taken place in the first week (v. 8). Although the present text of *Jubilees* is somewhat obscure when it comes to precise the creation of the woman,[19] the priority of Adam is nevertheless clear. Halachic differences pertaining to male and female are legitimized by reference to the creation of man and woman. The correspondences between creation acts and purity laws for the woman who bears a child is defined by *Jubilees* in the following way:

Adam	*male child*
created in the first week	the mother unclean for seven days
brought to the garden of Eden	purification of her blood for 33
on the 40th day	days; altogether 40 days
Eve	*female child*
created in the second week	the mother unclean for fourteen days
brought to the garden of Eden	purification of the mother's blood
on the 80th day	for 66 days; altogether 80 days

The purity rules for the woman who bears a child are the same as those prescribed in Leviticus 12:1-5, but the connection with the divine creation act has been introduced by the Zadokite circles behind the *Jubilees*.

Zadokite priests were the constitutive element in the Essene movement and the Qumran writings are therefore imbued with Zadokite ideas. As in *Jubilees* 2-3, the use made of Genesis 1:27 in the Damascus Covenant is sprung from the wish to determine a law, this time not for women but for men. The author of the Damascus Covenant sharply criticizes the Hasmonean high priests and accuses them of marrying two women "during their lifetime" (i.e. the lifetime of the women).

The *Sibylline Oracles* books I-II, which are for the largest part of since YHWH "created them male and female." Obviously the Essene interpretation is that monogamy was enjoined already at the creation of man. The quotation of Genesis 1:27 is followed by the affirmation that "those who went into the ark, one pair they went into the ark" (CD V, 1), intended to support the prescription of monogamy. The claim for monogamy made by the Essenes has nothing to do with the idea of woman's god-likeness, but is a matter of holiness – for the man. Since the tendency for misogyny was evident among the Essenes (cf. below), one might interpret the interest in monogamy as an attempt to reduce defilement through woman to that necessary for procreation (one woman defiles less than two or three).

The texts to be treated next have the common aim to show that the first human person created was a male individual called Adam and that woman was shaped by YHWH from material taken out of Adam, in accordance with the Yahwistic creation account. Little interest is shown in the legal implications of this difference.

The *Sibylline Oracles* books I-II, which are for the largest part of Jewish origin, can be traced back to Greek-speaking Jews of Asia Minor about the turn of the era.[20] The creation account in I, 5-37 shows Adam as a youthful and beautiful man of divine appearance (νεὸν ἄνδρα καλὸν θεσπέσιον), shaped by YHWH and fashioned "after His own image" (lines 22-24). Adam felt himself alone and he prayed to behold another form (εἶδος) such as his own and so YHWH (θεός) made "the wonderful Eve" (26-28). Here god-likeness is reserved for Adam, whereas Eve has her resemblance primarily from Adam. The question whether woman shares through the man a likeness with YHWH is not considered.

The midrash on the six days of creation found in *Slavonic Enoch* 24-32 goes most probably back to a Jewish original composed during the first century C.E. within a diaspora community in the margins of mainstream Judaism.[21] The midrash follows the structure of the Priestly creation account. For the creation of man (30:8-18), however, it combines both Genesis accounts and adds much new material. The most striking idea is that YHWH entrusts Wisdom with the creation of man which she performs out of seven different components. YHWH gives the first human, Adam, a free will to choose between good and evil so that He might know whether man loves him or abhors him (v. 15). After the praise of Adam, the forming of Eve is briefly described according to Genesis 2:21-22 with the following conclusion: "I created for him a wife, so that death might come to him by his wife" (v. 17). There is no attempt to precise the constitution of the first woman as it was done for Adam. It might be inferred, however, that Eve as a creation out of the man's body was composed of the same elements as the man, given the same free will as he was given.

Haggadic traditions on the first human couple developed early and in the first century of our era they were expanded and collected in the *Life of Adam and Eve.*[22] The original collection was certainly of Jewish origin. The *Life* glorifies Adam as the image of YHWH and puts the blame on Eve for having brought the sin into the world. When Adam dies, the angels come down from heaven to the place where his body lies. They pray to YHWH that he might have compassion with Adam and bring his soul up to Paradise: "Yael, holy one, have pardon, for he is Thy image (εἰκών) and the creation of Thy holy hands" (*Life* 33: cf. also 35). In the *Life of Adam and Eve* the expression "image of God" is used almost as an epithet of the first man and his male lineage. Although we do not find any explicit denial of woman's god-likeness, it is nonetheless evident from the context that god-likeness i.e. being an "image of God" is thought of as a divine privilege reserved for the man and conveyed to him in the act of creation.

The *Life* tells of the illness of Adam and how Eve and Seth, on the request of Adam, go near to paradise where they shall pray to YHWH that he might give them of "the tree out of which oil flows" in order to bring it to Adam. On their way, a beast assails Seth, but Eve shouts to the beast: "You evil beast, don't you fear to assail the image of God?" (τὸν εἰκόνα τοῦ θεοῦ 10; cf. also 12). Eve here speaks of the "image of God" as something distinct from herself. Further on, the archangel Michael addresses Seth with the words "O, man of God" (ἄνθρωπε τοῦ θεοῦ, 13) which is to be understood in the light of the "image of God" concept.

The impact of Philo from Alexandria was not on subsequent Judaism but on the Christian tradition. Philo appears nevertheless as an important spokesman for the piety of many Greek-speaking Jews within the Egyptian diaspora in the early first century of our era. His exposition of man's creation in *De Opificio Mundi* stands in Jewish haggadic and homiletic traditions, but it is enriched with concepts borrowed from Greek religious thinking, particularly as brought out by Plato in *Timaeus*.[23] The Priestly account records, according to Philo, the origin of humankind as a genus (τὸ γένος ἀνθρώπων) in which the species (τὰ εἴδη) male and female are included (*De Opif. Mundi* 76). As shown by other passages in the same writing (134, 145), this first man "created in the image of God" (τοῦ κατὰ τὴν εἰκόνα θεοῦ γεγονότος πρότερον) represents the ideal man, the form (ἰδέα) of man, incorporeal and immortal and who was neither a male nor a female. The living copies of that form or archetype were shaped later and this is what is told in the Yahwistic account according to Philo. They have a body and a soul (ἐκ σώματος καὶ ψυχῆς συνεστώς) and are either male or female (134). Philo follows in his exposition the order in which man and woman is created in Genesis 2:7, 15-24. The first man (ὁ πρῶτος ἄνθρωπος) is thus Adam who potentially carries the woman in his body (cf. 134).

His beauty and excellency is described at length by Philo (136-144). However, says Philo, since mortal things necessarily are exposed to changes and reverses, even the first man had to suffer some bad fortune (κακοπραγία). The beginning of his blameworthy life was woman (151). Philo's assertion is rather a statement of fact than an expression of misogyny. But there is no doubt in Philo on the inferior status of woman. The story of the "fall" which Philo recounts and interprets in 153-165, has a deeper meaning and serves to illustrate the superiority of the male principle, the mind (ὁ νοῦς) over the female principle, the senses (ἡ αἴσθησις) in every man.[24] Adam representing the mind is seduced by Eve, the senses. This is so, says Philo, since pleasure (ἡδονή) associates itself first with the senses and through them cheats "the sovereign mind."

The treatment given to the origin of man by Josephus in his *Jewish Antiquities* I, 32-36 is based on the usual harmonization of the two Genesis accounts. Genesis 1:26-27 is reduced to the one phrase: "on this (sc. the sixth) day, he also fashioned man "which functions as a preliminary announcement of man's creation fully described in Genesis 2:7, 15-24. Josephus regards the Yahwistic account as the real creation story, which he relates rather extensively. The assertion "male and female he created them" of Genesis 1:27 is transferred by Josephus to the animals (I,32) and repeated again in I,35 for Adam's name-giving of the animals.

The messianic movement which followed upon the appearance of Jesus from Nazareth, got with Paul, a Cilician Jew, an energetic and ardent representative. His conversion took place *within* Judaism and the writings preserved from his hand[25] show no abandon of fundamental Jewish beliefs and practises. Paul's ideas on man and woman are in accordance with Jewish teaching. The passage in 1 Corinthians 11 :2-16[26] where Paul comes to speak about the creation of man (vv. 7-9) gives but another variant of the traditional interpretation of the Genesis accounts as set forth in the texts treated above. The man (ἀνήρ) alone is the image and the glory of YHWH (εἰκὼν καὶ δόξα θεοῦ) whereas woman is the glory of the man. Woman was made out of the man and she was created for his sake (vv. 8-9). Paul uses the reference to the creation with a similar purpose as that of the Zadokite groups in *Jubilees*. He wants to impose a teaching (παράδοσις cf. v. 2) on covering the head of the women in worship and he justifies it by pointing to the subordinate role of woman laid down already at the creation. This is not contradictory to that which follows in vv. 11-12. The essential thing is (cf. the πλήν in v. 11) that both man and woman are ontologically dependent on each other. If woman was fashioned from the man in the beginning, the man must come into this world through the womb of a woman. Ultimately all things come from YHWH, however. The reasoning of Paul in vv. 11-12 seems clear except for the expression "in the Lord" (ἐν κυρίῳ) at the end of v. 11. It stands parallel to the words "from God" (ἐκ τοῦ θεοῦ) in the structure of the passage (vv. 11-12) and "the Lord" may here mean YHWH, not the Messiah (ὁ χριστός).[27] The meaning of v. 11 would then be that the order of creation (hinted at with the words ἐν κυρίῳ) has made man and woman dependent on each other, as it is explicitly set out in the following verse (note the γάρ). There would accordingly be no mention in this passage of a new relation between man and woman in Christ. Anyway, the passage (vv. 11-12) cannot, in my opinion, be interpreted as an abrogation of the difference between man and woman in relation to the Divine as stated by Paul in vv. 7-9. The teaching given by Paul that women should not pray or prophesize with uncovered head (vv. 3-6) is supported with an appeal to what is natural (vv. 13-15) and with a reference to the "custom" (συνήθεια) of the communities of YHWH (αἱ ἐκκλησίαι τοῦ θεοῦ), and to the opinion of Paul himself (v. 16).

In the gospels of Mark 10:2-12 and Matthew 19:3-12 we find a saying of Jesus from Nazareth on divorce with elements from both creation accounts in Genesis. Some Pharisees approach Jesus and ask him if a man is allowed to divorce his wife. Jesus answers that YHWH created man from the beginning male and female, and that this is the reason why a man shall leave father and mother for his woman and the pair shall be one flesh. Consequently what YHWH has joined, man must not separate. Jesus goes on to say that divorce either on the part of the man or the woman to marry another is adultery.[28] This is the heart of the pericope on divorce in Mark and Matthew and it may well go back to Jesus himself[29] although the present versions presuppose different cultural environments.[30] The creation of man in the Genesis accounts is here, as in the Damascus Covenant IV, 21, taken to support monogamy in a strict sense. The ideal of monogamy was upheld also by the circles behind the *Testaments of the Twelve Patriarchs* which show many affinities with the teachings of the primitive Jesus-movement. The "aretalogy" of Issachar, a central parenetic passage, presents the patriarch saying:

"Except my wife, I have not known any woman,
I have not committed adultery by the uplifting of my eyes."
(Test. Iss. 7:2)

Fornication with "uplifting of the eyes" (μετεωρισμοῖς ὀφθαλμῶν) corresponds to what is intended by the logion in Matthew 5:28, where it is said that whoever looks on a woman with lust has already committed adultery with her in his heart.

In the Damascus Covenant IV, 21 and in the Jesus-logion on divorce the references to the creation of man are used to support the claim for strict monogamy, but without any mention of differences between the sexes in their relationship to the Divine.

Didactic Texts on the Nature of Woman

As is well known, Jewish wisdom tradition sometimes expresses a contemptuous attitude towards woman (e.g. Qoheleth 7:26-28; Ben Sira 9:1-4, 8; 25:19, 24; 42:14). This attitude, which is not connected with the opposition between the good and the bad wife, comes close to a topos in wisdom literature. It seems to be based on the idea of a constitutional inferiority of woman.

In the didactic literature there are some passages in which such an idea is set out in more detail.[31] One of the most important of the didactic writings is the *Testaments of the Twelve Patriarchs* mentioned above. The original was composed in the first half of the first century B.C.E. among Jewish levitical sages of northern Palestine.[32] The Greek text of the present collection constitutes, as it seems, an abbreviated and reworked version. Its Jewish character cannot be denied, however.

The author of the *Testaments* often admonishes against adultery (πορνεία) and this is the main theme of the exhortations in the *Testament of Reuben*, the first testament of the collection. The parenesis against "adultery" culminates in a short "homily" on the nature of women, especially their seductive wails (*Test. Reub.* 5:1-7). They are constantly possessed by thoughts of how to seduce the man. By their adornment they sow poison in the man's mind. The author exhorts his male listeners (or readers) to forbid their wives and daughters to adorn their heads and faces. Women who do this will be kept for eternal punishment. According to the *Testament of Reuben*, woman has an inclining for adultery which is constitutional and stronger than any corresponding desire in the man: "women are inferior in the spirit of adultery than men are" (5:3). Since the affirmation cited is introduced as a divine revelation transmitted by an angel, it is likely that the author considers woman's moral weakness to go back ultimately to her creation by YHWH. No such legitimizing introduction would have been necessary, if the "fall" was seen as the cause, because Eve's seduction of Adam is plainly stated in Genesis 3. The "homily" is completed with a reference to the haggadah of the Watchers also known from other Jewish writings.[33]

The misogynic tendency is particularly at home among the Essenes and the circles influenced by them.[34] It is not surprising that they tried to justify their contempt for women by obscure references to a constitutional weakness, present already from the creation of the first woman.

The Sacrificial Worship and Women

The system of values inherent to a religious culture like early Judaism can be grasped from its basic ideas and rituals. For the Jews in the Second Temple period the cult at the Jerusalem sanctuary was of utmost importance in maintaining a close and secure relationship between the community and its supreme god, YHWH. The concepts underlying the Jewish sacrificial system may help to elucidate the position of woman in relation to the Divine.

The issue whether women were allowed to act as sacrifiers[35] is for our purpose less revealing than to look at the structure of the central cult-place and the types of victims used for the offerings.[36]

The Jerusalem temple was holy through the presence of YHWH. Yet the holiness of the temple varied with its different parts. From the centre, the cella (the Holy of Holies), where in all probability some symbols of the divine presence were deposed, the holiness character decreased gradually towards the outer parts and with it also the levels of purity. This concentric outflow of holiness is most clearly seen in the ideal picture of the Jerusalem temple as it is outlined by the Zadokites in the *Temple Scroll* from Qumran.[37] An analysis of the sources for the Second Temple reveals a holiness structure which is related to different categories of worshippers and includes the following areas (each higher ranking cult category was, of course, permitted to enter the areas for lower ranking categories as well):

areas of holiness	*entrance allowed to*
Holy of Holies (*qōdeš qodāšīm*)	only the high priest
the Holy Place (*hēkāl*)	officiating priests
priestly cult area	officiating priests
outer priestly area	male members of priestly families and Levites
court of the Israelites	adult male members of the Jewish community
court of the women	Jewish women and children; proselytes since few generations

This hierarchical order of worshippers reflects a religious value system correlated with nearness and distance to the Divine in which women are placed in *one* category low in the holiness and purity scale.

In offerings, generally seen, the sacrificial matter has a particular significance as the object which establishes that relationship between God and man intended by the sacrificial ritual. The kind of victims offered in animal sacrifices may have a bearing upon the religious ideology in its relation to sexual and social differentiation.

To this purpose I have investigated the distribution of male and female victims among the various sacrifices in the early Jewish cult. Such an investigation may illustrate the part played by the female element in the communication between YHWH and his worshippers.

The sources on the sacrificial worship during the Second Temple period[38] are found in the Priestly code of the Pentateuch (Leviticus 1-7 and Numbers 28-29 being the most important passages), in Zadokite texts from the Hellenistic period (*Temple Scroll, Apocryphon of Levi, Jubilees*) and in some Mishna tractates (e.g. *Zevaḥim, Middot, Tamid*).

The Jewish sacrifices can be divided into two general categories a) public sacrifices and b) private sacrifices.[39] The public sacrifices offered at the festivals, the sabbath days and in the daily *tamid*-offering were of particular importance. As to the different kinds of sacrifice, Jewish tradition distinguishes three main types which require each a specific ritual: a) the burnt-offering (*ʾōlāh*), b) the sin-offering (*ḥaṭṭāt*) and the closely related guilt-offering (*ʿāšām*), and c) the shared-offering or communion sacrifice (*zebaḥ šēlamîm*). The first two types were considered more sacred and termed "most holy" (*qōdeš qodāšîm,* cf. Leviticus 6:25, 30; 7:1, *Zevaḥim* 5:4). The following survey of the early Jewish sacrifices is based on the groups of sources indicated above and aims at giving a picture of the distribution of male and female victims related to types of sacrifice and partly also to social differences (female victims have been italicized).

types of sacrifice	*victims*	
	private sacrifices	*public sacrifices*
burnt-offering from the cattle	a male	bulls, young bulls, calfs
burnt-offering from the flock	a male	rams, he-goats, young male lambs, and kids
sin-offering from the cattle	on behalf of a priest: young bull, calf	bulls, young bulls
sin-offering from the flock	on behalf of a man of standing: a he-goat on behalf of any person from the common people: a *she-goat* or *ewe*	he-goats
guilt-offering from the flock	a ram	
shared-offering from the cattle or the flock	male or *female*	

It appears that in the public sacrifices considered the heart of the temple cult there is a total dominance of male victims. In the most sacred sacrifices, the *ʾōlāh* and the *ḥaṭṭāt* — *ʾāšām* offerings, female victims were used only for private sin-offerings from persons belonging to the common people. Higher up on the social scale male victims are a rule. In the shared-offerings which constituted a sacrifice mainly for the common people, the choice between male and female victims was left free. Thus, the cultic relationship with the Divine was in early Judaism largely mediated by the male element.

Conclusions

The Jewish sources do not raise the questions with which many modern scholars approach the texts, e.g. are women god-like or not? What is, more precisely, the position of woman in relation to the Divine?

The creation of man is most often referred to in general terms without attention to sexual distinction. The human person is usually represented by the first male individual. In some texts, where particular concerns are involved, precisions are found which reflect a religious and moral evaluation of women, almost in all cases leading to the conclusion of an inferior status for women. This can be considered representative for early Jewish religion in view of the wide variety of texts and milieus investigated. Although the two creation stories in Genesis are treated as statements on one and the same event, the Yahwistic account sets the interpretative norm and provides the justification for the subordinate role assigned to women by the Jewish society and its male-shaped ideology. When occasionally, as in the Damascus Covenant and in the Jesus-saying on divorce, Genesis 1:27b is allowed to stand for itself, it is cut off from the idea of man's god-likeness in 1:27a. This supports the conclusion that women are implicitly regarded as not being created in the image of YHWH.

The place of women in the holiness structure of the Temple and the inconspicuous role of the female element in the sacrificial worship is completely in accordance with the interpretations of man's creation made in the written documents. With respect to God and image of woman the Jewish system of values is thus strikingly well-balanced as an expression of a strongly androcentric culture. A greater appreciation of women's relationship to the Divine might have existed among some Jewish groups (the primitive Jesus-movement and other messianic and baptismal groups?). The sources that have come down to us cannot make this evident, however.

(1990)

Notes

1. This span of time corresponds roughly to what is termed the Second Temple period.
2. It is difficult to state exactly when primitive Christianity detaches itself from Judaism and becomes a religion of its own. One may consider the first Christians a Jewish movement as long as the majority and the leading persons regarded themselves as Jews ethnically and culturally. Towards the end of the first century this was certainly no longer the case. Sayings and teachings (within and outside the New Testament) which go back to Jesus himself or to the primitive community, as well as the genuine writings of Paul can be said to represent sources belonging to the Jewish stage of the history of Christianity.
3. Cf. also Smith 1971, especially pp. 1–14.
4. The expression is taken from Smith 1971.
5. As far as I know, there are virtually no written records extant, which can be shown to have been formulated by women living within the culture of early Judaism.
6. In the period with which we are concerned the *sōfēr* and the *ḥākām* represented the same category of religious authority, cf. Hultgård 1982 pp. 215–219.
7. An influence of the Greek concept ὁ θεός or τὸ θεῖον may already be present in the use of *ʾĕlōhîm* in Qoheleth as argued by Bickerman 1962 p. 66.
8. The worship of other deities beside YHWH in the Exilic, Persian and Hellenistic periods is attested in several sources e.g. Jeremiah 44:15–19 (the Queen of heaven), Isaiah 65:11 (Gad, a god of fortune, and Mani, a goddess giving happiness and wellbeing), the Elephantine papyri (Anat-yahu and possibly other deities). For a discussion on such forms of worship within early Judaism, see Patai 1966, Delcor 1952, Smith 1984.
9. The biblical creation stories are not analyzed here. Interesting analyses of the sexual distinction at the creation according to the Genesis account are found in Trible 1978, Mikaelsson 1980 and Bird 1981.
10. Psalm 8 describes the creation of man along the same lines of thought as the Priestly creation story in Genesis 1. There are, however, no direct literary borrowings in this psalm from the Genesis account. The creation texts in Psalm 139 and Job 10:8–12 which are independent of those in Genesis, have had little impact upon the early Jewish accounts.
11. The translation is that of Andersen 1983.
12. The Hebrew original probably had *ha-ʾādām* which in the context of 7:70 and 6:54 rightly was rendered by the Latin and Syriac versions (through the intermediary of the lost Greek text) with Adam.
13. On the origin and date of the *Book of Tobit,* cf. Grintz 1972 and Greenfield 1981.
14. Translated after the Greek text of codex Sinaiticus.
15. Cf. Bickerman 1976.
16. In the post-exilic period the difference between Aaronite and Zadokite priests

was merely theoretical, the former representing the line of Ithamar and the latter the line of Eleazar.

17. This characterization is that of Caquot 1985. The *Book of Jubilees* was most probably composed during the latter half of the second century B.C.E. Fragments of the Hebrew original have been found at Qumran.

18. The absence of the "image"-concept seems to characterize a particular form of early Jewish creation accounts which may go back to an early midrash summarizing the creation of the six days, cf. Jervell 1960 pp. 19-21.

19. The creation of the first woman, Eve, is told in the context of the events of the second week 3:1-7, but in 3:8 the text states that Adam was created in the first week together with "the rib, his wife" and that she was shown unto him in the second week (*basab⁽ĕt qadamit taffaṭĕra ʾadām wagabo bĕʾesitu wasab⁽ĕta kĕlita ʾarayo kiyā lotu*). The meaning may be that the woman was potentially present in Adam, but was not fashioned until the second week. A corruption of the text in 3:8 is perhaps a more probable explanation.

20. Cf. Kurfess 1941 and Collins 1983 pp. 330-334.

21. The origin and date of the *Slavonic Enoch* is much debated. Some authors consider the work a Christian compilation from the early Middle Ages e.g. Milik 1976. Its Jewish character is, in my opinion, manifest. For the date and provenance proposed here, cf. Bugge & Hammershaimb 1974 and Andersen 1983 pp. 94-97.

22. The title *Life of Adam and Eve* denotes in the first place the Greek text called "Apocalypsis Mosis" and edited by Tischendorf 1895 and in the second place the Latin writing known as "Vita Adae et Evae" which complements the Greek text in some passages. For composition, date and origin, cf. Nickelsburg 1984 pp. 110-118, Bertrand 1985 and 1987.

23. Cf. Fossum 1985 pp. 203-208.

24. For an overall treatment of the categories male and female in Philon, see Baer 1970.

25. These are the Letters to the Romans and the Galatians, the First and Second Letters to the Corinthians, the First Letter to the Thessalonians, and the Letter to Philemon, cf. Vielhauer 1975.

26. For a commentary on the whole pericope, see Conzelmann 1981 pp. 222-234.

27. The Pauline formula ἐν κυρίῳ is generally taken to refer to the Messiah (Christ) but it may not be so in every passage. In 1 Cor 7:22 the first mention of kyrios (ἐν κυρίῳ) is best interpreted as meaning YHWH (cf. v. 17), whereas the second one (κυρίου) refers to the Messiah. The passage vv. 11-12 is discussed in detail by Jervell 1960 pp. 309-312. On the basis of rabbinical parallels, he interprets v. 11 as an allusion to the god-likeness of both man and woman "in the new eon" in Christ.

28. The version of Mark is closer to the original saying than the text of Matthew, which by the addition of μὴ ἐπὶ πορνεία in v. 9 makes an exception to the general condemnation of divorce intended in the reference to the creation act.

29. It is referred to by Paul in 1 Cor 7:10; cf. also Luke 16:18.
30. See the discussion of the Jesus-logia on divorce and remarriage by Lövestam 1978.
31. An instructive passage is 4Q184 "The wiles of the wicked woman." Irrespective of which word stood in the lacuna at the beginning (*zônāh* or *ᵓiššāh*) the target seems to be woman in general and not specifically the harlot, cf. for this interpretation Dupont-Sommer 1967 and Philonenko 1982. The allegorical interpretation of 4Q184 is less convincing.
32. On the composition, origin and date of the *Testaments of the Twelve Patriarchs*, see Hultgård 1982.
33. On the myth of fall of the Watchers and its connection with the idea of women as source of sin, see Prusak 1974.
34. An excellent survey of the problem of misogyny among the Essenes is given by Philonenko 1982.
35. For the distinction in early Judaism between sacrifiers and sacrificers, cf. Hultgård 1987.
36. In the Jewish society of the Second Temple period the sacrifiers were usually men, but women were permitted to bring offerings, as is shown for the *ᵓōlāh* by *Zevahim* 12:2.
37. The Temple Scroll dates from approximately the same time as the *Book of Jubilees*, cf. Yadin 1977 and Caquot 1985. The earliest manuscript fragment of the Scroll is on palaeographical grounds dated to the end of the 2nd cent. B.C.E.
38. For a discussion on the sources of the sacrificial cult in early Judaism, see Hultgård 1987.
39. This distinction is made also by Philo *Spec. Leg.* 168 and Josephus *Antiquities* II, 224.

Works Consulted

Andersen, F. I. 1983. "2 (Slavonic Apocalypse of) Enoch, a new translation and introduction." In *The Old Testament Pseudepigrapha*, ed. James H. Charlesworth, vol. 1. New York.

Baer, R. A. 1970. *Philo's use of the categories male and female.* Leiden.

Bertrand, D. A. 1985. "Le destin 'post mortem' des protoplastes selon la "vie grecque d'Adam et Ève." In *La Littérature Intertestamentaire*, Paris, pp. 109–118.

———. 1987, "Vie grecque d'Adam et Ève." in: *La Bible, écrits intertestamentaires*, ed. A. Dupont-Sommer and M. Philonenko (Bibliothèque de la Pléiade, Éditions Gallimard) pp. 1767–1796.

Bickermann, E. 1962. *From Ezra to the last of the Maccabees, foundations of post-biblical Judaism.* New York.

——. 1976. *Studies in Jewish and Christian History*. Part One. Leiden.

Bird, Ph. 1981. "'Male and Female He Created Them': Gen 1:27b in the Context of the Priestly Account of Creation." *Harvard Theological Review* 74:129–159.

Bugge, A. & Hammershaimb, E. 1974. "Anden Enoksbog." In *De Gammeltestamentlige Pseudepigrafer*, pp. 791–826.

Caquot, A. 1985. "Éléments aggadiques dans le livre des 'Jubilés.'" In *La Littérature Intertestamentaire*, Paris, pp. 57–68.

Collins, J. J. 1983. "Sibylline Oracles, a new translation and introduction." In *The Old Testament Pseudepigrapha*, ed. James Charlesworth, vol. 1. New York.

Conzelmann, H. 1981. *Der erste Brief an die Korinther*. 2 Aufl. Göttingen.

Delcor, M. 1982. "Le culte de la 'Reine du Ciel' selon Jer 7,18; 44,17–19.25 et ses survivances." In *Von Kanaan bis Kerala, Festschrift van der Ploeg*, pp. 101–122.

Dupont-Sommer, A. 1967. "L'Essénisme à la lumière des manuscrits de la Mer Morte: le Maître de justice et son Évangile." In: *L'Annuaire du Collège de France, 66ᵉ Année*, pp. 347–358.

Fossum, J. 1985. "Gen. 1,26 and 2,7 in Judaism, Samaritanism, and Gnosticism," *Journal for the Study of Judaism* 16:202–239.

Greenfield, J. 1981. "Ahiqar in the Book of Tobit." In *De la Tôrah au Messie, études d'exégèse et d'herméneutique bibliques offertes à Henri Cazelles*. Paris, pp. 329–336.

Grintz, Y. M. 1972. "Tobit, Book of." In *Encyclopaedia Judaica* 15:1183–1186.

Hultgård, A. 1982. *L'eschatologie des Testaments des Douze Patriarches* vol. 2. Uppsala.

——. 1987. "The Burnt-Offering in Early Jewish Religion, sources, practices and purpose." In *Gifts to the Gods*, ed. by T. Linders & G. Nordquist. Uppsala (Boreas 15), 83–91.

Jervell, J. 1960. *Imago Dei, Gen 1,26 f. im Spätjudentum, in der Gnosis und in den paulinischen Briefen*. Göttingen.

Kurfess, A.-M. 1941. "Oracula Sibyllina I/II." *Zeitschrift für die neutestamentliche Wissenschaft* 40:151–165.

Lövestam, E. 1978. "Divorce and Remarriage in the New Testament." *The Jewish Law Annual*, 4:47–65.

Mikaelsson, L. 1980. "Sexual Polarity: An Aspect of the Ideological Structure in the Paradise Narrative, Gen. 2,4–3,24." *Temenos* 16:84–91.

Milik, J. T. 1976. *The Books of Enoch, Aramaic fragments of Qumran cave 4*. Oxford.

Nickelsburg, G. W. 1984. "The Bible rewritten and expanded." In *Jewish Writings of the Second Temple Period*, ed. Michael E. Stone, Assen/Philadelphia, PA. pp. 89–156.

Patai, R. 1969. *The Hebrew Goddess*, New York.

Philonenko, M. 1982. "Essénisme et misogynie." *Académie des Inscriptions & Belles-Lettres, comptes rendus des séances de l'année 1982, avril-juin*, pp. 339–353.

Prusak, B. 1974. "Woman: Seductive Siren and Source of Sin?" In: *Religion and Sex-*

ism. *Images of Woman in the Jewish and Christian Traditions,* ed. Rosemary Radford Ruether. New York.

Smith, M. 1971. *Palestinian Parties and Politics That Shaped the Old Testament.* New York and London.

——. 1984. "Jewish Religious Life in the Persian Period." In: *The Cambridge History of Judaism,* ed. W. D. Davies and Louis Finkelstein. Vol. 1, Introduction; The Persian Period, pp. 219–278.

Tischendorf, K. von. 1866. *Apocalypses Apocryphae.* Leipzig.

Trible, P. 1978. *God and the Rhetoric of Sexuality.* Philadelphia, PA.

Vielhauer, P. 1975. *Geschichte der urchristlichen Literatur.* Berlin.

Yadin, Y. 1977. *Megillat ha-Miqdaš. The Temple Scroll.* Vol I and II, Introduction, Text and Commentary. English edition 1983. Jerusalem.

4

IMAGE OF GOD AND GLORY OF MAN: WOMEN IN THE PAULINE CONGREGATIONS

℅ Lone Fatum

What was the role attributed to women by Pauline theology, and what was their status in the Pauline communities? What were the conditions imposed upon Christian women of the early missionary congregations, and were they given any opportunity to develop fully as Christians and as women in a fellowship based on freedom and equality?

These questions are by no means new. They have been asked many times and in many ways, and though generally meant to serve a common positive purpose, they have admittedly in the course of time been interpreted and treated in different ways. Rarely, however, have they been treated in their full consequence with sufficient seriousness and without prejudice. Mostly referred to as merely a detail, an isolated and rather inferior problem in the traditional interpretation of Paul, they have often been subjected to a desultory and unsatisfactory treatment, having thus been explained away rather than explained.[1]

The reason for this may be found in the fact that traditional interpretation of Paul is based on an overall gender-blind theology which makes it difficult even to discern the full consequence of critical questions concerning gender roles and sexual motifs. It may also be that the majority of Pauline interpreters so far have not just had a traditional approach to him, their basic attitude has been dogmatic rather than analytic; this may well put an effective limit to their critical attention, perhaps even cause an aversion towards going into problems relating to sexual discrimination or downright suppression of women in Paul and among the early Christians. First and foremost, though, there has been – and still is[2] – a tendency to look upon these questions, even in their most persevering and critical shape, as predefined expressions of a set task: that of interpreting Gal 3,28 as a reflection of an absolute affirmation of women, and thus the questions have in every respect been determined by Gal 3,28 as an eschatologically qualified primary text on gender, sexuality and women.

This one verse, taken to be part of a pre-Pauline baptismal formula,[3] on the abolition of gender differences in Christ, has been given a theoretical and normative value in questions of sexual and feminist concern; its content has been fully accepted and taken at face value, and the verse has been used to prove beyond dispute that every distinction between man and woman has been overcome in principle, that equality in Christ has been established as a theological fact, and that gender-critical questions are no longer needed among human beings in Christ. Few will contest the fact that sexual discrimination exists, or that suppression of women occurs; indeed, Gal 3,28 does seem to be contradicted by 1 Cor 11,2-16 within the Pauline context itself. But in Christ this can be asserted to be without importance; in Christ Gal 3,28 once and for all has turned the problems of Christian women into sham problems – relative, temporary, inferior, in relation to what really matters: as a human being in Christ to belong to God without any provisions or limitations. Phenomena like sexual discrimination and suppression of women may exist, even to Christian women they may represent unavoidable and socially destructive experiences; but according to Gal 3,28 the critical questions have been clearly delimited. In view of the superior apologetical purpose it has been asserted that neither practical circumstances nor social consequences can lay claim to a theological, not to speak of a christological, relevance or interest in the interpretation of Paul.

Thus, on the one hand, Gal 3,28 is seen unequivocally as an expression of an absolutely positive affirmation of women *coram deo*, while, on the other hand, 1 Cor 11,2-16 may be interpreted negatively, although this text, in an indistinct and theologically confusing way, is seen to represent an acceptable compromise. The apparent need of confining the lives of the Corinthian women and subjecting them to common gender models and social norms may be regretted. On the other hand this can be explained, even defended, as a sensible precaution on the part of Paul when he, in Cor 11,2-16, seems prepared to make concessions at the cost of the women, partly out of regard to the unity of the congregation as a whole, partly with a view to the strategy of further missionary activities.[4] The obvious contrast between Gal 3,28 and 1 Cor 11,3-9 does of course underline the difficulties of a harmonization, and great pains have been taken to veil or modify it. Gal 3,28 has been used as an undisputed measure of the importance of Paul's argumentation in

1 Cor 11,3-9, and the apologetical interest has been given free rein in the attempts to neutralize the unambiguous words about women's inferior rank and secondary role in the order of creation as well as of salvation.[5]

Sometimes it can be difficult to say whether the apologetical efforts are meant to save Paul for women or women for Paul. But there is no mistaking the often very uncritical treatment of Gal 3,28 at the cost of a satisfactorily consistent understanding of 1 Cor 11,2-16. Far too many have taken Gal 3,28 at its word and used it as an ideal norm at its face value. Only very few have examined it more closely in search of its social consequences or have questioned seriously the practical implications of an eschatologically loaded saying about the abolition of gender differences. No one has ever contested the basis for speaking about the overcoming of sexual discrimination in a patriarchal society, which was completely adapted to androcentric sexual motifs and values. So far the interpretation of Paul has left unanswered a number of questions on the status of Christian women and on their circumstances and conditions as women in Christ.

It is one thing what interpreters have so far been able to agree upon, because they have chosen to be content with finding in Gal 3,28 a positive expression for what is ideal and eschatologically fundamental in Christ; but it is quite another thing – and already some women in the Corinthian congregation felt this[6] – that the practical circumstances and conditions imposed on the lives of Christian women within the social context of the community were not meant by Paul to conform to this ideal or this eschatological principle. On the contrary; although the Corinthian situation would have led one to expect that Gal 3,28 was now to be put to the test in practice, it appears that it has not been applied on 1 Cor 11,2-16 at all. Instead of using Gal 3,28 as a basis for his argumentation Paul resorts to other devices to serve his moral purpose regarding the Corinthian women. By means of 1 Cor 11,3-9 he marks out the fundamental theological basis[7] of his clearly restrictive women's *paraenesis*.

In continuation of this it is unsatisfactory from a critical point of view that an apparent conflict between Gal 3,28 and 1 Cor 11,2-16 is so often taken for granted though theologically harmonized and reduced to being just a conflict between theory and practice: between that which is absolutely valid and a necessary compromise which is only relative. Apart from being the justification for a theological neutralization of 1 Cor 11,3-9 by means of Gal 3,28 this reduction leads to an overall distorted and diffused approach to 1 Cor 11,2-16. Exegesis has been preconditioned by *eisegesis* and the emphasis in 1 Cor 11,2-16 has accordingly been allowed to rest upon the practical *parae-*

nesis, tied up with the actual situation and thought to be of but relative interest from a theological point of view.[8] All things considered, however, 1 Cor 11,2-16 consists of both theory and practice, and vv. 3-9 are, theologically assessed, as much fundamental theory as Gal 3,28. Only theological prejudice can decide that one theory should be accorded greater normative importance than the other, or that one fundamental saying on the relationship between man and woman *coram deo* should take precedence of another and be accepted at face value as the eschatological ideal par excellence.

The fact that Paul argues for a certain practice on the basis of 1 Cor 11,3-9, without involving Gal 3,28, calls for a reconsideration of what, in his own view, were the theological and practical consequences of Gal 3,28? What did a saying about the abolition of gender differences in Christ imply within the boundaries of Paul's own theological assessments and of his own cultural and social universe?

Bearing this in mind it becomes a necessity to reconsider both the theological and practical significance of 1 Cor 11,3-9. These verses call for an independent and unbiased interpretation, putting aside Gal 3,28 as the key text and asking instead for Paul's opinion in 1 Cor 11,3-9, free of preconceived ideas on what Paul ought to mean. There is nothing in those two texts to reasonably support the view that Paul himself held Gal 3,28 for more important or of greater fundamental value than 1 Cor 11,3-9, and wishful thinking always was an unreliable interpretation motive. To the extent that 1 Cor 11,3-9 is a fundamental theological saying expressing a theological principle concerning the relationship between man and woman *coram deo*, it should, like Gal 3,28, be subjected to an unremittingly critical approach as a saying in its own right and of its own theological value within the Pauline context.

It is no wonder that the apologetic interpretation of both Pauline texts has had such an impact within patriarchal theology, and that it has been decisive for the views on gender, sexuality, and women in an androcentrically biased exegesis. What surprises is that a regrettable number of feminist theologians of recent years has come out with exactly the same theological and exegetical attempts to explain away, harmonize or minimize the problems, and that these attempts are given a positive value even by the more critical and hermeneutically reflected feminist theologians doing Pauline research.[9] It is a pity that so many feminist theologians today shrink from asking critical questions and persevere instead in their apologetical endeavours, hardly ever seriously disputing them.[10] Many seem almost too willing to settle for too meager a result when they ought to be asking again and again whether the inferences on Christian women's involvement in the Pauline congregations can in fact and actual practice be said to be positive and affirmative from the point of view of the women themselves.[11]

So far there is hardly any influential exegesis within recognized Pauline interpretation that concerns itself specifically with theological criticism and analysis of the social and practical context of the Pauline congregations, and the attention lavished on questions relating to feminist and gender matters is accordingly negligible.[12] This does of course put an extra demand on feminist theologians not only for theological and exegetical discernment, but for analytical and critical perseverance and a certain stamina when it comes to uncovering the circumstances of Christian women as women to be considered in a text material, a congregational and social context, and an established tradition of interpretation, all of which are dominated theologically and hermeneutically as well as historically and socially by sexual discrimination and the suppression of women.

Evidently, feminist exegesis is no easy task. At times it may even seem impossible, since one has to penetrate into text and tradition just as assiduously, as they will always seem to contradict any feminist approach. Nonetheless, the necessary questions of feminist theologians about the conditions of Christian women can only be solved by looking for information and convincing answers in a material which, like the Pauline letters, is androcentrically biased and in a theological as well as a social respect patriarchally organized and authorized.[13] The difficulties are tangible and should not be turned into excuses by a timid and scrupulous feminist theology, ready to make apologetical compromises with its own critical discernment and thus running the risk of being too easily satisfied with inconsistencies and half-solutions.

The difficulties will of course become more acute and even develop into existential questions of a very personal and pressing character, if the critical approach of the feminist theologians is not only motivated by a subjective interest, but also by subjective scruples inherent in Christian women who are still today being made to suffer from a misogynist and anti-feminist theology, excluded from office and recognized leadership and restricted in their personal commitment and development by a misogynist and anti-feminist church tradition and establishment.[14] Circumstances like these may easily provoke an apologetic attitude and make it seem tempting to interpret even the slightest and most ambiguous traces of a presence and an active participation of women in the Pauline congregations as a sure guarantee that there was indeed a time when Christian women were present in their own right and had their own roles to fulfill in Christ – both as Christians and as women; with the implicit argument that what was in the beginning should of course be so again today.

However, it is one thing to be able to understand a given situation, quite another to accept it. And so, it must be maintained that a feminist theology, dominated by apologetic interest, runs the risk of doing more harm than good to everybody concerned. It is never satisfactory to give up half-way, but this is what happens if the questions of feminist theologians are escaping the critical issue and made into a theological project of utopian quality. It is essential to pay critical attention to the fact that, according to its very essence, feminist theology is heuristically determined and hermeneutically invested.[15] But if we allow our scruples at a negative consequence of critical analysis to lead us and leave us content with any seemingly positive detail, the outcome will be an unserious and unimportant exegesis and a theological work of no avail either to women or to Paul.

If the feminist theological discernment is one-sidedly tied to the necessary questions and the ensuing arguments for their heuristic value, theological interest will be distracted from the persevering and consistent criticism of the possible answers. In that case feminist theological interpretation will be in serious danger of stagnating as a project of mere postulations. Subjecting Pauline texts to critical questions one must be prepared to face both negative and positive answers, and questions as well as answers must be critically tested within the Pauline context to prevent a definite "was" or "is" from being confused with an eschatological "should" or an utopian "must."

Summing up, it seems regrettable that feminist theological work with Pauline texts is so greatly influenced still by apologetic endeavours. For even though the purpose has shifted from androcentric and patriarchal to feminist motivation, and though the exegetical and theological tools are handled today by some feminist theologians with another consciousness and a clearly defined subjectivity,[16] it seems as if, by some sad irony, the ghost of tradition is still haunting. Somehow feminist theological exegesis seems to be attracted by the very same temptations and willing to run the very same risks as androcentric interpretation and patriarchal theology, hitherto so dominant.

When disinclination to take the consequences of a thoroughly critical clash with established theological tradition is sufficiently deep-rooted and the possibilities of a personal breach with current dogmatic and confessional consciousness sufficiently overhanging, even feminist theologians may choose to turn a blind eye to facts. And then, even among feminist theologians, theological and ecclesiastical prejudices may forestall the critical elaborations of exegetical analysis in a way that both determines and limits their results. Suppression of women may be thrown down the front stairs with drums beating and flags flying; sooner or later it will sneak in again through the back door only to settle down the more comfortably, because now it can get to work in its most efficient shape, that of self-suppression and denial.[17]

When feminist theologians minimize what is socially concrete and practical in the Pauline context, and when they pass lightly over or even bypass the actual circumstances and conditions under which Christian women lived in the social context of the missionary congregations, they contribute to the reduction of Paul's words about freedom and equality in Christ to idle talk and eschatological rhetoric. Once again, one thing is theological principle and eschatological ideal, but quite another is the sheer and uncompromising reality of Christian women then and now as Christians and as women. The former is looked upon as an absolute and is seen to be analogous with the meaning of faith and the definition of hope, whereas the latter is seen as a relative and changing phenomenon of this world. And here, apparently, we have to be satisfied with life in all its relativity without faith and without hope?

Can it really be satisfactory to feminist theologians to stop here? Is this all that feminist theology has to offer? Is it in fact what feminist theological interpretation is prepared to be content with?

Considerations of this kind have caused me once more to subject Gal 3,28 and 1 Cor 11,3-9 to a critical feminist theological evaluation. I shall not pretend to be able to produce satisfactory answers to all the questions asked on the status of women in Christ and the role of Christian women as members of a fellowship of freedom and equality. But I do hope to be able to demonstrate what these questions actually imply when they are examined closely and dealt with consistently within the Pauline context with due respect for Paul's Jewish-Christian pattern of motifs and values.

I have chosen not to focus on the possibilities of being a Christian woman today, as I find such consideration misleading to the interpretation at hand. Only when exegesis and theological interpretation have been carried through, and both negative and positive results have been tested in their full hermeneutical consequence, will it be possible to revert to today's situation on a reasonable and defendable basis. Only thus will it be possible to detach oneself from the apologetic limitations and try to understand the significance of Gal 3,28 as well as 1 Cor 11,3-9. Each text must be consistently examined before it becomes possible to compare them and maybe find a common denominator for them within the limits of Paul's universe. For of course it is indeed within this it makes sense to state, on the one hand, that sexual difference no longer exists in Christ, and, on the other, that woman is the glory of man. Against the Pauline background and within Paul's theological universe these questions will have to be asked: What do the texts mean exactly? What preconceived ideas made them what they are in the Pauline context? And what were their implications on Christian women in the Pauline missionary congregations?

Gal 3,28: In Christ There Is No Sexual Differentiation

In his illustrative description of the contrast between law and faith Paul, in Gal 3,19–29, characterizes the law as the tutor whose task it is to lead unto Christ, v. 24. His intention is clearly to reveal the relative and temporary purpose of the law in God's plan of salvation. In its role as a tutor the law has been given a purpose outside itself, and it follows that when the task has been accomplished and the purpose fulfilled the function and meaning of the law is at an end, v. 19 and v. 25.

From this, however, Paul cannot deduce that there is anything wrong with the law as such, nor does he see it as contradictory to the promises to Abraham and his seed, v. 21. The decisive factor to Paul is that the law has proved ineffective as a means of redemption from sin, which, according to v. 22, the world and all worldly existence is definitely consigned to. It is precisely this inefficiency towards sin that has been demonstrated to Paul by the inevitability of the death of Christ; he has once and for all atoned on the premises of the law, thereby breaking the power of sin as well as the authority of law.[18] Thus the concepts of law and faith are clarified as theological opposites, the cross of Christ being literally the *crux* not only in Paul's system of symbols and theological values, but also in consistent Pauline interpretation. He can now proceed to preach the death of Christ as the conditional anticipation of a life in Christ.[19] Christ crucified is maintained throughout as the authorization of a fellowship which is to be based and realized on the concepts of freedom and equality in Christ.[20]

Against this background Paul can argue that through Christ the law has been annulled by God himself in accordance with his plan to save by faith and not by law, law-abidingness and justification by law, vv. 19, 22 and 24. The law has seen its time and played its part. Abraham's seed has come, and with it, with Christ, the relationship to God has become one of faith no longer subjecting anyone to a tutor, v. 25. Thus the promise to Abraham has been fulfilled, and the inheritance has been realized in Christ in a way that makes everyone belonging to Christ heirs of God by promise, v. 29. But to those baptized unto Christ this implies a union with Christ as well as with all other

Christians, vv. 27–28. Detached from their past and their separate backgrounds those who are baptized unto Christ have been set free in order to be one body and to live with one another on equal terms of commitment, because now only Christ, not the law, is significant to them. To belong to Christ means in fact being embodied in a fellowship of unity comparable to a newly established fellowship of life,[21] in which all take part in Christ, and accordingly, all have become sons of God[22] in a union with Christ, based on faith, v. 26.

With vv. 27–28 Paul introduces a baptismal formula and, by three specific examples of existences hitherto incompatible, he elucidates the significance of belonging to Christ on the conditions of faith rather than law. This means: belonging to Christ in unity and solidarity irrespective of diversities and incompatibilities. And thus the Galatian brothers, who are the addressees of Paul's comprehensive paraenetic appeal in 3,15 and again in 4,12, are being committed to accept the fact that the moment he is baptized, a free-born circumcized Jewish male has no advantage as a Christian over other Christians. On the contrary, the free-born Jew is subjected to the same conditions in Christ as a Greek or as a slave, because the discriminatory regulations of the law have been nullified together with the temporary function of the law as a relative means of righteousness.

In so far as baptism unites the person baptized not only with Christ, but with other baptized Christians, v. 28d, the definitions of the law concerning clean and unclean are annulled along with the law as a prerogative and a normative pattern of separation values. To such an extent have the rules of discrimination been invalidated among the sons of God, that even distinction between male and female[23] is no longer significant in Christ, v. 28c. The concepts of unity and equality in the Christian fellowship of life are so independent of the law – and should thus also be applied by the brothers independently of the law[24] – as to include woman on the terms of man in exactly the same way as the Greek is included on the terms of the Jew and the slave on those of the free-born.

Thus Paul concludes his argumentation. Throughout he considers the conflict between law and faith from the point of view of the free-born Jewish male; throughout he remains true to his Jewish background and addresses himself to his Galatian brothers in consistency with his own Jewish-Christian universe. His Christian arguments on the annulment of the law and the ensuing nullification of circumcision are based on Jewish categories reflecting a concrete and consistent interpretation of Jewish motives and their theological implications.[25] This factor has of course also been decisive for his paraenetic use of the baptismal formula in vv. 27–28 and should be hermeneutically appreciated, before v. 28 is singled out for special analysis.

The very fact that Paul in his letter to the Galatians argues against the law in general and circumcision in particular must be recognized to be of consequence to his use of the baptismal formula. It delineates a very specific but limited approach to a very specific, but equally limited pattern of motifs; and this of course is bound to have a decisive impact on the comprehension of what Paul considered to be the consequence of baptism as well as of the practical implications of v. 28. The inference is that vv. 27–28 cannot be said to be absolutely unique and independent of the context, nor can v. 28 be isolated theologically from the Galatian argumentation as a whole. Vv. 27–28 should be considered as one of many arguments, all adjusted to the general theme of admonishing those Galatian brothers who accept circumcision. In other words, what Paul is concerned about is not the introduction of a sacrosanct quotation of purely dogmatic or performative value,[26] but rather to remind the Galatians of the implication of their baptism by applying it with a direct paraenetic reference to those brothers who are about to forfeit the freedom of faith by their reversion to the bondage of the law.[27]

In so far as belonging to Christ in faith means being the sons of God in union with Christ, this faith cannot and should not be supplemented by law. The moment baptism has definitely replaced circumcision as a token of the relationship to God, what was formerly a prerogative in the eyes of a Jew has been definitively turned into a temptation[28] and an impending curse.[29] To submit to the law again with all its commandments and regulations, thus disavowing and in actual practice compromising Christ, is to Paul tantamount to espousing sin and death again by means of the law;[30] this is what the brothers in Galatia are about to do. What is really at stake is that a return to lawabidingness means that freedom of faith will be lost and Christ not adhered to utterly and uncompromisingly as the only means of salvation.[31] So all encompassing is the perspective in the Jewish pattern of motifs, in which vv. 27–28 are used, and so utterly uncompromising and radical in their either/or quality are Paul's ideas of freedom from the Law and equal terms through faith in Christ for all sons of God.

Paul could hardly have expressed more clearly that it is his relative and circumstantial interpretation of the Jewish presuppositions which decides the use of the baptismal formula in the context, just as the necessity for a final disposal of circumcision and, with it, the Jewish prerogatives hitherto valid, decides the significance of the three examples in v. 28, their theological scope as well as their practical implications.

All three examples relate to the annulment of distinctions, thus illustrating the idea that dissimilarities and incompatibilities must be overcome before Christian unity can be attained. None of the examples make sense, though, if it is not readily acknowledged that the basis of this idea and of the mutually opposing contrasts, is to be found in the self-understanding of the free-born Jewish male, which is indeed prescribed by law to be both exclusive and discriminating. His assessment of the relationship between clean and unclean alone invests the examples mentioned with meaning, and his prerogatives and rules of discrimination hitherto valid are alone able to bind the examples together in a comprehensive concept of a union with Christ, as a union which should be exercised in ways and places among those with whom formerly a union would have been practically inconceivable.

The examples have all been contextually exploited by Paul according to Jewish motifs and preconceptions. The commandments of the law on clean and unclean limit the outlook in the same way as the exclusive ideals of the free-born Jewish male definitely limit the implications of freedom and equality. When trying to understand v. 28 all this should of course be taken into account. It conveys that Paul's conception of the consequence of baptism is here closely tied up with his conception of the nullification of the law and the invalidity of circumcision. The ensuing interpretation and the critical assessment of the normative impact of the examples in v. 28 must be dependent on this.

This assessment does not give much trouble in v. 28a and b. These examples of mutual contrasts are immediately understandable and easy to concretize socially, because they connect in nounal categories Jew with Greek and slave with free-born as social types whose distinctly social features in opposition to each other are mutually annulled by double negations. In both cases a social basis has been established on which it is possible to compare these aspects of equality, and the obvious aim is to demonstrate the meaning of unity on a social level as social compatibility instead of the discrimination hitherto accepted.[32]

The difficulties connected with v. 28c are far more substantial, because this third example differs so decisively from the others.[33] In the first place the contrast between male and female is expressed by adjectives in the neuter characteristic of biological gender and the function of sexual reproduction.[34] Secondly the gender difference is annulled at a stroke by means of a single negation. This negation does not, as in v. 28a and b, aim at a comparison between two parties on a social level, but seems rather to presuppose that the abolition of the sexual distinction will be synonymous with a gender unity.

The social consequence of this is not pursued and not even implied by the gender categories. In other words, v. 28c does not relate to social categories. Man and woman are not considered here as social modes or types in relation to each other, but male and female are viewed together as one comprehensive expression of human sexuality. An annulment of this sexuality is tantamount to an annulment of gender differentiation.[35]

Whereas the first examples thus aim at a unification in Christ of opposite social types inducing them to associate in the congregation on a common basis of social fellowship, it remains difficult, if not impossible, to say exactly what v. 28c was meant to convey in a social context. The reason why c deviates so markedly from v. 28a and b both conceptually and grammatically is due to the fact that c with its "male and female" quotes Gen 1,27b (LXX); therefore v. 28c must necessarily be distinguished from v. 28a and b, even though this distinction may seem both vexatious and unsatisfactory for a comprehensive notion of the full implication of the baptismal formula for Paul as well as his congregation; even though it is tempting, not the least for dogmatic reasons, to try to find a common denominator somewhere.[36]

The implication of v. 28c can, however, only be determined exactly on the basis of Gen 1,27b (LXX), and this certainly does not in itself imply any social consequence of the saying on sexuality in v. 28c, nor is it forthwith possible to concretize what the Pauline context understands by the abolition of gender differentiation considering the normative impact of this in Christ. Instead of making the concepts of v. 28c more comprehensible, the dependence on Gen 1,27b (LXX) confirms the impression that, with regard to v. 28c, there is no way of convincingly harmonizing the three examples of the baptismal formula. Any efforts to establish harmony in order to be able to treat v. 28 as a principal unity, only underestimate the significance of the exceptional position of v. 28c as the third part of a sequence, which elsewhere is used by Paul with its first and second sections only, though with different social associations added.[37] It is, however, also to underestimate Gen 1,27b (LXX) as the presupposition of the concept of sexuality expressed in v. 28c as a measure of gender differentiation. There is no denying that Gen 1,27 (LXX), as a Pauline presupposition, holds the clue to a more precise definition of Paul's views on sexuality and sexual negation.

Gen 1,27b (LXX) defines the sexual categories of male and female by separating the female from man in terms of the differentiation between male and female in continuation of the creation of man, the human being, in v. 27a. Characterization as gender differentiation into male and female is thus an addition to the creation of the man in 1,27a, as man in God's image. And as apparent from what follows in 1,28 with its blessing and commandment to be fruitful and increase, the purpose of a sexual differentiation in 1,27b is obviously functional: it is meant to serve the reproduction of humanity, i.e. man. The sexual characterization in male and female adding female as a secondary component to the man of creation is thus, according to the contextuality of Gen 1,26–28, not only an addition to the idea of man created in God's image, it is also a breach with the idea of man as a human entity and, as such, at one with God's creation.[38] Thus, when Gal 3,28c speaks of the annulment of sexual differentiation, it must be taken to mean both that the addition has been annulled, and the breach healed; through Christ man has again become what he originally was, a unity and an entity in God's image.

As Gal 3,28c is founded on Gen 1,27b (LXX), it expresses that in Christ there is neither male nor female. It does not say that there is neither man nor woman such as a conceptual and grammatical agreement with v. 28a and b might have suggested. What is indicated by a sexual rather than a social terminology is that among Christians who have become sons of God, male or female purposes and functions are no longer valid, because man has been reverted to his original status and is no longer subjected to reproductive measures.[39] When it is accepted that the consequence of Gal 3,28c is based on the Pauline understanding of Gen 1,27 (LXX), and when this consequence is further related to Paul's view in Gal 3,19–29 generally, then a pattern of motifs becomes apparent, whereby it is possible to concretize the importance of v. 28c in a way compatible with the dominant values of Paul's Jewish-Christian universe. That he wrote within the limitations of this background and universe should be allowed for, if Paul's way of thinking is to be given a fair treatment and respected for its own worth in its own right, and the importance of v. 28c is to be evaluated in a way that is analytically and critically defensible and pays due regard to the Pauline conditions and presuppositions.

Obviously the idea of the annulment of sexual differentiation is very difficult to handle as a concrete definition. In a social respect its practical implication is elusive. The temptation to qualify it as an eschatological ideal and speak of androgyny is therefore great as this would at least allow us to rubricate it among myths and religious symbols.[40] However, this will lead us down the wrong trail. To name it *andro-gyny* is to hint, although in a veiled and tentative manner, at sexual duality as some adjusted form of indistinct but dual social category. And this is precisely what v. 28c says is not to be found in Christ. What has been abolished is not male and female in relation to the social roles and categories of man and woman, but as gender aspects and sexual functions in relation to the differentiation into male and female of man, the human being of creation.

To Paul sexuality and duality both belong to the secondary human functions of reproduction according to Gen 1,27b–28 (LXX). Sexuality as well as duality ought therefore to be non-existent to man in Christ. This fits in well with Paul's characteristic preference for asexuality and actual celibacy,[41] qualified ways of life which anticipate the realization of salvation in an eschatological existence in which God is everything to everybody, and where unity and fellowship between God and his creation is complete and all-encompassing.[42] Within the boundaries of Paul's thinking, however, this means in practice that male and female gender are both annulled as a sexual duality in favour of male/man as an entity of asexuality, according to Gen 1,27a. It seems irrelevant and misleading to try to impose on the text the conception of a third sex, even as a kind of synthesis of the two[43] when for Paul it is decisive that being one with Christ presupposes that gender and sexuality as such is discarded, and what was originally the first and only aspect of humanity is re-established before God.

If the male-centered or androcentric basis of Paul's sexual assessment is thus fully maintained along with his persistent sexual repudiation so typical of his dualistically ascetic attitude to life, it becomes evident that Gal 3,28c, in contrast to v. 28a and b, does not convey a positive interest in social determination, but, on the contrary, it reveals a negative interest in sexual determination. As an illustration of the practical consequences of baptism, v. 28c is not at all positive, but rather, it is a negation in so far as sexuality and sexual activity to Paul are negative concepts in themselves. Accordingly, the impact of the eschatological normativity of v. 28c does not at first[44] extend beyond the biological gender aspect; the practical implications stop short of the abolition of sexual differentiation, which to Paul is synonymous with the abolition of sexuality and thus with a freedom possessed by the sons of God in Christ.

Obviously it is hermeneutically unfeasible to want to draw extensive social and practical conclusions from v. 28c in an attempt to define the circumstances of women as Christians and as women in the Pauline communities. This, certainly, is not at all what Paul is after. V. 28c is part of the context as just one example of the freedom in Christ offered to the Galatian brothers, the object being to illustrate the conditions of this freedom, not as a freedom relating to women, but as a freedom relating to gender, i.e. a freedom that is synonymous with the annulment of sexuality. V. 28c is exploited by Paul to remind the brothers of how much they have been given in their baptism unto

Christ, and what accordingly they are in danger of losing. A return to law and circumcision will imply a return also to sexual differentiation and the bondage of the reproductive functions of sexuality, which in Paul's eyes is the unambiguous testimony of depending on and compromising with this world.[45]

It is of course possible to conclude from the nullification of the law and the invalidity of circumcision that the prerogative of the free-born Jewish male in his relation to God has been abolished in a way that opens up unknown opportunities for women. Circumcision being replaced by baptism, a male prerogative has been abolished, and the relation to God has been qualified by an admission card not exclusively reserved for man, the male; which is to say within the Pauline context that women may now also be sons of God in Christ. But what does this mean to the social relations of the missionary congregations? What does it imply in practice for the lives of Christian women? Neither text nor context allow us to jump to conclusions from v. 28c and speak of the equal rights of Christian women in freedom and solidarity with Christian men in the fellowship of the congregation. This would be seriously to misinterpret the overall negative character of Paul's sexual assessment as well as his actual concern respecting the Galatian brothers and their endangered freedom.

It is one thing when Paul in v. 28c, with the idea of the abolition of sexual differentiation in mind, defines the abolition of gender and sexuality as a freedom in Christ for the sons of God. Another is whether this definition can be termed positive to both men and women? Practically speaking, asexuality is qualified as the equal terms that will allow a woman to be regarded as a full human being, i.e. a man or a son or a brother before God. The freedom and equality of asexuality as the consequence of baptism thus implies that in Christ the woman is no longer at one with her sexuality and her reproductive functions,[46] but on the contrary, as a son of God she has become like a man in God's image. She is no longer female in relation to male; she is male. But, again, what does this mean to her personal and social life?

While v. 28c is only concerned with an eschatological assessment of biological gender and sexual aspects, addressed specifically to the Galatian brothers, it is no use questioning the social and practical implications for Christian women. What matters here to Paul is the annulment of the negative aspects for men rather than a possible confirmation of the positive aspects concerning women. If the Jewish androcentric limitation so closely associated with the Pauline background is maintained, and if it is further acknowledged how far this limitation has been intensified by Paul's dualistically ascetic attitude to social life in general but to sexuality in particular, then it will be quite clear that v. 28c offers no basis from which it is possible to ask for the social consequences to Christian women as women. Such questions will never find their solution in v. 28c, due to its androcentric orientation. But they will in fact disregard the importance assigned by Paul to the abolition of the sexual differentiation as a re-establishment of man's original and proper existence as the image of God. And they will definitely overlook the fact of Paul's altogether negative view on gender and sexuality, which makes abolition of sexuality in itself synonymous with freedom in Christ and thus an eschatological quality, not leading to a social practice, but, on the contrary, deviating the affairs of this world and opposing them as a means of Christian self-affirmation.

1 Cor 11,3–9: But Woman Is the Glory of Man

Interpreters of 1 Cor may disagree on many things respecting the integrity of the letter as a compositional unity,[47] but as to its background and the purpose of the *paraenesis* in its various sections the agreement is widespread; the Corinthians, whom Paul addresses, are considered to be a congregation in a crisis. Evidently they are a mixed constellation of Christians at loggerheads with each other as well as with their apostle because of diversities and social tensions.[48] Throughout the letter Paul uses his authority to explain, admonish and commit the Corinthians on one issue after the other, clearly rooted in existing discordances of various kinds; clearly the disagreements are theological as well as practical.

However, it is characteristic for 1 Cor that the preoccupation with social issues is overwhelming. Paul's persistent efforts to organize the conduct of the congregation and the social activities of its members throw light on the Corinthians' relationship to Christ, but it also reflects Paul's own. His admonitions to the Corinthians emphasize very clearly that he does not think it possible to separate the confession of faith from daily life and congregational behaviour. To Paul hope and faith are definitely an issue of congregational consequence demonstrated in a life in union with Christ, in which the social aspect is in practice designed to constitute and confirm the theological values. The practical application thus serves to give the significance of the confession to Christ credibility[49] as a value of life as well as a law for life. However, since this significance is invariably eschatologically invested,[50] Paul's efforts throughout the letter are concentrated on restraining the Corinthians to the common commitment of the congregation to live in accordance with the eschatological realization of faith and hope,[51] thus anticipating salvation in their social life together. By his active engagement in the social and moral diversities of the congregation Paul reveals both what the Corinthians have misunderstood christologically and ecclesiologically and what in his own theology are the constituting eschatological motifs.

In most of his very concrete and practical admonitions Paul seems intent upon solving directly the complaints and enquiries from the congregation concerning its actual problems, which have been brought to his knowledge by members from Corinth either orally on in writing.[52] Some discrepancies may have been reported by way of rumours, but the majority seems to have been submitted to him by representatives of the congregation or by personal contacts, who have expressly asked for his apostolic intervention to solve a problem or patch up a quarrel; more generally his guidance may have been asked for in a number of administrative issues.[53] Within this framework Paul very consistently devotes all his efforts to the conditions of the Corinthian Christians, as seen from his basically eschatological attitude to the congregation as a socially committed fellowship of life in Christ. 1 Cor 11,2-16 seems to be logically and naturally integrated in this framework as a piece of women's *paraenesis:* a piece of social and moral guidance concerning the behaviour and appearance required of Christian women within the life and worship of the congregation.

However, the relation between text and context is in fact only seemingly harmonious. The harmony only skirts the social surface and the differences below are greater and more significant than the concordances. What interests Paul in 11,2-16 is not at all the social aspect in relation to Christ, but the existing code of gender policy and sexual morality which is socially valid outside the congregation independently of Christ. Thus the central issue of the *paraenesis* in 11,2-16 is the social aspects of women's conduct in relation to gender and sexuality rather than in relation to Christ. As a social admonition this women's *paraenesis* is thus singled out theologically and has been given a stamp of its own within the context of the letter.

A comparison between the theological basis for the argumentation in 11,2-16 and Paul's theological reasons for a practical and socially paraenetic argumentation in the other sections of 1 Cor emphasizes the exceptional position of the women's *paraenesis* even in the paraenetic context of the letter. One thing is that the social intention behind the *paraenesis* in 11,2-16 may seem to agree with the social demand for unity and fellowship so characteristic of Paul's paraenetic efforts in 1 Cor as a whole, another is that Paul in this case, where the conduct of the Christian women is in dispute, resorts to very different measures, both theologically and paraenetically, to gain his social purpose within the practical social application.

Paul's endeavours to re-introduce and maintain a moral order of sexual discrimination among the Corinthians may very well, in their ultimate practical aim, be due to his predominant concern about the unity of the congregation.[54] How Paul became aware of the circumstances dealt with in 11,2–16 is not quite clear, but there can be no doubt that he takes the matter very seriously; the behaviour of the Christian women has obviously become a social strain both within and outside the congregational life and has caused both scruples and indignation.[55] However this cannot do away with the fact that what Paul wants to reinforce in the congregation is male sexual control. No matter how much he wants to strengthen the solidarity of the congregation out of regard to the strategy of his missionary work and to the vulnerable social status of a minority group,[56] the singularity of 11,2–16 cannot be disguised; what Paul tries to do is to settle the question of the irregular conduct of the Christian women, not as an eschatologically invested question of status and obligations in Christ,[57] but, on the contrary, as a social and moral question relating specifically to the sexual status and obligations of women as women according to the sexual order of creation and the hierarchic arrangement of patriarchal society.[58]

This is to say that, faced with an actual problem concerning the behaviour of Christian women as active and independent[59] members of the Christian fellowship, Paul chooses to rebuke the women as females, i.e. as sexual beings; he does not treat them or even relate to them in 1 Cor 11,2–16 as Christians. This is apparent from the way he bases his argumentation on creation theology instead of christology and eschatology as elsewhere in the letter; instead of being christologically organized and clearly structured on the basis of eschatological motifs, Paul's arguments are here allowed to dissolve into something remarkably incoherent and awkward,[60] and the women's *paraenesis* has thus none of the theological and paraenetic consistency otherwise so typical of 1 Cor. This means that Paul is unable to lay emphasis on his moral appeal in 11,2–16; his *ad hoc* argumentation does not leave room for a decisive support of his demand in Christ, since his arguments are not of Christ and accordingly not in practice equivalent to a command to follow Christ.[61] On the contrary, in 11,13–16 he has virtually to let go. Evidently in the end he can only refer to custom, and his decision as to the issue of the women is consequently epitomized in a rather vague reference to what is deemed common sense by the androcentric standards, usually resorted to where patriarchal control has the administering power over the lives and opportunities of women. With vv. 13-16 Paul emphasizes that his women's *paraenesis* is a sexually biased social admonition imposed on women, not addressed to women. The Corinthian women in question are disregarded as independent Christians and as persons in their own right by Paul's decision, because as Christians and as members of the congregation with their own individual status in Christ they are simply not visible to Paul. As women and as females they have no right and are not entitled to make any claims for themselves; they are not entitled to any respect or personal recognition, and therefore, to Paul, they are actually no parties in this case. He is unable to consider them as he does those who are strong, who can be urged to renunciation and compromise, nor is he able to consider them as he does those who are weak in faith and conduct in need of understanding and indulgence in Christ. He is altogether unable to see and relate to these women in Christ.[62]

Not surprisingly, the difference between the *paraenesis* of 11,2-16 and that of the other sections of the letter is remarkable, and since it is a matter of principal discrepancy between text and context, it should be more closely considered on a number of points essential to the understanding of 11,3-9.

The context of the women's *paraenesis* is first and foremost chapters 11-14, which Paul incorporates directly in the eschatological application by means of the joint introductory and transitional verse 11,1. This emphasizes the fact that to Paul eschatological application means following Christ, which again is synonymous with imitating the apostle authorized by Christ. On this basis Paul urges to unity and solidarity in honour and recognition of the congregation as the temple of God.[63] In most of the concrete questions he also argues on this eschatologically qualified basis for the social commitment of all Christians to live together in mutual concern and tolerance as befits those who are now, as an eschatologically founded fellowship, intimate with the special demands for brotherly love which is the law of Christ.[64] This way and on this basis the object of their entire lives is eschatological: to exist before God as members of the body of Christ.[65]

The general paraenetic theme of chapters 11-14 is thus the homiletic appeal for love and edification so characteristic of 1 Cor;[66] but it is applied on practical admonitions directly respecting the meetings of the congregation, the order of worship and the administration of the spiritual gifts.[67] It is conspicuous that in these questions Paul sees no reason to contest the Corinthian Christians' relation to confession and tradition,[68] on the contrary, he praises them for their standing firm on what they have received as right and true. Thus, when he insists that the confession of Christ should be applied to the common good in ways of love,[69] he is not paraenetically occupied with problems of belief and attitude, but always with the way in which this belief and attitude express themselves in conduct and behaviour. Very consistently he winds up his detailed argumentation in chapters 11-14, maintaining the christological motif of appeal with unabridged and unabated authority, because the eschatological purpose which is being insisted on so vigorously is in fact the following of Christ in the concrete demands for renunciation, consideration and solicitude, demands which in every single case mean taking care, compromising and letting love manifest itself.[70] In every single case, that is, except 11,2-16 which differs in all respects.

While Paul in chapters 11-14 on the whole is engrossed in matters in which two or more parties are sought reconciled by means of love's forbearance in the form of a patient both/and,[71] he seems disposed in 11,2-16 to settle matters by an either/or. Here, there is no talk of reconciliation, no arguments for manifestations of love within the congregation. While Paul in the context pleads for self-denial based on the humility and self-denial of Christ,[72] his entire *paraenesis* in 11,2-16 is concentrated on dominant control, hierarchic status and manifestations of authority.[73] In this passage his sole concern is to preserve the *status quo* of gender and sexuality, for social rather than eschatological reasons.[74] Accordingly he is intent upon guarding male order and preserving the balance of power by maintaining its once and for all delineated distinctions and boundaries.

While in chapters 11-14 Paul's main concern is to commit the members of the congregation to new and unaccustomed norms of conduct, which they will have to learn to co-ordinate and administer in common practice for the strengthening of their life in Christ, the purpose in 11,2-16 is the very opposite, namely to completely reject all that is new and unaccustomed. It is one thing for Christian women to participate actively in the Pauline congregations,[75] another that, even so, they remain women bound to the terms of sexuality, when viewed on a social level and measured by the moral standard of sexual relation, which is precisely what Paul does in his women's *paraenesis*. He sees the Christian women as women and females instead of as Christians and is thus unable to tolerate their new and unaccustomed conduct; for seen from a social and sexual angle such conduct cannot be incorporated in the context of the congregation. It simply does not fit in with the common purpose of Christian life, which to Paul is invariably anti-sexual in its full eschatological perspective.[76] The conduct of the women must therefore be rejected as a cause of scandal and moral indecency, and, ironically, it must be rejected on a non-eschatological, non-christological basis as apparent in 11,3-9.

What gives offence is not that women are praying and prophesying, but that they worship unveiled;[77] that way their behaviour transgresses the social limits befitting to their sex. These limits are presumably respected in the social context of the Corinthian congregation[78] and, according to Paul, they are still to be enforced within the congregation as norms and measures for women's conduct. Paul sees the discrepancy from his androcentric point of view, and without hesitation he identifies himself with the male members of the congregation, reducing the problems of the Christian women to being a matter of dispute between the Christian men and their women.[79] The implicit, dualistically androcentric presupposition is thus that as females women are in particular[80] bound to terms of sexuality and thus dependent also on the social structure of sexual organization. In the accepted patriarchal categorization of gender roles and sexual identity this is tantamount to saying that women are inferior and administratively subordinated to the men they belong to. For that reason women may not by their appearance, their dress or their social conduct whatsoever violate the social bounds and transgress the limits appropriate for their sex.[81] If they do so after all, they go beyond the sexual distinction, which is a normative social frame of reference, invested with values of symbolic and political meaning to both sexes. In other words they contest the established moral order and sexual policy[82] and threaten the social and moral privileges due to the male because of his being sexually and morally superior. To maintain that this is the order acceptable to God as required among human beings is simply to safeguard social relations by means of creation theology and a fundamental sense of religion; and it is precisely what Paul is doing in 11,3-9.

According to Paul, the dualistically androcentric foundation for the male organization of patriarchy is absolutely verified by the normativity inherent in the concepts of creation theology. In 11,3-9 his theological starting point is therefore that of power and authority, rather than that of powerlessness and renunciation qualified by Christ himself as the normative paradigm of life and fellowship among Christians. Sexual relations reflect androcentric domination and are treated accordingly as relations of male power and supremacy. Consequently, the proper androcentric administration of sexuality on a social level is a practical question of control and hierarchic structure.[83] To Paul as a man as well as to the male Corinthians sexuality is for men to organize and deal with, in so far as it is in reality a question of ownership and owner's rights, arranged and agreed upon among men.

Thus in 11,3-9 Paul gives his support to the established order of male superiority and male sexual power structure before the world in general and the Christian congregations and their women in particular; the women of the congregation are at one with their sexuality and restricted by their gender characteristics both outside and inside the Christian community. Literally in 11,3-9 Paul pleads for male control in the shape of practical suppression of women, and he does so on the social terms of gender and sexuality even though these terms, in all other sections of 1 Cor, have been deprived of their binding significance to those who have been given a new life in Christ on eschatologically qualified conditions.[84] This means that Christian women as women are referred to the male power structure of sexuality in social subordination and dependence on the symbolic values of sexual discrimination, notwithstanding the fact that these symbolic values have indeed been abolished through Christ; also notwithstanding the fact that Paul is firmly convinced that sexuality is an anti-eschatological aspect, relating only to the temporary existence of this world and therefore without any purpose or quality in Christ, since he considers sexuality and sexual activity as incompatible in principle with the eschatological commitment to devote oneself to Christ by imitating his most favoured apostle.[85]

It has often been maintained that 11,3-9 only indirectly or implicitly denies the participation of woman in the human prerogative of being created in the image of God, and that it is due to a later, more misogynist tradition that the Pauline formulations in vv. 3 and 7 have been turned into an explicit and exclusive doctrine of the imperfection and inferiority of woman.[86] However, this interpretation of the Pauline intention, as expressed in 11,3-9, but in vv. 3 and 7 particularly, cannot be substantiated. Not only is it apologetically misleading to Paul's moral purpose, but it also distorts Paul's argumentative point, that the image of God is an expression of superiority and hierarchic order. The image of God as a theological and anthropological concept as such is no concern of Paul's, for likeness of God is simply not under debate. On the contrary, Paul considers the category an absolute, just as he accepts that likeness of God is in fact a token of a definite and absolute order of creation reflecting the qualitative difference between man and woman. The question of whether woman is wholly or only partly and relatively an image of God is not under debate either. On the contrary, Paul takes for granted that woman is indeed not of God's image; for he relates 11,3-9 to Gen 1,26-27a instead of 1,27b-28,[87] indicating without any discussion that woman is not included in original humanity nor, of course, in God's image. Thus, his intention is here not to defend a certain doctrine, but to maintain common knowledge and clarify its consequences. His moral purpose is to explain the implication of the order of creation as a structure of superiority and a qualitative succession on the terms of gender and sexual distinction.

In v. 7 Paul states that man alone is the image of God and thus also exclusively to be considered as the direct reflection of the divine power and quality.[88] The man is man in the primary and proper sense of the word as in Gen 1,27a, whereas woman was created as an addition, related to and dependent on man as in Gen 1,27b and 2,22-23. In so far as the man as man was stamped directly by God this stamp determines his relationship both to God and Christ on the one hand,[89] and to all the rest of creation on the other as emphasized by the hierarchic order in v. 3. To Paul this is undoubtedly a question of qualitative definitions. The purpose of v. 3 is obviously not just to list a chronological sequence, but to maintain theologically the significant succession of creation, which is also in fact the significant order of hierarchic precedence and quality. Thus, the central issue in v. 3 as well as in v. 7 is the question of domination, and the man is qualified by the fact that he as man is both subordinate and superior, whereas the woman is only subordinate.

The consequence of being created in God's image is to Paul a mark of qualitative value, reflecting at once man's special distinction as a creature in relation to God and the distinction of the man, his gender role and status, in relation to woman. Woman's status as a creature subordinated to man makes her subordinated and dependent on him also in her relationship to God. Before God she is always the secondary creation, in so far as she is restricted in her activities by the terms of her sexuality, according to Gen 1,27b-28. But further, as emphasized by vv. 8-9, based on Gen 2,18-24 as well as 3,16, woman is being kept in her place by Paul as a tool for man's endeavours; not only created from man, but for the man, v. 9.

In this way Paul reasons unambiguously for the man's primacy as the lord of creation and as the head of woman. As the head of woman, and as head explicitly,[90] the man is, without reservation, invested with a superior status as norm and measure of the social order of creation on the terms of gender and sexual differentiation. As a direct consequence of his being the image of God the man has been given the religious as well as the social authority over the woman, which, in the terms of gender and sexuality, reflects two aspects of the same issue, in practice asserted as suppression of women. What is decisive to Paul is that in a social sense suppression of women is a theological necessity according to the order of creation, and, consequently, inseparable from male control in a religious and moral sense. Paul's main concern is thus to make certain of man's primacy in all respects by means of woman, i.e. by maintaining a double consequence of the image of God, positively as a quality inherent in the man, and negatively as a deficiency inherent in the woman. Thus sexual discrimination must be acknowledged by both parties and publicly complied with, as apparent from vv. 4–5. The demand on both, however, has one common aim in the primacy of man, the man; it is only justified by the man's superiority and should be submitted to by both out of regard to man and his being the image of God. Paul's way of qualifying the duty of the woman to confirm the man in his superiority by acknowledging herself inferior and dependent on him is, as noted above, founded on Gen 1,27b–28. Here woman is clearly defined as a creature of secondary status, because she was created as a sexual addition and, in concordance with Gen 2,22–23, made after man as a part of man for his benefit and to serve his purpose of self-affirming reproduction. Throughout his argumentation this duty to confirm the man in his self-affirmation is maintained by Paul as a consequence of sexual differentiation.

By insisting on the acknowledgment of these implications of sexual differentiation in vv. 4–5, Paul does in fact plead for the male control inevitable if man's exclusive status as the image of God, participating in God's power over all the rest of creation, is to be upheld. Thus, woman is in fact being confined to her inferiority for the sake of superiority. The insistence on a woman's duty to wear a veil during worship, vv. 5–6, is actually just the consequent demand for a practical or social testimony of her submission to the distribution of power and authority institutionalized by creation. Being veiled she signifies to God and to the world, on social and sexual terms,[91] that she knows her place at the bottom of the hierarchy and acknowledges that she does not exist for her own sake, but to belong to a man. A woman may only appear before God in conformity with her status as male property, and the veil as token of the rights of power and authority of the man, whose possession she is, is to Paul a pledge both of the man's proprietary right and of man's status before God as the head of woman. On the terms of gender and sexuality the veil serves to confirm man in his dignity by revealing woman's indignity and guarding her in it. Only if sexual differentiation is maintained this way as a qualitative difference, will the significance of the order of creation be duly acknowledged and revered as an order of precedence. Without her veil the woman inflicts shame not just on the man who is her head, but more comprehensively, also on man as the lord of creation, and thus the woman's glory, as is evident from the relation between vv. 4 and 7.

Whereas a man as a consequence of his being the image of God and as a pledge of his full humanity has the right to appear before God without covering his head, a woman must be veiled. In practice this means that apart from her long hair[92] she is to wear the prescribed token that she, being sexually distinguished from man, is inferior to him and dependent on him also *coram deo.* Thus, in relation to divinity a woman is completely subordinated to man in his humanity, and this implies for her worship and prayer that she is, like a reflection in the mirror, dependent on man as the image of God.[93] Paul makes this abundantly clear in v. 3, when he refers to the order of precedence, with God as the head of Christ, Christ as the head of man, and finally man as the head of woman.

It is of no avail to try to distinguish here between God and Christ. In v. 3a Christ takes God's place not as a saviour, but as a creator, i.e. like God himself partaking in the act of creation.[94] V. 3c is most of all like an afterthought, added by Paul for the sake of completeness. In the relation between God and Christ the concordance is here essential, and based on this Paul can therefore qualify the decisive difference on two levels as it were: on a religious and theological level between divinity and humanity and on a social and gender level with respect to sexual morality between male/man and female/woman.[95] The mention of Christ is thus without specific significance to Paul in this connection, just as the parenthesis in vv. 11-12 on the mutual value of man and woman to each other in marriage[96] remains a parenthesis left out of account and not at all applied in the *paraenesis.*

Summing up, it seems that the consequence of vv. 3 and 7 is unavoidable: a woman who was not created in the image of God cannot pray or prophesy before God in her own right or by her own status, for she possesses neither. On the terms of gender and sexuality this is tantamount to saying that she is literally without personal identity or human value. On her own she has no head, in so far as her head is a man; because she has not got a head of her own, she must be under authority. As a sexual creature she has no legitimate independence authorizing her to act freely and to make her own choices with regard to her conduct and appearance, for as a sexual creature she is indeed without influence on her own activity. Created for the sake and purpose of the man, she has no purpose in herself or in a life of her own, as vv. 8-9 say so pointedly.

Because man's superiority controls the opportunities and sets the conditions of a woman's life, woman ranks as the lowest and most inferior creature within the qualitative order of precedence established by creation. Therefore her head must be veiled, to confirm the man in his being superior. When her metaphorical head is the superior man, any attempt on her part to make her head visible by casting aside her veil or by shearing her long hair is equal to being disgraced and shamed, for this is to assume a right and an honour not due to her. Where the man has rights, a woman has only duty,[97] and her most vital duty is to persist in her own unworthiness and inferiority as a consequence of her not being the image of God.

In practice, of course, a woman might well have her hair shorn and thus possess herself of a gender characteristic which, according to Paul, rightly belongs to the man, but this does not make such a step either imaginable or excusable on Paul's social and moral premises. On the contrary, the sarcastic reference in v. 6 to what is possible in practice only serves to emphasize what is socially considered absolutely out of the question and morally unforgivable according to v. 5. Being completely unable to imagine a woman who would want to have her hair cropped, Paul is bound to deem it even more inexcusable, morally considered, were she to cast aside the veil which signifies her imperfection as a sexual creature in a way that enhances the man's perfection as man, the human being.

Thus Paul develops his idea of the importance of the image of God in the order of creation. It is the image of God which authorizes man's status of superiority and by contrast, woman's lack of status. Without the image of God a woman is without human quality; as a secondary creature she is only a reflection, i.e. the glory of man. As the least and lowest creature in the hierarchy of creation she is bound to remain without a head, i.e. without independence and human individuality, before God and all other powers as a token of her sexual dependency and lack of human status. There is certainly no question here of unity and equality. On the contrary, to Paul the terms of sexuality will remain the terms of hierarchic power and sexual control basically arranged to secure the supremacy and superiority of the man. Paul's women's paraenesis is concentrated on this one purpose[98] and is consistently composed in accordance with the pre-christological argument that sexuality prevails in this world, and that a woman must therefore be socially controlled on the androcentric conditions of sexual discrimination as a creature of sexuality.

Asexuality and the Lives of Women in the Pauline Congregations: A Summary and Some Conclusions

It is possible to regard Gal 3,28c as the historical basis of the situation behind 1 Cor 11,2-16. Partly because the pre-Pauline formula must have been in existence prior to both Pauline texts; and partly because it seems reasonable to assume that an expression so characteristic of Pauline baptismal theology as Gal 3,27-28 must indeed have been well known to the Corinthian

Christians, this congregation being more than any other a cause of anxiety to Paul and a test of his apostolic liability.[99] Finally, some congregational teaching of sexual liberation in Christ must somehow be taken for granted, as otherwise major parts of 1 Cor in general and 11,2-16 in particular would not seem understandable. On the one hand Gal 3,28c provides the justification for Christian women's right to participate actively in the service of the congregation, on the other hand Gal 3,28c may explain why some Christian women have wanted to be able to pray and prophesy without being obliged to wear a veil. However, it is of course one thing to state how Gal 3,28c may be used, or perhaps misused, but quite another thing to imply what Gal 3,28c does in fact convey in its own theological and contextual connection, and how this may be supposed to have influenced the conditions and personal lives of Christian women. Viewing Gal 3,28c as a historical prerequisite underlying the circumstances of 1 Cor 11,2-16 does not of necessity make 1 Cor 11,2-16 either theologically or thematically dependent on Gal 3,28c in so far as a historical explanation is not sufficient reason for speaking as a matter of course of a thematic dependency, much less of a theological compatibility.

A historical explanation is no guarantee at all for a thematic connection and should not be mistaken for a theological explanation. External chronology cannot be juxtaposed with internal causality, and a historical consequence ought never to be confused with a theological intention.[100] Thus, it is not legitimate to infer Paul's intention in Gal 3,28c from the consequence taken by some Christian women at Corinth, any more than it is legitimate to assume that the women's *paraenesis* advanced by Paul in 1 Cor 11,2-16 is theologically dependent on his statement in Gal 3,28c about the annulment of sexuality.

The fact that 1 Cor 11,2-16 is a women's *paraenesis* implying a group of Christian women with an emancipated awareness of themselves as women does not invariably transform the address to brothers in Gal 3,27-28 into a positive and liberating address to women, any more than it makes Paul a positive and liberating affirmer of women and sexuality. For though it is true that Gal 3,28c deals with liberation in Christ, there is no indication whatsoever, either positively or affirmatively, of its liberating consequence for Christian women as women. Rather the opposite. Because sexual liberation to Paul is synonymous with an eschatological affirmation of life based on the annulment of sexual differentiation, sexual liberation is in fact liberation from sexuality; and it follows that to Christian women sexual liberation means not only a denial of their female gender and bodies, but practically speaking also, as a direct consequence of Gen 1,27b (LXX), an actual self-denial. Thus, to a Christian woman liberation from sexuality means that she is no longer at one with her sex and her reproductive purpose; she is in fact no longer bound to be female because in Christ it is possible for her to become male. Consequently the liberating conditions of Christian women, as based on Gal 3,28c, which again depends on Gen 1,27b (LXX), not only imply a negative evaluation of sexuality, they also confine Christian women as well as men to a negative evaluation of women as females. To Paul sexual liberation is indeed eschatologically qualified; but this does not mean, however, that the prerequisites and consequences of sexual liberation are not still androcentrically dualistic and thus in practice suppressive of women as well as of sexuality.

Thus it is one thing that Gal 3,28c may have been well known to the Christian women at Corinth, and that by refusing to be veiled they may have wanted to act expressly on Paul's talk of sexual liberation in Christ for all the sons of God. Another thing is of course whether these women understood Paul properly? Did they fully apprehend his preconceived theological ideas? Did they conform to the conditions he thought necessary for a woman in Christ to be incorporated into the fellowship of the sons of God on the terms of eschatological asexuality? Were the practical consequences they drew at all compatible with Paul's theological intention when he, in Gal 3,28c, speaks of sexual liberation in Christ from his androcentrically dualistic point of view?

These questions are not rhetorical. On the contrary, they serve the purpose of underlining what is exegetically unreasonable about the widely spread idea that Paul should be divided against himself and his view of women in the relationship between Gal 3,28c and 1 Cor 11,2-16, because in the former he speaks of liberation from sexuality in Christ as an eschatological affirmation of life, whereas in the latter he argues on the basis of creation theology and pre-christology for the suppression of women and sexual hierarchy.

However, as I have attempted to substantiate, it will not do to uphold Gal 3,28c as the ideal canonical text of women's emancipation any more than 1 Cor 11,2-16 can be depreciated or simply written off as an actual testimony of the life conditions of Christian women. The fact that 1 Cor 11,2-16 is based on creation theology and thus pre-christological in its argumentation does not mitigate its significance as a theological testimony, in the same way as its being explicitly and downright suppressive of some Christian women cannot diminish its value when it comes to an assessment of Paul's attitude to women. For, as I have also tried to establish, 1 Cor 11,2-16 holds within itself its own unambiguous and principal point which is averse to being either explained or reasoned away by means of Gal 3,28c.

The incompatibility of the texts remains and is bound to remain, if the texts, each in its own right, are to be done justice to exegetically as well as theologically. Only the persistent apologetic desire of finding at least one passage in Paul which might justify the idea of the unconditional freedom of Christian women within the first congregational fellowship, admits of a canonization of Gal 3,28c at the cost of 1 Cor 11,2-16, which in itself is so intricate to handle. And so the exegesis becomes eclectic, evasive, and superficial. A blind eye is turned upon the obvious facts, and one fails to see that liberation on Paul's conditions is androcentrically as well as dualistically determined and therefore not as a matter of course available to Christian women as women, i.e. as females. What is undesirable is left unnoticed in order to establish a connection and to find a compromise between the texts, where no theological connection can be demonstrated, and where consequently a compromise is indefensible.

This way not only is the significance of each text seriously weakened, but the decisive and principal discordance between them is left unamplified and exegetically unexploited for a more profound understanding of what may, according to Paul, be termed the dual conditions of the lives of Christian women. The principal discordance will, on the other hand, lend itself to an amplification if the very duality is adhered to and fully acknowledged in both its shapes, i.e. in Gal 3,28c as well as in 1 Cor 11,2-16. The peculiarity of Paul's view of women is, indeed, that instead of one, he advocates two different views, although he holds only one coherent negative view of the female gender and of sexuality as a whole. This means that to Paul women remain beings bound to and limited by their sex, only to be allowed direct access to God in Christ by the annulment of sexuality, whereas in this world they will, for as long as sexuality rules and makes its demands, generally be committed as females to the terms of sexuality and thus subordinated to the control of the males to whom they belong.

Thus considered, Paul is not divided against himself or against his view of sexuality and women. On the contrary, the discordance between Gal 3,28c and 1 Cor 11,2-16 is a logical consequence of a consistently negative attitude to sexuality which, on an androcentric basis, allows women the alternative of two different ways of life: asexuality and the eschatologically qualified asceticism, which would seem to be the implicit consequence of Gal 3,28c, or sexuality and the social and moral dependency on worldly norms and institutions in a pre-christological and non-eschatological respect, as apparent from the explicit concern of the women's *paraenesis* in 1 Cor 11,2-16. Either the Christian woman is exempted from her sexuality, i.e. her femaleness, in Christ and given the opportunity to be reckoned among the sons of God like a Christian male, or she remains bound to her body and female gender with the result that she is literally left behind in this world and its sexual hierarchy, belonging to a man before she may be said to belong to Christ, and thus socially as well as theologically of course dependent on the superior male also in her relation to God. To a Christian woman life is either conditioned by asceticism or it is determined by gender and sexuality, thus being maritally organized and institutionalized.

So in Gal 3,28c there is no indication of Paul having once and for all established the absolute eschatological ideal respecting women's free and equal lives in Christ – an ideal which unfortunately he was himself the first to desert in 1 Cor 11,3-9 overwhelmed by the demands of the Christian women in real life. On the contrary, the indication is that Gal 3,28c and 1 Cor 11,3-9 merely display two different aspects of one and the same issue, namely: the suppression of women and sexuality on a conservative Jewish-Christian basis. The consequences of the two texts for Christian women are therefore not mutually exclusive, on the contrary, they are mutually confirmative, precisely on the basis of their common background in Paul's androcentric dualism. Against this background the following conclusions are thrown into relief:

A comprehensive assessment positive to women cannot be extracted from Gal 3,28c, because the verse, like Gen 1,27b (LXX) behind it, rests on a negative view of sexuality and of women as females, defining the annulment of sexuality in Christ as the eschatological affirmation of life, i.e. as the eschatological re-establishment of Gen 1,27a (LXX). This does not allow Christian women any opportunity of being affirmed as women, but fixes them in a state of asexuality dependent on the androcentric concept of human normality. The Christian women at Corinth are therefore debarred from citing Gal 3,28c as a reason for their unwillingness to be veiled; apparently they already belong to men and live in this world on the terms of gender and sexual hierarchy. Thus, Paul can only see them as females in so far as they, according to the implicit consequence of Gal 3,28c, cannot be reckoned as males and thus treated in Christ as independent agents. It is thus completely in tune with Paul's altogether negative attitude to women and sexuality when he, in his *paraenesis* of 1 Cor 11,2-16, disregards Gal 3,28c and instead argues on the pre-christological and non-eschatological basis of creation theology. Seen from an androcentrically dualistic perspective a both-and, meaning asexuality as well as sexuality, is of course out of the question for the Christian women at Corinth; they are referred instead to an absolute either-or: either an eschatologically qualified asceticism and freedom in Christ, or the sexual hierarchy and the socially established order of creation theology in conformity with the purpose of sexuality and the casting of sexual differentiation.

Either a Christian woman belongs completely to Christ unrestricted by gender and sexuality, and she lives as a virgin or as a widow with the possibility of participating like a Christian male in the work for Christ and for the fellowship of the congregation;[101] or she belongs to a man and is at one with the purpose of her sexuality in such a way and to such an extent that her life and her opportunities both as a woman and as a Christian are in all respects limited by sexual functions, sexual values, and sexual institutions, as apparent from 1 Cor 11,2-16 along with 14,34-36 and 7,10-24, 39-40. The fact that the dualism of this either-or between what is eschatologically qualified and what is sexually restricted and socially organized is to be ascribed to Paul himself, seems indeed to be testified unambiguously and characteristically by 1 Cor 7; and so this dualism should not be put aside as a secondary formulation made rigorous only by Paul's successors.[102] The incompatibility of Gal 3,28c and 1 Cor 11,3-9 is clearly discernible in 1 Cor 7 as a duality of two equally consistent trends all through e.g. vv. 8-11, 26-40, with vv. 29-31 as an eschatological pivot in the dualistic assessment of what is asexuality and what is socially justified sexuality. Thus 1 Cor 7 is not only illustrative of the logical discordance between the consequences contained implicitly in Gal 3,28c and explicitly in 1 Cor 11,2-16; but the many detailed directions of 1 Cor 7 substantially underline in what a profound and integrated sense these consequences emanate from and are rooted in Paul's own ascetically eschatological outlook.[103] Of necessity this outlook will result in an antagonistic attitude to the conditions of women when female asceticism is organized on an unequivocally androcentric basis at the same time as female sexuality is laid down as a sphere of life subjected to androcentric control and administration.

In practice this means that sexual control in the form of male control of women has been institutionalized by Paul in a dual sense. The control is exercised differently, of course, on unmarried and on married Christian women, concerning an eschatological level and a social or non-eschatological level, dependent on whether it is exercised by the woman herself in Christ, or whether it is being exercised by the man who is the head of the woman, according to the order of creation and sexual morality. In both shapes it is a question of male control, however, control of sexuality and control of women. This should be acknowledged if the full significance of the incompatibility of Gal 3,28c and 1 Cor 11,3-9 is to be clarified without bias. More particularly it is a point that should be faced when trying to evaluate the apparent discordance of two opposed consequences for the lives of Christian women. Logically seen the two consequences have but one source and one justification, namely the negative attitude to sexuality and to woman which is Paul's theological prerequisite in both cases.

This way Paul's view of women becomes explicable and definable in dependence on both Gal 3,28c and 1 Cor 11,3-9. Both texts have had their say, both have been treated fairly in all theological respects to an extent which not only confirms the duality of the determination of Christian women's lives in Paul's own congregations, but also throws light on the development among Paul's successors. The trend from Gal 3,28c may be followed via 1 Tim 5,11-15 to e.g. Thecla,[104] and in the same way the trend from 1 Cor 11,3-9 may be pursued with the same amount of logic and with the same practical consistency via Col 3,18 and Eph 5,22-33 to 1 Tim 2,9-15.

According to the present interpretation there is no longer any excuse for investing Paul with the legitimization of an apologist of feminist theology, nor is there any basis for seeing the development after Paul as a regrettable fall from the pinnacle of former freedom. The discordance endures and to all appearances has existed from the very beginning of congregational life. Beyond any doubt those Christian women who practised qualified asceticism and thus were able to come forward and work like the Christian brothers, did for a time[105] experience a hitherto unknown freedom of movement and action. But it was always a freedom on androcentrically dualistic terms, which basically serves to emphasize to what a far-reaching extent Christian women's lives were from the very first organized as a denial of their female gender and their own selves and thus theologically institutionalized as the suppression of women.

(1988)

Notes

1. Both in commentaries and in monographs examples are legion; two of these will suffice as typical: Heinrich Schlier, 1965, pp. 174f., emphasizes in Gal 3,28 the sacramental perspective and accentuates the real, though hidden, consequence of the new creation of baptism. In note 4, however, he warns emphatically against drawing concrete conclusions with regard to religious and political reality. The body of Christ is not, nor was ever meant to be identified with political society. The word women is not even mentioned in his exegesis. See also Wolfgang Schrage 1980, pp. 111-73, and 1982, pp. 208-20. Quite obviously his preoccupation with a legitimization of the marriage morale of conservative middle-class establishment both predisposes and limits his view of sexuality and women.

Lone Fatum

2. Of profound influence on the recent debate is Krister Stendahl, pp. 25-43; rightly disputed by Madelaine Boucher, pp. 55-58. Conspicuously many women priests accept Gal 3,28 as supportive of a positive and affirmative view of women's status within the church, although the question of a possible practical consequence of the verse is still very far from a clarifying solution. Cf. Ulla Carin Holm, pp. 8 and 70f. See characteristic examples of the normative use of Gal 3,28 in Dautzenberg 1983, Fitzer, Jewett 1979b, Scroggs 1972 and 1974 and Walker 1975 and 1983. But cf. also Evans, Schüssler Fiorenza 1983, Heine, Heister, Kähler, Parvey and Schottroff 1980 and 1985.

3. Cf. Rom 10,12; 1 Cor 12,13; Col 3,11 and, for an elaborated version, Eph 2,11-22. The idea of baptism as a clothing, a new creation and a new spiritual life commitment is the constituent eschatological motif in Paul; cf. Rom 6,1-14; 13,11-14. Although male and female is only mentioned in Gal 3,28c, there is sufficient basis for taking the entire verse as an expression of a baptismal theology, accepted and developed by Paul, and v. 28c may thus be assessed as a saying in concordance with e.g. 2 Cor 5,16-17; Rom 8,1-17, where the idea of a new creation in an eschatological and ecclesiological sense is irretrievably tied up with the idea of a new life in Christ and a new growth with Christ as model and example; cf. Rom 8,29 and Phil 2,1-11.

4. Cf. the demand for unity and solidarity in 1 Cor 11,33; 12,4-26 and for intelligible and edifying talk in 14,22-25. See Conzelmann, pp. 213 and 225f., Luise Schottroff 1980, p. 118 and Schüssler Fiorenza 1983, pp. 228-30.

5. Apologetic efforts often unite in the attempt to find in Gal 3,28 the absolute verification of equality, thus to be able to insist upon a similarity between this verse and 1 Cor 11,11-12 expressive of what is genuinely and principally Pauline. Examples are numerous, but representative among them are Dautzenberg 1983, pp. 209-24, Schottroff 1985, pp. 104f. and Scroggs 1972, pp. 298-303. Jewett 1979b, pp. 64-77, cements his idea of Paul's sexual liberalism by means of the radical re-organization of the Corinthian correspondence. An extreme course is taken by Walker by his viewing the entire section, 1 Cor 11,2-16, as a post-Pauline interpolation; ctr. Murphy-O'Connor, who, in conjunction with the majority of exegetes, is content just to leave out 14,34-36. On the relationship between Gal 3,28 and 1 Cor 11,11-12, see also Lone Fatum 1976 for an earlier and more cautious view.

6. The fact that Paul uses the baptismal formula in different versions in Gal 3,28 and 1 Cor 12,13 gives reason for a consideration of the complicated question of the relative chronology of the Pauline material. Ctr. to e.g. Dautzenberg 1983, p. 219, it seems reasonable to acknowledge Gal 3,28 as the older version and 1 Cor 12,13 as a cautious adaptation adjusted to the special circumstances of the Corinthian situation. This permits us to see Gal 3,28c as a prerequisite for 1 Cor 11,2-16 without having to take into account prematurely whether or not the behaviour of the Corinthian women may in fact be considered concomitant with the Pauline point of argument in Gal 3,28. See Betz, pp. 199f., and Jervell, pp.

292-95, who is seconded by Hyldahl, pp. 64-75. Cf. also Jewett 1979b, p. 58, in continuation of 1979a, pp. 59f. and his Graph of Dates and Time-Spans. For a detailed discussion of a different view of the Pauline chronology, see Gerd Lüdemann 1980.

7. When the theological preference is concentrated on 1 Cor 11,11-12 the theological significance of vv. 3-9 is severely depreciated; see e.g. Conzelmann 1969, pp. 214-23. who refuses to accept the sexual concern in Paul's argument and thus is unable to see that rabbinic Jewish creation theology is the prerequisite of Paul's sexual paraenesis. Somewhat differently Jervell, pp. 296-313, and Barrett, pp. 247-52. On the necessity of crediting also the evidence that explicitly suppresses women with a theological and principal significance, see Boucher, pp. 57f.

8. So long as it is maintained that only Gal 3,28 and 1 Cor 11,11-12 are eschatologically qualified sayings, all the rest of 11,2-16 together with 14,34-36 and e.g. the material from the household-codes may too easily be disregarded as secondary, practical adjustments, results of a patriarchal institutionalization of but minor historical interest. And so, obviously, no theological value need be attached to these texts much less any normative significance. Cf. e.g. Stendahl, pp. 32-37, and Parrey, pp. 136f. For a detailed discussion of the development after Gal 3,28, see Schüssler Fiorenza 1983, pp. 245-84.

9. Elisabeth Schüssler Fiorenza stands out as the feminist theologian, who has contributed most substantially and most influentially towards the critically reflected feminist exegesis as well as to the necessary debate on feminist hermeneutics and methodology. But other names deserve mention, e.g. Bernadette Brooten, Susanne Heine, Carolyn Osiek, Karin Friis Plum, Rosemary R. Ruether, Letty M. Russel, Katharine Doob Sakenfeld, Turid Karlsen Seim, Susan Brooks Thistlethwaite, Mary Ann Tolbert and Phyllis Trible. In various ways these women have all been working in a critically conscious way with feminist theory of exegesis. In particular, however, they have all in their own ways been apologetically intent upon proving in practice that biblical texts may leave a room for both affirmation and liberation of women, if only they are made comprehensible by exegetical means compatible with women's subjective religious interests and alternative values of theological interpretation. Their common basis is thus the supposition that Christian faith and biblical religion and spirituality are in themselves neither suppressive nor misogynist. But does this not seem to delineate a set task of feminist exegesis that is affirmative of women in a way that will somehow allow the end to justify the means and let purposes and presuppositions together determine the results? All interpretation and biblical exegesis is conducted within a hermeneutic circle. But does not the specific feminist interest imply that the cycle of the feminist hermeneutical circle becomes so narrow as to make the exegesis predictable and self-affirmative? Cf. the definition of feminist hermeneutics as hermeneutics of suspicion, unwilling to accept what the text says, but, deliberately, focussing on what it does not say. If both purpose and presupposition are inherent in the experiences and personal beliefs of the feminist exegete, the text

will have serious difficulties in making itself heard and respected as a self-contained interlocutor in the dialogue of interpretation, and it will in effect be unable to function as a necessary dialectical corrective within the frames of the continuous historical discourse that is theological exegesis, constituting theology as a dynamic process of identification and transformation. Among feminist theologians it is widely accepted that feminist exegesis is not to be limited to texts explicitly relating to women. And yet, e.g. Prisca, Phoebe and Junia are again and again being resorted to in repeated attempts to find textual affirmation. Again, according to formal agreement it is not the object of feminist theology to isolate a canon within the canon; but nevertheless especially Gal 3,28 is repeatedly exploited in exactly this way as a particularly qualified impact of eschatological liberation in Christ and the revolutionary and transformative power of the Word of God, of the messianic prophetic message or even the testimony of womanchurch. To speak of the historically proto-typical meaning of a given text instead of insisting on the mythically arche-typical value of biblical texts as such implies, of course, a liberating and creative encounter with the absolute authority of Bible tradition and with the strategies of male domination of church and established theology. None the less the current dilemma of feminist theology still seems to be rooted in the traditional obsession of biblical theology, that feminist theological insight and experience has to be authorized by Scripture; when the text will not allow this, it will have to be effected against the text; for nothing can be made valid, or so it seems, without text? This way feminist hermeneutics is still divided against itself, and the actual feminist exegesis does not live up to its own hermeneutical intentions. Cf. for this the sharp criticism of K. Barth's exegesis launched by Phyllis A. Bird, pp. 130–32, which not only hits the author herself like a boomerang in her apologetic conclusion, pp. 158f., but also hits feminist theological interpretation and application in general, so long as the relationship between a critically analytical exegesis and a critically theological (re)-construction has not been made sufficiently clear, and so long as the very personal relationship of feminist theologians to biblical authorization and legitimization remains one of dependency. In this Boucher is right, p. 58. See also, referring to the above, Schüssler Fiorenza 1983, pp. 26–36 and 41–64 and 1984, pp. 66–115. Further contributions by Schüssler Fiorenza and Ruether in: Letty M. Russell ed. 1985, pp. 125–36 and 111–24 with a commentary by Russell, pp. 137–46.

10. To a remarkable degree Luise Schottroff e.g. seems able to obtain affirmative feminist results although she applies an exegesis based on social and material history. Because she does not focus specifically on the categories of gender and sexuality from a socio-cultural and anthropological point of view, though obviously she prefers to work with texts explicitly dealing with women's social status, her positive exegesis does not differ substantially from the apologetic contributions by e.g. Alfons Weiser, Dautzenberg and Claus Bussmann in: Dautzenberg 1983. Exegetically quite unacceptable examples of uncritical apologetics are

found in Catharina J. M. Halkes and Elisabeth Moltmann-Wendel, both partially emphasizing as their aim of interpretation present women's personal experiences and religious needs. This partial and cursory use of biblical texts, adapted to meet present feminist ends, seems to prevail also among Eastern Asiatic feminists, see e.g. Sun Ai Park. See also Magdalene Bussmann in: Dautzenberg 1983, pp. 339-58, which should be compared with the note in Schüssler Fiorenza 1980, pp. 83f.

11. Is it positive for women possibly to have been generically included by male designations such as brothers and sons? Is it compatible with the idea of women's self-contained dignity to acquiesce to the fact that a small number of affluent women may have been allowed to serve among the early Christians, cf. Luke 8,1-3, if this kept even these women tied to their traditional roles of subordination and institutionalized their dependent status of caring and attending? Or if the rights of women in Christ were preconditioned by their ascetic denial of body and sexuality in acceptance of women's secondary nature and imperfect human quality as compared to man as the norm and standard of humanity? Is it positive for women still to accept the assessment of what in Christ is right and eschatologically ideal, when this in effect in every respect – textually, traditionally, institutionally – is being contradicted by all that is socially and politically realized and ecclesialistically practised? All these critical questions and many others like them ought justly to be put to Else Kähler, Mary Evans and Luise Schottroff 1980 and 1985. But also to e.g. Bernadette Brooten, and not least to Schüssler Fiorenza 1983, pp. 41-67 and 160-204. Quite noteworthy is the claim by Dautzenberg 1982, pp. 196ff., that Gal 3,28 is to be seen as the evidence of revolutionary experience. See an equivalent enthusiasm about the uniquely radical and revolutionary potentials in very early Christianity in Jewett 1979b, Scroggs 1972 and, less hampered by clichés, Meeks, 1974. For a summing up, see Tolbert, p. 124: "Can feminists remain satisfied with the discovery of the occasional or exceptional in a patriarchal religion?"

12. Cf. Banks, pp. 122-30; Gager, pp. 34f.; Kee, pp. 88-91; Meeks 1983, pp. 23-25 and 70f. The sociological interest will concentrate on class instead of focusing on gender. When questions are asked about social identity among the early Christians primarily on a class or material basis, women still appear as an inferior side-topic, often referred to the footnotes. In sociological exegesis of this sort gender neutrality equals gender blindness and androcentric texts and contexts are left unchecked by androcentric questioning. Quite different results may be obtained when exegesis and early Christian social analysis utilize insights from cultural anthropology; cf. Malina 1981, pp. 25-48 and 94-118. Here sexuality is seen as a constituent symbol of social value and gender is acknowledged accordingly as a religious and political factor in the social process of identification and institutionalization. See Mary Douglas 1976, pp. 140-158.

13. See especially the hermeneutical reflections on the necessity of a radical feminist reconstruction as a conscious evasion of the androcentricism dominant in patri-

archal canonization by Schüssler Fiorenza 1983, pp. 26-95. But cf. also 1979, 1981 and 1984.

14. Characteristically, feminist theological debate has reached considerable herme-neutical as well as exegetical results in its confrontation with the misogynist tra-dition and the deprecating view of women still prevailing in the Catholic church. Cf. representative contributions by e.g. Schüssler Fiorenza, Bernadette Brooten, Madeleine Boucher, Adela Y. Collins and Sonya A. Quitslund in: *Women Priests,* eds. L. and A. Swidler 1977. See also Rosemary R. Ruether 1983, pp. 122-26, 139-52 and 193-213. Moreover, cf. the pioneer work by Kari Elisabeth Børresen from 1968.

15. On the heuristic and contra-cultural approaches as expressions of the feminist hermeneutical shift of paradigm, see Schüssler Fiorenza 1979, pp. 39ff. and 1984, especially pp. 66-115. It should not be overlooked, however, that the heuristic approach as a self-contained theological project runs the risk of ending up as a self-fulfillment of wishful feminist thinking or as a gynocentric mythology on a par with speculations in pre-historic matriarchies and thealogies and with a- or anti-historic goddess-spirituality. If androcentric texts and patriarchal tradi-tion are not squarely faced in their full implications as the historic conditions given for feminist living as well as for feminist interpretation, feminist heuristic hermeneutics are in danger of reducing themselves to a self-affirming sub-culture and will in the end have nothing to offer but postulates about the specialness of women and of feminist efforts.

16. On the subjectivity of feminist exegesis, see Tolbert, pp. 114-21. But cf. already Elizabeth Cady Stanton together with the discussion by Schüssler Fiorenza 1983, pp. 7-40. The confrontation with the dogma of analytical objectivity and with the whole idea of the unbiased interpreter and his value-free approach to the questions of exegesis and their possible theological consequences has, of course, been both justified and of great importance. However, this does not legit-imatize feminist subjectivity as an aim in itself, which it tends to become in Schüssler Fiorenza 1983, pp. 41-95. When subjectivity is maintained on its own as a hermeneutical principle and thus is programmed exclusively in relation to what in a text has not been said and to that in tradition which is not reflected, this subjectivity seems to be eluding analytical judgment and critical correctives and may end up facing arbitrariness.

17. It seems like self-oppression when feminist theologians accept Gal 3,28 as a canon in canon and, thus, as the guarantee of an eschatological ideal, the practi-cal consequence of which is found to be maintained by the eschatological value of the terms brothers and sons in Christ, assessed as generically inclusive desig-nations, although the implications for Christian women are quite impossible either historically to substantiate or socially to realize. Generally speaking, self-oppression is characteristic of the heavy dependency with which most feminist theologians accept the biblical view of women and gender as a normative view. An extreme example of this dependency is Phyllis Trible's attempt to make the

sacrificed women of biblical tradition come alive as an inspiration for present women in their ongoing struggle against the patriarchal God-Head, cf. 1984, pp. 93-116. As opposed to this Cady Stanton is much to be preferred, cf. Part II, pp. 25-27.

18. Cf. Gal 3,10-14; 4,1-7; Rom 7,7-25. See Donaldson, pp. 105f.; Hahn 1976, pp. 41-47 and 54-57; Wilckens, pp. 76-82.

19. See Rom 7,1-6 in the light of 5,12-17; 6,1-11. Cf. Gal 3,1 along with 1 Cor 1,17-25; Gal 3,19-4,7 with Phil 2,1-13. See Käsemann 1969, pp. 82-93 and 106f. and 1972, pp. 55ff. and 86-102; Wilckens, pp. 71f.

20. See Gal 2,15-21 along with 4,8-11; 5,1. On the imperative as a constituent motif in Paul also after the termination of the law in Christ, cf. Schlier 1965, pp. 176-88. See also Gal 6,2 in the light of 5,13-15. Cf. Kertelge, pp. 382f. and 389-91; Käsemann 1969, pp. 196-210 and 1972, pp. 82ff., 138-42 and 156-63; Paulsen, pp. 75f. and Wilckens, pp. 77ff.

21. Cf. 2 Cor 5,14-17 together with 1 Cor 12,4-27. See Paulsen, pp. 86-89 and 94; Wilckens, pp. 78-80; Kertelge, pp. 385f.; Käsemann 1969, pp. 76ff., 181ff. and 203ff. On the millenarian aspect, see Gager, pp. 34f.

22. Neither text nor context give support to a translation of sons in v. 26 into children. With the examples in 3,16-18 and 4,1-7 Paul explicitly refers to the male child and the male heir, and when in 4,19 he addresses the Galatians as children, this is not a generically inclusive designation but one determined by the birth metaphoric in 4,19-21. The fact that Paul consistently focuses on sons and thus on the conditions and obligations of sons to develop and grow according to the purpose and measure of Christ, is emphasized by the reference to the sons of Abraham in 4,22 and by the address to the brothers in 4,28. In this connection 5,1-12 serves to clarify and concretize the obligation in 4,21-31 in a way which shows brothers and children in v. 31 to be synonyms. Cf. to this Rom 8,12-30. See Kertelge, pp. 386-88; Wilckens, pp. 68ff.; Paulsen, pp. 89-93; Hahn 1976, pp. 39-41 and 55ff. But see also Becker, pp. 44f.; Lietzmann, pp. 23f.; Mussner, p. 262 and Oepke 1984, p. 124.

23. To translate v. 28c by man and woman is incorrect and serves to obscure the fact that male and female are sexual designations, dependent on Gen 1,27b. Against Schüssler Fiorenza 1983, p. 211. Also dependent on Gen 1,27b are Mark 10,6; Matth 19,4 along with the condemnatory references to sexuality in Rom 1,26-27. Luke 2,23 speaks of the male sex in the absolute sense, implying by the very exclusiveness of the designation glory as well as quality, and this is underlined by Apoc 12,5. Obscuration or repression of the sexual signification of v. 28c is deeply rooted in the lexicographical tradition of theological abstraction and a-historic intellectualizing. Cf. Oepke 1966a and b along with Jeremias and Greeven. Within this tradition it is possible to deal with human conditions in the world as well as in Christ without ever reflecting on the significance of gender; cf. symptomatically Bultmann, pp. 232-46 and 332-53, along with Jewett 1971, pp. 95-116 and 119-34. Obviously, this abstract and a-historic approach to v. 28c helps to interpret Paul's view on sexuality and women apologetically.

24. That Paul in Gal addresses the male members of the congregation with an urgent and rather palpable purpose is testified by 5,1-12. Since, obviously, it is not women who are on the point of letting themselves be circumcized, it is not women either who are in the actual danger of separating themselves from Christ; cf. 1,6-9; 5,4. In effect, Gal nowhere gives reason to believe that Paul is concerned at all with the circumstances of women. Thus there is no textual evidence for the assumption of Witherington, pp. 597-602, that Paul's aim in opposing the Judaistic demand for circumcision is to come to the rescue of the women of the congregation. Besides, see Kertelge, pp. 383f.; Donaldson, pp. 94 and 100ff.; Hahn 1976, pp. 57ff.; Wilckens, pp. 68ff. and 75ff. But see also Oepke 1984, pp. 125f., who finds Paul's real concern in v. 28a and considers the rest of the verse irrelevant in the Galatian context. Lietzmann, pp. 23f., underlines the eschatological perspective by his reference to Rom 8,23 but does not reflect on gender and sexuality. Cf. Becker, pp. 45f.

25. The prerogative of the Jew is manifest in Gal 4,4-5, but is maintained also by e.g. 2,5; Rom 3,2; 9,4-5; 11,25-32. In spite of the termination of the law, Paul's positive view of the law is upheld in Gal 3,19-24; Rom 7,7-19. In relation to the matter of equality and liberation it is especially noteworthy how persistently Paul in fact puts the Jew before the Greek in Rom 1,16; 2,9-10; 3,9; 1 Cor 1,24; 10,32 as well as in Rom 10,12 and 1 Cor 12,13. Col 3,11 is an interesting exception, although circumcision is mentioned before foreskin. Besides, see Hahn 1976, pp. 51-57 and 59; Kertelge, pp. 385f.; Donaldson, pp. 97-99; Paulsen, pp. 84f. and 90ff.

26. Meeks 1974, p. 182, defines the present tense of the verb in v. 28 as a performative statement based on the dramatic ritual of baptism. He is supported by Betz, pp. 189ff., who emphasizes the fact that Paul is using the formula secondarily in a polemic situation; cf. pp. 184-86. Cf. Bouttier, pp. 6-8 and 15-18, along with Paulsen, pp. 84-89. The difference between formula and admonition, however, needs clarification. Because it seems obvious that v. 28 retains neither the pronouncement quality nor the immediate effect of transformation experience, the Pauline purpose in v. 28 should be found in the polemic adjustment of paraenetic admonition and not in the performative formula in itself. Through the verb in the present tense Paul is in fact looking back, just as he is in v. 27, and thus his admonition becomes accusation and appeal in one. In a similar way Paul employs liturgical formulas in 1 Cor 11,23-26; 15,1-11 for his immediate paraenetic purposes. See also Phil 2,1-11. The liturgical indicative is not maintained in a self-contained dogmatic form for its own sake, but it is applied by Paul as the well-known and recognizable tradition and thus made to serve as the common ground on which a concrete imperative can be formulated, related directly to the congregational situation. In effect, Paul is concerned neither with baptism nor with the baptismal formula in itself in Gal 3,27-28; he is concerned only with the consequences of baptism and intent on securing these among the brothers in Galatia.

27. The Galatian situation is characterized by 1,6-9; 3,1-3; 4,8-11.21; 5,1-12; 6,12-13, showing the former Gentiles to be under pressure from a group of Jewish Christians. Obviously, the main issue is circumcision, advocated by the Judaizers as a necessary supplement to baptism. But that which to the Galatians seems to be a both-and, baptism as well as circumcision, is to Paul a radical either-or: it is Christ or the law, spirit or flesh, life or death, freedom or bondage. Cf. Schlier 1965, pp. 39, 73, 125, 237 and 280f. It is interesting to note that Paul's accusation in 4,9 becomes a parallel to the accusation against Kephas in 2,14; cf. Betz, p. 216. Besides, see Kertelge, pp. 386-88; Donaldson, pp. 104f.; Käsemann 1969, pp. 26ff. and 67ff.

28. Cf. Gal 3,3; 5,4; 6,12-13 together with Rom 2,17-29. See Schlier 1965, pp. 233f. To Paul the former Jew, fanatic in his religious activity and ardour, putting one's trust in personal achievements always remains the great temptation, radically to be opposed by the motif of merit and boast in Christ, i.e. according to the reversed criteria of the *theologia crucis* paradigm; cf. 1 Cor 1, 1,18-31. See Hahn 1976, pp. 34-41 and 58.

29. Cf. Gal 5,3-4 in the light of 2,19; 3,10-14. On Paul's view of the Galatians as evidence of rabbinic Jewish superiority, see Betz, pp. 259f. Cf. Phil 3,2-11. Besides, see Donaldson, pp. 102ff.; Hahn 1976, pp. 54ff.; Kertelge, pp. 384 and 387f.; Wilckens, pp. 74f.

30. See Gal 3,21-22 together with Rom 3,19-20; 7,12-14. Thus, Gal 5,4 should be taken at face value. Cf. Schlier 1965, p. 232. That Paul's radical view, however, is just one among others, is rightly stressed by Betz, p. 261. Cf. e.g. Gal 2,11-14 along with 2 Pet 3,16. See also Kertelge, pp. 383f. and Wilckens, pp. 80ff.

31. To be in Christ is to Paul the consequence of having put on Christ during the divinely transforming process of baptism, and so it is hereafter to exist in the power sphere of life instead of death. See Rom 5,12-19; 6,3-11 in connection with Gal 2,19-20. Decisive, however, is the fact that Christ to the Christians constitutes the ground, the conditions and the obligations of life all in one. Thus, Schlier 1965, pp. 173f., seconded by Mussner, p. 263, is rightly opposed by Betz, pp. 186-89, because of his sacramentalistic interpretation. Betz finds support in W. Meeks 1974, pp. 181f. and 189-97, and sees baptism in Paul as a christocentric rite of adoption. Those baptized in Christ are qualified to be sons of God through Christ and are hereafter directly dependent on Christ for their lives in a way that implies the obligation to grow after the measure of Christ, if they are to reach the final realization of Christ's glory. Cf. to this note 22 and see in Gal 3,3; 4,19; 5,7 how the motif of birth and growth, beginning and development, is used by Paul to apply the claim of a growing likeness in the form of a still more perceptive similarity between Christ and the Christians; cf. Rom 8,1-21 and Col 1,14-20; 2,6-15; 3,1-4. The androcentric standard of this Christ-motif should not be underestimated. It is indeed an evidence of the fact that androcentric normativity is deeply rooted not only in the theological paradigm of creation, according to Gen 1,27a, but also in the ideal of *imitatio Christi* as the encompassing

paradigm of Christian existence. Thus the androcentric concept of normality finds its point of fixation in the Adam-Christ typology which as an *Anthropos* speculation is maintained by Paul in the son and heir motif, but applied throughout not as an aspect of the androgyne but, on the contrary, as a pattern of life, invested with androcentric quality personified by the male figure of Christ, cf. e.g. Gal 4,4; Rom 9,4-5 as applied in 2 Cor 5,14-21; Rom 6,1-11. See generally Donaldson, pp. 97f. and 105f.; Hahn 1976, pp. 57ff.; Kertelge, pp. 386ff.; Wilckens, pp. 67 and 73ff.; Käsemann 1969, pp. 20ff., 67-79, 181-85 and 199-204, and 1972, pp. 107-14.

32. This is emphasized in 1 Cor 12,13 by the body metaphoric and in Col 3,11 by the addition of the ethnic specifications. That social change is not what Paul intended is made clear in 1 Cor 7,20-24 in connection with 12,14-26. See also 11,20-21.33 where Paul pleads for different ways of congregational gathering but certainly not for a change in social conditions or ways of earthly living. Cf. Bouttier, pp. 6-8 and 11ff. along with Paulsen, pp. 76-79. It is a weakness in Wilckens, pp. 78ff., that he does not even come near the question of the socially concrete; in this respect Mussner is also symptomatic, cf. pp. 264ff.

33. See e.g. Schüssler Fiorenza 1983, p. 211, along with Dautzenberg 1982, pp. 182f. and 1983, pp. 216f. Cf. also Bouttier, pp. 10f. and 15ff.; Becker, p. 45f.; Oepke 1984, p. 125.

34. Betz, p. 195, sees a biological motif implied by the neuter of the adjectives, but he insists all the same on the social connotation of v. 28c. Dependent on Meeks 1974, he seeks for an explanation in Gnostic Hellenistic and rabbinic Jewish mythology on the androgynous Original Man or *Anthropos*-Urmensch, pp. 196-200. However, the social implications of this in regard to women remain unclarified, cf. Betz, p. 197. Ctr. Schüssler Fiorenza 1983, pp. 211-14, who is able to deny the restrictive meaning of the reference to biological gender as well as the anthropological-cosmic interpretation. Relating v. 28c to Gen 1,27 as a whole and not just to v. 27b as opposed to v. 27a, Schüssler Fiorenza insists on the happy aspects of procreation and fertility, marriage and family. Thus, Gal 3,28c becomes a very positive affirmation of sexual as well as social life, although, of course, the verse is said to imply a warning against patriarchal misuse and exploitation. Characteristically, Schüssler Fiorenza is not concerned with clarifying the anthropological, but focuses only on the ecclesiological. For similar unrealistic interpretations on the basis of Gen 1,27 as a whole, see e.g. Evans, Kähler, Heine, Heister and Schottroff; cf. the apologetic purpose in Leipoldt and Paul K. Jewett, but see also Jervell, pp. 231ff. along with the interpretation of e.g. Rom 8,29 and 1 Cor 15,35-47 by Larsson; for further examples of gender-blind exegesis, see the contributions by Koehler, Schmidt, Kürzinger, Schlink and Loretz in: *Der Mensch als Bild Gottes*, ed. Leo Scheffczyk.

35. Against Schüssler Fiorenza 1983, pp. 211 and 218. To maintain that the biological sex differences have lost their constitutive meaning but that sexual differentiation still remains as a positive human value, is like wanting to eat your cake and

have it. If the discrepancy between v. 28a–b and v. 28c as well as the dependence
of v. 28c on Gen 1,27b are to be fully acknowledged, v. 28c gives no reason
within the Pauline context to speak positively of either sexuality or marriage.
See further note 39. Also against Dautzenberg 1982, pp. 194–96 and 1983, pp.
217–21. Conspicuously contradictory is Scroggs 1972, pp. 288f. and 295f., but
seconded all the same by Jewett 1979b, p. 65, in his attempt to find a basis for
the peculiar argument that Paul was anxious to stimulate sexual activity through
a positive concept of sexuality as a conscious countermeasure against ascetic
androgynous inclinations; cf. pp. 70 and 72f. See further Paulsen, pp. 85–89 and
92f.; Käsemann 1969, pp. 22ff.

36. Because v. 28c is considered to be the most difficult part of the verse, a common
denominator must be found in a–b when an interpretation implying social consequences is envisaged. See e.g. the ecclesiological emphasis put on the perspective of liberation by Schüssler Fiorenza 1983, pp. 209–11. Cf. Betz, pp. 190–95.
who, like Oepke 1984 and Mussner, does not exploit the possibilities of a comparison between slaves and women in relation to 1 Cor 7,24.29–31. For an interesting attempt to find in v. 28c the freedom for women to choose for themselves
whether or not they want to marry, see Witherington, pp. 597–99. Decisive to
Paul, according to this interpretation, emphasizing the agreement between a–b
and c, is the freedom within the Christian fellowship to be different, cf. pp.
600–02. Although Thecla is rightly seen as a possible consequence of c, Witherington's argument carries little conviction; partly because it cannot be supported
directly by textual evidence, cf. note 24; and partly because it considers Gen 1,27
as a whole to be a positive pattern to Paul and thus presupposes the purpose of c
to be sexuality instead of asexuality. Generally, an uncritical view of Gen 1,27 as
a positive basis for c is characteristic of apologetic interpretation; but it is worth
noting how often this interpretation is advanced, more or less overtly, in defence
of the Christian marriage, thus authorizing matrimonial sex; see examples in
Dautzenberg, Scroggs, Jewett and Schüssler Fiorenza in continuation of note 34.
For an extreme example of marriage apologetics based on Gen 1,27a–b, see the
contribution by Walter Dürig in: *Der Mensch als Bild Gottes*, ed. Leo Scheffczyk;
presumably by the same token but without substantiation, Oepke 1984, p. 126,
uses v. 28c against the threat of ascetic interpretation of 1 Cor 7,1ff. Besides,
Bouttier, pp. 15–18; Paulsen, pp. 94f.

37. See Betz, pp. 181–85; Scroggs 1972, p. 292; Meeks 1974, pp. 180–83; Witherington, pp. 596f.; Bouttier, pp. 3ff. and 8ff.; Paulsen, pp. 78ff.

38. Cf. Phyllis Bird, pp. 147–51. Against attempts to see the androgynous *Anthropos*-Urmensch behind v. 28c, the masculine designation of the unity in v. 28d is
rightly emphasized by Witherington, p. 597; but he does not reflect critically the
implications to women of the androcentric Christ-motif in his own assessment of
d. Schüssler Fiorenza 1983, p. 213, apparently finds no importance attached to
the masculine designation in d; to her it seems exceedingly essential to dissociate
v. 28 altogether from Gnostic asceticism; cf. p. 218. See also Mussner, pp. 265f.

and Oepke 1984, p. 126. Ctr. Jewett 1979b, p. 65. See also Paulsen, pp. 82-84. On the Jewish background, see further Strack/Billerbeck III, pp. 557-63.

39. Scroggs 1972, p. 288, is rightly rejected by Elaine Pagels, pp. 540-43. It does seem impossible for a critically consistent analysis to avoid the impression that Paul's view on sexuality is fundamentally negative, that, accordingly, his eschatological ideal is ascetic, and that this has an effect on his view of women. Cf. 1 Cor 7,1.7.26.32.34.37.40. Against Jewett 1979b, pp. 71-73. In accordance with Meeks 1974, pp. 193-97, but against his conclusion regarding Paul's view, pp. 199-202 and 208.

40. Cf. Meeks 1974, pp. 180-83, 189-97 and 208, followed by Betz, pp. 186-200. However, in his comprehensive analysis of the myth of the androgyne, Meeks isolates the baptismal formula from the Pauline context and deals primarily with the social implications of rite itself, cf. note 26. By doing this, he not only obscures the connection within the Pauline context between Gal 3,28c and 1 Cor 11,2-16; he also misses the significance of Paul's dependence on Gen 1,27b. As a result, Meeks is able to emphasize the bisexual aspect of the (re)united androgyne instead of the asexual impact of the androcentric *Anthropos*-Urmensch in accordance with Gen 1,27a. See Bird, pp. 137-46. If Paul's rabbinic Jewish interpretation of Gen 1,27b is referred to as the basis of a negative view of sexuality and women, it is impossible to argue with Meeks for an antagonism between Gal 3,28c and 1 Cor 7 and 11; on the contrary, it seems reasonable to argue for a coherence between Gal 3,28c; 1 Cor 7,7 on one hand and 11,2-16; 14,34-36 on the other; a coherence, i.e., defined and consistently applied by Paul in consideration of the superior ideal of eschatological existence according to the special charisma of asceticism. For a collective interpretation of the *Anthropos*-Urmensch motif in concordance with the body metaphoric of 1 Cor 12,12-26, cf. Paulsen, pp. 87-93. This, of course, could be seen as just another way of avoiding the issue of the sexually specific in androcentric Christology, cf. note 34.

41. Against Meeks 1974, pp. 199-202 and 208; but also generally against Walker, Scroggs, Dautzenberg, Jewett and Schüssler Fiorenza, who all seem anxious to reduce the signs of asceticism in Paul to something dubious and of a clearly non-, pseudo-, or even anti-Pauline character and origin. It remains highly suggestive, though, that an eschatological key passage like 1 Cor 7,29-31 may in fact be interpreted convincingly as a direct confrontation with the social and moral normativity of sexuality, characterized by the patrilinear control and the defensive marriage strategy of patriarchal society; cf. Derrett, pp. 184-92, along with B. Malina 1981, p. 103. Moreover, see Niederwimmer, pp. 121-24.

42. Cf. 1 Cor 7,32-35 together with Rom 5,12-19; 6,1-14; 8,18-21; see on the motif of growth and its androcentric implications in note 31.

43. To comprehend fully the consequences of v. 28c and d, it seems necessary to speak of likeness in the specified sense of uniformity instead of unity or union. And this allows for no speculation on the bisexuality of the androgyne. Thus, the Thecla-figure is not androgynous, but virile; cf. Meeks 1974, p. 196. Therefore,

the masculine designation in v. 28d should be respected as an androcentric designation of exclusiveness instead of inclusiveness. Cf. notes 22 and 23. Only by
maintaining the male exclusiveness of the Christ motif in v. 28d along with the
concept of androcentric normality in v. 28c according to Gen 1,27a, is it possible
to grasp the full impact within the Pauline context of the fundamental either-or
which in the form of clean ctr. unclean constitutes his Jewish-Christian universe.
Cf. the presupposed discrimination against the unclean, i.e. Greek, slave and
(female) sexuality, in v. 28 with the presuppositions of Paul's argument in 1 Cor
5,9-13; 6,15-20; 10,14-33. See Mary Douglas 1976, pp. 49-57; Malina 1981, pp.
125-50. Many interpreters have found it necessary to point out the difficulty or
even irrelevance of v. 28c; so e.g. Meeks 1974, p. 181, emphasizing the fact that c
seems unmotivated in the Galatian context. The irony is, however, that c only
seems contextually unmotivated when interpreted without contextual consistency. When isolated from the Galatian argument and not recognized as an integral part of the admonition to the Galatian brothers, c, of course, cannot be seen
for what it is, namely a statement concerning clean and unclean; a statement, i.e.,
exemplifying the consequences of baptism to the benefit of the former Gentiles
and thus asserting the fact that the threat of the unclean is invalidated in Christ.
The incompatibility between clean and unclean is the reason behind the Judaistic
demand for circumcision in Galatia, and accordingly it is Paul's belief in the inval-
idation in Christ of this incompatibility that is his reason for arguing as he does,
in v. 28 a-d, for unity and likeness in the sense of uniformity between Christ and
the Christian brothers. See Bird, pp. 137-44.

44. As a statement of annulment and negation in relation to sexuality and reproduction v. 28c is not a social text. In every respect it serves in the Pauline argument
as an eschatological paradigm and should therefore be recognized as an antisocial text. Cf. Meeks 1974, pp. 193-97. Thus it is both misleading and oddly
unrealistic when e.g. Betz, pp. 188 and 200, emphasizes the social and political
implications. Cf. Paulsen, pp. 88f. and 94f.; Bouttier, pp. 18f. Against Jewett
1979b, pp. 72 and 76f.; Scroggs 1972, pp. 288 and 293-96, it must be maintained
that Paul is not advocating a positive sexual revolution. The reservation of 1 Cor
7,20 applies, of course, to all parts of v. 28a-c. It should be explicitly noted, however, that the reservation may be applied very differently to men and to women.
When concretized in deference to the androcentric motif in v. 28d, v. 28c obviously cannot be made to render a positive possibility of social identification to
the Christian woman in the same way as v. 28b may be said to render immediately a positive possibility of social identification to the Christian slave, by referring him to the established social value of the free-born. But this seems to be
only further evidence of the assessment that v. 28c is an eschatological assertion
which in its immediate context carries a positive meaning only to the male Christians in Galatia. Only indirectly and implicitly is it meaningful to speak of consequences to Christian women, and the question remains, whether these
consequences deserve to be called positive? It must not be overlooked that the

virgin-ideal in a social respect is but a temporary compromise with this world, and thus eschatological asceticism is in a special way antisocial when applied to women; the very nature of the compromise seems illustrated by the as if-designations in 1 Cor 7,29-31, since the asexually masculinizing categories of virginity and widowhood represent the possibilities of ascetic negation of femaleness, if the androcentric standard is to be recognized. Contrary to a slave who may have the possibility of social freedom and may even choose not to use this possibility, the ideal of eschatological asceticism seems to leave the Christian woman with something rather less than freedom; for either she is married and ought to stay married, and her head is then her husband *coram deo;* or she is unmarried and may stay so, if she has the means, and if her father will allow it, cf. 1 Cor 7,36-38; but does an unmarried woman take the consequence of v. 28c, she chooses in fact to become non-female or non-woman, according to the androcentric standard of the Christ motif. Cf. 1 Cor 7,20-24 along with Philem 8-20; see Stuhlmacher, pp. 43f.

45. Cf. Gal 3,3; 4,3; 5,3 in connection with e.g. 1 Cor 7,1-2.9.26.32-35 and Rom 7,14-25. It is decisive to acknowledge how flesh to Paul comprises sexuality and reproduction together on the preconditions of sin and death; so, that which is eschatologically qualified is that which effectively opposes this world and its institutions by negating its criteria and values. See 1 Cor 5-6 in the context of 1,18-25; 7,29-31. Moreover, cf. Niederwimmer, pp. 80-97 and 106-20. See further Maurer and Kümmel along with Oepke 1966b, especially p. 785, where sexuality is maintained as the curse of woman with reference to Mark 12,18-27 par. This clearly discriminating way of defining a woman negatively by her sex shows Oepke to be more in line with Paul himself than his modern interpreters of the apologetic school.

46. By v. 28c and d Paul has in fact himself established the eschatological ideal of asceticism which, when applied in social practice, means androcentric annulment of femaleness and thus implies androcentric discrimination towards unmarried as well as married women in the Pauline congregations. Against Meeks 1974, pp. 197-202; there is no textual evidence to support the assumption that Paul was less conservative and less discriminating in his attitude towards women than e.g. Philo; also against Meeks 1974, pp. 176f. and Scroggs 1972, p. 290. The possibility remains that the independent women who serve as Paul's co-workers were in fact leading lives of eschatological asceticism; against Meeks 1974, pp. 197f. and Schüssler Fiorenza 1983, pp. 208-18. This possibility should have been considered pp. 160-204; but see for a similar want of critical reflection Schottroff 1980, pp. 113-21. Cf. Earle Ellis 1971.

47. Excessive is Schmithals, cf. 1969, pp. 84-89, and 1973. He is followed by Jewett 1971, pp. 23-41; see also 1979b, p. 59. See further Walker and Trompf. Moderate spokesmen for accepting integrity are Conzelmann 1969, pp. 13-15, and Barrett, pp. 11-17. A weighty contribution to the discussion in favour of unity is given by Merklein.

48. Especially Gerd Theissen has contributed substantially to the socio-historical assessment of the Corinthian situation; cf. his articles, pp. 231-71, pp. 272-89, and pp. 290-317. See also Meeks 1983, pp. 74-192, along with N. A. Dahl, Holmberg, pp. 58-95, and Schütz, pp. 187-248. For an anthropological assessment, see Barton and Neyrey; also dependent on Mary Douglas, cf. Malina 1986, pp. 112-56. For an approach based on rhetorical criticism, see Schüssler Fiorenza 1987, along with Bünker, pp. 72-80. A useful clarification of the congregational context as well as of the fundamental diversity between Paul and the Gentile Christians at Corinth is given by Hasler. See further Käsemann 1964 I, pp. 109-34, par. to contribution in Kertelge ed., pp. 173-204.

49. If 1 Cor is regarded as one compositional unity, characterized by thematic and contextual coherence, the interpreter's key to the letter may well be found in 1,18-25. On the relationship between indicative and imperative and on the implications of Paul's own role as the personal representation of his *theologia crucis* paradigm, see e.g. Schütz, pp. 187-203. Cf. generally Bultmann, pp. 324-53. together with his article: "Das Problem der Ethik bei Paulus," in Rengstorf ed., pp. 179-99. Compare Käsemann 1972, pp. 79-114. See further Lone Fatum 1971.

50. A useful clarification of the eschatological discrepancy between Paul and the Corinthian enthusiasts is given by Thiselton, in continuation of Barrett, p. 109. The principal agreement between the parties, which Paul himself seems to take for granted, is rightly stressed; cf. e.g. 1 Cor 1,4-10; 3,10-17; 4,14-17 in connection with 11,23-25 and 15,1-11. Not only should Paul's clash with the charismatic individualists be understood on this common basis, but 11,1.2.16.17 should be concretely evaluated within this context.

51. Against the Corinthians' enthusiastic beliefs in present eschatological fulfillment, based on sacramentalism and tending towards pneumatic Gnosticism, Paul all through 1 Cor consistently emphasizes an eschatological imperative which is qualified by hope and future expectations, thus implicating the collectivity of the body of Christ both in its present representation in the congregation and in its anticipation of the coming fulfillment at the *parousia* of Christ. Thus life in Christ to Paul is a life of commitment and collectivity, orientated towards an eschatological future of final affirmation and identification, cf. 1 Cor 13; but see also the characteristically Pauline dialectics in the correlation of that which is "already" and that which is "not yet," exploited as the twofold motivation in 5,6-13; 6,12-20; 7,26-35; 8,9-13; 9,15-23; 10,23-11,1; 11,27-34; 12,14-26.31-14,5; 15,12-34. See von Soden: "Sakrament und Ethik bei Paulus," in Rengstorf ed., pp. 338-79. Cf. generally Lampe along with Käsemann 1969, pp. 61-107 and pp. 178-210, together with 1972, pp. 79-114. Thus, decisive of the interpretation of Paul's main paraenetic concern in 1 Cor is the insistence on the thematic coherence not only of 1 Cor itself, but between 1 Cor and the other letters of Paul, especially Gal and Rom; the characteristic imperative of Gal 5,25 and Rom 6,1-14 implies exactly the same eschatological motivation as 1 Cor

7,29-31 and e.g. Gal 2,15-21; Rom 7,1-8,4 hold the same Christological prerequisite as 1 Cor 1,18-25; see further Phil 2,1-13. The fact that first Paul urges
the Galatian brothers to absolutely and unabridgedly assert their Christian freedom, whereupon, shortly afterwards, he literally does everything in his apostolic
power to persuade the strong and self-confident Corinthians to compromise their
freedom and reduce their trust in the present state of salvation is not the result
of a reversed theological policy but, on the contrary, the logical evidence of
Paul's consistent endeavours to uphold and put into practice one and the same
kerygma in very different congregational situations; cf. 1 Cor 9,19-23, the practical implications of which especially within the Corinthian context can hardly be
overestimated.

52. Cf. the mention of those of Chloe in 1,11 together with the introductory formu-
    las in 7,1.25; 8,1.4; 12,1; 16,1.12, all pointing to the fact that Paul was presented
    with a number of questions in writing; cf. also the mention of Stephanas and his
    colleagues, apparently present with Paul in Ephesus at the closing of 1 Cor
    according to 16,15-18. Generally, chapters 1-6 seem to be concerned with mat-
    ters of which oral information was given, while chapters 7-14 possibly 15 and
    parts of 16 contain Paul's reaction to a letter from the congregation. See Hurd,
    pp. 61-209, for a copious discussion and some very ingenious attempts at recon-
    structing the correspondence prior to 1 Cor.

53. Evidently, a letter from Paul as well as a letter from the congregation are implied
    by 5,9; 7,1. But it is highly problematic to decide who brought the letter from
    Corinth to Paul at Ephesus, since the assessment both of 1,11 and of 1,16;
    16,15-18 is encumbered by uncertainty and mere guesswork. It seems a reason-
    able supposition that those of Chloe are house slaves or dependent clients; they
    may have brought both the letter and the oral information, or they may have
    brought only the oral information, staying just for a short visit in Ephesus which
    is why they are not mentioned in chapter 16. It is equally reasonable to suppose
    that Stephanas, obviously one of the patrons of the congregation and a loyal sup-
    porter of Pauline authority, was the official deliverer of the letter together with
    his travelling companions; they are mentioned in chapter 16 with words of praise
    and recommendation because they are to carry 1 Cor back with them, and
    because the letter as well as its deliverers are included in Paul's persistent
    attempts to (re)establish his supreme apostolic authority in relation to a dis-
    rupted and non-homogeneous group of fervent Christians; cf. 1 Cor 1-4 along
    with Dahl, Theissen, pp. 231-71, and Meeks 1983, pp. 57-59 and pp. 118-20.
    For further discussion, cf. Hyldahl, pp. 42-51. For a general discussion of the
    problem of charismatic authority and roles of leadership, see Rohde, pp. 43-56,
    along with the contributions by von Harnack, Sohm, Lietzmann, Käsemann and
    Schelkle in Kertelge ed. See also Bünker, pp. 74-76, together with Theissen, pp.
    272-89, and Barton, pp. 229-42. Schüssler Fiorenza 1987, pp. 394-99, does not
    contest Paul's personal affiliation to the patrons of his congregations, but seeing
    Chloe as an affluent, active and socially independent Christian woman she

assumes her to have been one of the Corinthian leaders. Thus, those of Chloe are neither slaves nor client freedmen but followers of Chloe and as such the official delegates of the congregation. Though the conjecture is interesting, it seems rather difficult to substantiate in any convincing way. Once again the allegation of Paul's generically inclusive language is put forward; cf. the discussion in notes 11 and 22. However, in view of the fact that Paul in 1 Cor finds reason to appeal directly to the "brothers" altogether 20 times, compare 9 times in Gal and 10 times in Rom, it is hard to accept 1 Cor especially as Paul's reaction to questions put to him officially and matters communicated to him personally by a certain female Christian leader and her followers – a certain female Christian leader, i.e., whose position and personal influence among the Corinthians equal those of Peter, Apollos, Paul and Christ himself, if the parallel of the genitives in 1,11 and 1,12 are taken at face value; see pp. 394f. This interpretation seems an unhappy, but characteristic result of feminist exegesis bolting into feminist apologetic reconstruction and conjecturing at a pace neither socio-historical analysis nor cultural anthropological insights can keep up with. See a deserved criticism of gynecocentric analysis, Malina 1986, p. 161, in continuation of discussion in notes 9 and 34. A solution which completely ignores the social conflict among the Corinthians between patrons and clients is proposed by Conzelmann 1969, p. 358. The fact that women are administered by men also among Christians is evidenced by 7,36-38; cf. Derrett, pp. 184-92. See Hurd, p. 185, for a reconstruction of the question behind 11,2; cf. Lietzmann, p. 53, and Weiss, p. 269. See also Hasler, pp. 113-21; further in note 62.

54. Cf. 11,2.16 in connection with the motif of congregational commitment and common practice in 1,2; 4,14-17; 7,17; 11,1.23; 14,33-34; 15,1-2.11. Even though 11,6.13-15 concerns custom and socio-sexual morality of the conventional sort, confusing nature with culture in order to maintain institutionalized culture as true and uncompromised nature, v. 16 gives no reason to spurn the matter in question as "trifles," so Barrett, p. 257. Paul, obviously, is concerned with upholding order on a serious basis, and his endeavour should be taken seriously in view of the fact that his guidance concerning women and sexuality occupies a considerable part of 1 Cor, and especially in 7 and 11 Paul is reacting to questions from the Corinthians with a *paraenesis* which must be assessed accordingly as an integrated moral attempt, symptomatic of the fundamental clash of eschatological paradigms and their pneumatic implications by way of personal freedom and a self-confident authority. Barton, pp. 229-34, rightly emphasizes the seriousness of the authority problems involved, pointing to the congregational dependence on the private house for official meetings and sacred worship, thus necessitating an investment in symbolic separation and a rule of qualifying discrimination to mark a difference and a set of boundaries in time and space between the sacred and the profane. This, obviously, creates a special problem concerning married women in 14,33b-36, but it seems no less to be the root of the conflict of gender roles and social authority in 11,2-16. However, just as it is

an avoidance of the issue to see in 11,2–16 only a mere trifle about women's head-gear and hair-do, so it is equally an evidence of gender-blind interpretation to see the text not as a matter of married women's subordination but generally as a positive affirmation of the socio-sexual relationship between men and women; cf. the view of e.g. Barrett, Evans, Hooker, Kähler and Swidler; and on the side-track of explicit homophobia, Scroggs 1972 and Murphy-O'Connor 1980. See rightly Trompf, p. 226, in continuation of Lietzmann, p. 55. The unwillingness found e.g. in Heine, Heister, Schüssler Fiorenza 1979 and 1983 and Schottroff 1980, to accept 11,3–9 theologically at face value as Paul's argument in favour of married women's subordination during worship is due partly to the canonical use of Gal 3,28 and partly to the apologetic preoccupation with 11,11–12. See further in note 96. The principal importance of 11,3–16 as a midrashic teaching of socio-sexual order, based independently on creation theology, should be emphasized against Jervell, p. 295, and Kähler, p. 53 and p. 66, in continuation of note 7.

55. See 10,32–11,2 as the contextual basis of the women's *paraenesis* along with especially 14,2–5.22–23 as the formulation of the demand for common edification, summarized in 14,40. Representatives of the widespread agreement among interpreters are Weiss, pp. 268f., Lietzmann, p. 52, Kähler, pp. 43f., seconded by Evans, pp. 82f. See also Cartlidge. The social aspect is rightly stressed by Schottroff 1980, pp. 117–20, and Heine, pp. 103–05; the probability of a class conflict between strong and weak women is emphasized by Heister, pp. 168–70, who sees the insistence on the conservative Jewish veil as Paul's deliberate support of the socially weak and insecure women; cf. further Schüssler Fiorenza 1983, pp. 227–30, who acknowledges a conscious missionary strategy in Paul's attempts to limit ecstatic behaviour among female Sophia-worshippers; crucial for her interpretation is 14,23. But for a detailed discussion of v. 2, see Blass/Debrunner/Rehkopf, § 154, along with Moule, p. 35, both emphasizing the coherence between 11,2 and 10,33. However, the implication in v. 2 seems to be the qualification: as regards congregational worship, partly necessitated by the parallel references to *paradosis* in v. 2 and v. 23 and yet partly allowing for the divergence between the praise in v. 2 and the explicit withholding of praise in v. 17. But compare discussion in Trompf, pp. 201ff.

56. See especially chapters 5–6; cf. Barton, pp. 225–28, and Neyrey, p. 130, p. 134 and pp. 151–56. See also Malina 1981, pp. 51–68 and pp. 122–51, along with 1986, pp. 112–65. Thus Gal 6,10 in connection with 1 Cor 7,29–31 hold the interpreter's key to e.g. Gal 5,13–26 and Rom 13; cf. Meeks 1983, pp. 85–103 and pp. 117–25; generally Schrage 1982, pp. 202–08, along with Furnish 1973, pp. 91–118. It is rightly emphasized by Schüssler Fiorenza 1983, pp. 224–26, that by personally favouring the ascetic ideal Paul goes directly against official marriage policy, thus in practice contesting the prevailing social order of the *paterfamilias* institution. On this basis it seems highly inconsistent to characterize his claim in 1 Cor 7,17–24 as mere social prudence and anti-revolutionary

precaution. Neither 7,17-24 nor 11,2-16 are explained satisfactorily as practical modifications of Gal 3,28; so e.g. Cartlidge along with Schottroff 1980, pp. 119f.; and no more can social inequality be made non-existent by the mere rhetoric of ideal equality, so generally Boucher, Feuillet, Hooker, Jaubert and Paul K. Jewett. Schüssler Fiorenza 1983, p. 219, owes to explain why Gal 3,28c is omitted in 1 Cor 12,13; cf. also Heister, pp. 169f., who compares Paul's insistence on the veil with the demand for circumcision in Galatia, seeing, however, one as the result of social consideration and the other as restraint.

57. Against the extremely widespread tendency to see in 11,11-12 a christological affirmation of gender and sexuality as a fully equal and mutual state of human interdependence, expressing Paul's fundamentally positive assessment of the Christian marriage either alongside or in contrast to 1 Cor 7,1-7, it must be stressed that neither Christ in v. 3 nor the reference to Christ as the Lord in v. 11 play any part in Paul's argumentation in 11,2-16. See Earle Ellis 1986, pp. 491-94, but also critical observations by Meyer 1856, p. 234, and Weiss, p. 275; to v. 3 as well as vv. 11-12 by Conzelmann 1969, p. 216 and p. 224, and Jervell, p. 297 and pp. 310-12. It seems decisive of an unprejudiced interpretation to maintain that 11,2-16 as a whole is based on arguments from creation theology, dependent on conservative, rabbinic Jewish tradition of interpretation and midrashic teaching. Thus, Christ in v. 3 is a secondary insertion, evidenced partly by the fact that God is added at the end of the verse at variance with the hierar-chical structure of the power paradigm and partly by the peculiarity thus effected, implying Christ in place of God as the head of every man in a clearly inclusive, i.e. non-christological or creation theological sense. In addition, vv. 11-12 represents an inserted parenthesis, neither contradicting nor revoking vv. 3-10, but supplying a concession in direct continuation of vv. 8-9, v. 12 like vv. 8-9 presupposing Gen 2,18-24, while vv. 3-7 is based on the implications on sexual differentiation according to Gen 1,27a-b. An adversative conjunction in the concessive sense opens v. 11; cf. Phil 1,18 along with Bauer 1963, pp. 1327f., and Blass/Debrunner/Rehkopf, § 449,1 and not § 449,2 as stated. This implies that vv. 11-12, instead of introducing the motif of the new creation in Christ, this being anticipated by the Christ reference in v. 3, simply admits sexuality a place in human life out of respect for the order of creation and the will of God. Thus, as a concession, vv. 11-12 holds exactly the same meaning as the admis-sions expressed in 7,1-7.38.39 and should be estimated on the same back-ground, namely Paul's insistence on the ascetic way of life as an eschatologically qualified life in Christ, cf. 7,29-35. See Delling 1931, pp. 62-66 and pp. 106ff. Thus, Paul cannot admonish in Christ in 11,2-16, because the married women in question do not live their lives in Christ in the qualified sense; a socio-sexual problem of order and authority is to Paul a problem of the old and not of the new creation. But compare Meyer 1856, p. 241, Weiss, p. 275, Lietzmann, p. 55, Barrett, p. 248 in spite of p. 255, Dautzenberg 1982, p. 199. and 1983, pp. 211f., Scroggs 1972, pp. 300-02, Parvey, p. 127, Heine, p. 108, and Schüssler Fiorenza

1983, p. 229; all considering vv. 11-12, almost unanimously, to be Paul's christological corrective by which he deliberately wants to safeguard against the negative consequences of vv. 3-10. But if so, why does Paul continue in vv. 13-15 exactly as in vv. 3-10 with the intention of keeping married women subordinated? And why, after all, does he resort to arguments from creation theology and midrashic interpretation if he himself is uneasy about the impact and means to say something radically different? Certainly his letters generally speaking give no apparent reason to doubt either his authority or his ability to admonish in Christ, if admonishing in Christ is what he wants and deems appropriate. See also note 60.

58. On hair and women's hair-do as an area of socio-sexual symbolism administered by patriarchal control within an androcentric system of cultural values, see Derrett, pp. 170-75. Cf. also Schottroff 1980, pp. 117f., and Barton, pp. 229-34, along with Strack/Billerbeck III, pp. 427-34. But compare Bultmann, pp. 193-211 and pp. 232-54, contested by Käsemann 1969, pp. 9-60, and somewhat corrected by Jewett 1971, pp. 95-166 and pp. 248-87, with no sign whatever of a critical reflection on gender or of sexual differentiation and discrimination having been taken into account. See Delling 1931, pp. 57-119, for a general warning against value neutrality in Paul's concepts of worldly and bodily existence and for a consistent assessment of the non-Christian values of sexuality and their negative implications for women. On gender-blind exegesis, cf. Heine, pp. 49-54.

59. On the relatively liberated conditions of Graeco-Roman women of the urban society, see Schottroff 1980, pp. 113-21, thus explaining the clash with Paul's conservative Jewish patriarchalism; cf. 1985, pp. 106f. Also Oepke 1966b and 1967, along with Delling 1931, pp. 2-56, and Heine, pp. 102-05; Heister, pp. 168-70, rightly emphasizes the women's emancipated behaviour as an evidence of their affiliation to the socially as well as pneumatically strong among the Corinthians. Cf. Theissen, pp. 272-89, and Thiselton, pp. 511f. Schmithals 1969, pp. 225-30, sees the women's emancipation as the result of Gnosticism, and is seconded by Kähler, pp. 49f., and Parvey, p. 125; see also for discussion Wendland, pp. 90f., and Meeks 1974, pp. 201f. However, Evans, p. 83 and p. 94, rightly stresses the probability that the Corinthian women are merely putting into practice what they believe to have learnt from Paul himself, thus implying Gal 3,28 as the prerequisite of 1 Cor 11,2-16; cf. note 6. But compare Parvey, p. 133. See further Schüssler Fiorenza 1983, pp. 227f., who finds in v. 2 the key to the understanding of Paul's admonition.

60. The text has been characterized as a *crux interpretum* by Caird, p. 17, and has in the course of time and discussion called forth a great number of rather emotional reactions, from an indulgent shake of the head to bitter scorn and frustrated sarcasm; see Heine. Most interpreters have chosen to see Paul in a dilemma, unable to connect his radical theory with his conservative practice; see e.g. Parvey, p. 123, and Heine, p. 109; cf. Lone Fatum 1976, pp. 118-29. Scroggs 1972, p. 297, goes as far as to assume the existence of a "hidden agenda," hid-

den, i.e., to Paul as well as to the Corinthians, but, of course, not to the enlightened interpreter. Thus emergency solutions abound and the reflection asserts itself whether the experiences of embarrassment, uneasiness, dilemma and contradiction, apparently caused by Paul's straightforward demand for married women's social subordination, do not in fact rest only with Paul's interpreters? For illustration, see Weiss, pp. 268-77, Conzelmann 1969, pp. 212-26, Barrett, pp. 246-58, along with Delling 1931, pp. 96-105, and Schrage 1982, pp. 215-17. Cf. also Walker and Trompf. The fact that the idea of Christian liberation is ambiguous and that Paul in 11,2-16 clearly is on the defensive should, of course, not be disputed; cf. Käsemann 1964 II, pp. 215-18, Characteristically Schüssler Fiorenza 1983, p. 219 and p. 227, cf. 1980, p. 69. Further Schmithals 1969, pp. 226f. Thus, generally speaking, the dialogue between Paul and his interpreters at this point has been hampered by a massive incongruity of interests. Symptomatic are the verdicts by Jewett 1979b, p. 67, that Paul's arguments in 11,2-16 are "curious" and "contradictory," and by Meeks 1974, p. 200, that "11,3-16 is not one of his most lucid patterns of logic," both testifying to the difficulty that will arise when it is in the interpreter's interest to ask for the final affirmation of sexuality and the equality of gender which Paul certainly is not prepared to supply. The result is an interpretation of Paul which looks precariously like manipulation, as when e.g. Jewett chooses to find in Paul an advocate of the liberation of sexuality, when in fact Paul on his own eschatological terms is advocating consistently a liberation from sexuality. See further pp. 36f.

61. Cf. Jervell, pp. 292-312, and Earle Ellis 1986, pp. 493f. In contrast to the Christ reference in v. 3, see the typically Pauline use of the christologically qualified imperative in passages like 1 Cor 15,12-34; Rom 5,12-6,14; Phil 2,1-13. The fact that the reference in v. 3 is not exploited as the eschatological motivation for growth and development in Christ according to the implications of faith and baptism corresponds with the fact that in 11,2-16 Paul is concerned exclusively with the life of the body in a socio-sexual sense and not, as in 1 Cor 5-6, with the congregational life of the body of Christ in an eschatological sense. Thus Paul's arguments in 11,2-16 are not concerned with purity and holiness but, on the contrary, with the moral decency and social order of this world. See the discussion in Käsemann 1964 II, pp. 198-222.

62. Paul is not speaking to but of the women concerned; see rightly Weiss, p. 269, against e.g. Evans, p. 83. The coherence of 11,1.2.17 is an indication that all through the chapter the patrons of the congregation are addressed and personally appealed to, because it is their responsibility to provide order and some social fairness during worship and sacramental fellowship taking place in their houses. The connection between the address to the "brothers" in v. 2, supported by a large number of textual witnesses, and the final appeal in 11,33 should not be overlooked. See also 7,27.32-33 as an evidence of the consistency with which Paul adheres to the male Christian as his addressee as well as his normative reference, even though, as in 11,3-10, he is concerning himself directly with the

conditions of women. The significant change in 7,28 from male address to female reference corresponds with the references in 7,8.36–38.39–40 and leaves 7,16 as the interesting exception; see for further discussion in note 101. The apologetic endeavours by Kähler, pp. 14–43, are quite unsatisfactory, taking neither social nor anthropological considerations into account; see also Banks, pp. 124f., and Schrage 1980, pp. 128–47. For an illustration of the fact that women are invisible also to Paul's interpreters, see e.g. Bultmann, pp. 193–203, and Jewett 1971, pp. 254–87. If the conditions of women are to be properly assessed within the Pauline context of normative values, not only must the qualitative difference between *sarx* and *soma* be upheld, but the special female affiliation to *sarx* must, indeed, be faced squarely as the implication to Paul of Gen 1,27b. See Weiss, p. 276, along with Sand, pp. 165–217, and Bauer 1971, pp. 67–130.

63. Cf. 3,16–17 and 6,19 along with 2 Cor 6,16. The temple metaphor coheres with the metaphors of body and building as the common basis of Paul's use of commitment motifs like growth, development and edification. Consequently, he presents himself with apostolic authority either as founder, cf. 3,10–15, or as father, cf. 4,14–21, but always as the special representative and personal intermediary of Christ, called and qualified to work as the dedicated agent of God's spirit, cf. 1,17; 2,1–21; 4,1.8–13; 15,8–10. The apostolic calling grants him the superior status of a personal example, cf. 4,17; 7,7; 9; 11,1; 14,18–19, along with the obligation to admonish authoritatively those Christians whom he considers to be the product of his missionary achievement and thus, literally, his territorial responsibility and "ground" for his efforts to attain the final praise in Christ, cf. 16,1–4.10–11.15–16 along with 3,10–15; 4,1–5; 9,13–23 and 2 Cor 3–4; 10–13. See generally Schlier 1972, pp. 147–59, together with the contributions by von Campenhausen, Greeven and Schürmann in Kertelge ed.; cf. also von Campenhausen 1965, pp. 13–39, in continuation of 1963, pp. 1–29. On the authority conflict in relation to the Corinthian pneumatics, cf. Barton, pp. 232–34 and pp. 239–42, along with Malina 1986, pp. 131–38. On the question of fronts and opponents, cf. Schmithals 1969, pp. 217–30, and Lüdemann 1983, pp. 105–25. That Paul by his metaphoric usage and by his personal interpretation of his apostolic role has laid the foundation of a hierarchic patriarchalization of Christian tradition is emphasized strongly by Schüssler Fiorenza 1983, p. 76; cf. Schottroff 1985.

64. See chapter 13 in connection with Gal 5,6.13–15; 6,2; cf. pp. 10–12. See generally Furnish 1968, pp. 208–41, and 1973, pp. 91–118 and pp. 205–18.

65. Cf. 12,4–27. It must not be overlooked that here as always Paul is concerned with unity and not with equality. It is rightly stressed by Neyrey, pp. 154–56, that Paul adheres to a basic idea of differentiation, hierarchically organized; see also Malina 1981, pp. 60–67. For a closer assessment of the implications of Paul's body metaphoric, however, it is necessary to consider the eschatological perspective of judgment, present in 1 Cor 5–6 in the motifs of purity and purification and in 10,1–13; 11,27–32 in the motifs of retribution and chastisement. Thus it

seems evident that Paul expects eschatological development and not social change, cf. the connection between 11,2–16 and 11,34 on the thematic basis of 12,14–26, especially v. 23. See further Delling 1931, pp. 120–29, along with the commentary on 6,12–20, pp. 62–66; cf. also Käsemann 1964 II, pp. 198–204.

66. Cf. Conzelmann 1969, p. 167, p. 207, pp. 273–79 and p. 288; see also Merk, pp. 122–31, and Thiselton, pp. 514–23.

67. It is important to maintain the observation that 11,5.10 does not contest the right of women to participate actively in official congregational worship; on the contrary, women's contribution in the form of prayer and prophecy is taken for granted, apparently both by Paul and by the Corinthians; cf. the use of Joel 3,1ff. in Acts 2,17ff. But the important question remains, almost totally neglected by interpreters, whether all Christian women enjoyed the same right and were given equal opportunity to exercise it? See further in note 77. The surface problem, obviously, concerns the way in which women should pray and prophesy, and it is dealt with by Paul as a principal question of women's role and social behaviour. A satisfactory assessment of Paul's admonition, however, must consist of an enquiry below the surface as to which women and why those, why some, i.e., if not all. According to 12,10.13 charismatic gifts are involved, bestowed upon the women in connection with their baptism and to be counted among the highest *charismata*, cf. 12,30–14,1; thus, the women's contribution during worship is practiced in concord with the superior purpose of love as well as with the concrete demand for unity and edification, cf. 14,3.5.12–19. This charismatic context is not respected by Schüssler Fiorenza 1983, pp. 227f., who seems hypnotized by 14,23 and assumes as a matter of course the women's display to have been one of *glossolalia*. But nothing in 11,2–16 is indicating that this is what Paul is worried about. Schüssler Fiorenza seems to be carried away by her picture of Sophia-worshippers in orgiastic ecstacy, hair unbound and wildly streaming. See, however, Derret, pp. 171ff. Against Trompf, pp. 198ff., and Delling 1931, pp. 102–05 together with the inconsistency of pp. 110–14.

68. See 11,2 in connection with 11,23–25 and 15,1–7. The observation that Paul finds reason for praise only in v. 2 in contrast to 11,17.22 and 15,12.35–36 does not contest the general impression of fundamental agreement about the common tradition. Thus, admonishing the Corinthians is to Paul a matter of practical guidance in ways, means and consequences of Christian faith; in continuation of note 50, cf. Thiselton, pp. 511–20. Rightly also Trompf, p. 210 in spite of pp. 210ff.; against Meeks 1974, pp. 201ff.

69. The insistence on the thematic coherence of chapters 8–14 is conclusive, showing 13 to play the same principal part within the structure of 11–14 as 9 within 8–10 and thus elucidating the correlation between the demand for consideration for the weak brother in 8 and 10 and for unity and edification in 12 and 14. Consistently, Paul is concerned with strength contra weakness socially as well as pneumatically, clearly identifying with strength in his choice of perspective both in 11,21–22.34 and in 12,14–24, in order to argue for renunciation and self-limi-

tation on the basis of hierarchic authority and apostolic example. Cf. von Soden in Rengstorf ed., pp. 338–69, along with Theissen, pp. 290–317, who, somewhat resigned, calls attention to the fact that a homogeneous group might have made a better fellowship of love; see also Theissen, pp. 231–71, pleading for love patriarchalism as a fitting characterization, but rightly contested by Schüssler Fiorenza 1983, pp. 76–80. See also Meeks 1983, pp. 51–73, pp. 117–31 and pp. 157–62. See further Schrage 1983, pp. 155–208, but compare Delling 1931, pp. 120–29.

70. See the excellent characterization by Hahn 1981, emphasizing, although unintentionally, the degree to which the *paraenesis* of 11,2–16 does not fit into the typical pattern, since in this one case Paul neither takes his point of departure in the commitment motif of baptismal recreation nor argues on the basis of the love relationship, thus exploiting the motif of eschatological fulfillment; cf. especially pp. 90ff. Compare Merk, pp. 131–35, not thematically integrated in the context of pp. 81–149; see further Wendland, pp. 85–89, not serving as a thematic introduction to pp. 90–94, because the anthropological presuppositions are as exclusively androcentric as those of Paul; see especially p. 89. Cf. Conzelmann 1969, pp. 215ff., in continuation of 1966, pp. 240f., along with Schrage 1983, pp. 213–20.

71. Paul's wish to avoid the radical either-or solutions in his opposition to the pneumatically self-confident and seemingly over-zealous Corinthians is evidenced by 5,11; 7,2–6; 8,4–13; 10,23–33; 11,34; 14,5.15.18–19.39–40; exceptions from the rule are then 5,1–8; 6; 10,14–22 all, characteristically enough, concerned not only with the congregation, internally, as the body of Christ, but also externally as a social minority group with pressing problems of identification in its relationship to surrounding society and former practice. Here, therefore, the body metaphor is exploited by Paul in a way clearly emphasizing the need of a restricted social code, applied as a system of symbolic values and practised as a measure of socio-sexual body control, at the same time delimiting the boundaries and confirming the qualitative difference which must exist between old and new, outside and inside. The uncompromising claim on the Galatian brothers to preserve their freedom in Christ belongs within this thematic context, cf. note 27. But since sexuality and sexual differentiation in a fundamental sense imply the socio-sexual problem of boundaries and qualitative difference, 11,2–16 also belongs within this context although from a social and not from an eschatological point of view; not because of a specifically christological assessment but, on the contrary, on the basis of creation theology and pre-christological criteria held by Paul to be universally valid as the strategy of control of moral order. See Delling 1931, pp. 62–66, Pagels, p. 544, and Neyrey, pp. 138–56. On the subject of restricted social code as the basis of classification system symbolically organized in a strong group, low grid, high classification combination, see Mary Douglas 1973, pp. 48ff. and pp. 80–110, along with 1976, pp. 7–40 and pp. 114–58. The immediate conclusion to the authority clash between Paul and the

Corinthian pneumatics, the women of 11,2-16 included, seems to be found in the clash between a high and a low classification system.

72. It must be considered that the principal *theologia crucis* motif of 1,18-25 is not adopted at all in 11,2-16, although it dominates throughout chapters 8-10 and 12-14 and is exploited effectively in 11,1 in continuation of 2,1-5; 4,1-17 as well as of chapter 9. Cf. Hasler, pp. 113-21, and Kittel 1967b, pp. 394ff. The implication is that 11,2-16 represents an exception within the christological and eschatological *paraenesis* of the letter, thus invalidating christological and eschatological interpretation of the veil demand by stressing instead the fact that to Paul the case of married women's subordination under the social control of their husbands is, indeed, a matter of social power and moral order and is not to be handled as a question of renunciation and love's foregoing out of consideration for a weaker party. The women concerned are seen as females, i.e. as beings created without power, superiority and strength and thus with nothing of their own to renounce. No doubt, their charismatic authority during worship tells more, according to Paul, about the freedom and unpredictability of God's spirit than about the actual social freedom of married women in the Pauline congregations. Against the apologetic endeavours of e.g. Hooker, Parvey, Kähler, Evans, Heine, Schottroff and Schüssler Fiorenza caution is necessary lest spiritual activity be confused with social independence and personal autonomy even in the case of a Prisca or a Junia. Compare Delling 1931, pp. 66-72 and pp. 105-16.

73. *Exousia* means power, authority, dominion; in v. 10 the noun is used by Paul in full compliance with ordinary usage as a designation of the active power of a ruling subject, and nothing in the text permits the deduction that Paul is here, exceptionally, implying a passive meaning or referring to the authority of the woman herself. On the contrary, it is a matter of someone's active authority claim upon the woman, and as an indication of something on or perhaps hanging from the woman's head *exousia* depends primarily on vv. 3 and 7, implying the sign of authority by which the married woman ought to demonstrate her married state in subordination under the rule of her husband as the object of his control. Cf. Foerster, pp. 570f., Strack/Billerbeck III, pp. 435f., Meyer 1856, pp. 238f., Lietzmann, p. 54, and Schottroff 1980, p. 116, along with 1985, p. 104, all in principle accepting v. 10 to be a matter of male authority and female subordination. However, Foerster, p. 571, finds comfort in Kittel's emergency solution of a translation error, while Strack/Billerbeck and Schottroff rightly suggest a case of metonymy; see also Fitzmyer, p. 50, along with the obviously secondary, but quite logical textual evidence for a replacement of *exousia* with *kalymma* in full agreement with the impact of symbolic meaning in this context of socio-sexual control, applied in practice as male control of female behaviour and role characteristics. V. 10 sums up the argument from creation theology in vv. 3-9, cf. the opening "therefore"; thus the demand on the woman to comply with custom concerning the coiffure of decent wives should be seen, according to Paul, both as the consequence of her subordinated position at the bottom of the hierarchy in

v. 3 and as the implication of her lack of *imago dei* quality due to her secondary creation in v. 7. Thus the social subordination for which Paul is arguing is closely connected with the theological concept of woman's inferiority; the two are correlative expressions, and together they constitute the defensive marriage strategy equivalent to the restricted social code of sexual morality, characteristic of rabbinic Jewish conservatism. The over-subtle discussion among interpreters whether the veil demand is owing to woman's deficiency, which needs to be hidden, or to her natural weakness, which needs to be covered and protected, seems rather superfluous, inasmuch as the decisive point of concern is to guard the status and rightful claim of the husband as the superior owner of his wife. Accordingly, it is as the property of her husband the wife is to be protected. And when this is maintained, it is evident that the reference to the angels does not introduce a new argument; let alone a theological contradiction. "Because of the angels" should be assessed on the basis of Gen 6,1-4 in line with the argument in vv. 3-9 to secure socio-sexual order, emphasizing the duty of the husband to guard his property in the effort to uphold the boundaries of creation. The reference to the angels is the mythological trump card by which Paul rounds off his argumentation trying to play his point through by the combination of a threat and a warning; cf. especially Hendel. V. 10, therefore, is directly concerned with the implications of male power expressed in symbols of male authority and applied by women in dress and behaviour in terms of male sexual ownership and social control. Thus *exousia* is used by Paul, here as elsewhere, in an androcentric perspective as the designation of superior male status and activity; the husband is seen as the socio-sexual proprietor, and the text does not admit of any positive assertion of female authority, let alone of a general proof of Christian women's godgiven dignity and personal integrity within the new order of creation. The solution of Hooker, pp. 415f., must be rejected as quite untenable, theologically as well as socially and anthropologically. Partly, it seems incompatible with the socio-sexual implications of vv. 3 and 7, thus not fully appreciating the importance and the thematic consistency of Paul's midrashic dependence; partly, it is in conflict with the reference to shame and dishonour in vv. 4-6, thus unable to assess this reference to the motifs constituting the social strategy of sexual control within the patriarchal code of restriction and subordination; finally, it seems to disregard the opening "therefore" in favour of "because of the angels," thus shifting the conclusive weight of the argument away from vv. 3-10a to v. 10b, isolating i.e. v. 10b from its thematic context in order to use it as the basis of independent eschatological speculations, which not only are at variance with the mythological reference in itself, but also with Paul's negative view of sexuality and gender differentiation as a whole. Summing up the many differing interpretations of 11,2-16, the reluctance to take v. 10 at its words is conspicuous; much energy and ingenuity have been invested to make the aspect of male superiority less blatant and, accordingly, the demand for women's subordination less offensive: if interpretation has not quite succeeded in proving in vv. 3 and 7 that discrimination and inequality read affirmation and equality, at least it is working hard to detect the good excuses and most well-meaning intentions behind v. 10. Illustrations are found in Weiss, p. 273, Wendland, p. 93, Lietzmann, p. 54, Conzelmann 1969, pp. 222f., Kähler, p. 63, Evans, pp. 90f., Parvey, p. 126, Heine, pp. 107f., Heister, pp. 170f. See further Jaubert and Feuillet 1973, and compare Padgett. The fact that Hooker's solution has been met with so much approval seems in itself to indicate the unwillingness among interpreters to deal with v. 10 without apologetic bias; cf. Barrett, pp. 253–55, Scroggs 1972, p. 301, Murphy-O'Connor 1980, p. 497, and even Schüssler Fiorenza 1983, p. 228. The attempts to see v. 10 as supportive of women and, especially, as an affirmation of Christian women's personal authority must, however, in any case be characterized as a result of wishful thinking, thus diverting or even deluding critical explanations, as seems evident from the many conjectures and unclarified assertions they have to rely on. Both Kähler, Evans and Schüssler Fiorenza e.g. are oddly evasive and equivocal in their determination of cause, implications and practical purpose of the *exousia*. More consistent is Meier, pp. 220–22, maintaining against Hooker the sexual aspect as well as the social control motif in v. 10, although he, too, prefers to speak positively about protection. Interesting in this connection is his observation on "faulty methodology," p. 226, but the objections raised towards eclectic exegesis, wanting to work on the basis of historical criticism and yet out of ideological or dogmatic interests prepared only to be a little bit critical, certainly apply to several other interpreters of 11,2–16 besides those responsible for the declaration against ordaining women in the Catholic church, *Inter Insigniores*.

74. Against the attempt at qualifying *exousia* as a positive concept of eschatological impact in order to find in v. 10 the reference to creation as well as to re-creation and thus securing for women a compensation in Christ for the lack of *imago dei* quality in the old order. In adherence of this attempt, the angels are seen as guardians either generally of the order of creation or more specifically of the order of worship and the cultic assembly, but in both cases as the representatives of the old, now challenged and provoked by the new in the form of liberated Christian women with charismatic authority of their own. See Caird, pp. 18ff., along with characteristic examples in Kähler, pp. 59–63, Hooker, pp. 414–16, Scroggs 1972, p. 300. Not quite clarified is Delling 1931, pp. 98–104. A remarkable interpretation is offered by Fitzmyer, pp. 55–57, emphasizing the parallel between an unveiled woman and a bodily defect and finding in both an adequate reason for holy angels to be cultically if not morally scandalized. The fact that Paul is able to regard angels as non-eschatological beings without a legitimate place within the order of the new creation is evidenced by 1 Cor 6,3; 2 Cor 11,14; 12,7; Gal. 3,19; but compare Rom 8,38; 1 Cor 4,9; 13,1; Gal 1,8; 4,14 for illustrations of the ambiguity of eschatological perspective. Conclusive of the interpretation of the angels of v. 10 is the contextual evidence that Paul is arguing from creation theology on a traditional midrashic basis; thus his usage of Gen 1,27;

2,18-24 corresponds closely with his usage of Gen 6,1-4, both depending on rabbinic Jewish usage of protohistory; cf. Hendel along with Earle Ellis 1986, pp. 492ff., and Meier, pp. 220f.

75. No doubt that at Paul's time in Graeco-Roman society, and in urban areas especially, women had attained a greater amount of social and individual freedom than had Jewish women from a conservatively restricted and socially secluded milieu. This, of course, is relevant at least as part of the explanation of the presence of women among Paul's coworkers as well as of the conflict behind 11,2-16. It does not follow, however, that 11,2-16 is merely the result of a clash between emancipated women among the Corinthians and Paul's Jewish Christian conservatism. Cf. Oepke 1966b, along with Parvey, pp. 118-23, Schottroff 1980, pp. 117f. See generally Leipoldt and Greeven along with Delling 1931, pp. 105-14; compare Brooten. Although many have emphasized the number of qualified women among Paul's close colleagues, few have been interested in a further examination of the role and lives of these women. Heine, pp. 102-05, Heister, pp. 168-70, and Schüssler Fiorenza 1983, pp. 218-26, rightly emphasize the probability of a social conflict among Christian women themselves since, obviously, it seems more likely for the unmarried, affluent woman to have participated actively in mission work and congregational support than for the married or the less affluent. But none of the three seems willing to draw the logical conclusion and ask further, whether this does not in fact imply that e.g. a Phoebe must have been both unmarried and affluent? And whether the significant designation of her role and vocation in Rom 16,1 does not presuppose precisely the ascetically qualified way of life prescribed by the implications of Gal 3,28c; 1 Cor 7,32-35 about the annulment of gender and the eschatological ideal of asexuality in Christ? See further note 101 in continuation of note 44. Cf. the use of Joel 3,1ff. in Acts 2,17ff.; cf. Acts 16,16f. along with the mention of the unmarried daughters in Acts 21,9. See Strack/Billerbeck III, pp. 435f., and not consistently clarified by Delling 1931, pp. 76-79 and pp. 84-86, with the inconsistency emphasized in 1966, p. 835.

76. Seeing married women in dependence of their husbands in 11,2-16 and not of Christ, Paul is merely maintaining his view from 7,32-35 in coherence with his point in 7,1-7, establishing marriage as a concession, secondary in charismatic value compared to the ideal asceticism. As a way of social order marriage is defensible in Christ, but this does not amount to the conclusion that marriage as a sexual relationship has its purpose let alone its justification in Christ; on the contrary: sexuality remaining to Paul both the temporary prerequisite and the temporary rationale of married life, marriage is exclusively a matter of sexual control and social order and thus a state in need of defensively intensified purity restrictions, if all that is carnal and of this world only is to be kept within its limits out of deference for that which is ideal and eschatologically qualified; cf. 1 Thess 4,3-8 along with 1 Cor 6,12-20; see Collins 1983 and Niederwimmer, pp. 64-74 and pp. 121-24. However, as marriage as a socio-sexual state is taken

for granted in 11,2-16, cf. the direct reference to marital sexuality in vv. 11-12, it is seriously misleading to interpret this text as Paul's attempt to ensure heterosexual practice among the Corinthians, either against ascetic androgyny or against homosexuality; against Jewett 1979b, pp. 67f., along with Barrett, pp. 256f., Evans, p. 93, Scroggs 1972, pp. 297f., and Murphy-O'Connor 1980, pp. 483-88. See also Schüssler Fiorenza 1983, p. 230. In 11,2-16 Paul is concerned with gender roles and socio-sexual status, applied by social symbols of gender characteristics; but he is not concerned with sexual practice. According to his basic androcentric understanding, of course, Paul regards the women in question as the object of control and not the men. By introducing the male example in v. 4 he is simply stating the androcentric norm, but he is not referring to actual male activity; thus, the attempts to exploit Rom 1,26-27 in this context as a menacing parallel to the threat, present at Corinth, seem considerably like overshooting the paraenetic mark of 11,2-16. Compare for discussion Padgett on vv. 4-7. But see also Delling 1931, pp. 57-95 in spite of p. 104; against e.g. Heine, pp. 110-16.

77. 11,2 seems to warrant the conclusion that the right of Christian women to participate actively in congregational worship was motivated directly through Paul's missionary preaching and personal mediation of Christ; cf. Schüssler Fiorenza 1980, pp. 76ff., and 1983, pp. 234-36, along with Kähler, pp. 43ff., rightly pointing out the importance here of Gal 3,27-28. According to 14,1-12 prophesying is the equivalent of teaching and according to 14,13-17 prayer is an activity comprised by the general demand for a conscious edification of the congregation as a whole. Thus, the charismatic activity of the women during worship is a central and not a marginal display of gifts, bearing the stamp of pneumatic qualification as well as authorized leadership, and therefore not to be confused with ecstatic *glossolalia*. Against Schüssler Fiorenza 1983, pp. 227f. In chapter 11 Paul is concerned with social order and not, as in chapter 14, with the charismatic discipline necessary if the congregation is to benefit collectively from the administration of gifts so variously bestowed. Within this context 14,33b-36 does represent a problem, but hardly one of incompatibility. For the discussion, see Fitzer, Walker and Murphy-O'Connor 1986. But compare Schüssler Fiorenza 1983, pp. 230-33, along with Barton, pp. 229-34. If it is maintained that in 14,33b-36 as well as in 11,2-16 Paul is concerned with patriarchal administration of married women, it may be inferred that his predicament in both cases is how to allow for the charismatic authority of the wives during worship without compromising the socio-sexual authority of the husbands, thus jeopardizing male superiority in general and the patriarchal order of the household institution in particular. In both texts, accordingly, Paul is intent on keeping a very delicate balance of authority by drawing a line of distinction based on criteria which in principle are mutually exclusive, namely, on the one hand, deferring to that which during worship is eschatologically qualified and thus not only defensible in Christ, but in fact exemplary and, on the other hand, that which is maritally valid and binding, thus from

a socio-sexual point of view still indispensable. Now supposing Gal 3,28c to be the cause of the role and authority conflict in both texts, thus implying that unmarried Phoebe was allowed to act and dress in a way that married Prisca was not, and, further, taking into account the accentuation of the socio-sexual problem due to the clash between official/sacred and private/profane during congregational worship, it seems clear that the issue Paul is dealing with is the fundamental problem of how to integrate married women into the Christian fellowship, when in fact only unmarried women are fully qualified to take their part and play their roles among the brothers. Thus, taken together, the two texts not only testify to sexual discrimination in the relationship between men and women, nor simply to a class conflict among women themselves, but more complicated still to charismatic discrimination, administered on the socio-sexual basis of the patriarchal household and thus implying the moral duty of the husband to control uncompromisingly both the socio-sexual behaviour and the charismatic activity of his wife when his own authority is at stake. The suggestion is that 14,33b–36 is neither concerned with prayer and prophecy nor merely with idle talk and interruptions, but deals specifically with married women's participation in the official duty of testing the spirits, according to 12,10; this involves charismatic authority as well as the right to question and discuss. But if only unmarried Phoebe may have had the privilege to appear unveiled, it follows that she only may have enjoyed the right to partake in the testing of the spirits, since the participation of a married woman implies the possibility of an open breach of patriarchal household authority: she might sit in judgment on men, including, of course, her own husband. Preferring to see all of 14,26–36 concerned primarily with *glossolalia*, Schüssler Fiorenza comes close to obscuring the complexity of the patriarchal control strategy applied here, unwilling, apparently, to face squarely the role and authority conflict in all the discriminating implications of the socio-sexual dichotomizing of Christian women's lives. See observations by Delling 1931, p. 97, p. 103 and p. 113, on the qualitative difference between gender role restriction and sexual renunciation; inconsistently, however, he is unable to acknowledge the prerequisite of charismatic authority behind married women's right to pray and prophesy and so almost discards the problem dealt with in 14,33b–36; cf. pp. 110–19 on the background of pp. 57–69; see also note 67. But compare further Parvey, pp. 133ff., and Schottroff 1980, p. 117, in continuation of Meyer 1856, p. 237. Cf. note 101.

78. Although Paul's demand for a veil undoubtedly is dependent on conservative Jewish custom, there is no grounds for the assumption that his demand in 11,2–16 is totally new and unfamiliar to Graeco-Roman women of the urban congregation at Corinth; cf. 11,2.13.16, presupposing a unity, based on Christian tradition as well as on social custom of gender role behaviour, thus enabling Paul in the same breath, so to speak, to appeal to natural judgment in vv. 13–15 and to normative congregational practice in v. 16. That Paul does not altogether trust the persuasive effect of his creation theological arguments in relation to non-Jew-

ish urban Christians is, however, also evidenced by vv. 13-15 and v. 16. Thus, in continuation of note 60, it should be noted that Paul's embarrassment does not relate to the demand itself that married women must be subordinated and must demonstrate their married state by symbols of inferiority and social dependence; on the contrary, it is only a matter of uncertainty whether or not his *paraenesis* on midrashic tradition will carry weight and achieve its practical purpose. Against von Campenhausen 1965, pp. 23f., in continuation of Schmithals 1969, p. 226; cf. Parvey, p. 125; against Conzelmann 1969, p. 225, but in agreement with Weiss, pp. 276f., emphasizing the brachylogy in v. 16 and the ind. realis of the conditional clause. However, Weiss, p. 277, is too subtle in his attempt to explain a clash between Jewish and Hellenistic Christians behind the normative double reference in "we" as opposed to "the congregations of God"; once again he resorts to the emergency solution of the gloss. With Lietzmann, p. 55, an explanation could be to find in "we" a reference to the congregation at Ephesus, from where Paul is writing, in order to localize specifically the pointed reference to Paul himself and those similarly disposed, cf. Meyer 1856, p. 243, leaving "the congregations of God" to refer comprehensively to all Christians, irrespective of whether or not the congregations in question were founded by Paul himself; cf. 1,2 along with 15,11; see Barrett, p. 258. In any case, the most important observation is that Paul in his argumentative uncertainty chooses to resort to the concept of comprehensive Christian normativity to help support his own local authority; cf. Wendland, p. 93, against Kähler, p. 66, and Evans, p. 93. Rightly Schüssler Fiorenza 1983, p. 226. Cf. also Derrett, p. 173, in continuation of Oepke 1966b and 1967, while the discrepancy between Jewish and non-Jewish seems exaggerated by Jewett 1979b, p. 67, and Schottroff 1980, p. 117; see also Heister, p. 170; quite untenable is Heine, pp. 106f., seeing "we" referring to Jews as opposed to Christians. Generally against the apologetic solution by Hurley.

79. On the social aspects of gender role characteristics and sexual symbolism, see Malina 1981, pp. 42-47 and pp. 102-16, in continuation of note 73 on *exousia*. See also Meeks 1974, p. 201.

80. See p. 16 on Gen 1,27b in connection with 2,18-24; 3,16; cf. Bird; this deserves to be thrown in relief by 1 Thess 4,4 in spite of the motif of mutualness in 1 Cor 7,2-6 as well as in 11,11-12; the trend may be followed to 1 Tim 2,8-15 over 2 Cor 11,3. Cf. Mary Douglas 1976, pp. 140-58. But it belongs within this context that Oepke 1966b, p. 785, is able still to refer to the female sex as the woman's curse. Cf. Delling 1931, pp. 96-119, and Pagels, pp. 543f. While 1 Cor 7,21-24; Philem 16 implies a positive reference to the slave role, cf. Gal 2,19-20; 2 Cor 4,10-11; 5,14-17; Rom 14,7-9, the case is very different where the role of woman is concerned; defined by her sex, her natural sphere of life is *sarx* and not without self-denial in a comprehensive sense may she attain a position, qualified by *soma;* see Delling 1931, pp. 93f. But see also Heister, pp. 170f., in continuation of Delling 1931, pp. 57-66, rightly emphasizing the coherence between 1 Cor 6,16; 7,1-7.32-35 and 11,2-16; 14,33b-36; against e.g. Collins 1983 and Maurer.

81. On hair as an area loaded with symbolic values and socio-sexual meaning, see especially Derrett, pp. 170–73. Meeks 1974, pp. 202f., is oddly unclarified. It should not be overlooked, of course, that Paul nowhere speaks directly of a veil, but only of having something on or hanging from the head, v. 4, as opposed to being uncovered, v. 5, epitomized in v. 6: a woman must be covered. The reason why it is shameful to a woman to be uncovered appears from the harsh comparison in v. 6, presupposing the utter scandalization of a cropped or shorn female. Opposite, another concord is presupposed in v. 15 between long hair and a head covering, both defined to be in keeping with the natural order of creation. Thus Paul is concerned here with the coiffure of decent wives, but not demanding a full veiling, and the purpose of his *paraenesis* is not that a woman's head should be hidden nor her face covered, since her long hair may serve as an example in the sense of a shawl or a cloak. On the meaning of *anti* in v. 15, see Moule, p. 71, along with Meyer 1956, p. 242, Weiss, p. 276, and Barrett, p. 257; against Heine, pp. 108f., whose outstripping sarcasm prevents a defensible exegesis; see also Caird, pp. 18–22. On the elaborate coiffure with the use of *himation*, cf. Strack/ Billerbeck III, pp. 428f., and Schottroff 1980, p. 117. on the meaning of *kata* in v. 4, see Moule, p. 60, along with Blass/Debrunner/Rehkopf § 225. That Paul is not concerned with a separate headgear is rightly underlined by Barrett, pp. 249f., using veil as a convenient paraphrase; this usage has been adopted here. See also Scroggs 1972, pp. 298f., but especially Murphy-O'Connor 1980, pp. 484ff., taking off from v. 4 and using homophobia as his lever, he finds the text to be primarily concerned with male homosexuals; cf. note 76. To speculate in Paul's disapproval or personal loathing of lesbians, taking off from vv. 5–6, is, however, equally misleading. As a specific label, lesbianism may easily be rejected, of course, as a cultural and historical anachronism in the Pauline context. If it must be used at all, it requires as its presupposition the concept of an autonomous sexual activity among women, defined and administered by the women themselves to meet their own needs for affirmation, identification and satisfaction, indifferent to the pressure from patriarchal institutions and independent, too, of the androcentric stereotypes of female normality and gender role socialization. But the assertion of such a concept of female autonomy seems more than doubtful in the anthropological and theological universe of Paul and his congregations. In 1 Cor 7,2-6 he does ascribe the female party her own needs and rightful demands, but the fact that the purpose and perspective of sexual activity are left with the male is evident e.g. in 11,8-9.11-12. The implication is that to Paul as well as to any other androcentric man a woman's role is either to be passive, receptive or reactive, her socio-sexual status being either that of virgin and daughter, wife and mother or prostitute and socially disqualified. Within this context sexual autonomy among women is non-existent, because women's autonomy in general is non-existent. Thus, what may be called lesbianism, in misleading deference to later feminist policy, should perhaps rightly be called voyeurism in an effort to emphasize the androcentric interest in the socio-sexual administration of labels, evident in Paul as well as among his interpreters.

An indiscriminate use of the label, lesbianism, may in fact serve to obscure the extent to which women's socio-sexual relevance, whether they come in ones, in twos or in crowds, are estimated through male eyes and defined according to male standard. Cf. the very consistent interpretation by Derrett, pp. 184-89, against Delling 1931, pp. 86-91, and 1966, p. 835, along with Kümmel. The suggestion is that Paul not even in Rom 1,26-27 is concerned with lesbians, as to him and his contemporaries it is a label void of meaning and the potential of association. Thus, also in Rom 1,26-27 the androcentric perspective predominates, and it is Paul's purpose to exemplify illegitimate male behaviour, i.e. non-marital sexuality in the form of an alliance with prostitutes, v. 26, cf. 1 Cor 6,12-20, and of male homosexuality, v. 27, cf. 1 Cor 6,9. Note also the androcentric perspective e.g. in Lev 18,19-23; 20,10-21. The socio-sexual order to be upheld is tied up inseparably with male ownership and the rights and property of reproduction within patriarchal organization; in comparison, an alliance between women is simply irrelevant, because socially as well as sexually it is immaterial and the women therefore, literally, invisible: their alliance implying neither a parallel nor a replacement, they represent neither a threat nor a challenge to the male order of androcentric assessment; thus, within the Pauline context, an alliance between women cannot come into focus as an independent activity of autonomous value and socio-sexual implications, and neither men nor women, sharing Paul's presuppositions, have been able to relate to a label like lesbianism. Cf. Fadermann, pp. 147-313. On this background the conclusion is that in vv. 5-6.10 Paul is neither concerned with lesbianism, nor with unwomanly slovenliness; but against Schüssler Fiorenza 1983, pp. 227f., it must be maintained that floating ecstacy and orgiastic frenzy are not his problem either. The situation at Corinth, to Paul, is far more fundamentally upsetting. For if wives are allowed to disregard the rights and control of their husbands, male supremacy is at stake and the patriarchal hierarchy of creational order is compromised. The parallel of motifs between 11,5-6.10 and 12,22-25 is remarkable in this connection, and Paul's hierarchic pattern of socio-sexual values must be emphasized also in 11,7; against e.g. Hooker and Feuillet 1974. The married woman, defined by her gender role, lacks an *imago dei* quality of her own in the old as well as in the new order of creation; thus she must be covered to be honourable, to which her long hair is nature's testimony; if she is uncovered, she is shamed, implying, literally, that she is unveiled in her lack of honour; cf. the illustrating examples in Strack/Billerbeck, in spite of Conzelmann 1969, p. 218, the decisive point being that a married woman thus unveiled is a dishonour first of all to her husband. See the ambiguity in v. 5 along with the ambiguous use of *doxa* in v. 7 and v. 15; a woman's hair, then, is not just her special adornment, primarily it is sign and proof of her virtue, cf. Meyer 1856, p. 236, and Derrett, pp. 171f., against the inconsistency in Delling 1931, p. 104, Wendland, p. 83, and Murphy-O'Connor 1980, pp. 488f., not at all attentive to the social implications of v. 15. Cf. Strack/Billerbeck III, pp. 442f.

82. That Paul is concerned with the symbolism of gender roles and not at all with sexual activity, is underlined by vv. 5-6; on the conspicuous use of *to auto* in the neuter and the sociative dative in the feminine in v. 5b, cf. Blass/Debrunner/ Rehkopf, § 131 and § 194, along with Meyer 1856, p. 236, and Weiss, pp. 271f. On the social implications of the gender symbolism, see Strack/Billerbeck III, pp. 427-35. It is Paul's obvious presupposition that a shorn or cropped woman's head is equal to a dishonoured and shameless female, socially the worse to her husband, since losing at once her virtue and her adornment she is in effect violating his social status. That Paul is not formulating a request, but drawing up a caricature of a warning image, should be self-evident. Yet, the usefulness of anthropological insights to critical exegesis may well be emphasized in an effort, hopefully, to obtain still wider acceptance of the principal assertion that body control is the means of social control. However, to realize fully the discriminating implications of Paul's control strategy in 11,2-16 and elsewhere, perhaps it needs to be emphasized also that the socio-sexual code system, applied by Paul, is a system of sexual restrictions and social sanctions, based on male values of affirmation and administered to safeguard male purposes of identification. The implications are then that patriarchal organisation as well as androcentric normality are upheld according to the standard of male dominance and male group identity, which means that sociosexual behaviour is a question of appearance, measured, controlled and perhaps condemned according to social status and institutionalized role characteristics. On this background it is understandable why Paul means to uphold the order of creation by controlling the coiffure of married women at Corinth. But on this background it is generally worth noting how in the cultural history of sexism, discriminating restrictions and heavy social sanctions have always been exercised on women as regards their appearance in dress and posture, movement and behaviour, while their private practice and personal projects have been deemed officially unimportant. See Fadermann, pp. 21-61 and pp. 233-340. In continuation of note 81, the observation suggests itself that Deut 22,5 is concerned with the violation of male role characteristics, thus warning against the infringement on the privileged territory of male identity and socio-sexual supremacy in an effort to uphold, like Paul in 1 Cor 11,4-6, the androcentric system of gender roles and symbolic values. Cf. the illustrating example of Thecla: her adoption of short hair and a man's attire is the consequence of her break with the marital order of patriarchal society; and yet, the characterization of Thecla shows no interest whatever in the role and gender characteristics themselves, let alone the sexual activity of Thecla; cf. *Acta Pauli et Theclae*, chapters 5-6, 11-12, 15-17, 25 and 40 in Heinz Kraft ed., pp. 235-72. Summing up, the system of gender roles and symbolic role characteristics is fundamentally a system of social organization, and thus in practice a social concern, not a matter of sexuality or a sexual concern. In 11,4-6.10 Paul testifies to this, concerning himself neither with sexuality at Corinth nor with the married women themselves, but, much more comprehensively, with the patriarchal

order of androcentric identification and male supremacy. Only homophobia will confuse the issue and disregard the complexity of the gender role system. The logic of the Pauline control strategy should not be underestimated, but nor, of course, should the discriminating consequences in women's lives. The Christian life of Thecla is characterized as a life, qualified eschatologically by asceticism and self-denial; personifying the implication of Gal 3,28c, she is not merely transgressing gender role boundaries but, in practice, exemplifying the eschatological transcendence of sexual differentiation, which means that she is free in Christ to act and work like a man as well as to look, dress and behave like a man. And by exactly the same token, the married women in 11,2-16, not living their lives immediately in Christ but defined and restricted still by their female role, must by all means be prevented from transgressing the role boundaries and taking possession of the social advantages, which are tied exclusively to the male role. Thus, the logical way of demonstrating the eschatological freedom of Thecla is to ascribe to her the social characteristics of male supremacy, while the logical way for Paul to safeguard male supremacy in 11,2-16 is to insist on the social subordination and the lack of eschatological freedom of married women. However, the important point is that in both cases the logic of the argument depends on Gal 3,28c.

83. Against Evans, pp. 83-93, effecting her idea of equality so consistently that in v. 3 she sees no hierarchy, but only analogous parallels. Also against the tendencies to obscure the implications of the power structure in Boucher, Feuillet 1974 and Scroggs 1972. See further the apologetic endeavours in Barrett, p. 248, Hooker, p. 410, and Heine, p. 107; more cautious Schüssler Fiorenza 1983, p. 227, but see especially p. 229, in continuation of 1979, p. 48.

84. Cf. the social reservation in 7,28.34 as the prerequisite for the noneschatological *paraenesis* of 11,2-16; see also the *status quo* motif of 7,12-24, and note especially v. 21 as an accentuation of Paul's social *status quo* demand. Against Schüssler Fiorenza 1983, p. 221; but see for discussion Stuhlmacher, pp. 42-49. When it is maintained, against e.g. Evans, p. 85, that Paul in 11,2-16 is arguing for the subordination of married women, it seems evident that in their socio-sexual situation there simply is no basis for an eschatological appeal in accordance with 7,29-31; cf. Derrett, pp. 184-92, in continuation of Delling 1931, pp. 57-84.

85. Cf. 7,1.7 along with 11,1 as the background for the paraenetic address in 11,2-16 to Christian husbands concerning their wives; see Weiss, p. 269, against Evans, p. 83. Because Schüssler Fiorenza 1983, pp. 218-30, has chosen to consider chapter 7 as well as 11,2-16 as mere "modifications" of Gal 3,28c, she is unable to distinguish clearly between that which is eschatologically qualified and that, on the other hand, which belongs to this world, is limited by *sarx* and must be socio-sexually restricted. In her interpretation the principal difference between asceticism and marriage is considerably weakened. Cf. p. 223. It must be stressed, however, that from a social point of view neither married women nor

slaves have any power to renounce, and therefore Paul's eschatological appeal cannot be addressed to them directly, nor can they apply the motif of love in their social practice in any immediate way; cf. 7,10-11.20-21 along with Philem 13-16 as a contrast to the paraenetic appeal in chapters 9 and 13; cf. also notes 62 and 69.

86. Cf. the apologetic usage of Gal 3,28 as the canonical blueprint of liberation theology in general and of feminist theology in particular; see rightly Neyrey, p. 154. See further note 5. But cf. on misogyny as a fully integrated part of Paul's cultural background, predisposing him for the unrelenting maintenance of patriarchal order, in Earle Ellis 1986, pp. 491-94, Meeks 1974, pp. 176-80, Niederwimmer, pp. 64-74, Scroggs 1972, pp. 289-91, and Parvey, pp. 118-23. Cf. also Delling 1931, pp. 105-19, against the conclusion by Walker and Trompf. See for comparison the contributions by Bird, Prusak, Ruether, Hauptmann and McLaughlin in Ruether 1974 ed., along with Børresen, pp. 15-35, pp. 147-78 and pp. 315-41. An unbiased and unsentimental assessment of the sexist purpose of 1 Thess 4,4; 1 Cor 11,2-16; 14,33b-36; 2 Cor 11,3 on the one hand and Col 3,18-4,1; Eph. 5,22-6,9; 1 Tim 2,8-15 on the other renders untenable the detection of a certain qualitative difference between Paul and non-Paul, regarding the prevailing demand for patriarchal control; instead, it serves to demonstrate the consistency with which this demand is formulated throughout as a claim, based on the concept of male supremacy and exercised, of course, with direct reference to those women whose social conditions are defined by sexuality and whose moral destination, accordingly, is restricted to the role of wife and mother. For a different estimation, see Schüssler Fiorenza 1983, pp. 247-79, and Heister, pp 170f. Meeks 1974, pp. 197-206, rightly underlines the importance of the gender role symbolic in 11,2-16; seemingly preconditioned, however, by his idea of a conflict between Paul and androgyny, his interpretation cannot realize the full impact of the *paraenesis* nor meet the complexity of the power motif in the Pauline demand for patriarchal control. See also Schrage 1980, pp. 150-73, and Parvey, pp. 126ff.

87. The fact that Gen 1,27a-b contains the aspect of a sexual hierarchy in full agreement with Gen 2,18-24 is rightly emphasized by Earle Ellis 1986, p. 493; against Meier, p. 219. See also Meyer 1856, pp. 237f., and Weiss, pp. 269f., against e.g. Barrett, p. 252f., and Scroggs 1972, pp. 300f., who wrongly traces Gen 2,18-24 already in 11,7 instead of in 11,8-9, thus unable to realize the point of Paul's exploitation of Gen 2,18-24 in 11,8-9 as a clarification of 11,7 and, behind it, of Gen 1,27a-b. Cf. pp. 15-16. The uncertainty in Wendland, p. 92, seems symptomatic; cf. Evans, pp. 89f., who insists on speaking positively of difference in the form of complementarity. Seeing 11,7 as a reference to the equality of the human couple, and finding this affirmed christologically by 11,11-12, is the main aim of Kähler, pp. 56ff. It must be said to be a serious weakness in the interpretation of *eikon* and the Pauline use of Gen 1,27 that no attempt is made by e.g. Jervell and Larsson, cf. note 34, to distinguish between 27a and 27b. First, of course, it

serves to obscure the specific point of the sexual differentiation; but, second, it has cleared the road for the marriage rhetoric of equality and complementarity, unrestrained, apparently, by the evidence from texts as well as from experience; cf. characteristically Kähler and Evans.

88. Cf. Meyer 1856, pp. 237f., Weiss pp. 272f., and Lietzmann, pp. 53f., against Conzelmann 1969, p. 219, Kähler, pp. 58f., and Heine, pp. 107f. In spite of her own apologetic interest even Evans, p. 90, finds Feuillet 1974 to have gone too far. See further Jervell, pp. 292–312, especially pp. 299f.

89. Although Christ is mentioned in v. 3 it should be maintained that he is not introduced as a part of the argument, and he has no role to play in v. 7, which only serves to emphasize Paul's dependence here on rabbinic Jewish creation theology; cf. Jervell, p. 297, and Hooker, p. 411. For a dependence on Hellenistic Jewish school tradition, see Conzelmann 1966, p. 240, and 1969, pp. 215f. Against Meyer 1856, p. 235. But see Weiss, pp. 273f., and Barrett, pp. 252f. Again, uncertainty prevails in Wendland, pp. 90–92; see also Scroggs 1972, p. 299, and Murphy-O'Connor 1980, pp. 494ff. It is worth noting that Paul in 11,7 refers to man as *aner* and not as *anthropos;* but far from demonstrating generic inclusiveness this usage, on the contrary, attests to the androcentric exclusiveness already present in Gen 1,27a and fully established within the traditional context of Jewish interpretation. Thus *aner* merely states explicitly the concept of male supremacy, what Gen 1,27a already implies, showing the extent to which Paul adheres to his Jewish presuppositions. Cf. 2 Cor 11,2-3, and see Oepke 1966a, p. 364; see further Jeremias. On this background, the contrast between *ouk opheilei,* v. 7, and *opheilei,* v. 10, should be given its full due, and it should be noted how the use of *gar* in vv. 7.8.9 both demonstrates the coherence of the argument, beginning with the *hoti*-clause in v. 3, and leads on to the final purpose in v. 10, accentuated by the opening *dia touto.* Against the attempts to break this coherence by Kähler, pp. 48–53, and Evans, pp. 84–90, also against the conclusion *e silentio* by Hooker, p. 441, and Schüssler Fiorenza 1983, p. 229. Compare Oepke 1966a, p. 364, and 1967, p. 564; see further Jewett 1979b, p. 68. The Adam–Christ typology in Rom 5,12-19 and 1 Cor 15,20-28 serves together with Rom 8,29; 1 Cor 15,49; 2 Cor 3,18; 4,4; Col 1,15 to demonstrate by comparison that Paul's concern in 11,7 is not, indeed, christological, but prechristological or creation theological. In continuation of note 34, see generally Jervell and Larsson for illustrating examples of an interpretation that, first, obscures the androcentric perspective of *eikon,* tied up with the inherently hierarchic structure of Gen 1,27a-b, and, second, perhaps as a result, is unable to recognize the qualitative difference between Paul's concept of eschatological growth in Christ, on the one hand, and the socio-sexual conservatism of his prechristological use of midrashic Genesis tradition, on the other. Obviously, it is significant to observe that Col 3,10-11 has left out a parallel to Gal 3,28c; but it ought to be given equal recognition that Eph 5,22-33 actually holds a parallel to 11,7 in the sense that both attest to the concept of male supremacy, inherent in Gen

1,27a–b, without applying the Christ motif in its eschatological perspective of Gal 3,28c, both argue for the subordination of married women on the basis of socio-sexual conservatism, and, finally, both underline their argument by a reference to woman's inferiority or imperfection; thus the reference to defects and blemishes in Eph 5,27 serves to clarify the implications of Paul's point in 11,7 as well as to emphasize, of course, the discriminating concord between a Pauline and a non-Pauline *paraenesis* of women's subordination. Interesting in this context is Heister, p. 169.

90. When the hierarchic structure of power and authority in v. 3 is fully recognized, "head" as the designation of man's qualified position as the superior of woman holds, all tied up in one symbolic pattern, both the socio-sexual and the theological criteria necessary to permit the argument in vv. 4–6.10 to shift with such ease from the literal to the metaphorical sense of *kephale*. To point out a logical flaw in this pattern is of no avail and may just obscure the coherence of Paul's purpose. That he is arguing for hierarchic order on the solid basis of creation theology should, of course, be conclusive for the understanding of "head" in all its implications, whether they overlap, as in v. 5, or they may be held apart, as in v. 4 and v. 6. Thus, while man may dishonour his "head" in a twofold sense, i.e. a literal as well as a metaphorical, a woman may only dishonour her superior, and in that sense her husband is her true "head," literal and metaphorical in one, because dishonour occurs within the hierarchy, literally and metaphorically, upwards from below. Cf. Meyer 1856, pp. 234ff., Lietzmann, pp. 53f., Wendland, pp. 90ff., and Conzelmann 1969, pp. 215ff. Cf. also Weiss, pp. 269ff., although he decides to give up on v. 3. Against Barrett, p. 251, Kähler, p. 55, and Evans, p. 89; see also Caird, pp. 19ff., Schmithals 1969, p. 226, and Heine, p. 107; against the christological interpretation in Jervell, pp. 301f., and Schlier 1967. Apparently, Schüssler Fiorenza 1983, pp. 228f., does not want to formulate any definite attitude to the power motif of the gender role symbolic, but seems content with a reference to ambiguity in continuation of Hooker, pp. 410ff., and Feuillet 1973; cf. Feuillet 1974, pp. 165ff. It may well be stressed that source, cause or origin is a more appropriate translation of *kephale* in the metaphorical sense, and that the collectivity implied by "head," according to ordinary use, seems peculiar in this context. However, this gives no ground for explaining away the consistency in Paul's argument for male supremacy and patriarchal control in the form of androcentric authority all through vv. 3–10 against Scroggs 1972, pp. 298f., and Murphy-O'Connor 1980, pp. 491ff. More cautious is Barrett, pp. 248f.; cf. also Heister, pp. 167f. For an anthropological assessment of "head" as a socio-sexual designation of male superiority, see Malina 1981, pp. 60–64, along with Neyrey, pp. 151–56. A significant illustration of Paul's point in vv. 3–10 is found in 1 Cor 12,14–25: just as a married woman must be covered, so must the *genitalia* of the body, literally as well as metaphorically; and in both cases in an effort to prevent dishonour from spreading upwards from below. Thus a close comparison between 11,3–10 and 12,23; Eph. 5,27 serves to underline the socio-sexual

impact of dishonour as a gender role concept of hierarchic control, to be applied individually as well as collectively according to the alliances of the dyadic structure. So, rightly Fitzmyer, p. 56, although his conclusion as regards v. 10 is untenable; see notes 73 and 91.

91. It is obvious from vv. 2.4–5.13.16 that Paul is dealing directly with the congregational situation during worship, cf. e.g. Kähler, p. 53. This is a poor excuse, however, for disregarding the principal attempt of Paul to legitimate male supremacy in order to uphold the patriarchal organization of his congregations. His demand for married women's subordination is based on arguments from creation theology and the order of nature, cf. vv. 3.7–9 and vv. 6.13–15, in a way that attests to the absolute universality of his control strategy, not permitting a belittling into something relative, merely a local detail of worship practice. Accordingly, the reference to the angels should be interpreted in consistency with the comprehensive principle of patriarchal order in general and not limited to worship order in particular; cf. note 73. When Gen 6,1–4 is maintained as the mythological prerequisite of v. 10 the conclusion suggests itself that the angels are demonic challengers who, like the powers of chaos or non-ordered nature, represent the non-controlled aggressiveness of sexuality in the form of violence, conquest and male competition. Just as the reference to the dishonoured female in v. 5 is meant as a warning caricature, so the reference to the unrestricted sexual aggression in v. 10 is used by Paul as a threat, emphasizing the essential point of his argument: that the duty of the husband to uphold patriarchal order as regards his own wife is principally the duty of man to uphold the sociosexual organization of established society, maintaining and defending the cosmos of God against the powers of chaos; the implication is, of course, that patriarchal organization and a defensive marriage strategy, based on male alliances, are part and parcel of God's creational intention according to Gen 1,27b–28; 2,18–24. Cf. Hendel, pp. 22–26, along with Mary Douglas 1973, pp. 78–108 and pp. 132–77, and 1976, pp. 94–158. See also Malina 1981, pp. 25–47 and pp. 75–90. Thus the angels of v. 10 are the threats of sexual aggression enlarged; in the context they serve to impress on the husband the role of superior as well as the rights of proprietor. The reference to the angels, then, helps to clarify how consistently Paul is dealing here with man's duty to stand out for his right and protect his property in a way that is plainly contradicting his general demand in 1 Cor for renunciation and compromise, attesting to the presupposition that matters of gender and sexuality are in themselves a contradiction of Christ, belonging to this world of pre-christological order and, therefore, not to be regulated immediately by eschatologically qualified *paraenesis*. See Meeks 1983, pp. 94–103, for comparison and contrast. Cf. further Weiss, p. 274, Lietzmann, pp. 54f., Meier, p. 221, Schottroff 1980, p. 116, Heine, p. 108, and Heister, pp. 170f.; against Strack/Billerbeck III, pp. 437–40, Caird, p. 18, Fitzmyer, pp. 52–57, Hooker, pp. 412ff., Barrett, pp. 252ff., Kähler, p. 61, Evans, p. 91, Scroggs 1972, p. 300, Schüssler Fiorenza 1983, p. 228, Neyrey, p. 153; see also the discussion in

120

Trompf, pp. 205–09. The very widespread preference for seeing the angels as good and friendly or, indeed, protective powers is closely linked to the equally widespread attempt to gain a foothold in v. 10 for the affirmation of Christian women, based on christological and eschatological interpretation. See Jervell, pp. 306ff., along with Kittel 1966, p. 85, who appears to be puzzled, and Conzelmann 1969, p. 223, more or less giving up on Paul's behalf. The objection that normally in Paul a specific reference to angels implies a positive reference carries little weight; see in continuation of note 74 the possible connection between Rom 8,22–27; 1 Cor 13,1; 14,2 and 2 Cor 12,4. However, when it is recognized how consistently Paul is arguing in 11,3–10 on the basis of midrashic interpretation of Genesis protohistory, it should easily be accepted that the angels are introduced in v. 10 as a matter of course, due to the tradition of the material; so, precisely because Paul depends so heavily on arguments from traditional creation theology and mythology he can allow himself to take for granted the Genesis motif of the angels, representing socio-sexual disorder and thus, by their threatening example, emphasizing effectively the need for patriarchal control.

92. On the meaning of *anti* in v. 15, cf. note 81. That Paul is not implying that long hair is a sufficient replacement to be worn instead of a veil is obvious from the context in general as well as from v. 10 in particular, and it is underlined by the acknowledgment that this is a matter of coiffure, hair being an important area of socio-sexual symbolism, and not at all of veiling in form of head-dressing in order merely to conceal. Against the discussion by Lietzmann, pp. 53f., and Conzelmann 1969, pp. 222f.; but also against the presentation of the problem by Foerster, pp. 570f.; see further Oepke 1967, along with Strack/Billerbeck III, pp. 442f.

93. Cf. Kittel 1967a, p. 240, against the attempts to establish a parallel between *eikon* and *doxa;* see further Kittel 1967b, pp. 393–95, on *eikon* as the expression of the archetype, original and therefore exclusive in a qualitative sense. See further, in continuation of note 89, the christological use of *eikon* in Rom 8,29; 1 Cor 15,49; 2 Cor 4,4; Col 1.15 in contrast to the usage, based on the line of arguments from creation theology, in 11,7. For an illustration of the intricate relationship between original, on the one hand, and image as reproduction and as reflection, on the other, see 1 Cor 13,12 and 2 Cor 3,18; both emphasize the principal contrast between glory reveiled and glory covered or hidden, and only glory reveiled, obviously, corresponds with the concept of eschatological re-creation in Christ, thus excluding a christological interpretation of v. 10, if the coherence of vv. 3–10 is to be maintained. Hooker, p. 415, reaches her peculiar conclusion as regards the eschatological affirmation of Christian women's god-given authority by disregarding the principal difference between *eikon* and *doxa* and by introducing into v. 10 the perspective of the new creation. Cf. further Meyer 1856, pp. 237f., Jervell, p. 300, Weiss, pp. 272f., Lietzmann, pp. 53f., and Heine, p. 107; against Barrett, p. 252, Wendland, p. 92, Evans, p. 90, Kähler, pp. 57ff., Schmithals 1969, p. 226, and Scroggs 1972, pp. 299ff. Rightly, the meaning

of the contrast in v. 7 is stressed as a consequence of the hierarchic order of v. 3 by Heister, pp. 167f.; see also Conzelmann 1969, pp. 219ff.; but against Feuillet 1974 and Schüssler Fiorenza 1983, p. 229.

94. Cf. Meyer 1856, p. 234, Weiss, p. 269, and Heister, pp. 167ff.; against the various attempts to interpret christologically, by Barrett, pp. 248f., Conzelmann 1969, pp. 215f., Kähler, pp. 48-53, Evans, pp. 84ff., Hooker, pp. 410f., Murphy-O'Connor 1980, p. 491ff., and Schlier 1967. Cf. also Jervell, p. 297 against p. 305. Decisive for a contextually valid interpretation of v. 3 is the recognition that the mention of Christ adds nothing to the relationship between God and man, directly stated in v. 7; so, the implication is that in v. 3 there is no christological point introduced by the mention of Christ as the head of man, and this is attested by the non-christological use of *eikon* in v. 7. See also note 89.

95. While Paul in Gal 3,28c speaks about the annulment of gender and sexuality on a qualified basis of eschatological re-creation, he, on the co..t.ary, in 11,7-10 is insisting on the social and moral consequences for those Christians who live their lives in this world, restricted by gender roles and sexual commitment; the socio-sexual impact of Paul's use of *aner* in v. 7 instead of *anthropos* is underlined by the shift of reference from Gen 1,27a contra b in v. 7 to 2,18-24 in vv. 8-9; cf. note 87. The reproduction of Adam as the purpose of sexual differentiation is attested to by the use of *dia* in v. 9, legitimating the creation of the female, thus, once again, emphasizing the coherence of Paul's argument from creation theology and midrashic tradition; see on *dia* in Blass/Debrunner/Rehkopf § 222.

96. Taken literally at its own words the text gives no ground for regarding vv. 11-12 as Paul's conscious retreat in an effort to correct himself and his use of rabbinic Jewish tradition in vv. 3-10; see on the opening "yet" in v. 11 as a concessive conjunction and, accordingly, on the whole parenthesis of vv. 11-12 as a concession in note 57. Cf. also Trompf, p. 197. While Paul in vv. 3-10 concerns himself implicitly with the sociosexual order of marriage by dealing explicitly with the hierarchic structure of creation and the power relation inherent in sexual differentiation, applied in practice through the gender role symbolics, he interposes in vv. 11-12 an explicit comment on the mutual interdependency of reproduction, thus concerning himself explicitly with the organization as well as the purpose of marriage. Therefore, v. 11 is not a contradiction, let alone a retrievement, but, on the contrary, an accentuation, especially of vv. 8-9, to be recognized against the consensus of interpreters on this point. And still on the basis of vv. 8-9, v. 12 is the accentuation made concrete. Against the attempt by Kurzinger to revise the interpretation of *choris* in v. 11 in order to legitimate the Christian ideal of human equality and mutual solidarity, instead of merely adhering to the concrete matter of sexual interdependence. However, Kurzinger is followed by Murphy-O'Connor 1980, p. 497, and Schüssler Fiorenza 1983, pp. 229f.; but see Neyrey, p. 154, for an important modification. On the meaning of *choris*, see Bauer 1963, columns 1760f.; cf. also Meyer 1856, p. 234 against p. 241; see Jewett 1979b,

p. 68, and Earle Ellis 1986, p. 494; against Hooker, p. 414, Kähler, pp. 53ff., Evans, pp. 85ff., and Scroggs 1972, pp. 300ff. Oddly ambiguous is Jervell, p. 302 and pp. 310-12; cf. also Parvey, p. 127, along with the unconcluding deliberations by Weiss, pp. 270f. and pp. 275ff. The widespread view that in vv. 11-12 Paul is purposely trying to safeguard against misunderstanding or even misuse of vv. 3-10 remains highly unconvincing, since, obviously, the argument in vv. 3-10 is continued and emphasized in vv. 13-16; but see e.g. Lietzmann, p. 55, and Heine, p. 108, in continuation of notes 57 and 76; cf. Trompf on the coherence of the argument, against Walker 1975. The suggestion is that the parenthesis of vv. 11-12 is introduced by Paul in dependence of chapter 7, in order to establish marriage and the purpose of reproduction as the legitimation of sexuality among Christians; cf. Delling 1931, pp. 57-72; against Jervell, p. 302. Therefore, "in the Lord" in v. 11 implies neither contradiction nor correction as regards vv. 3-10, but concession and restriction in the form of Christian specification. So, "in the Lord" in v. 11 does not imply a reference to the new creation in Christ, let alone an eschatological qualification of sexuality; on the contrary, it allows for the concession that sexuality may be practiced even among Christians in the form of marriage, though sexuality itself belongs to the old order of creation. Thus, although sexual practice is not in accordance with the eschatological ideal of a life in Christ, marriage, as a compromise with this world, is defensible "in the Lord." In vv. 3-10 the universal order of socio-sexual organization has been established, and in vv. 11-12 this is accentuated with specific address to Christian couples in order to emphasize the restricted commitment which binds the two partners together; cf. the negative wording of v. 11. So, in spite of the direct warning by Murphy-O'Connor 1980, p. 499, it should be acknowledged that the inference of vv. 11-12 concerns the marriage relationship, defensible in Christ, in full agreement with the concessions of 7,7.10-11.17.36-38.39-40; the mutual dependency of sexual activity, concretized in v. 12, is anticipated by 7,2-6. But it is worth noting that in v. 12 Paul resorts explicitly to his argument from creation theology by emphasizing God himself as the ultimate legitimation of reproduction and maintaining, i.e., reproduction as the sole purpose of gender and sexual differentiation in accordance with his interpretation of Gen 1,27b-28, cf. the use of Gen 2,18-24 in vv. 8-9. This underlines the point that the mention of Christ, the Lord, in v. 11 implies concession in the form of specification and restriction but is no more an integrated part of the argument of vv. 11-12 than is the reference to Christ in v. 3. The mention of Christ carries no christological impact within this context and there is, accordingly, no basis on which to establish an eschatological coherence between vv. 11-12 and Gal 3,28c; cf. Weiss, pp. 275f., and see further note 57. Against the typical endeavours to find in vv. 11-12 a trace of Gal 3,28c in e.g. Boucher, Feuillet, Jaubert, Heine, Scroggs 1972 and Schüssler Fiorenza 1979, 1980 and 1983; see corresponding attempts, although in a different version in Dautzenberg and Parvey. It should not be overlooked that Paul's negative view on sexuality includes gender as well as marriage, both being in principal discord with the ideal of eschatological qualification and total commitment in Christ; cf. on the contrast between *sarx* and *pneuma* Gal. 4,21-31 in connection with 4,4 on the parallel roles of woman and law as the essence of the curse; see 3,10-14; and compare this with Phil 2,7-8 on self-denial and death in connection with v. 6 and vv. 9-11. In fact, it seems that Paul comes very close to Schmithals' idea of the Gnosticism at Corinth, cf. 1969, pp. 206ff.; see discussion by Thiselton and Hasler, along with Barton and Neyrey. So, rightly Delling 1931, pp. 62-66, emphasizing the negative coherence between 1 Cor 6,12-20 and 7,5.32f. as the negative presupposition of 11,2-16.

97. Cf. the contrast between *ouk opheilei* of man in v. 7 and *opheilei* of woman in v. 10; see note 89. The inconsistency, symptomatic of the apologetic solutions, is manifest in Hooker, pp. 413-16; she is unable to commit herself directly on the implication of *ophelei* in v. 10, the naked demand for duty and obligation being, of course, incompatible with her interpretation of *exousia* as the specific guarantee of Christian women's god-given authority as well as with her conclusion that the old reflection on a women's head of the *eikon* quality of man is to be hidden in order to allow Christian women's new glory to shine in its own right. A characteristic move has taken place here away from duty and obligation to the idea of women's right and autonomous authority, compromising the contrast between the terms of v. 7 and v. 10 but, also, disregarding v. 3 as the prerequisite of both v. 7 and v. 10 and, finally, overlooking the connection of *dia touto* and *opheilei* in v. 10 dependent, again, on both v. 3 and v. 7. Cf. note 73, and compare Meyer 1856, p. 237, Jervell, p. 304, and Barrett, p. 252. See further Malina 1981, pp. 44-47, and 1986, pp. 154-65, along with Barton, pp. 229-34, and Neyrey, pp. 155f. The attempt to distinguish between compulsion and obligation appears in Foerster, p. 570, to be a splitting of hair since, in any case, it is a matter of women's subordination by means of the patriarchal strategy of socio-sexual control. The reference to the possible exceptions of 1 Cor 5,10; 7,36 is interesting, but it serves rather to underline the point that Paul does not take his stand in v. 7 and v. 10 on the basis of his apostolic authority, cf. v. 16, but is in fact arguing on the terms of v. 3 and the Jewish concept of God's hierarchic order of original creation; thus vv. 3.7.10 as well as vv. 14-15.16 only serve to emphasize the difference of Paul's argumentation in 11,2-16 compared to the rest of 1 Cor; see note 70.

98. All things considered, the thematic coherence between 11,2-16; 14,33b-36 and Col 3,18; Eph 5,22-33; 1 Tim 2,8-15 is too striking to be made light of or still to be explained away; cf. notes 77 and 86. In all cases the matter is a demand for patriarchal control, legitimating the fundamental concept of male superiority, exercised on married women since they lead their lives in this world on the conditions of sexuality and must be made responsible for the gender role order. But then the ironic conclusion suggests itself that the debate on women's ordination and full access to priesthood or ministry has, in fact, been conducted on a wrong

basis even by the most faithful adherers to the evidence of Scripture. The real problem is not women in general but only married women in particular. Thus the question to be debated on a Pauline basis is whether married women are to be excluded from ordination on the grounds of Gal 3,28c and 1 Cor 7,34a? The assertion is that the discriminating women's *paraenesis*, consistently directed against married women, only draws the logical and practical conclusion of 7,34b, implying the socially realistic corrective to Gal 3,28c which, in any case, seems officially invalidated by 1 Tim 5,11-15; cf. note 104. Against e.g. Stendahl, pp. 28-43, whose positive endeavours are characteristic of feminist apologetics, turning a blind eye on the socio-sexual implications of the androcentric values organized and administered through the symbolic structure of gender roles, and thus unable or unwilling to see the extent to which sexism is functioning as an integrated strategy of organization and control also among the early Christians. See also for discussion the contributions in Ruether et al. eds. 1979 and A. and L. Swidler eds. 1977.

99. Cf. 1 Cor 1,17; 2,1-5; 3,1-11; 4,14-16.21.

100. Cf. my use of the concept: intention and consequence, in Lone Fatum 1976; see also Karin Friis Plum, p. 30.

101. It seems a reasonable assumption that Phoebe, the *diakonos*, was leading an eschatologically qualified life of asceticism, cf. Rom 16,1-2. In continuation of note 77 it may not be inferred, however, that e.g. Prisca and Junia, cf. 16,3.7, must also have been qualified ascetically to have been among Paul's co-workers; see Earle Ellis 1971. On the contrary, to married women like a Prisca and a Junia 1 Cor 7,20 remains valid on the basis of 7,1-6.10-11, although juxtaposed with 7,7. And this implies that even a Prisca would have been restricted in her charismatic activity and would in fact have been subjected to the socio-sexual control measures of 11,2-16; 14,33b-36; cf. note 98. A Phoebe, on the other hand, together with e.g. Euodia and Syntyche in Phil 4,1 would have been exempted from these measures, provided that they had become asexual and non-female and thus, according to the eschatological assessment of Paul, directly in and dependent on Christ. The Greek is not to become a Jew and a slave is not to seek his social freedom; in Christ the slave will be free and the Greek will be as good as a Jew and by the same token the asexual and non-female woman may count as a male, *anthropos* being the eschatological concept of human quality, but *aner* the social interpretation. Cf. the illustrating example of Thecla, note 82. Only once in 1 Cor 7 are the women in question addressed by Paul directly, although representatively in the singular, namely in 7,16. While in other parts of the chapter as well as e.g. in 11,2-16 Paul consistently addresses the Christian men who are the social administrators of their women, be they wives or daughters, apparently Christian women in mixed marriages represent a special case and can be admonished personally. Thus it is tempting to conclude from 7,15-16 in relation to 11,2-16 that a non-Christian husband is not regarded by Paul as a proper and competent head of a Christian woman, and therefore divorce is to be welcomed if

he so wishes; but therefore, also, it is not only possible but indeed necessary for Paul to admonish directly in the same way he admonishes his co-workers e.g. in Phil 4,1. 1 Cor 14,36 is not admonition in this way but, rather, a sarcastic sneer of intimidation and non-approval, thus making another exception. Cf. for discussion the argument of Witherington, pp. 598-602, and compare e.g. Betz, p. 200, along with Stuhlmacher, p. 67.

102. Against the general tendencies of apologetic interpretation by Jewett, Walker, Meeks, Scroggs, Schüssler Fiorenza and so very many others.

103. Against any attempt to explain away the value of 1 Cor 7,1 as an expression of Paul's own attitude towards asceticism in accordance with 7,7. Cf. Niederwimmer, pp. 74-124, against e.g. Jewett 1979b, p. 71, and Scroggs 1972, pp. 294-97, in spite of Snyder, Phipps and Whitton. See also Schrage 1976, pp. 228-34; but for further discussion, cf. generally Delling 1931 against Baltensweiler and Niebergall.

104. Cf. Jouette Bassler, pp. 33-36; see also Castelli. It is thought-provoking that the ascetic trend was made suspicious very early; cf. the discriminating characterization in 1 Tim 5,13. The ascetic was marginalized and later became analogous to the sectarian and dangerously heretical, but actually the trend is broken already by 1 Tim 5,14 to the obvious advantage of the other trend, allowing, of course, direct instead of indirect patriarchal control of female sexuality; cf. 1 Tim 2,15. See further Crouch, pp. 75-151, for an assessment of the conservative Hellenistic Jewish origin of Christianized socio-sexual morality, in general agreement with Niederwimmer, pp. 67-74, pp. 121-24 and pp. 162ff.

105. Cf. Meyer 1985. See also Bassler, pp. 36-41, where the development illustrated by 1 Tim 5,11-15 is assessed as a question of eschatological attitude as well as social and economic conditions. The fact that the ideal of virginity is maintained, however, as the quintessence of purity, based on the annulment of female sexuality, cf. Luke 1,26-38; 11,27-28, emphasizes the connection between 1 Cor 6,19; 2 Cor 11,2 on the one hand and Eph 5,26-27 on the other, and it serves to make 1 Tim 2,15 stand out in relief. See quite unsatisfactory commentaries by Delling 1966, p. 835, and Stählin, pp. 441ff. Cf. notes 77, 86, 98.

Works Consulted

Baltensweiler, Heinrich (1967): *Die Ehe im Neuen Testament: Exegetische Untersuchungen über Ehe, Ehelosigkeit und Ehescheidung.* Zürich: Zwingli 1967.

Banks, Robert (1980): *Paul's Idea of Community. The Early House Churches in their Historical Setting.* Exeter: Paternoster 1980.

Barrett, C. K. (1986): *A Commentary on the First Epistle to the Corinthians.* London: Black 1968, 1971.

Barton, Stephen C. (1986): "Paul's Sense of Place: an Anthropological Approach to Community Formation in Corinth." in: *NTS* 32,1986; pp. 225-46.

Bassler, Jouette M. (1984): "The Widow's Tale: A Fresh Look at 1 Tim 5,3–16." in: *JBL* 103, 1984; pp. 23–41.

Bauer, Karl-Adolf (1971): *Leiblichkeit, das Ende aller Werke Gottes*. Gütersloh: Gerd Mohn 1971.

Bauer, Walter (1963): *Griechisch-Deutsches Wörterbuch zu den Schriften des Neuen Testaments und der übrigen urchristlichen Literatur*. Berlin: Töpelmann 1958.

Becker, Jürgen (1976): *Der Brief an die Galater*. Göttingen: Vandenhoeck & Ruprecht 1976.

Betz, Hans Dieter (1984): *A Commentary on Paul's Letter to the Churches in Galatia*. Philadelphia, PA: Fortress 1979.

Bird, Phyllis A. (1981): "Male and Female He Created Them: Gen 1,27b in the Context of the Priestly Account of Creation." in: *HTR* 74,1981; pp. 129–59.

Blass, Friedrich/Albert Debrunner (1979): *Grammatik des neutestamentlichen Griechisch*. Bearbeitet von Fr. Rehkopf. Göttingen: Vandenhoeck & Ruprecht 1976.

Boucher, Madeleine (1969): "Some Unexplored Parallels to 1 Cor 11,11–12 and Gal 3,28: The NT on the Role of Women." in: *CBQ* 31, 1969; pp. 50–58.

Bouttier, Michel (1976): "Complexio Oppositorum: sur les Formules de 1 Cor 12,13; Gal 3,26–28; Col 3,10–11." in: *NTS* 23, 1976; pp. 1–19.

Brooten, Bernadette J. (1985): "Frühchristliche Frauen und ihr kultureller Kontext. Überlegungen zur Methode historischer Rekonstruktion." in: *Einwürfe* 2, ed. F.-W. Marquardt et al. München: Kaiser 1985; pp. 62–93.

Bultmann, Rudolf (1961): *Theologie des Neuen Testaments*. Tübingen: Mohr (Siebeck) 1958.

Bünker, Michael (1983): *Briefformular und rhetorische Disposition in 1. Korintherbrief*. Göttingen: Vandenhoeck & Ruprecht 1983.

Børresen, Kari Elisabeth (1981): *Subordination and Equivalence. The Nature and Role of Woman in Augustine and Thomas Aquinas*. Washington D.C.: University Press of America 1981 (1968).

Caird, G. B. (1967): *Principalities and Powers: a Study in Pauline Theology*. Oxford: Clarendon 1956.

von Campenhausen, Hans (1963): *Aus der Frühzeit des Christentums*. Tübingen: Mohr (Siebeck) 1963.

——. (1965): *Die Begründung kirchlicher Entscheidungen beim Apostel Paulus*. Heidelberg: Universitätsverlag 1957.

Cartlidge, David (1975): "1 Corinthians 7 as a Foundation for a Christian Sex Ethics." in: *JR* 55, 1975; pp. 220–34.

Castelli, Elizabeth (1986): "Virginity and Its Meaning for Women's Sexuality in Early Christianity." in: *JFSR* 2, 1986; pp. 61–88.

Christ, Carol P. and Judith Plaskow eds. (1979): *Womanspirit Rising. A Feminist Reader in Religion*. New York: Harper & Row 1979.

Collins, Adela Yarbro, ed. (1985): *Feminist Perspectives on Biblical Scholarship*. Chico, CA: Scholars 1985.

Collins, R. F. (1983): "The Unity of Paul's Paraenesis." in: *NTS* 29, 1983; pp. 420-29.

Conzelmann, Hans (1966): "Paulus und die Weisheit." in: *NTS* 12, 1966; pp. 231-44.

——. (1969): *Der erste Brief an die Korinther.* Göttingen: Vandenhoeck & Ruprecht 1969.

Crouch, James E. (1972): *The Origin and Intention of the Colossian Haustafel.* Göttingen: Vandenhoeck & Ruprecht 1972.

Dahl, Nils A. (1967): "Paul and the Church at Corinth according to 1 Corinthians 1-4." in: *Christian History and Interpretation, FS John Knox,* ed. W. R. Farmer et al. Cambridge University Press 1967; pp. 225-48.

Dautzenberg, Gerhard (1982): "Da ist nicht männlich und weiblich. Zur Interpretation von Gal 3,28." in: *Kairos* 24,1982; pp. 181-206.

Dautzenberg, Gerhard et al. eds. (1983): *Die Frau im Urchristentum.* Quaestiones Disputatae 95. Freiburg: Herder 1983.

Delling, Gerhard (1931): *Paulus' Stellung zu Frau und Ehe.* Stuttgart: Kohlhammer 1931.

——. (1966): "*Parthenos* im Neuen Testament." in: *Th. Wb.* V, 1954; pp. 832-35.

Derrett, J. Duncan M. (1977): *Studies in the New Testament, I.* Leiden: Brill 1977.

Donaldson, T. L. (1986): "The 'Curse of the Law' and the Inclusion of the Gentiles: Gal 3,13-14." in: *NTS* 32, 1986; pp. 94-112.

Douglas, Mary (1973): *Natural Symbols.* New York: Vintage Books 1973.

——. (1976): *Purity and Danger.* London: Routledge & Kegan Paul 1966.

Ellis, E. Earle (1971): "Paul and His Co-Workers." in: *NTS* 17, 1971; pp. 437-52.

——. (1986): "Traditions in 1 Corinthians." in: *NTS* 32, 1986; pp. 481-502.

Evans, Mary (1983): *Woman in the Bible.* Exeter: Paternoster 1983.

Fadermann, Lillian (1985): *Surpassing the Love of Men.* London: The Women's Press 1981.

Fatum, Lone (1971): "Det paulinske imperativ." in: *DTT* 34, 1971; pp. 20-39.

——. (1976): "Paulus og den socialpolitiske konsekvens." in: *DTT* 39, 1976; pp. 106-33.

Feuillet, A. (1973): "La signe de puissance sur la tête de la femme (1 Cor 11,10)." in: *Nouv. Rev. Théol.* 55, 1973; pp. 945-54.

(1974): "'L'homme gloire de Dieu' et la femme 'gloire de l'homme' (1 Cor 11,7 b)." in: *RB* 81, 1974; pp. 161-82.

Fiorenza, Elisabeth Schüssler (1978): "Women in the Pre-Pauline and Pauline Churches." in: *USQR* 33, 1978; pp. 153-66.

——. (1979): "The Study of Women in Early Christianity. Some Methodological Considerations." in: *Critical History and Biblical Faith. New Testament Perspectives,* ed. T. J. Ryan. Villanova, PA: College Theology Society 1979: pp. 30-58.

——. (1980): "Der Beitrag der Frau zur urchristlichen Bewegung." in: *Traditionen der Befreiung 2,* ed. W. Schottroff et al. München: Kaiser 1980; pp. 60-90.

——. (1981): "Toward a Feminist Biblical Hermeneutics: Biblical Interpretation and Liberation Theology." in: *The Challenge of Liberation Theology,* ed. Brian Mahan et al. Maryknoll, NY: Orbis 1981; pp. 91-112.

——. (1983): *In Memory of Her. A Feminist Theological Reconstruction of Christian Origins*. London: SCM 1983.

——. (1984): *Bread Not Stone. The Challenge of Feminist Biblical Interpretation*. Boston, MA: Beacon 1984.

——. (1987): "Rhetorical Situation and Historical Reconstruction in 1 Corinthians." in: *NTS* 33, 1987; pp. 386-403.

Fitzer, Gottfried (1963): *Das Weib schweige in der Gemeinde. Über den unpaulinischen Charakter der mulier-taceat-Verse in 1 Korinther 14*. München: Kaiser 1963.

Fitzmyer, Joseph A. (1958): "A Feature of Qumran Angelology and the Angels of 1 Cor XI,10." in: *NTS* 4,1958; pp. 48-58.

Foerster, Werner (1967): "Exousia." in: *Th. Wb.* II, 1935; pp. 559-72.

Furnish, Victor Paul (1968): *Theology and Ethics in Paul*. Nashville, TN: Abingdon 1968.

——. (1973): *The Love Command in the New Testament*. London: SCM 1973 (1972).

——. (1979): *The Moral Teaching of Paul. Selected Issues*. Nashville, TN: Abingdon 1979.

Gager, John G. (1975): *Kingdom and Community. The Social World of Early Christianity*. Englewood Cliffs, NJ: Prentice-Hall 1975.

Greeven, Heinrich (1958): "Frau. Im Urchristentum." in: *RGG* II, 1958; pp. 1069-70.

Hahn, Ferdinand (1976): "Das Gesetzesverständnis im Romer- und Galaterbrief." in: *ZNW* 67, 1976; pp. 29-63.

——. (1981): "Die christologische Begründung urchristlicher Paränese." in: *ZNW* 2, 1981; pp. 88-99.

Halkes, Catharina J. M. (1980): *Gott hat nicht nur starke Söhne. Grundzüge einer feministischen Theologie*. Gütersloh: GTB Siebenstern 1980.

Hasler, Victor (1984): "Das Evangelium des Paulus in Korinth. Erwägungen zur Hermeneutik." in: *NTS* 30, 1984; pp. 109-29.

Heine, Susanne (1986): *Frauen der frühen Christenheit*. Göttingen: Vandenhoeck & Ruprecht 1986.

Heister, Maria-Sybilla (1986): *Frauen in der biblischen Glaubensgeschichte*. Göttingen: Vandenhoeck & Ruprecht 1984.

Hendel, Ronald D. (1987): "Of Demigods and the Deluge: Toward an Interpretation of Genesis 6,1-4." in: *JBL* 106, 1987; pp. 13-26.

Holm, Ulla Carin (1982): *Hennes verk skall prisa henne. Studier av personlighet och attityder hos kvinnliga präster i Svenska kyrkan*. Vänersborg: Plus Ultra 1982.

Holmberg, Bengt (1978): *Paul and Power. The Structure of Authority in the Primitive Church as Reflected in the Pauline Epistles*. Lund: Gleerup 1978.

Hooker, Morna D. (1964): "Authority on Her Head: An Examination of 1 Cor 11,10." in: *NTS* 10,1964; pp. 410-16.

Hurd, John J. (1965): *The Origin of 1 Corinthians*. London: SPCK 1965.

Hurley, J. B. (1972): "Did Paul Require Veils or the Silence of Women?" in: *Westminster Theol. Journ.* 35, 1972-73; pp. 190-220.

Hyldahl, Niels (1986): *Die Paulinische Chronologie.* Leiden: Brill 1986.

Jaubert, Annie (1972): "Le Voile des Femmes (1 Cor 11,2–16)." in: *NTS* 18, 1972; pp. 419–30.

Jeremias, Joachim (1966): "Anthropos" in: *Th. Wb.* I, 1933; pp. 365–67.

Jervell, Jacob (1960): *Imago Dei. Gen 1,26f. im Spätjudentum, in der Gnosis und in den paulinischen Briefen.* Göttingen: FRLANT 76, NF 58, 1960.

Jewett, Paul K. (1975): *Man as Male and Female.* Grand Rapids, MI: Eerdmans 1975.

Jewett, Robert (1971): *Paul's Anthropological Terms: A Study of Their Use in Conflict Settings.* Leiden: Brill 1971.

——. (1979a): *A Chronology of Paul's Life.* Philadelphia, PA: Fortress 1979.

——. (1979b): "The Sexual Liberation of the Apostle Paul." in: *JAAR Supplement* 47, 1, 1979; pp. 55–87.

Kähler, Else (1960): *Die Frau in den paulinischen Briefen.* Frankfurt, Zürich: Gotthelf Verlag 1960.

Käsemann, Ernst (1964): *Exegetische Versuche und Besinnungen I–II.* Göttingen: Vandenhoeck & Ruprecht 1964.

——. (1969): *Paulinische Perspektiven.* Tübingen: Mohr (Siebeck) 1969.

——. (1972): *Der Ruf der Freiheit.* Tübingen: Mohr (Siebeck) 1972 (5. Auflage).

Kee, Howard C. (1980): *Christian Origins in Sociological Perspective.* London: SCM 1980.

Kertelge, Karl ed. (1977): *Das kirchliche Amt im Neuen Testament.* Wege der Forschung CDXXXIX. Darmstadt: Wissenschaftliche Buchgesellschaft 1977.

Kertelge, Karl (1984): "Gesetz und Freiheit im Galaterbrief." in: *NTS* 30, 1984; pp. 382–94.

Kittel, Gerhard (1966): "*Aggelos* im Neuen Testament." in: *Th. Wb.* I, 1933; pp. 81–86.

——. (1967a): "Der neutestamentliche Gebrauch von *doxa*." in: *Th. Wb.* II, 1935; pp. 240–56.

——. (1967b): "*Eikon.*" in: *Th. Wb.* II, 1935; pp. 391–96.

Kraft, Heinz ed. (1959): *Acta Apostolorum Apocrypha, I.* Darmstadt: Wissenschaftliche Buchgesellschaft 1959.

Kümmel, W. G (1965): "Verlobung und Heiratung bei Paulus." in: *Heilsgeschehen und Geschichte I.* Marburg: Elwert 1965 (1954); pp. 310–27.

Kurzinger, J. (1978): "Frau und Mann nach 1 Kor 11,11–12." in: *BZ* 22, 1978; pp. 270–75.

Lampe, G. W. H. (1967): "Church Discipline and the Interpretation of the Epistles to the Corinthians." in: *Christian History and Interpretation, FS John Knox,* ed. W. R. Farmer et al. Cambridge University Press 1967; pp. 337–61.

Larsson, Edwin (1962): *Christus als Vorbild. Eine Untersuchung zu den paulinischen Tauf- und Eikontexten.* Uppsala: ASNU 23,1962.

Leipoldt, Johannes (1965): *Die Frauen in der antiken Welt und im Urchristentum.* Leipzig: Kohlert & Ameland 1965 (1954).

Lietzmann, Hans (1931): *An die Korinther I–II.* Tübingen: Mohr (Siebeck) 1931.

——. (1932): *An die Galater.* Tübingen: Mohr (Siebeck) 1932.

Lüdemann, Gerd (1980): *Paulus, der Heidenapostel, I. Studien zur Chronologie.* Göttingen: Vandenhoeck & Ruprecht 1980.

——. (1983): *Paulus, der Heidenapostel, II. Antipaulinismus im frühen Christentum.* Göttingen: Vandenhoeck & Ruprecht 1983.

Malina, Bruce J. (1981): *The New Testament World: Insights from Cultural Anthropology.* Atlanta, GA: John Knox 1981.

——. (1986): *Christian Origins and Cultural Anthropology.* Atlanta, GA: John Knox 1986.

Maurer, Christian (1966): *"Skeuos."* in: *Th. Wb.* VII, 1964; pp. 359-68.

Meeks, Wayne A. (1974): "The Image of the Androgyne: Some Uses of a Symbol in Earliest Christianity." in: *HR* 13,1974; pp. 165-208.

——. (1983): *The First Urban Christians. The Social World of the Apostle Paul.* New Haven, CT: Yale University Press 1983.

Meier, John P. (1978): "On the Veiling of Hermeneutics (1 Cor 11,2-16)." in: *CBQ* 40, 1978; pp. 212-26.

Merk, Otto (1968): *Handeln aus Glauben.* Marburg: Elwert 1968.

Merklein, Helmut (1984): "Die Einheitlichkeit des ersten Korintherbriefes." in: *ZNW* 75, 1984; pp. 154-83.

Meyer, Heinr. Aug. Wilh. (1856): *Kritisch exegetisches Handbuch über den ersten Brief an die Korinther.* Göttingen: Vandenhoeck & Ruprecht 1856.

Meyer, M. W. (1985): "Making Mary Male: the Categories 'Male' and 'Female' in the Gospel of Thomas." in: *NTS* 31, 1985; pp. 554-70.

Moltmann-Wendel, Elisabeth (1980): *Ein eigener Mensch werden. Frauen um Jesus.* Gütersloh: GTB Siebenstern 1980.

——. (1982): Evangelische Theologie 42, 1: Zur feministischen Theologie, ed. Elisabeth Moltmann-Wendel. München: Kaiser 1982.

Murphy-O'Connor, J. (1976): "The Non-Pauline Character of 1 Corinthians 11, 2-16?" in: *JBL* 95, 1976; pp. 615-21.

——. (1980): "Sex and Logic in 1 Corinthians 11,2-16." in: *CBQ* 42, 1980; pp. 482-500.

——. (1986): "Interpolations in 1 Corinthians." in: *CBQ* 48, 1986; pp. 81-94.

Mussner, Franz (1977): *Der Galaterbrief.* Freiburg: Herder 1974.

Nestle, E./K. Aland (1979): *Novum Testamentum Graece.* 26. Auflage. Stuttgart: Deutsche Bibelgesellschaft 1899 und 1979.

Neyrey, Jerome H. (1986): "Body Language in 1 Corinthians. The Use of Anthropological Models for Understanding Paul and His Opponents." in: *Semeia* 35, 1986; pp. 129-70.

Niebergall, A. (1985): *Ehe und Eheschließung in der Bibel und in der Geschichte der alten Kirche.* Marburg: Elwert 1985.

Niederwimmer, Kurt (1975): *Askese und Mysterium.* Göttingen: FRLANT 113, 1975.

Oepke, Albrecht (1966a): *"Aner* im Neuen Testament." in: *Th. Wb.* I, 1933; pp. 363-64.

——. (1966b): *"Gyne."* in: *Th. Wb.* I, 1933; pp. 776-90.

——. (1967): *"Katalypto."* in: *Th. Wb.* III, 1938; pp. 563-65.

——. (1984): *Der Brief des Paulus an die Galater. Bearbeitet von Joachim Rohde.* Berlin: Evangelische Verlagsanstalt 1937, 1957.

Padgett, Alan (1984): "Paul on Women in the Church: the Contradictions of Coiffure in 1 Cor 11,2-16." in: *Journ. NT Stud.* 20, 1984; pp. 69-86.

Pagels, Elaine (1974): "Paul and Women: A Response to Recent Discussion." in: *JAAR* 42, 1974; pp. 538-49.

Park, Sun Ai (1986): "Understanding the Bible from Women's Perspective." in: *In God's Image.* Singapore, 106, Dec. 1986; pp. 22-28.

Parvey, Constance F. (1974): "The Theology and Leadership of Women in the New Testament." in: *Religion and Sexism,* ed. Rosemary R. Ruether 1974; pp. 117-49.

Paulsen, Henning (1980): "Einheit und Freiheit der Sohne Gottes: Gal 3,26-29." in: *ZNW* 71,1980; pp. 74-95.

Phipps, William E. (1982): "Is Paul's Attitude toward Sexual Relations Contained in 1 Cor 7,1?" in: *NTS* 28, 1982; pp. 125-31.

Plum, Karin Friis (1987): "Kvindehermeneutik og bibelsk eksegese." in: *DDT* 50 1987; pp. 19-41.

Rahlfs, Alfred ed. (1965): *Septuaginta, I-II.* Stuttgart: Württembergische Bibelanstalt 1935.

Rengstorf, K. H. ed. (1969): *Das Paulusbild in der neueren deutschen Forschung.* Wege der Forschung XXIV. Darmstadt: Wissenschaftliche Buchgesellschaft 1969.

Rohde, Joachim (1976): *Urchristliche und frühchristliche Amter.* Berlin: Evangelische Verlagsanstalt 1976.

Ruether, Rosemary R. ed. (1974): *Religion and Sexism. Images of Women in the Jewish and Christian Traditions.* New York: Simon & Schuster 1974.

Ruether, Rosemary R. et. al. eds. (1979): *Women of Spirit: Female Leaders in the Jewish and Christian Traditions.* New York: Simon & Schuster 1979.

Ruether, Rosemary R. (1983): *Sexism and God-Talk. Toward a Feminist Theology.* Boston, MA: Beacon 1983.

Russel, Letty M. (1974): *Human Liberation in a Feminist Perspective. A Theology.* Philadelphia, PA: Westminster 1974.

Russel, Letty M. ed. (1985): *Feminist Interpretation of the Bible.* Philadelphia, PA: Westminster 1985.

Sand, Alexander (1967): *Der Begriff "Fleisch" in den paulinischen Hauptbriefen.* Regensburg: Friedrich Pustet 1967.

Scheffczyk, Leo ed. (1969): *Der Mensch als Bild Gottes.* Wege der Forschung CXXIV. Darmstadt: Wissenschaftliche Buchgesellschaft 1969.

Schlier, Heinrich (1965): *Der Brief an die Galater.* Göttingen: Vandenhoeck & Ruprecht 1949.

——. (1967): *"Kephale* im Neuen Testament." in: *Th. Wb.* III, 1938; pp. 677-81.

——. (1972): *Die Zeit der Kirche. Exegetische Aufsätze und Vorträge.* Freiburg: Herder 1955.

Schmithals, Walter (1969): *Die Gnosis in Korinth*. Göttingen: Vandenhoeck & Ruprecht 1956.

——. (1973): "Die Korintherbriefe als Briefsammlung." in: *ZNW* 64, 1973; pp. 263–88.

Schottroff, Luise (1980): "Frauen in der Nachfolge Jesu in neutestamentlicher Sicht." in: *Traditionen der Befreiung 2*, ed. W. Schottroff et al. München: Kaiser 1980; pp. 91–133.

——. (1985): "Wie berechtigt ist die feministische Kritik an Paulus?" in: *Einwürfe 2*, ed. F.-W. Marquardt et al. München: Kaiser 1985; pp. 94–111.

Schrage, Wolfgang (1976): "Zur Frontstellung der paulinischen Ehebewertung in 1 Kor 7,1–7." in: *ZNW* 67, 1976; pp. 214–34.

——. (1980) "Frau und Mann im Neuen Testament." in: *Frau und Mann*, ed. Erhard S. Gerstenberger und Wolfgang Schrage. Stuttgart: Kohlhammer Taschenbucher 1980; pp. 92–188.

——. (1982): *Ethik des Neuen Testaments*. Göttingen: Vandenhoeck & Ruprecht 1982.

Schütz, John H. (1975): *Paul and the Anatomy of Apostolic Authority*. Cambridge University Press 1975.

Scroggs, Robin (1972): "Paul and the Eschatological Woman." in: *JAAR* 40, 1972; pp. 283–303.

——. (1974): "Paul and the Eschatological Woman: Revisited." in: *JAAR* 42, 1974; pp. 532–49.

Seim, Turid Karlsen (1982): "Maria har valgt den gode del. Kvinnelige disipler Lukasskriftene." in: *Andre Linjer, FS Kari Elisabeth Børresen*, ed. Kari Vogt et al. Oslo: Solum 1982; pp. 68–85.

——. (1985): "Når sløret fjernes. Kvinneblikk på bibeltekster." in: *Riv ned Gjerdene, FS Jacob Jervell*, ed. R. Berg et al. Oslo: Gyldendal 1985; pp. 85–95.

Snyder, Graydon F. (1976): "The Tobspruch in the New Testament." in: *NTS* 23, 1976; pp. 117–20.

Stanton, Elizabeth Cady ed. (1972): *The Woman's Bible, I–II*. New York: Arno 1972 (1895–98).

Stählin, Gustav (1973): "*Chera*," in: *Th. Wb*. IX, 1973; pp. 428–54.

Stendahl, Krister (1979): *The Bible and the Role of Women*. Philadelphia, PA: Fortress 1966 (1958).

Strack, H. L. und Paul Billerbeck (1922–28): *Kommentar zum Neuen Testament aus Talmud und Midrasch I–IV, 1–2*. München: Beck 1922–28.

Stuhlmacher, Peter (1981): *Der Brief an Philemon*. Zürich: EKK 18, Benziger/Neukirchener 1975.

Swidler, A. and L. eds. (1977): *Women Priests. A Catholic Commentary on the Vatican Declaration*. New York: Paulist Press 1977.

Swidler, Leonard (1979): *Biblical Affirmation of Women*. Philadelphia, PA: Westminster 1979.

Theissen, Gerd (1979): *Studien zur Soziologie des Urchristentums*. Tübingen: Mohr (Siebeck) 1979.

Thiselton, A. C. (1978): "Realized Eschatology at Corinth." in: *NTS* 24, 1978; pp. 510-26.

Tolbert, Mary Ann (1983): "Defining the Problem: The Bible and Feminist Hermeneutics." in: *Semeia* 28, 1983; pp. 113-26.

Trible, Phyllis (1978): *God and the Rhetoric of Sexuality*. Philadelphia, PA: Fortress 1978.

——. (1984): *Texts of Terror. Literary-Feminist Readings of Biblical Narratives*. Philadelphia, PA: Fortress 1984.

Trompf, G. W. (1980): "On Attitudes towards Women in Paul and Paulinist Literature: 1 Corinthians 11,3-16 and Its Context." in: *CBQ* 42 1980; pp. 196-215.

Walker, William O. (1975): "1 Corinthians 11,2-16 and Paul's View Regarding Women." in: *JBL* 94, 1975; pp. 94-110.

——. (1983): "The 'Theology of Woman's Place' and the 'Paulinist' Tradition." in: *Semeia* 28, 1983; pp. 101-12.

Weiss, Johannes (1970): *Der erste Korintherbrief*. Göttingen: Vandenhoeck & Ruprecht 1910.

Wendland, Heinz-Dietrich (1972): *Die Briefe an die Korinther*. Göttingen: Vandenhoeck & Ruprecht 1936,1968.

Whitton, J. (1982): "A Neglected Meaning for SKEUOS in 1 Thessalonians 4,4." in: *NTS* 28,1982; pp. 142-43.

Wilckens, Ulrich (1976): "Christologie und Anthropologie im Zusammenhang der paulinischen Rechtfertigungslehre." in: *ZNW* 67, 1976; pp. 64-82.

Witherington, Ben (1981): "Rite and Rights for Women: Galatians 3,28." in: *NTS* 27, 1981; pp. 593-604.

Supplementary Bibliography

Castelli, Elizabeth A. (1991): *Imitating Paul. A Discourse of Power*. Louisville, Kentucky: Westminster/John Knox Press, 1991.

Fatum, Lone (1992): *Kvindeteologi og arven fra Eva*. København: Gyldendal, 1992.

——. "Women, Symbolic Universe and Structures of Silence. Challenges and possibilities in Androcentric Texts." in: *Studia Theologia* 43, 1989; pp. 61-80. Reprinted in: *Kan vi tro på Gud Fader? Tro & Tanke*. Red. Hanna Stenström. Uppsala: Svenska kyrkens forskningsråd, 1992; pp. 263-83.

Macdonald, Margaret Y. (1990): "Women Holy in Body and Spirit: The Social Setting of 1 Corinthians 7." in: *NTS* 36, 1990; pp. 161-81.

Oster, Richard E. (1988): "When Men Wore Veils to Worship: The Historical Context of 1 Corinthians 11.4." in: *NTS* 34, 1988; pp. 481-505.

Wire, Antoinette Clark (1990): *The Corinthian Women Prophets: A Reconstruction through Paul's Rhetoric*. Minneapolis, MN: Fortress Press, 1990.

5
IMAGE OF GOD
AND SEXUAL DIFFERENTIATION
IN THE TRADITION OF *ENKRATEIA*

∽ Giulia Sfameni Gasparro

Protological Motivations

Numerous sectors within early Christianity gave strong emphasis to *enkrateia* both in the sense of "virginity" and "marital continence"[1] as a central value of the Christian life. These various sectors therefore came together within a sufficiently homogeneous and specific context even though this context included diverse motivations for and uses of this discipline.[2] With regard to these uses, a precise distinction can be made between a rejection of marriage based upon its outright condemnation and a voluntary renunciation of marriage which at the same time recognises it as divinely instituted and hence lawful for the Christian. Consequently, one can identify both a radical and a moderate expression within the *enkrateia* tradition.

Traditionally, "encratism" has referred specifically to a radical, extremist position, and Irenaeus included the teachings of those whom he called "encratites" in his lexicon of heresies.[3] What is termed the "moderate" interpretation coincides in large measure with the position of the Catholic Church. Although this latter interpretation offered enthusiastic support for what it considered the preponderant dignity of virginity, it nevertheless consistently asserted the biblical basis for the divine origin of the institution of matrimony and its legitimate place in the lives of Christians.

Given this distinction, however, there remains the far more complex and delicate problem of clarifying the various motivations involved.

Indeed, the extremist position condemning marriage brings together historical figures as different as Tatian and Julius Cassianus.[4] It found expression within some apocryphal literature[5] and within certain anonymous texts inspired by the encratic ideal,[6] which generally assert the biblical notion of a unique divine demiurge to which the salvific activity of Jesus was applied. On the other hand, condemnation of marriage is found in some Gnostic currents where, as the discovery of the Hag Hammadi writings has confirmed, proponents of a dualistic ontology were greatly concerned with the whole question of continence: sexual as well as dietary.[7]

Within Gnostic writings, the outright rejection of physical union and generation found its primary and decisive justification by affirming the intrinsic negativity of matter and corporeality, which constitute the second "principle" of reality, irremissibly opposed to the spiritual or divine sphere. As for the non-ditheist "encratites," a whole series of motivations comes into play as a basis for abstinence, motivations which should be evaluated in relation to each other in order to determine the ideological framework. The exalted position which the Catholic Church afforded virginity and continence arose as a result of a number of motivations within the different contexts. Hence, the essential distinctions drawn between radical and moderate *enkrateia* are important. Furthermore, it is essential to distinguish those more or less explicit and detailed theoretical reasons providing justification for such diverse practices.

It is possible to identify three chief motives behind the *enkrateia* tradition in addition to the dualistic, ontological one mentioned before. While these motivations frequently concur in different proportions, they can be distinguished by their respective characteristics, and are further differentiated by the exclusive or predominant roles they sometimes exercise in one or another of the contexts. These roles allow for sufficient homogeneity when examined with reference to the overall tradition.

The Gospel notion of "eunuch for the sake of God's reign" (Mt. 19,12) depicts a spirituality of voluntary renunciation of worldly goods for a religious ideal, and introduces thereby an ascetic tension transcending, without depreciating, certain positive intramundane values.

An outlook strongly characterized by an eschatological waiting arises from the Pauline formulation in 1 Cor. 7, a text which is fundamental for the *enkrateia* tradition in its multiple expressions. In this text, in fact, the exhortation to use worldly goods with detachment, couples with the notion of the urgent *kairos* of Christian salvation. Virginity and continence appear as the privileged means to reach this purpose. This eschatological waiting, then, assumes different connotations within different contexts resulting sometimes in the suggestion of a "realised eschatology."[8]

In any case, the eschatological motivation of *enkrateia* appears well-defined in character and qualifies a vast gamut of positions relative to the theme. Nevertheless, in some cases the privileged eschatological value of virginity and continence within Christian experience is joined to a protological perspective, that is, one that links *enkrateia* with the fall of Adam. Consequently, *enkrateia* represents one of the decisive premises and a privileged "sign" of that beatific "end" which is intended as the restoration of the original condition of humanity characterised by virginity. Thus, the third motive of this tradition, the protological one, is identified and located within various forms of the *enkrateia* tradition in both its radical and moderate forms.

The character of this protological motivation follows from certain anthropological considerations. There is, in fact, an inescapable theoretical linkage between the practice of *enkrateia* and the initial condition of the original parents or protoplasts in paradise before sin. This initial condition had the *status* of integral virginity, a status interrupted by sin itself. Such linkage applies both in the sense that this sin is constituted in marriage, as the encratites viewed it, as well as in the sense that this practice, neither necessary nor useful within paradisiacal perfection, has been permitted by God for a humanity by now mortal and weak. Matrimony is therefore both a "remedy" for that concupiscence accompanying sin, and indispensable for guaranteeing the propagation of the human species and the realisation of the plan of salvation. Such are the positions taken by numerous authoritative representatives of the Catholic Church which, in spite of giving forceful support for the liceity of marriage against the encratites and Gnostics, considered it instituted in consequence of the fall.

Within this framework, in both its radical formulation with marriage as the first sin, and its moderate formulation with marriage as the result of the first sin, the practice of virginity and continence is defined as the restoration of prelapsarian integrity based upon a specific protological motivation, one which relates virginity to the condition of the first parents in paradise. This sort of thinking reveals an anthropology with a graduated structure. Consequently, what is affirmed is the extraneousness of sexual activity and of physical generation to the original constitution of the human being as projected by the Creator. Such activity is a specific consequence of Adam's sin. A double-tiered anthropology results in which the second level in ontological and chronological order correlates with the initial debasement. Often this second level from which marriage and procreation emerge is considered to be "animal" in nature, in contrast with the original "angelic" character of the human being. This original character, fully restored in the eschatological perspective, is realised in the virgin in which the paradisiacal *arche* (beginning) is bound to the eschatological *telos* (fulfillment).

In some contexts, the "double creation" structure[9] is systematically articulated. In certain cases the notion of the soul's pre-existence along with its subsequent embodiment is expressed; at other times what is described is the passage of the body from a celestial condition to a terrestrial one, with resulting biological functions. In yet another theory propounded by Gregory of Nyssa, sexual differentiation suggests a reality "added" by the Creator in anticipation of humanity's future sin. This addition represents a change from the original divine intention to provide the human being with a body having no sexual character. Within Gregory's anthropology, sexual differentiation even prior to its functioning, is directly correlated with the first sin. Other formulations of the *enkrateia* tradition which have a protological foundation for defining the place of marriage and procreation also involve, in various ways, sexual differentiation prior to and together with sexual activity.

Early Christian anthropology in its variety of expressions constantly appeals to the biblical notion of creation of the human being "in the image and likeness" of God.[10] Yet, this notion occurs within different currents of the *enkrateia* tradition and it is oftentimes placed in relation with matrimony, corporeality or, more precisely, with the sexual differentiation characterising it. Even without examining here each context, by means of certain soundings, the role which creation "in the image" of God plays in the *enkrateia* tradition can be verified. This tradition praises the value of virginity and continence while it appeals to certain primordial events of history and attributes to Adam's sin a negative or "downward" effect, resulting in the origin of sexual attributes and activities which define the human ontological structure.

One of the more noted supporters of the radical encratite position is Tatian, whose ideological framework seems more correctly situated in a non-ditheist encratism than Gnosticism.[11] For a correct evaluation of these characteristics beyond the merely heresiological data which define their encratite quality,[12] the contribution of his *Discourse to the Greeks* is indispensable, since he couples his unique trichotomic anthropology (spirit-soul-body) with a harsh critique of paganism.

Tatian's exposition was adapted to the biblical account of creation which, though never explicitly cited, is clearly perceptible as a warrant for his own account.[13] This exposition of the primordial events of cosmic and human history views the Logos as creating a human being, "the image of immortality," "according to the imitation of the Father who generated it" (i.e., the Logos itself). Nevertheless, this human being became mortal at the very moment in which, having listened to diabolic suggestions, it was abandoned by the "more powerful spirit."[14] In fact, Tatian's anthropology suggests the presence in the human being of two *pneumata,* one mortal, the *psyche* (animal soul), the other superior: *theou eikon kai homoiosis* (image of God and likeness). Together, these form one *syzygia* (couple), and salvation depends upon their harmony since the corporeal human being by means of this harmony constitutes a "temple" in which God dwells through the *pneuma*-image. If the equilibrium is lost the *psyche* is left alone, resulting in its "darkening," and dies along with the material *sarx* (flesh).[15]

Humanity, called to a consciousness of its own dignity and to a restoration of the equilibrium of the two *pneumata,*[16] is, however, defined and determined by the primordial event of a fall. This vicissitude is expressed by two parallel formulations which, although certainly distinguishable from one another, are otherwise connected by the events described in each and by the effects which they bring about in the human being. The first formulation employs the Platonic image of the "wings" of the soul, and views the fall of the *psyche* as a separation through its own fault from the "perfect spirit," resulting in the loss of "celestial union" (*synousia*) and a desire to participate in inferior realities.[17] The second formulation adheres more closely to a biblical format and shows the protoplasts far removed from a superior "land" after their sin.[18]

This same formulation calls to mind that "celestial" paradise which is at odds with the terrestrial world reserved for the sinner.[19] It also implies a vertical gradation of cosmological levels, with the result that once the *pneuma* is detached from the *psyche* the latter falls from union with a celestial substance (*pneuma-eikon*) to participation (*metousia*) with inferior reality. Tatian's anthropology identifies this inferior reality with the material *sarx* which constitutes his third element in the trichotomic human composite.

In its figurative, allusive and scarcely systematic method, Tatian's argumentation leaves unclear the original condition expressed in the relation between the *syzygia: pneuma* and *psyche.* Nor does it clearly delineate the situation of the protoplasts before or after the "fall," given the somatic and terrestrial realities which constitute the human being's present condition. Neither of the formulas here described completely presupposes the notion of the pre-existence of the soul and its successive embodiment as fully as it is suggested by Julius Cassianus.[20] Rather, they suggest a condition of "light" corporeality compatible with the harmony of the spiritual *syzygia* or with the condition of the protoplasts in paradise. In neither case, however, is any biological function assumed. It is only after the "fall" that the human being as we now know it, "massive" and physiologically determined, arrived on the scene. A clear tension and opposition between the "harmonic union" which is finalised in prayer, and the "union of corruption" (*koinonia phthoras*) or marriage is, however, certainly affirmed in the only existing fragment of Tatian's work *On perfection according to the Saviour* which, according to Clement of Alexandria, spelled out Tatian's encratite presuppositions. The well-known Pauline passage 1 Cor. 7,5 is joined in this context with a reference to Mt. 6,24 on serving two masters. Both texts are interpreted in the light of the encratite condemnation of marriage as a diabolical invention.[21]

Symphonia, which is service to God, is contrasted with *asymphonia* which is disruption of the "harmonic accord" and as such equivalent to the "union of corruption" understood as service to "incontinence, fornication, and the devil." The antithesis between *symphonia* and *asymphonia* once again evokes the anthropological scheme of the *syzygia: pneuma-psyche*. The ruinous association of the soul with the material *sarx* follows from this disruption. The result is an irremissible incompatibility between the superior quality of the "image" in which the human being participates by virtue of the *pneuma* of those sexual distinctions which characterise the body.

The human being defines its nature in terms of the notion: *eikon kai homoiosis theou* (image and likeness of God), the loss of which, according to the *Discourse to the Greeks*, degrades that nature to the animal level.[22] At the same time, marriage is regarded as *asymphonia* or degradation of a spiritual harmony which is complete only in religious life. Sexual differentiation which makes marriage possible is pictured as a reality opposed to the "image" of God that characterises the human being in its deepest structures although the *pneuma*-image is a divine gift, added to two "natural" human components, soul and flesh.

Yet another trichotomic anthropology with remarkable similarity to Tatian's doctrine is clearly present in the *Teachings of Silvanus* contained in Codex VII of the Nag Hammadi documents. In this tractate a strong encratite tension is expressed in the exhortations against all passions, particularly carnal love.[23] This tension is linked with the notion of a divine element in the human being reminiscent of a Gnostic dualistic ontology.[24] However, the complex, mythical accounts particular to Gnosticism are nowhere to be found here. Instead, *Silvanus* affirms that "the divine mind has substance from the Divine,"[25] a position consistent with the Gnostic doctrine of divine consubstantiality with a spiritual component of the human being. This assertion is not accompanied by any condemnation of the body or of the cosmos as being creations of an inferior demiurge; nor is it accompanied by the notion of the intrinsic negativity of matter. Thus, it seems that the author, without accepting the dualistic, anti-cosmic and anti-somatic doctrine of Gnosticism, chose to emphasise the dignity and superiority of the intellectual element in the tension between the spiritual and corporeal levels because the intellect expresses a profound affinity with the divine. The intellect realises this affinity by contrasting itself clearly with the physical component which is subject to various strong passions.

It is with this in mind that the author utilises the biblical account of creation in the image of God. The superior component of the human being, the *nous* (mind), is identified with that element which is *kat' eikona*. "Understand that you have come into being from three races," *Silvanus* declares, "from the earth, from the formed (*plasma*), and from the created (*poiesis*)."[26] The distinction between *plasma* and *poiesis* recalls that interpretation of Gen. 1,26–27 and Gen. 2,7 which refers to "two human beings" or to two components, the spiritual and physical respectively. It is this interpretation, rooted in Philo of Alexandria,[27] that Origen will continue to modify and utilise.

The *Teachings of Silvanus* offers a trichotomic anthropology in which the body is the terrestrial element, the *plasma* is the *psyche* and the *poiesis* is the *nous* born "according to the image" of God.[28] As in Tatian, human salvation depends upon the correct relationship of these elements, implying the absolute pre-eminence of the intellect[29] to which the soul must be subordinated while it lies in close approximation to the body. The *psyche*, in fact, stands in a middle position and can become similar to one or the other of the opposite components. The human being, in this case, becomes either "noetic" or "carnal."[30]

The relationship between *nous* and *psyche* is structured like a marriage.[31] Interior human nature is understood as a male-female structure in which the first element which is of divine origin grounds and guarantees the salvation of the entire human composite. If the human being rejects this "male" divine element and distances itself even from the "female" soul, it assumes "animal thought and likeness." "You have become fleshly," Silvanus declares, "since you have taken on animal nature."

Philo's use of this male-female symbolism to express the relationship of the various human components is well-known; the male represented by the *nous* while the *psyche* represents the female. Once again the male component is superior to the female.[33] In the text from Silvanus, the biblical notion of the image of God, although not explicitly combined with the account concerned with sexual differentiation, suggests the radical subordination of the somatic sphere to the spiritual. This inferior, physical realm is left with its burden of passions among which the "sins of lust" constitute a particularly clear expression.[34] Just as in Philo and Tatian, the two Genesis accounts of creation:

1) "in the image and likeness" of God, and 2) of "male and female," are used by this author merely to define the quality of entirely spiritual components and their interrelationship without any regard whatsoever for the application of these biblical texts to creation of physical men and women. This results in an implicit but clear depreciation of the human physical structure which is scorned as "animal" because it was sexually differentiated and radically opposed to the divine "image" characterising human nature. The body along with its passions belongs, in fact, to the terrestrial sphere.

One need not dwell here on the presence of strong encratite tendencies within many Gnostic currents. Yet, the number and complex variety of the biblical themes concerning human creation which are incorporated into their anthropological speculations ought not to be passed over without mention.[35] It should also be noted that Gnostic abstinence, as was emphasised earlier, is grounded primarily in a dualistic ontology which in turn evaluates negatively the physical matter in which the body with its sexual and reproductive functions is rooted. The ditheism inspiring Gnostic exegesis leads to the identification of the Creator with an inferior demiurge. This further depreciates creation "in the image and likeness" to demiurgic activity, clear traces of which are then found in both the physical and spiritual components of the human being.[36] The motive for divine exemplarity with respect to cosmic reality has direct bearing on Valentinian's as well as other Gnostics' speculations concerning divine substance present within the human being in the form of an "image" of pleromatic entities. In these writings it is difficult to distinguish between what is undoubtedly Platonic philosophy, and the biblical theme of creation "in the image and likeness" of God. Close examination though suggests that the biblical theme is transposed here to illustrate the notion of a substantial community between divine and human nature.

One ought to note just how in Saturninus[37] or even in such strongly mythological texts as the *Apocryphon Johannis*[38] and *The Hypostasis of the Archons*[39] the theme of "image" is applicable to both levels mentioned above. For in both of these latter works, and in Saturninus' system the encratite motif rejecting marriage and reproduction appeals to protological motivations beyond those which merely stem from a dualistic ontology.[40] One application of the "image" theme illustrates an aspect of Archontic creation, in which inferior powers work to trap a divine spark in material *plasma* which reflects their animal "image."[41] In yet another application, the theme expresses the relationship which is established against the will of these powers, between the human creature and that supreme entity extraneous to the

Giulia Sfameni Gasparro

world whose "luminous image" is reflected in cosmic waters, thereby arousing the covetousness of material beings.[42]

Both the duality of the sexes and their specific functions appear in this context as privileged instruments of the Archons as they struggle to dominate the divine substance which descended in order to give true life of the spirit to the human being.[43] At the same time, the theme of the spiritual "couple" or androgyny, regarded as a completion or a totality in the Gnostic framework,[44] is brought into contact with the "image" motif and is related both to the divine and human levels. One need only recall the Naassenes' system in which man, the "image" of the celestial Anthropos who was formed by Archontic Powers, receives life through a soul as androgynous as is the Divine Man from which it is derived.[45] In this scenario an affirmation of the androgyny of the "Man who is in all," disguised by a corporeal covering,[46] precedes a condemnation of physical marriage[47] expressed contemptuously as "the work of pigs and dogs."[48]

This connection of marriage and procreation with Adam's fall provides specific protological support for the exaltation of virginity and continence within the patristic tradition. The anthropological theories of Origen and Gregory of Nyssa concerning the theme of creation "in the image" of God emphasise the problem involved in defining the relationship of this "image" motif to the corporeal and sexual dimensions of the human being. Origen follows the exegetical line of Philo[49] and Clement of Alexandria[50] disdaining literal and anthropomorphic positions,[51] while affirming the relevance of the "image" quality within the spiritual component of the human being. Beginning with *Peri Archon* and continuing throughout his biblical commentaries and homilies directed to the simple faithful, all of Origen's intellectual and religious activity gravitates around the certainty that the rational creature in its essence lies in the *eikon* structure of the first and unique image of God, the divine Logos.[52] This specific approach is consistent with Origen's overall anthropology and cosmology, affirming as it does a gradation of levels and of the intelligent creatures which inhabit them. Included among these creatures are angels, demons and human beings, all of which were involved in the primordial event which initiated the gradual decline away from God's perfect creation. Origen's complex thought structure is sustained by an intensely ascetic and mystical spirituality drawing continually upon the Scriptures. At the same time, this system rests upon the fundamental "hypothesis" of the pre-existence of rational creatures.

The notion of pre-existence recurs in Origen's thought as a solution to certain Gnostic positions, taken up during polemical discussions concerning the origin of evil and the diverse conditions of spiritual beings. Origen's solutions to these problems employed rational arguments and conformed to the true faith by safeguarding both the inalienable principles of God's unity and justice along with the freedom of intelligent creatures.

This same hypothesis grounds the structure of "double creation." Accordingly, creation of cosmic matter and of the weighty corporeality of rational beings represented the fruit of a "second divine intervention," and followed upon the commission by these creatures of variedly serious sins. Yet, this "second" creation was finalised in a manner providential for salvation.[53] In this framework, the notion of the "image" of God thus assumes the role of both nerve centre and propeller. The first creation correlates with the *noes*, intelligences brought into existence on a mutually equal and free basis by an absolute and gratuitous act of divine goodness. This is creation "in the image," that is, in the Logos. These intelligences consequently possess the *logikos* (rational) character deeply inscribed in their being.

The question of the presence of some form or other of corporeality in the first creation was a problem with which Origen was himself concerned,[54] and one which has sparked a number of scholarly interpretations of his intentions.[55] It is sufficient to note that the primordial *noes* which constitute humanity progressively assume a form of corporeality characterised by a series of physiological attributes completely extraneous to their original condition. In fact, if instead one acknowledges a continuity between the "ethereal" body of pre-existence and the material body, the characteristics assumed by the latter result only in a defect, one of the typical and characteristic marks of which is sexual differentiation.

Origen's notion of the "double creation," for the most part associated with Gen. 1,26 and 2,7, finds one of its most vivid and cogent elaborations in a passage from his *Commentary on John*. Here he distinguishes the human being's "primordial essence" as being "in the image of the Creator" and as such contrasting itself with that component which stems from guilt, fashioned as it is by the earth's clay.[56]

Given the relevance for Origen of the divine "image" to the spiritual dimension of the human being, otherwise expressed as "that one who is interior, invisible and incorporeal, incorrupt and immortal,"[57] Origen defines his position in the context of other factors. These issues clarify the ways in which the divine "image" and corporeality are related to each other, especially in terms of the implied male-female differentiation.

Origen's anthropological language does not present a rigid, systematic fixity, but turns out to be richly varied even given the persistence of rather consistent and homogeneous fundamental notions in his thought. This conclusion can be demonstrated notwithstanding the Latin translations through which much of Origen's work has been filtered.

His affirmation in *Peri Archon* that the original *nous* separated itself from the "warmth" of love for God and subsequently "cooled down," thus becoming *psyche*,[58] results in the *psyche*'s becoming for him the centre of the rational element *kat' eikona* in the human being.[59] However, he frequently employs the terms *nous/mens* to define the rational element. Occasionally, he makes reference to an "inferior soul and friend of corporeal substance,"[60] which as a result of passions is capable of inclining itself toward corporeality and even of ending up more or less completely absorbed in carnality. In his dichotomous scheme, Origen refers to the body as both *soma* and *sarx*, the latter including its own biblical connotations of passion and sinfulness. The dichotomy inherent in the soul/intellect-body structure was, however, frequently substituted by a trichotomous one which incorporates the *pneuma/spiritus* dimension supporting religious life.[61] This latter formula permitted Origen to transpose the biblically-attested male-female distinction to the spiritual level, thereby placing it in immediate continuity with creation "in the image and likeness" of God. At the same time he is able to utilise the symbolism of marriage, equally familiar to Tatian, in order to specify more clearly the relationship between soul and spirit. In his first *Homily on Genesis*, Origen moved beyond the literal sense[62] to explain "allegorically how the human being made in the image of God is male and female" (*per allegoriam quomodo ad imaginem Dei homo factus masculus et femina est*). He subsequently declares: "Our inner human being consists of spirit and soul. One calls the spirit male and the soul female" (*Interior homo noster ex spiritum et anima constat. Masculus spiritus dicitur, femina potest anima nuncupari*)."[63]

In a clear reference to the Pauline theme of *symphonia* between spouses, Origen indicates in the *concordia* and *consensus* of the two elements (i.e., *spiritus* and *anima*) the necessary conditions for the "generation" of offspring, those good thoughts capable of inhabiting the "earth" identified as "the sense of the flesh subject to itself (i.e. the spirit") (*subiectum sibi sensum carnis*).[64]

The overall system which he adopted induced Origen to develop his discourse in such a way as to incorporate both marriage symbolism and the female character of the soul which he had subordinated to *spiritus*. Responsibility for the eventual descent into corporeal passions, a descent represented as adultery, resulted eventually in a deserved punishment for "the soul which gives completely in to flesh sense and to corporeal desires, deserting the union with the spirit" (*anima quae Spiritus coniunctione deserta sensui se carnis at desideriis corporalibus tota prosternit*).[65]

Yet, the male-female distinction when applied to the interior human structure, keeps Origen's exegesis of biblical texts consistent with his own anthropological presupposition, i.e., the notion of the *"eikon"* as a quality peculiar to the human spiritual essence. At the same time, it leaves open the problem of the relationship between this *eikon* and the sexual differentiation peculiar to the somatic structure. This problem is particularly unavoidable when viewed in the light of the above-mentioned "double creation" doctrine. The material human body along with its physiological activities, while created by God and consequently substantially good, is connected in some meaningful way to the original fall in pre-existence. This human body is, therefore, a place of humiliation for intelligent creatures and a source of those impurities which can be removed only in an eschatological perspective.

One of the principal causes and the focus for such contamination lies in the sexual arena in as much as the body inevitably originates from a physical union which even in chaste Christian marriages results in impurity for parents and offspring alike.[66] Contamination from sexual activity stems from two sources: 1) the material body itself which results from the fall of a rational creature from the status of original integrity and perfection, and 2) the sin of the first human couple. Origen in fact combines two schemes of human beginnings. The first is related to the destiny of the *noes* and is indicated by a fall from the perfect condition of pre-existence. The second, a strictly human one, is explained by the biblical narration of the historical process which the protoplasts underwent.

Once Origen joins marriage and procreation with Adamic sin in the *Commentary on the Epistle to the Romans*[67] and in a fragment of the *Commentary on the First Epistle to the Corinthians*,[68] the concern of the second level's protology with *enkrateia* becomes apparent. The human body in paradise was destined for virginal integrity in order to constitute a pure "temple" for the Lord. The soul inhabiting this body was to be "pure and blessed and totally prepared to venerate the Holy Spirit," itself destined to become a "minister of the Holy Spirit" present within the human being.[69]

Only after Adam's fall and the consequent *astheneia* (weakness) of the human condition did God concede marriage to the species.[70] While legitimate for the Christian, marriage nevertheless marks the lowpoint in the creaturely fall, given Origen's concept of a graduated protology descending from preexistence into corporeality and finally arriving at sexual activity. Origen's constant adulation of virginity[71] reveals the power which the symbol held for him as a state of integrity and "incorruptibility,"[72] which not only restores the initial Adamic condition, but even anticipates the final perfection to be achieved by the resurrection.

Putting aside those notoriously controversial issues relative to Origen's teaching on the theme,[73] one aspect that deserves attention is the abolishment of sexual distinction following the resurrection of the dead. In his *Commentary on Matthew*, Origen argues against the materialistic, Millenarian position which presupposed the continuation of marital relations among the resurrected, relations which he rejected as producing "pollution" and a "certain impurity."[74] In consequence, he explicitly insisted on the absence of sexual differentiation in the resurrection. Jesus' teaching on the likeness of the resurrected to angels and on the relative absence of marriage in that condition suggested to Origen a much deeper mystery, one which his interlocutors were incapable of understanding. For that reason he maintained that the *isangelia* (angel-likeness) of the redeemed will witness, in addition to the abolition of marriage, a profound transformation from the form of their "bodies of humiliation" which will become like "angelic bodies, ethereal and refulgent."[75]

The elimination of sexual differentiation in the resurrection, expressed as similarity to an angelic condition, is asserted as well in a passage from Jerome's *Commentary on the Epistle to the Ephesians*. Accused by Rufinus of complete adherence to condemned Origenistic theses, Jerome later attributed this passage to Origen. Rufinus, as is well known, was violently attacked by Jerome for translating the *Peri Archon*,[76] and for that reason was determined to demonstrate just how Jerome in the aforementioned commentary not only made ample use of Origen's commentary but went on to make himself spokesman for theories that had by then come to be viewed as "heretical." Included among these was the abolishment of sexual differentiation following the resurrection. In this *Apologia* Rufinus cites a passage from that commentary in which the author includes this notion within the general framework comprising a process of transformation of woman into man and of body into soul: "In the third book of the Commentary on the Epistle to the Ephesians, with reference to the passage where is written: 'who loves his wife loves himself; nobody in fact hated his flesh,' after a few words, he speaks like that: 'We husbands must love our wives as our souls (must love) the bodies, so that the wives will change into males and the bodies into souls, and there will not be any difference of sex; but, as well as among the angels there is neither male nor female so we who will be like the angels begin at present to be what is promised us in the heavens.'"[77]

For his part, Jerome tried unsuccessfully to clear himself of the charge of professing this opinion and claimed that the passage was borrowed from Origen's work in question.[78]

Aside from this important influence of Origen on Jerome,[79] it is interesting to note that the formula of transformation which is employed does in fact parallel the passage from woman to man with the spiritualisation of the body. As such it alludes to *logion* 114 of the *Gospel of Thomas*, which likewise proposes the transformation of Mary Magdalene from woman to man as a condition of her assumption into the "reign of God" in which she becomes a "living spirit," "resembling a man,"[80]

Thus Origen's complex anthropology belies an irresolvable tension between the divine "image" within the rational creature and its physical body along with sexual differentiation and activity. The tension here consists in an explicit incompatibility and opposition located as well in other texts of his *Commentary on Matthew*. Returning once again to the two biblical accounts of human creation, Origen distinguishes the substantial diversity between the two couples discovered there.[81] In speaking of the creation of the "male and female" (*arsen, thelu*), the Bible likewise refers to the notion of creation "in the image and likeness." However, when the Scripture is concerned with marriage (Gen. 2,24), it speaks of a man formed from clay and a woman from Adam's rib. This second "couple" comes into existence "after" the first, and they are termed *aner* and *gyne* (man, woman) in reference to those characteristics of a sexual nature which make marital relations possible. The subtle reference to both the chronological sequence and ontological difference between the two creations, while clearly an allusion to pre-existence, establishes a sharp dichotomy between the human being *kat' eikona* and sexual differentiation particular to the human being "formed from clay."

In the passage in question, the exegesis of the terms "male" and "female" as particular qualities of the human being created "in the image" of God, are not worked out in relation to the interior human structure, but only in terms of a Christological function. The two are seen as representing Christ and the Church in pre-existence, the couple endowed with a character *kat' eikona*.[82]

Among patristic authors whose notion of *enkrateia* develops out of a protological foundation, Gregory of Nyssa offers the most limpid and dramatic assessment of the radical incompatibility in the human being between its quality as image of God and its sexually differentiated structure with the resulting functions and attributes. Gregory's doctrine concerning "image,"[83] its strong Platonic component and its larger anthropological context have each been amply studied.[84] Similarly well-known is the weight of the influence which Origen exerted among the Cappadocians. Gregory of Nyssa, in rejecting the "hypothesis" of pre-existence, nevertheless revealed tendencies toward Origenist thinking by formulating an original scheme of "double creation" in *De hominis opificio.*[82]

Without going too far into the details of the problematic related to Gregory's anthropology, it is clear that after his early tractate *De virginitate,* in which there is no hint of a "double creation," his anthropological reflection is dominated by a tension between the themes of human dignity as "image of God" and the fall. His mature work was intended to "complete" Basil's *Hexameron* by filling out the account of human creation. This work along with all of his later writings is subject to the same anthropological tension.[87] The fall is evidenced by the present condition of humanity, which is both corruptible and mortal. Sexual functions with the inarrestable rhythm of *genesis-phthora* (generation-corruption)[88] on which they depend, thus represent the privileged ground of reproduction for the passion itself.

The quality of "work and imitation of divine nature without mixture" which for Gregory is expressed by the biblical affirmation of creation "in the image and likeness" of God, leads him to hold that in its *protegenesis* (initial condition) the human being was deprived of the "capacity to suffer and die."[89] This is due, as the author points out, to the fact that the image is not real unless it actually reproduces its model in such a way that the image reflects a perfect resemblance to the original.[90] The sin of the first human being consisted in an estrangement for virtue and a descent into vice. This alienation introduced corruption by obscuring the original beauty of the soul as it slid into the "mud" of passions.[91]

The tractate "On virginity" reveals its protological foundation by describing the Adamic condition as one in which the divine "image" was not yet obscured "by the contamination of the flesh."[92] The first man was in fact naked, without the "tunics of skin" (*dermatinoi chitones*)[93] which for Gregory represents the mortal, passionate corporeal condition along with all the functions of the biological cycle from birth to death.[94] Adam alone enjoyed the complete security of divine contemplation while the woman was given to him as a spiritual helper.

As is the case in so much of the *enkrateia* tradition based upon a protological foundation,[95] the perfect paradisiacal condition is represented as continual and blessed religious activity free from any corporeal cares or stimuli. In such a condition sexual differentiation was irrelevant, deprived as it was of any existential impact. Such efficacy, on the other hand, comes into play as a result of the offense and subsequent ejection from paradise. Gregory, in line with so many other ecclesiastical writers, interpreted as cause and effect the sequence of biblical narratives which places the marriage of the protoplasts only after their expulsion from paradise.

The author discovers an *akolouthia* (consistency)[96] in these primordial and decisive events in human life, and reasons that there ought to be a corresponding inverse movement restoring the human being to its earlier beatitude: "At the same time a form of pleasure introduced through trickery was the beginning of decadence. It was followed by shame, fear and an incapacity to stand before the eyes of the Creator, or to do anything more than to hide in the foliage, in darkness. After this they covered themselves in dead animal skins and were sent into exile in the unhealthy and toilsome land in which marriage was invented as a consolation for death,[97] i.e. to counteract mortality by carnal fecundity.

Given this tight linkage of events, *parthenia* (virginity) seemed to Gregory to be the first step toward original human perfection. Since it posed an insuperable limit to death, it broke the generation-corruption cycle which was initiated by sexual activity. This activity, unnecessary in paradise, expressed through its own proper functions and effects the vast distance between the fallen human being and the perfect quality contained in the notion of "image."[98]

Gregory further developed his rigorously systematic approach to anthropology in *De hominis opificio*. Once again the decisive point of reference concerned the apparently irreconcilable tension between the biblical position of the human being created "in the image and likeness" of God and its current status as mutable, corruptible and subject to passions and death.[99] Given that the quality of "image" implies a real resemblance to the "incorruptible, pure and eternal" divine model, the author's conclusion was inevitable: "that which was made 'according to the image' is one thing, which is now seen in its affliction is another."[100]

This dichotomy appears to Gregory to be surmountable in as much as the biblical text can be interpreted as clearly distinguishing the expression, "God created the human being in the divine image," in which the one created *kat' eikona* was made perfect, from the later assertion: "male and female God created them."

Supported by Pauline authority in Gal. 3,28: "in Christ Jesus there is no male and female," Gregory reasoned that this distinction was excluded from the "prototype":

"Thus the creation of our nature is in a sense twofold: one made like God, one
divided according to the sexes: for something like this the passage obscurely
conveys by its arrangement where it first says, "God created the human being in
the image of God," and then, adding to what has been said, "male and female
God created them," a thing which is alien from our conception of God."[101]

Gregory's ample argumentation unfolds his two great anthropological
themes. Human beings are characterised by freedom, a sign of their affinity
to God, and by the intrinsic mutability of every created nature.[102] In this way
he delineates a singularly original anthropological vision through which he
overcomes Origen's hypothesis of pre-existence by recourse to divine foreknowledge. The time-lapse between the "two creations" becomes instead a
metaphysical gap between divine intentionality and human sin. In the former,
the human being is "projected in the image," that is a corporeal being but
incorrupt and asexual. In the latter, human sinfulness results in its descent
into corporeal passions. In the foreknowledge of this sin, God allowed for sexual differentiation in human beings as a means of bringing about the total
number of creatures constituting the *pleroma* (fullness). In this way, despite
its sin, a fallen humanity which had lost its "angelic" faculty of multiplication
could by means of marriage and physical generation bring about, during the
historical *diastema* (extension), the full number of human beings desired by
the Creator.[103]

Sexual differentiation was thus envisioned as a principal effect of a human
sin, not yet "historically" committed but foreseen by God and consequently
accounted for in that unique event of creation which extended to two distinct
ontological levels. Even though it is the product of a divine act, sexual differentiation was viewed as a typically "animal" prerogative.[104] Owing to sin, it
was "added"[105] to the original and essential structure of the human being, i.e.
to his quality of divine "image." This "image" will be restored in the eschatological *telos* (fulfillment) which is itself a reflection of the perfection of *arche*
(the beginning).[106]

The insistence on the animal quality of human birth, in addition to the
pathe (passions) which accompany biological functions,[107] clearly accentuates from Gregory's perspective the great distance which separates the dignity of creation "in the image and likeness" from sexual differentiation.
Enkrateia plays a decisive role in the long and difficult process by purifying
and restoring the original beauty of the *eikon* in which the perfect likeness
between the human being and the Creator is shown.

The final issue of this process is pictured by Gregory as a return to the
arche and is expressed in biblical terms as resurrection.[108] It is also expressed

through the complex formula of *apokatastasis* (restoration), which involves the complete elimination of evil with the reestablishment of the unity of the rational creation and with its "formation" according to the unique *morphe* (form) of Christ.[109] The two notions become clearer once Gregory declares in a significant definition in *De hominis opificio* that "the grace of the resurrection is announced to us as nothing more than a restoration to the ancient condition from which they fell."[110] Gregory expresses much the same conclusion in *De anima et resurrectione.*[111] Moreover, the eschatological perspective of the tractate *De hominis opificio* results in Gregory's articulating the "return" to that metaphysical *arche* which is the divine scope for humanity, modified radically from the foreknowledge of sin with the addition of the animal dimension to the *eikon.*

This *eikon* is therefore fully realised only in the beatitude of the *telos* following the necessary historical *diastema* signalled in the descent toward sensation. On the basis of biblical texts which represent the condition of the resurrected as *isangelia* (angel-likeness), Gregory grounds his conviction that human life before the fall was also angelic because the resurrection is an *apokatastasis* of the original condition; it is also a true mirror of the initial *angelikos* status of perfection.[112] In this perspective two essential dynamics give shape to human life: the angelic dimension of "image," and an "animal," "affective" dimension. The focus in which both dimensions converge and from which they diverge is constituted by sexual differentiation. Gregory, in fact, repeats the notion that sexual differentiation was "added" by God to the human *pleroma* "after" creation of the *eikon* in order to promote the multiplication of the species.[113] Thus human beings lost through sin the angelic faculty of reproduction and are now completely dependent upon an animal mode of generation to obtain the necessary *pleroma* of human souls brought into being by God in creation.[114]

As previously noted, Gregory intends the "periods": "before" (creation *kat' eikona*) and "after" (sexual modification) as a metaphysical succession corresponding to divine intentionality and ontological value. Hence, the human being comes into historical existence in a double construct of "image" and of corporeal creature, sexually differentiated like other animals. The human being's *apokatastasis* as divine "image" expresses its true nature and constitutes its *arche* in God's original plan. This factor, coupled with that corporeality which defines its particularly human creaturehood, allows the human being to "mediate" between intelligible and sensible natures. In the *apokatastasis* humanity thus abandons those sexual distinctions which stand for the animal affinity and exist only as consequences of its sinful decline into the sensible realm of passions.

De hominis opificio does not explicitly pose the theme of abolition of the male-female differentiation in the resurrection. Nevertheless, it is implied by the internal coherence of the anthropological vision analysed there, and hence supports the delicate argumentation of *anastasis* (resurrection) which Gregory connects with the theme of the nature and origin of evil. Gregory, in fact, demonstrates through his vast teleological vision the finite and perishable character of vice which, contrary to the nature of being, has its own precise limits. The human being, created for an infinite good, distances itself from evil in order to strive after its own end, the good which is God.[115] This movement is characterised as a return to paradise, to the tree of life and to the original dignity of the image.[116]

To illustrate the significance and the means of such a "return," Gregory examines creation, clearly showing just how the "grace of resurrection" rests upon an ontological foundation which is a primordial divine gift to the creature consisting in its creation "in the image." It is the creature's own sin, which God foresaw even if it was not yet historically occasioned, that brought on the animal condition of sexual differentiation.

Gregory returns to a discussion of Gen. 1,26-27 in terms analogous to the previous argument[117] and especially with reference to the modalities of the eschatological *telos*. He reveals here just how the transformation of humanity "from the corruptible, terrestrial condition to the impassible and eternal"[118] is connected to the theme of "differentiation according to male and female." This differentiation, a prerogative characteristic of animals, was adjoined to the "image" by the Creator in anticipation of its temporary corruption in the sensible realm. The eschatological abolition of sexual distinctions, however, is more or less explicitly affirmed in other texts beginning with an early work, the sermon *De mortuis*.[119] In this text Gregory seems to identify the "tunics of skin" of Gen. 3,21 with animal properties consisting in the passions.[120] Gregory is concerned here with the transfiguration of the bodies of the resurrected. Although fully conscious of the almost insurmountable difficulties facing the human being in imagining such a condition, he affirms that the differentiated, corporeal *idiomata* (qualities) now necessary for procreation will no longer be so. The final condition is thus expressed in terms of a "unification" of all creatures shining in the unique splendour of the "divine image" because they constitute the unique body and conform to the unique *charakter* of Christ.[121]

Divine "image" is once again represented as that which opposes the sexual differentiation typical of the present human essence and initiates the human being's eschatological transformation under the sign of the unity of the unique *morphe* of Christ.

Gregory's tractate *De anima et resurrectione* advances his firm conviction that "the resurrection consists in a return to the original condition of our nature."[122] It also confirms his own doctrine on the animal, irrational "addition" signified by the biblical expression "tunics of skin" completely at odds with the faculty of likeness to God.[123] The *dermatinoi chitones* are expressed as "intercourse, conception, childbirth, defilement, lactation, feeding, elimination of bodily waste, gradual growth, youth, old age, illness and death."[124]

Although sexual differentiation is not mentioned as such,[125] this *alogos* (irrational) element, displaced in the resurrection, is implied in the entire biological cycle. Gregory normally represents this cycle initiated by sexual differentiation in terms of *genesis* and *phthora*. At the same time the notion that procreation is an animal dimension added to the human being is central to his anthropology in which the human being was "projected" by God as an *eikon* endowed with a mysterious capacity for generation in a manner similar to angels. One may legitimately deduce from *De anima et resurrectione* that the mix is considered as primary characteristics of those "tunics of skins" displaced in the resurrection represent not only sexual functions, but sexual differentiation as well. Gregory once again mentions sexual differentiation in *Homily VII in Cant. Cant.* as an element extraneous to divine nature and as such destined to be displaced by the human being in the eschatological *telos*. He concludes by saying: "when we all become one in Christ, we will put off the signs of this difference together with the entire old human being."[126]

Conclusion

This brief essay has treated some of the most significant representatives of the *enkrateia* tradition with protological motivations. These authors have tried to combine the notion of human creation "in the image and likeness" of God with male-female differentiation. A few observations concern the specificity of the connection drawn between these two notions. These observations prescind from Gnostic dualism in both its radical and moderate forms. Although these features have yet to be analysed completely, one can detect the existence of two fundamental directions within which the authors here examined can be situated, even while acknowledging wide diversity in their approaches.

It was commonly understood among them that sexual differentiation was extraneous to the character of the human being as that intelligent creature brought into existence "in the image" of its Creator. Hence, biblical exegesis concerning male-female differentiation when following Philo sometimes resulted in a trichotomic anthropology. Such an anthropology recognised the body's own specific physiology as completely antithetical to the spiritual realm and attributed to this spiritual component both the characteristic of "image" as well as male-female differentiation. Furthermore, this anthropology, concerned as it was exclusively with the spiritual realm, assigned greater value to certain components of this interior-spiritual dimension over others. Thus, when the symbol of "couple" or "pair" is applied to this interior dimension of the human being, the "male" element, identified as *pneuma* by Tatian and by Origen, as *nous* in *The Teachings of Silvanus*, is given a superior position over the "female" element, the *psyche*. It is this latter component which is normally considered responsible for weakness, for the proclivity toward the sensible (Tatian), for the willingness to allow itself to be overpowered by passions and by vice (Origen, *The Teachings of Silvanus*). Consequently, sexual differentiation considered as a means of explaining the interior structure of the human being was also intended to express hierarchical relation between its constitutive elements. In this way both the equilibrium of these elements and the consequent salvation of the human being could be explained only by virtue of such subordination. Moreover, the *eikon* character of human being appears both in Tatian and in the *Teachings of Silvanus*, once again following Philo's model, as the exclusive prerogative of the "male" element, *pneuma* or *nous*. It is owing precisely to this reasoning that these formulations are connected in their own way with the well-known tradition restricting the divine image to the male.[127]

Even Origen's anthropology, while not reducible to fixed and uniform patterns, maintains an ambivalence in the application of male-female symbolism to the spiritual side of the human being. He, too, relates the characteristic of "image" to the intelligent creature of the first creation (*nous*), but continues to apply that quality to the human *psyche* resulting from the "cooling down" of primordial intellect. Nevertheless, Origen willingly distinguishes the same two levels in the human soul: a superior part, the element which is *kat' eikona*, and which is called the *nous* in order to show continuity with the pre-existent creature, and an inferior part often defined as the "soul" as such. The latter is actually situated in a middle position between the superior part and weighty, terrestrial corporeality. Thus, the peculiar weakness of the *psyche* is dialectically connected to its "female" quality.

Also found in Origen is the tendency to focus attention on the dichotomy of elements which make up the human being by attributing the divine "image" to the spiritual, thus securing a complete incompatibility between that characteristic and the male-female differentiation located in the somatic element. It is, however, Gregory of Nyssa who most clearly represents this perspective. For Gregory, the specific and most characteristic quality of the human is individuated in affinity with God expressed by the biblical expression of creation "in the image and likeness." Sexual distinction is thus extraneous to "true" human nature, though it is attributed to a providential, creative act of God. Yet, in that radical inferiority as an *alogos* element which is typically "animal," it is perceived as a sort of outgrowth which attaches itself to the perfected creature-image during a transitory historical *diastema*.

Thus, sexual differentiation is viewed as totally alien from the perfection of the *arche*, the unique and definitive creative event which brought the *pleroma* of humanity as *eikon* into existence. Sexual differentiation as it presently exists is destined to vanish in the eschatological *telos* in which the perfected form of the human *pleroma* will be recovered in the unique *morphe* of Christ. In this perspective, sexual activity is recognised as legitimate within marriage which is itself seen as necessary for the human being's own historical progress. However, the role of *enkrateia* remains essential and normative. Owing to virginity and continence, indeed, the cycle of *genesis-phthora* started with fault and sexual differentiation is broken. In the *enkrateia* two "moments" of perfection are seen as converging: the perfection of human beginnings within divine intentionality, and that perfection realised in the eschatological *telos*, the *apokatastasis* of the original, integral beauty of the creature: "image" and "likeness" of God.

(1987)

Notes

1. It is understood that the primary definition given for this Greek term is expressed as "self-discipline" and "temperance," both of which meanings extend beyond the sexual sphere in which the term is employed here, See W. Grundmann, art. *enkrateia* in G. Kittel, *ThWNT,* 2 (1935) c. 337–341; P. Th. Camelot art. *ENΓKPATEIA (Continentia)* in *DSp* 4:1 (1960) c. 357–370; H. Chadwick, art. *Enkrateia* in *RAC* 5 (1962) c. 343–365. Nevertheless, even though early Christian writers such as Clement of Alexandria understood the broader meaning of the term (*Strom.* III, VII, 57,1–60,4; Stählin, 3th ed., p. 222(14)–224(9)), they normally restricted its application to sexuality.

2. The reader is referred to my detailed study of this question in *Enkrateia e*

antropologia. Le motivazioni protologiche della continenza e della verginità nel cristianesimo dei primi secoli e nello gnosticismo. Studia Ephemeridis "Augustinianum," 20, Roma: 1984. Cf. also *L'Epistula Titi de dispositione sanctimonii e la tradizione dell'*enkrateia in *ANRW* II, 25,6, Berlin-New York: 1988, p. 4551-4664. Highly significant as well are the results of an international conference on this topic edited by U. Bianchi, *La tradizione dell'enkrateia. Motivazioni ontologiche e protologiche. Atti del Colloquio Internazionale, Milano, 20-23 aprile 1982,* Roma: 1985. Further important observations on this theme are found in E. H. Pagels, *Adam and Eve, Christ and the Church: A Survey of Second Century Controversies Concerning Marriage* in A. H. B. Logan and A. J. M. Wedderburn, eds., *The New Testament and Gnosis: Essays in Honour of Robert McL. Wilson,* Edinburgh: 1983, p. 146-175.

3. See F. Bolgiani, *La tradizione eresiologica sull'encratismo. I. Le notizie di Ireneo* in AAST 91 (1956-57) 343-419.

4. For these authors and texts consult my book *Enkrateia,* p. 23-79.

5. G. Sfameni Gasparro, *Enkrateia,* p. 87-101. For the *Gospel of Thomas* included in the Nag Hammadi discoveries and its complex problems of interpretation, consult ibid., p. 79-87. The theme of "unity" sometimes expressed by the term *monachos* constitutes in this text one of the nerve centers of religious reflection on the human being and its destiny. The theme is not connected with the biblical concept of "image" and therefore not directly related to the problem under consideration here. However, one ought not lose sight of the essential role which the theme of the duality of the sexes plays in the discussion of *monachos,* especially as regards the abrogation of that duality in the "unification" brought about once salvation is fully realised. Among the more relevant studies (see my *Enkrateia,* p. 79-87 for a fuller listing) are A. F. J. Klijn, "The 'Single One' in the Gospel of Thomas," *JBL* 81 (1962) 271-278; the magisterial work of H. Ch. Puech, *En quête de la gnose. II. Sur l'Évangile selon Thomas: Esquisse d'une interprétation systematique,* Paris: 1978: and J. J. Buckley, "An Interpretation of Logion 114 in the Gospel of Thomas," *NT* 27 (1985) 245-272. Buckley does not allow that the thematic of "unity" consisting in the transformation of woman into man and the insistence upon the inferiority of women expresses encratite tendencies. See also her *Female Fault and Fulfillment in Gnosticism,* Chapel Hill, NC: 1986, p. 84-104.

6. Among these are *Physiologus* and the tractate *De centesima, sexagesima, tricesima.* See my *Enkrateia,* p. 101-108.

7. Sfameni Gasparro, *Enkrateia,* p. 115-166.

8. Consult E. Peterson, "L'origine dell'ascesi cristiana," *Euntes Docete* 1 (1948) 195-204 (=*Frühkirche, Judentum und Gnosis. Studien und Untersuchungen,* Roma-Freiburg-Wien: 1959, p. 209-220; P. Nagel, *Die Motivierung der Askese in der alten Kirche und der Ursprung des Mönchtums,* (TU 95) Berlin: 1966, p. 2-55; Ton H. C. van Eijk, "Marriage and Virginity, Death and Immortality," in J. Fontaine and C. Kannengiesser, eds., *Epektasis. Mélanges patristiques offerts au*

Cardinal Jean Daniélou, Paris: 1972, p. 209-235. On the relationship between eschatology and sexuality in general, see B. Lang, "No Sex in Heaven: the Logic of Procreation, Death and Eternal Life in the Judaeo-Christian Tradition," *Alter Orient und altes Testament* 215 (1985) 237-253.

9. For the definition of this notion consult U. Bianchi, "La 'doppia creazione' dell' uomo come oggetto di ricerca storico-religiosa in id., editor, *La 'doppia creazione' dell'uomo negli Alessandrini, nei Cappadoci e nella gnosi,* Roma: 1978, p. 1-23.

10. For the exegetical history of Gen. 1,26, one of the key interpretative texts for early Christian and Jewish anthropologies, see A. Strucker, *Die Gottebenbildlichkeit des Menschen in der christlichen Literatur der ersten zwei Jahrhunderte. Ein Beitrag zur Geschichte der Exegese von Genesis 1,26,* Münster: 1913; R. McL. Wilson, "The Early History of the Exegesis of Genesis 1,26" in K. Aland and F. L. Cross, eds., *Studia Patristica,* 1 (TU 63), Berlin: 1957, p. 420-437; J. Jervell, *Imago Dei. Gen. 1,26 f. im Spätjudentum, in der Gnosis und in den paulinischen Briefen* (FRLANT 76, N. F. 58), Göttingen: 1960; P. Schwanz, *Imago Dei als christologisch-anthropologisches Problem in der Geschichte der Alten Kirche von Paulus bis Clemens von Alexandrien,* Göttingen: 1970. Consult also the research of H. Willms on Philo and his Platonic presuppositions: *EIKΩN Eine begriffsgeschichtliche Untersuchung zum Platonismus. I. Teil. Philon von Alexandreia. Mit einer Einleitung über Platon und die Zwischenzeit,* Münster: 1935. For Greek patristic authors in addition to these works: A. Meyer, *Das Bild Gottes im Menschen nach Clemens von Alexandrien,* Roma: 1942; R. Bernard, *L'image de Dieu d'après saint Athanase,* Theologie 25, Paris: 1952; and W. J. Burghardt, *The image of God according to Cyril of Alexandria,* Washington, D.C. and Woodstock, MD: 1957, see as well H. C. Graf, "L'image de Dieu et la structure de l'âme d'après les Pères grecs," *La vie spirituelle* Suppl. 22 (1955) 331-339; P. Th. Camelot, "La théologie de l'image de Dieu," *RScPhT* 40 (1956) 443-471; and, most importantly for the Alexandrian authors, W. J. Burghardt, "The Image of God in Man: Alexandrian Orientations," *The Catholic Theological Society of America. Proceedings of the Sixteenth Annual Convention.* Ottawa, Ontario (June 19-22, 1961) 147-160. As for Latin patristics, above all Augustine, a considerable amount of research has recently been published among the most important of which are: J. E. Sullivan. *The Image of God. The Doctrine of St. Augustine and its Influence.* London: 1963, and the more recent writings of G. Bonner, "Augustine's Doctrine of Man: Image of God and Sinner," *Augustinianum* 24 (1984) 495-514; and K. E. Børresen, "Imago Dei, privilège masculin? Interprétation augustinienne et pseudo-augustinienne de Gen. 1,27 et 1 Cor 11,7," *Augustinianum* 25 (1985) 213-234.

11. G. Sfameni Gasparro, *Enkrateia,* p. 23-56; 65-70.

12. These are given by Irenaeus in *Adv. Haer.* I,28,1 apud Eusebius, *Hist. eccl.* IV,29,2-3; *SCh* 264 (A. Roussel – P. Doutreleau) vol. 1:2, 354-357; *Adv. Haer.* III,23,8 *SCh* 211 (A. Roussel – L. Doutreleau) vol. 3:2, 466-469 and by Clement

of Alexandria (*Strom.* III,XII,79,1-85,2; Stählin, ed., p. 231, 1.16 – p. 235,1.20).
F. Bolgiani raises the possibility that other of Clement's arguments relative to
encratites reflect Tatian's positions even without their being explicitly mentioned. See Bolgiani, "La tradizione, II. La confutazione di Clemente di Alessandria," *AAST* 96 (1961-62) 537-664.

13. Consult G. Sfameni Gasparro, "Protologia ed encratismo: esempi di esegesi
     encratita di Gen. 1-3," *Augustinianum* 22:1-2 (1982) 75-89.

14. *Oratio* 7,1-3 in M. Whittaker, ed., *Tatian. Oratio ad Graecos and Fragments,*
     Oxford: 1982, p. 12-15. For an interpretation and French translation of Tatian's
     work, see A. Puech, *Recherches sur le Discours aux Grecs de Tatien,* Paris:
     1903.

15. Tatian, *Oratio* 12,1-13,2; Whittaker, p. 22-27.

16. Tatian, *Oratio* 13,3; Whittaker, p. 26-29. Cf. *Oratio* 11,2 (p. 22f.) where Tatian
     invites the reader to "die to the world, rejecting its madness" in order to live for
     God by putting aside "the old generation." In *Oratio* 20,2-3 (p. 40-43) he claims
     that it is possible for everyone to regain "the ancient relationship" between the
     soul and the spirit which will confer immortality upon the *psyche.*

17. *Oratio,* 20,1; Whittaker, p. 40-41.

18. *Oratio,* 20,1-2; Whittaker, p. 40-41.

19. Various Jewish and Christian speculations concerning celestial paradise are
     examined by J.-B. Frey, "L'État originel et la chute de l'homme. D'après les con-
     ceptions juives au temps de J.-C.," *RScPhTh* 5 (1911) 507-545; H. Bietenhard,
     Die himmlische Welt im Urchristentum und Spätjudentum, Tübingen: 1951, p.
     161-191; I. De Vuippens, *Le Paradis terrestre au troisième ciel. Exposé his-
     torique d'une conception chrétienne des premiers siècles,* Paris-Fribourg: 1925;
     E. Cothenet, art. "Paradis" in *DB Suppl.* VI, Paris: 1960, c. 1177-1220. Paradisi-
     acal symbols in patristic literature are examined by J. Daniélou, "Terre et Paradis
     chez les Pères de l'Église," in *EJb* 22 (1953) 433-472.

20. apud Clement of Alexandria, *Strom.* III, XIII,93,3; Stählin, p. 239, 1. 5-7. The
     author here affirms that the soul "being divine . . . having become female, fell
     downward from on high toward generation and corruption on account of its
     desire (*epithymia*)." *Strom.* III, XIV,95,2 (p. 239, 1. 26): "Cassianus thinks that
     the 'tunics of skin' are bodies."

21. *Strom.* III, XII,81,1-2; Stählin, ed., p. 232, 23-29.

22. *Oratio,* 15,1-3; Whittaker, ed., p. 28-31.

23. P. 84,16-21. Y. Janssens, ed., *Les leçons de Silvanos* (NH VII,4), Bibliothèque
     copte de Nag Hammadi – Section "Textes" 13, Québec-Louvain: p. 26f. English
     translation: M. L. Peel and J. Zandee, *The Teachings of Silvanus* (VII,4) in J. M.
     Robinson, ed., *The Nag Hammadi Library in English,* Leiden 1977, p. 346-361
     (1988[3] p. 379-395). On the ascetical tendencies of the work, see J. Zandee, "La
     morale des 'Enseignements de Silvian," *OrLovPer* 6/7 (1975-76) 615-630, and,
     more recently, Y. Janssens, "Les leçons de Silvanos et le monachisme" in H. Barc,
     ed., *Colloque international sur les Textes de Nag Hammadi (Québec: 22-25*

août 1978), Bibliothèque copte de Nag Hammadi Section "Etudes" 1, Québec-Louvain: 1981, p. 352-361.

24. Note the insistent call to return to one's proper "divine nature" through a repudiation of ignorance and passionate desires (P. 90,29f.; Janssens, ed., *Les leçons de Silvanos*, p. 38-39) and to protect the "divine which is within you" intended to inspire the reader to maintain "holiness" and "temperance" in soul and body (P. 91,34-92,6; Janssens, ibid., p. 40-43). See also P. 94,25-33 (p. 47-48) in which Silvanus exorts his interlocutors, telling them that as they are conscious of having been "born in the bridal chamber" they ought not to permit themselves to be "defiled by alien knowledge." This affirmation, coupled with the image of an "entering" into corporeal creaturehood and with the invitation to allow oneself to be illuminated by the intellect, calls to mind the Gnostic doctrine of the soul's divine origin. Nevertheless, the work does not seem to reflect a peculiarly Gnostic structural dualism. À propos see J. Zandee, "Die Lehren des Silvanus" also "Teil der Schriften von Nag Hammadi und der Gnostizismus" in M. Krause, ed., *Essays on the Nag Hammadi Texts in Honour of Pahor Labib* (NHS VI) Leiden: 1975, p. 239-252.

25. P. 92,25-27; Janssens, ed., *Les leçons de Silvanos*, p. 42-43; Peel-Zandee, p. 350,384[3].

26. P. 92,15-18; Janssens, ed., *Les leçons de Silvanos*, p. 42-43; Peel-Zandee, p. 350, 384[3].

27. Among the principal references in Philo proposing the distinction between biblical accounts concerned with "double creation" are *De op.* 69 and 134, and *Leg. All.* I,31 and 54. See C. Kannengiesser, *Philon et les Pères sur la double création de l'homme in Philon d'Alexandrie, Lyon: 11-15 Septembre 1966.* Colloques Nationaux du Centre National de la Recherche Scientifique, Paris: 1967, p. 277-296; A. M. Mazzanti, "L'aggettivo ΜΕΘΟΡΙΟΣ e la doppia creazione dell'uomo in Filone di Alessandria" in U. Bianchi, ed., *La 'doppia creazione'*, p. 25-42. On Philo's notion of "image" see H. Willms and I. Giblet, "L'homme image de Dieu dans les commentaires littéraux de Philon d'Alexandrie," *Studia Hellenistica* 5 (1948) 93-118. For further observations on Philo's anthropology in connection with *enkrateia* see my book *Enkrateia*, p. 323-341. While no evidence of any direct dependence of the latter upon the former is suggested, the use by Philo and *Silvanus* of Greek philosophers, especially Stoic and Platonic, in framing their respective biblical exegeses demonstrates some similarities. For a detailed analysis of a series of analogies between the two authors, see J. Zandee, "Les Enseignements de Silvanos et Philon d'Alexandrie," in *Mélanges d'histoire des religions offerts à Henri-Charles Puech*, Paris: 1974, p. 337-345. The author concludes that Silvanus most likely belongs within an Alexandrian theological ambient. On this possibility, consult J. Zandee, "'The Teaching of Silvanus' and Clement of Alexandria. A New Document of Alexandrian Theology," *Ex Oriente Lux.* Leiden: 1977.

28. P. 92,19-25; Janssens, ed., *Les leçons de Silvanos*, p. 42-43; Peel-Zandee, p. 350,384[3].

29. Cf. P. 93,3-5; Janssens, ed., *Les leçons de Silvanos*, p. 44-45; Peel-Zandee, p. 350: "Live according to the mind. Do not think about things belonging to the flesh. Acquire strength, for the mind is strong."

30. P. 93,24-94,22; Janssens, ed., *Les leçons de Silvanos*, p. 44-47; Peel-Zandee, p. 351, 385[3].

31. P. 92,29-31; Janssens, ed., *Les leçons de Silvanos*, p. 42-43; Peel-Zandee, p. 350: . . . For I think that it (i.e. the soul) exists as wife of that which has come into being in conformity with the image."

32. P. 93,7-21; Janssens, ed., *Les leçons de Silvanos*, p. 44-45; Peel-Zandee, p. 350-351, 384-385[3]: "If you fall from this other, you have become male-female. And if you cast out of yourself the substance of the mind, which is thought, you have cut off the male part and turned yourself to the female part alone. You have become psychic since you have received the substance of the formed. If also you cast out the smallest part of this so that you do not acquire again a human part but you have accepted for yourself the animal thought and likeness you have become fleshly since you have taken on animal nature."

33. Consult R. A. Baer, *Philo's Use of the Categories Male and Female*, Arbeiten zur Literatur und Geschichte des hellenistischen Judentums III, Leiden: 1970.

34. Cf. P. 104,31-105,26; Janssens, ed., *Les leçons de Silvanos*, p. 66-69 Peel-Zandee, p. 355, 389[3].

35. See H.-M. Schenke. *Der Gott "Mensch" in der Gnosis. Ein religionsgeschichtlicher Beitrag zur Discussion über die paulinische Anschauung von der Kirche als Leib Christi*, Göttingen: 1962. One particular biblical exegesis influenced by Simon Magus' circle is examined by J. Frickel, "Eine neue Deutung von Gen. 1,26 in der Gnosis," in *Ex orbe religionum. Studia Geo Widengren*, Leiden: 1972, vol. I, 413-423. On this theme consult as well G. Filoramo, "Aspetti del mito della creazione dell'uomo nello gnosticismo del II secolo," *Memorie dell'Accademia delle Scienze di Torino, Cl. Sc. Mor., Stor. e Fil.*, S. 4a, 35 (1977) 1-57.

36. Recall the Valentinian exegesis referred to by Irenaeus and substantially confirmed by the *Excerpta* of Theodotus whereby the human being "in the image" corresponds to the material soul while the human being "in the likeness" corresponds to the psychic (*Adv. Haer.* I,5,5; cf. *Exc. Th.* 50,1-3; *SCh* 23[2] (F. Sagnard) 162-165). These two inferior elements which correspond to the two "categories" of human beings are distinguished from the pneumatic substance coming from the divine Pleroma (Irenaeus, *Adv. Haer.* I,5,6; *Exc. Th.* 54,1-2; p. 168f.). Clement of Alexandria allows that the Valentinians identified the element which was κατ᾽ εἰκόνα with the psychic substance, whereas the καθ᾽ ὁμοίωσιν was the divine, spiritual seed (*Strom.* IV, XIII, 90,2-4; Stählin; p. 287,27-288,9).

37. Irenaeus, *Adv. Haer.* I,24,1-2; Rousseau-Doutreleau, eds., p. 320-325.

38. M. Tardieu offers a useful outline of the various editions of this text contained in the Codices of Nag Hammadi (CG II 1,1-32,9; CG III 1,1-40,11 and CG IV 1,1-49, 28) and in the *Cod. Berol.* 5082 (19,6-77,9) along with a translation and

commentary on the Gnostic tractates contained in the latter codex in his work *Écrits gnostiques. Codex de Berlin,* Paris: 1984.

39. For this text see B. Barc, *L'Hypostase des Archontes. Traité gnostique sur l'origine de l'homme du monde et des archontes* NH 11,4, Bibliothèque copte de Nag Hammadi Section "Textes" 5, Québec-Louvain: 1980.

40. In both tractates the theme of Eve's seduction by the Demiurge and Archons is present. This is due to the fact that the radical negativity of marriage and physical generation was emphasised in terms of both being inaugurated by aggressive, violent persons. See my *Enkrateia,* p. 117-139.

41. See *The Hypostasis of the Archons* (HA) P. 87,26-33; B. Barc, ed., p. 52-53. A useful synopsis of the anthropological narratives of the *AJ,* the *HA* and the *Tractate on the Origin of the World* is also given by Barc (p. 7-14). On this last work cited, see M. Tardieu, *Trois mythes gnostiques. Adam, Éros et les animaux d'Égypte dans un écrit de Nag Hammadi* (II, 5), Paris: 1974.

42. *Apocryphon Johannis* (AJ), B 47,14-49,9; CG III 21,16-22,18; CG II 14,13-15, 13 in M. Tardieu, *Codex,* p. 120-123. See also *HA* P. 87,1-23 (Barc, p. 52-53). The theme, already present in the "archaic" system of Saturninus, recurs frequently in various Gnostic systems.

43. *AJ* B 58,8-63,12; CG III 28,23-32,6; CG II 22,15-24,34 in M. Tardieu, *Codex,* p. 140-147; *HA* P. 89,3-91,11 (Barc, p. 56-61).

44. For the various accepted meanings of the motif consult E. L. Dietrich, "Der Urmensch als Androgyn," *ZKG* 58 (1939) 297-345; W. A. Meeks, "The Image of the Androgyne: Some Uses of a Symbol in earliest Christianity," *HR* 13 (1974) 165-208; M. Delcourt, "Utrumque-Neutrum" in *Mélanges d'histoire des religions offerts à Henri-Charles Puech, op. cit.,* p. 117-123.

45. Hippolytus, *Ref.* V, 7,7-15; GCS 26 (P. Wendland) 80-82.

46. Hippolytus, *Ref.* V, 8,4 (p. 89).

47. Hippolytus, *Ref.* V, 7,14 (p. 82).

48. Hippolytus, *Ref.* V, 8,33 (p. 95).

49. See above, n. 27.

50. The Logos as the "Image" of God, where "image" is the "true human being" or intellect, is found in Clement's *Protr.* X, 98,4; Stählin, ed., p. 71,24 ff.; *Strom.* III, 5,42,6 (p. 215,23-25); V, 94,5 (p. 388,14ff). In Clement, reference to *nous* as the biblical image is accompanied by explicit negation of *eikon* as an attribute of the body: *Strom.* II, 19,102 (p. 169, 16-21); VI, 14,114,4 (p. 489,14f.).

51. For Origen's critique of the anthropomorphic interpretation of Gen. 1,26, see *SelGen; PG* 12,93 A-96 A; *HomGen* I, 13; *SCh* 7 bis (H. de Lubac – L. Doutreleau) 58-59; *DialHer* 12; *SCh* 67 (J. Scherer) 80-81; *CoRom* I, 19; *PG* 14,871 A-872 A; *CCel* VI, 63; *SCh* 147 (M. Borret) 3:334-339.

52. For an extensive analysis of Origen's doctrine with its christological and anthropological applications, see H. Crouzel, *Théologie de l'image de Dieu chez Origène,* Paris: 1956.

53. For a detailed, documented presentation of this notion in Origen with particular

162 Giulia Sfameni Gasparro

reference to "double creation," the reader is referred to a number of my essays on the subject collected in *Origene. Studi di antropologia e di storia della tradizione*, Roma: 1984. A complete listing of the rich bibliography on Origen is offered by H. Crouzel, *Bibliographie critique d'Origène*, Instrumenta Patristica VIII. Hagae Comitis: 1971; Supplément I, Instrumenta Patristica VIII A, Hagae Comitis: 1982.

54. See in particular, *PArch* II, 3,1-7; *GCS* 22 (P. Koetschau) 106-112 and *SCh* 252 (H. Crouzel and M. Simonetti) 1:248-275; *PArch* III, 6,1-9; Koetschau, p. 279-291; *SCh* 268 (Crouzel-Simonetti), 3:234-255.
55. See H. Cornelis, "Les fondements cosmologiques de l'eschatologie d'Origène," *RScPhTh* 43 (1959) 32-80 and 201-247; M. Alexandre, "Le statut des questions concernant la matière dans le *Peri Archôn* in H. Crouzel, G. Lomiento and J. Ruis-Camps, eds., *Origeniana*. Premier colloque international des études origéniennes. Montserrat, 18-21 septembre 1973, Quaderni di Vetera Christianorum 12, Bari: 1975, p. 63-81; D. G. Bostock, "Quality and Corporeity in Origen," in H. Crouzel and A. Quacquarelli, eds., *Origeniana secunda*. Second colloque international des études origéniennes. Bari, 20-23 septembre 1977, Quaderni di Vetera Christianorum 15, Roma: 1980, p. 323-337.
56. *CoJoh* XX, 22(20), 182; *SCh* 290 (C. Blanc) 4:248-249.
57. *HomGen* I, 13; Doutreleau, p. 56-57.
58. *PArch* II, 8,3; Koetschau, p. 155,7-161,15; Crouzel-Simonetti, p. 344-347.
59. See *SelGen; PG* 12,96 A-C.
60. *PArch* II, 10,7; Koetschau, p. 181,13-19; Crouzel-Simonetti, p. 390-393
61. On Origen's doctrine of the spirit see J. Dupuis, *"L'esprit de l'homme." Étude sur l'anthropologie religieuse d'Origène*, Paris-Bruges: 1967, along with the observations of H. Crouzel, "Une nouvelle étude de l'anthropologie d'Origène," *BLE* 68 (1967) 273-277.
62. *HomGen* I, 14; Doutreleau, p. 64-67: Origen allows for this exegesis *secundum litteram* as long as it anticipates a future creation of the woman and of matrimonial blessing, *quoniam quidem crescere aliter et multiplicari non poterat homo, nisi cum femina.*
63. *HomGen* I, 15; Doutreleau, p. 66-67.
64. *HomGen* I, 15; Doutreleau, p. 66-67.
65. *HomGen* I, 15; Doutreleau, p. 66-69.
66. Consult the interpretation of these notions presented in my study "Le sordes (/rhupos), il rapporto genesis-phthorà e le motivazioni protologiche dell' enkrateia in Origene," in my book *Origene*, p. 193-252.
67. *CoRom* V, 9; *PG* 14,1046 B-1047 C.
68. *Fr. XXIX I Cor* in C. Jenkins, "Origen on I Corinthians. II," *JThS* 9 (1907-1908) 370,1-371,2.
69. *loc. cit.*
70. The concept of marriage as God's merciful "concession" to the weakness of a fallen humanity and its basis in a specific exegesis of 1 Cor. 7 extends through-

out the entire patristic tradition in various approaches wherever interest in the protological motivations of *enkrateia* is found. See my work *Enkrateia, passim,* for references.

71. H. Crouzel offers a detailed analysis of Origen's position on this theme in *Virginité et mariage selon Origène,* Paris-Bruges: 1962.

72. Among the numerous places in Origen's writings where, in contrast to the "corruption" inherent in sexual activity, *parthenia, katharotes* and *aphtharsia* are closely linked, are the following: *Fr. I Cor XVI* in Jenkins, *Origen,* p. 246,30–38; *"Fr. Eph.* XXXVII" in J. A. F. Gregg, *JThS* 3 (1901-1902) 576,11-25.

73. See H. Crouzel, "La doctrine origénienne du corps ressuscité," *BLE* 81 (1980) 175-200; 241-286 where the principal interpretations are presented.

74. *CoMt* VII, 35 *GCS* 40:2 (E. Benz and E. Klostermann) 698,33-699,12.

75. *CoMt* XVII, 30; p. 670,8-671,21.

76. On the terms of the debate between these two figures with respect to their respective Latin versions of Origen's tractate, consult my study "Aspetti della controversia origeniana: le traduzioni latine del *Peri Archon," Augustinianum* 26 (1968) 191-205.

77. *Apol.* I, 24; *CCL* 20 (M. Simonetti) 58,14-22: "In tertio commentariorum libro in epistula Pauli ad Ephesios, sub eo capitulo ubi scriptum est: *Qui uxorem suam diligit, seipsum diligit; nemo enim umquam carnem suam odio habuit,* post aliquanta ita ait: "Foveamus igitur et uiri uxores nostras, ut animae nostrae corpora, ut et uxores in uiros et corpora redigantur in animas, et nequaquam sit sexuum ulla diuersitas: sed quomodo apud angelos non est uir et mulier, ita et nos, qui similes angelis futuri sumus, iam nunc incipiamus esse quod nobis in caelestibus repromissum est."

78. Jerome, *Apol.* 1,28; *SCh* 303 (P. Lardet) 76-77. The passage cited by Jerome as coming from Origen's lost commentary contains expressions already included within his own without any indication of their source (later identified by Rufinus). It also contains a series of warnings over the care which the soul should exercise in relation to the body since this latter also is destined for resurrection. Jerome acknowledged his "debt" to Origen in the prologue to his own commentary where he stated that he had made use of Origen's *tria volumina* on the Pauline letter only *ex parte* (PL 26,472 B).

79. For the protological motivations for *enkrateia* as they appear in Jerome, see my *Enkrateia,* p. 290-300. I would add only that in a passage of *Adversus Iovinianum* the theme of continence is linked significantly with the *imago Dei* motif in as much as the author states: "*Imago Creatoris non habet copulam nuptiarum. Ubi diversitas sexus aufertur, et veteri homini exuimus, et induimus novo, ibi in Christum renascimur virgines." Adv. Iov.* 1,16; *PL* 23,246A.

80. *EvTh* 114 in A. Guillaumont, H. C. Puech, G. Quispel and W. Till-Yassah 'Abd al Masih, *The Gospel according to Thomas,* Leiden-London: 1959, p. 56-57: "Simon Peter said to them: Let Mary go out from among us, because women are not worthy of the life. Jesus said: See, I shall lead her so that I will make her

male, that she too may become a living spirit, resembling you males. For every woman who makes herself male will enter the kingdom of Heaven."

81. *CoMt* XIV, 16 (p. 321,23-322,22).

82. *CoMt* XIV, 17 (p. 325,27-32). Cf. XVII, 34 (p. 695,12-22).

83. J. B. Schoemann, "Gregors von Nyssa theologische Anthropologie als Bildtheologie," *Scholastik* 18 (1943) 31-53 and 175-200; J. T. Muckle, "The Doctrine of St. Gregory of Nyssa on Man as the Image of God," *MS* 7 (1954) 55-84; R. Leys, *L'image de Dieu chez Saint Grégoire de Nysse. Esquisse d'une doctrine*, Bruxelles-Paris: 1951.

84. H. F. Cherniss, *The Platonism of Gregory of Nyssa*, New York: 1930, 1971²; J. Daniélou, *Platonisme et théologie mystique. Doctrine spirituelle de Saint Grégoire de Nysse*, Théologie 2, Paris: 1944²; A. H. Armstrong, "Platonic Elements in St. Gregory of Nyssa's Doctrine of Man," *DSt* 1 (1948) 113-126; G. B. Ladner, "The Philosophical Anthropology of Saint Gregory of Nyssa," *DOP* 12 (1958) 59-94.

85. See U. Bianchi, "Presupposti platonici e dualistici nell'antropologia di Gregorio di Nissa in id., editor, *La doppia creazione*, 83-115; idem, "L'intention du Colloque. Analyse historico-religieuse" in U. Bianchi and H. Crouzel, eds., *Arché e Telos. L'antropologia di Origene e di Gregorio di Nissa. Analisi storico-religiosa*, Atti del Colloquio, Milano, 17-19 maggio 1979, Milano 1981, p. 9-27. Interesting observations on Gregory's anthropology are made by E. Corsini, "Plérôme humain et plérôme cosmique chez Grégoire de Nysse" in M. Harl, ed., *Écriture et culture philosophique dans la pensée de Grégoire de Nysse*, Actes du Colloque de Chevetogne (22-26 septembre 1969), Leiden: 1971, p. 111-126; idem, "L'harmonie du monde et l'homme microcosme dans le De hominis opificio," in J. Fontaine and C. Kannengiesser, eds., *Epektasis*, p. 455-462. For an analysis of the theme of creation "in the image" of God expressed in Gregory's tractate, see M. Naldini, "Per un'esegesi del "De hominis opificio" di Gregorio Nisseno (Cap. V e XVI)," *SIFC* n. s. 45 (1973) 88-123.

86. J. Gribomont, "Le Panégyrique de la virginité, oeuvre de jeunesse de Grégoire de Nysse, *RAM* 43 (1967) 249-266. For an analysis of this work see J. Stiglmayr, "Die Schrift des hl. Gregor von Nyssa 'Über die Jungfräulichkeit,'" *ZAM* 2 (1927) 334-359. For consideration of the problems of chronology in Gregory's life and works, consult J. Daniélou, "La chronologie des Sermons de Grégoire de Nysse," *RevSR* 29 (1955) 346-372; "Le mariage de Grégoire de Nysse et la chronologie de sa vie," *REAug* 2 (1956) 71-78; "La chronologie des oeuvres de Grégoire de Nysse," in F. L. Cross, ed., *Studia Patristica* VII, Part I (TU 92), Berlin: 1966, p. 159-169; "Orientations actuelles de la recherche sur Grégoire de Nysse," in M. Harl, ed., *Écriture*, p. 3-17; G. May, "Die Chronologie des Lebens und der Werke des Gregors von Nyssa," in M. Harl, ed., *Écriture*, p. 51-66.

87. The tension between the quality of "image" which implies an affinity with God through participation in the good, and the present condition of imperfection and misery which seems to contradict radically the biblical notion is once again

emphasised in the *Oratio catechetica*. This work focuses on the theme of liberty, the prerogative characteristic of the rational creature, on the problem of the origin of evil and on the theme of the intrinsic mutability of the creature itself (V, 1-VII, 4; *PG* 45, 20 D-32 D; cf. VIII, 1-20 *PG* 45 33 A-40 C). See J. Gaith, *La conception de la liberté chez Grégoire de Nysse*, Paris: 1953. On the affinity between the soul and God based upon creation "in the image," see a passage from *De mortuis* (*PG* 46,509 C-512 C; *GNO* IX, p. 41-43) where the divine attributes in which the soul participates (viz., intelligibility, immateriality, invisibility, incorporeality and intangibility: c. 509 C-D; *GNO*, p. 41-42) are enunciated and where the prospect of the final destiny of the creature is presented. The rational creature will lose its body at death just as if a "mask" (*prosopeion*) were taken off in order to draw nearer to that beauty "in which we were formed in the beginning having been made in the image of the archetype" (c. 512 A-B; *GNO* p. 42). In fact, Gregory concludes, the goal of the passage through the various phases of corporeal life is the *apokatastasis* toward the former condition which is nothing other than likeness to God (c. 520 D; *GNO*, p. 51). See also *In Ps* II, XII; *PG* 44,557 C; *GNO* V, p. 130): "The character proper to the human being is likeness to God"; *In Eccl. Hom.* I; *PG* 44,642 B; *GNO* V, p. 284: "The characteristic proper to the human being and conforming to nature is life made similar to divine nature." On this theme, see D. L. Balas, *ΜΕΤΟΥΣΙΑ ΘΕΟΥ. Man's Participation in God's Perfections according to Saint Gregory of Nyssa*, Studia Anselmiana 55. Rome: 1966.

88. See P. Pisi, *Genesis e phthorà. Le motivazioni protologiche della verginita in Gregorio di Nissa e nella tradizione dell'enkrateia*, Roma: 1981. For Gregory's notion of sin and its relationship with sexual differentiation, see E. V. McClear, "The Fall of Man and Original Sin in the Theology of Gregory of Nyssa," *ThS* 9 (1949) 175-212; F. Floëri, "Le sens de la 'division des sexes' chez Grégoire de Nysse," *EstEcl* 45 (1970) 203-235. This notion has influenced the anthropologies of such authors as Maximus Confessor and John Scotus Eriugena in whom the peculiar structure of "double creation" persists. Consult à propos my study "Aspetti di 'doppia creazione' nell'antropologia di Massimo il Confesseore," *Studia Patristica* VIII/I, Papers of the Ninth International Conference on Patristic Studies, Oxford 1983, Kalamazoo: 1985, p. 127-134, and amplified in *Studi in onore di S. Constanza*, Messina: 1991, p. 461-501; E. Jeauneau, "La division des sexes chez Grégoire de Nysse et chez Jean Scot Érigène," in W. Beierwalters, ed., *Eriugena*. Studien zu seinen Quellen. Vorträge des III. Internationalen Eriugena-Colloquiums Freiburg im Breisgau, 27.-30. August 1979 (Abh. Heid. Akad. Wiss., Philos-hist. Kl., Jahrg. 1980-3), Heidelberg: 1980, p. 33-54. See also M. Naldini, "Gregorio Nisseno e Giovanni Scoto Eriugena. Note sull'idea di creazione e sull'antropologia," *Studi Medievali*, S. III, 20 (1979) 501-533.

89. *De virg.* XII, 2; *SCh* 119 (M. Aubineau) 398-401. Other editions of the tractate in *GNO* VIII, 1:215-343 as well as W. Blum, *Gregor von Nyssa. Über das Wesen des christlichen Bekenntnisses. Über die Vollkommenheit. Über die Jungfräulich-*

keit. Bibliothek der griechischen Literatur 7, Stuttgart: 1977, p. 18–41 and 81–153.

90. *SCh* 119, p. 401–403. Cf. *De hom. op.* XI; *PG* 44,156A. Translated by J. Laplace, *SCh* 6, p. 122; *De hom. op.* XII; *PG* 44, 161 C (Laplace, p. 131).

91. *SCh* 119, p. 402–411. On the fundamental notion of *pathe* as an element extraneous to the quality of "image" and as a consequence of sin, consult *De beat. Or.* VI; *PG* 44,1269 B–1273 C, in particular c. 1273A; *In Ps. I,* VIII; *PG* 44,473 A–C; *GNO* V, p. 58–59; *In Ps. II,* XI; *PG* 44,544 A–545 B; *GNO* V, p. 116–118; *In Ps. II,* XII; *PG* 44,557 D–560A; *GNO* V, p. 130–131 where, on the basis of Ps. 48 (49), 13–21, the passions are defined as an animal prerogative assumed by human beings as sinners who had lost consciousness of their own dignity. See *De beat. Or.* V; *PG* 44,1257 D where the assumption of *pathe* is parallel with the loss of the original angelic condition and the fall toward "animal life."

92. For Gregory's notion of paradise see E. F. Sutcliffe, "St. Gregory of Nyssa and Paradise," *EcclRev* S. IX,4 (= 84) (1931) 337–350.

93. See J. Daniélou, *Platonisme,* p. 48–60; idem, "La colombe et la ténèbre dans la mystique byzantine ancienne," *EJb* 23 (1954) 390–393; "Les tuniques de peau chez Grégoire de Nysse," in *Glaube, Geist, Geschichte. Festschrift für E. Benz,* Leiden: 1967, p. 355–367. A history of this theme is given in P. F. Beatrice, "Le Tuniche di pelle. Antiche letture di Gen. 3,21," in U. Bianchi, ed., *La tradizione,* p. 433–482.

94. One of the texts which best clarifies this notion is the tractate *De anima et resurrectione,* in which a strong Platonic influence can be detected. See M. Pellegrino, "Il platonismo di San Gregorio Nisseno nel dialogo 'Intorno all'anima e alla resurrezione,'" *Rivista die Filosofia Neo-scolastica* 30 (1938) 437–474.

95. Thus, for example, on Athanasius and John Chrysostom, see my book *Enkrateia,* p. 202–212 and 249–253. For Chrystosom's doctrine of "image" in terms of male-female differentiation, see S. Zincone, *Il tema dell'uomo/donna immagine di Dio nei Commenti paolini e a Gn di area antiochena (Diodoro, Crisotomo, Teodoro, Teodoreto)* = Annali di Storia dell'Esegesi 2 (1985) 103–113.

96. See J. Daniélou, "ΑΚΟΛΟΥΘΙΑ chez Grégoire de Nysse," *RevSR* 27 (1953) 219–249; idem, *L'être et le temps chez Grégoire de Nysse,* Leiden: 1970, p. 18–50.

97. *De virg.* XII, 7; Aubineau, p. 420–21.

98. *De virg.* XIII, 1–XIV, 1; Aubineau, p. 422–437.

99. *De hom. op.* XVI; *PG* 44,180 A–C; *SCh* 6, p. 152–153. Cf. *De hom. op.* XX; *PG* 44,201A; *SCh* 6, p. 179.

100. *De hom. op.* XX; *PG* 44,181A; *SCh* 6, p. 154.

101. *De hom. op.* XX; *PG* 44,181 A–B; *SCh* 6, p. 154–155. English translation by H. A. Wilson, *Select Writings and Letters of Gregory, Bishop of Nyssa,* LPNF ser. 2, vol. 5, p. 405. Cf. *De hom. op.* XX; *PG* 44,181 C–D; *SCh* 6, p. 155–156.

102. *De hom. op.* XX; *PG* 44,184 A–D; *SCh* 6, p. 156–158.

103. *De hom. op.* XVI; *PG* 44,185 A–D; *SCh* 6,158–161; *De hom. op.* XVII; *PG* 44,188 A–192 A; *SCh* 6, p. 162–166.

104. *De hom. op.* XVI; *PG* 44,181 C; *SCh* 6, p. 155. After establishing the intermediate position of humanity between "divine, incorporeal nature and irrational, animal life," Gregory concludes: "in fact, as is easily verified, the human being participates in two orders: from divinity it has reason and intelligence and does not possess *in se* male-female differentiation; from irrationality it derives its corporeal constitution and a structure differentiated by male and female." Cf. *De hom. op.* XVI; *PG* 44,185A and *De hom. op.* XVII; *PG* 44,189 B-192 A; *SCh* 6, p. 165-166: Ὄντες γὰρ κτηνώδης ἐγένετο ὁ τὴν ῥοώδη ταύτην γένεσιν τῇ φύσει παραδεξάμενος, διὰ τὴν πρὸς τὸ ὑλῶδες ῥοπήν.

105. The use of the verbs ἐπιτεχνάσθαι (*De hom. op.* XVI; *PG* 44,185 A) and προσκατασκευάζειν (ibid.; *PG* 44,188 D) to indicate divine action περὶ τὸ ἄρρεν καὶ θῆλυ διαφορά, expresses completely this notion. Cf. also *De hom. op.* XVII; *PG* 44,189 B-C; *SCh* 6, p. 165.

106. *De hom. op.* XVII; *PG* 44,188 C; *SCh* 6, p. 163.

107. For his treatment of the passions in addition to *De hom. op.* chaps. XVI-XVII, consult chap. XVIII; *PG* 44,192 A-196 B; *SCh* 6, p. 167-172. The *pathe* existing within animal nature are communicated to human nature, from which they were previously extraneous in virtue of the latter's formation according to the divine *eidos*. This communication is grounded in that primary and essential, *alogos* component which was conjoined to the human being: the sexual dimension of generation still defined here as κτην ώδης γένεσις (*De hom. op.* XVIII; *PG* 44,192 A-C; *SCh* 6, p. 167f.). Furthermore, the quality acquired with sin is not intrinsically evil since, even though when subject to irrationality it can lead to vice, nevertheless, under the dominion of reason it can be turned to virtue (*PG* 44,193 B-C).

108. This is described by various expressions in *De anima et resurrectione:* "The resurrection consists in the return to the original condition of our nature," (*PG* 46,148A). "When God, by means of the resurrection, leads back nature to the original human constitution . . ." (*PG* 46,149 D). "The resurrection is nothing more than the return to our natural primitive state" (*PG* 46,156 C). ". . . the blessedness which will flourish in the resurrection will ascend once again to original grace" (*PG* 46,156 D). See J. Daniélou, "La resurrection des corps chez Grégoire de Nysse," *VigChr* 7 (1953) 154-170; M. Alexandre, "L'interprétation de Luc 16,19-31 chez Grégoire de Nysse," in J. Fontaine and C. Kannengiesser, eds., *Epektasis*, p. 425-441.

109. See, for example, *In Ps.* II,VIII; *PG* 44,525 C-528 A; *GNO* V, p. 101 where he concludes: "πάντες κατὰ Χριστὸν μορφωθήσονται καὶ μία πᾶσιν ἐξαστράψει μορφὴ ἡ ἐξ ἀρχῆς ἐπιβληθεῖσα τῇ φύσει," *In Ps.* II,XIV; *PG* 44,585 B; *GNO* V, p. 155; *De anima et resurrectione* (*PG* 46,72 B, 129 A-136 A, 156 B-160 C). On Gregory's notion of *apokatastasis*, consult the observations of J. Daniélou, "L'apocatastase chez Grégoire de Nysse," *RSR* 30 (1940) 328-347; idem, "L'être et le temps," p. 205-26. Gregory's complicated perspective is clearly explained by

M. Alexandre, "Protologie et eschatologie chez Grégoire de Nysse," in U. Bianchi, ed., *Arché e Telos*, p. 122-159.

110. *De hom. op.* XVII; *PG* 44,188 C-D; *SCh* 6, p. 163.

111. See above, note 108. "ὅτι ἀνάστασίς ἐστιν ἡ εἰς τὸ ἀρχαῖον τῆς φύσεως ἡμῶν ἀποκατάστασις" (*PG* 46,148 A); "Μηδὲν ἕτερον εἶναι ἀνάστασιν, ἢ τὴν εἰς τὸ ἀρχαῖον τῆς φύσεως ἡμῶν ἀποκατάστασιν" (*PG* 46,156 C).

112. In this sense the argument of chap. XVII confirms the notion of angelic similarity to the human creature in its prelapsarian integrity. The argument arises from the postulate that the end is equivalent to the beginning (*PG* 44,188 B-189 B; *SCh* 6, p. 163, ff.).

113. *PG* 44,189 B-C: "πῶς μετὰ τὴν κατασκευὴν τῆς εἰκόνος, τὴν κατὰ τὸ ἄρρεν καὶ θῆλυ διαφορὰν ὁ Θεὸς ἐπιτεχνᾶται τῷ πλάσματι." (*SCh* 6, p. 165).

114. *PG* 44,189 C-D; *SCh* 6,165 f.

115. Chap. XXI; *PG* 44,201 B-204 A; *SCh* 6, p. 180-182. On this theme consult J. Daniélou, "Comble du mal et eschatologie chez Grégoire de Nysse," in *Glaube und Geschichte. Festgabe Joseph Lortz*, edited by E. Iserloh and P. Manns, Baden-Baden: 1958, vol. 1, p. 27-45; idem, "L'être et le temps," p. 186-204.

116. *PG* 44,204A: "πάλιν τῆς εἰκόνος ἡ χάρις, καὶ ἡ τῆς ἀρχῆς ἀξία."

117. Chap. XXII; *PG* 44,204 A-205 B; *SCh* 6, p. 183-186.

118. *PG* 44,205 C.

119. See J. Daniélou, "La chronologie des oeuvres," p. 160 f.; M. Alexandre, "Le *De mortuis* de Gregoire de Nysse," *Studia Patristica* X (TU 107), Berlin: 1970, p. 35-43.

120. *PG* 46,524 D; *GNO* IX, p. 55: the properties of the *alogos physis*, (irrational nature) commingled with the human being because of its "decline (*rhopé*) toward the inferior" are indicated in the *hedoné* (pleasure), in the *thymòs* (anger), in the *gastrimargia* (gluttony), in the *aplestia* (insatiate desire) and in analogous passions. Such *pathe*, (passions) noted in *De hom. op.* (above note 107), are not intrinsically negative in as much as they are subordinated to reason and can be redirected to the exercise of virtue (*PG* 46,524 D-525 A; *GNO* IX, p. 55 f.). Gregory emphasised his point that evil and vice do not arise from the body but from bad will (*PG* 46,528 A-529 A; *GNO* IX, p. 58 f.).

121. *PG* 46,523 D; *GNO* IX, p. 53.

122. *PG* 46,148A.

123. *PG* 46,51 A-B, 89 B-C, 93 B-C, 97 B.

124. *PG* 46,148 C-149 A: "Ἔστι δὲ ἃ προσέλαβεν ἀπὸ τοῦ ἀλόγου δέρματος, ἡ μίξις, ἡ σύλληψις, ὁ τόκος, ὁ ῥύπος, ἡ θηλή, ἡ τροφή, ἡ ἐκποίησις, ἡ κατ᾽ ὀλίγον ἐπὶ τὸ τέλειον αὔξησις, ἡ ἀκμή, τὸ γῆρας, ὁ νόσος, ὁ θάνατος."

125. Sexual differentiation is characterised in the preceding discussion as useless in the bodies of the resurrected. At the same time objections to the doctrine of the resurrection are examined, and in this context the quality of the resurrected body is also discussed. The question of the consistency of the human body before and after the resurrection leads to the conclusion that those bodily organs pos-

sessing a precisely biological end, specifically reproductive organs, will have less reason to exist (*PG* 46,144 C–145 A).

126. *In Cant. Cant. Hom.* VII; *PG* 44,916 B; *GNO* VI, p. 213.

127. For a rapid summary of this tradition, see M. C. Horowitz, "The Image of God in Man. Is woman included?," *HThR* 72 (1979) 175–206. For a study of Antiochene writers on this question, consult the article of S. Zincone cited above (note 95), and for Augustine and his influence consult the study of K. E. Børresen also cited above (note 10).

6

"Becoming Male": A Gnostic and Early Christian Metaphor

၏ Kari Vogt

In certain Gnostic texts or texts that show unmistakable Gnostic influence, we find a sex-change metaphor[1] where "woman is turned into man" (*he gyne eis andra metatithestai*), or where the more general expression "becoming male" (*apandro*) is used. Apparently these terms can be regarded as parts of an anthropological and soteriological terminology.

A well-known example of such a sex-change metaphor is found in the Logion 114 of the *Gospel of Thomas*. This text comes out of the Nag Hammadi library Codex II, and probably springs from an encratite Gnostic-Christian setting. Logion 114 is set within the characteristic Gnostic frame of reference to the opposition between Peter and Mary Magdalene, "Simon Peter said to them, 'Let Mary leave us, for women are not worthy of life.' Jesus said, 'I myself shall lead her in order to make her male (*hout*), so that she too may become a living spirit resembling you males. For every woman who makes herself male (*hout*) will enter the Kingdom of Heaven.'"

The *Gospel of Thomas* is one of the most discussed texts of the Nag Hammadi library, and Logion 114, "ce fort étrange propos" as H.-Ch. Puech calls it, is often commented on.[2] The sex-change metaphor in Logion 114 is almost without exception regarded as a purely Gnostic metaphor. Only on rare occasions, as with G. Quispel, do we find that a parallel is drawn between it and the work of Philon and Porphyrios.[3]

In Porphyrios's *Ad Marcellam* as well as in Philon's work there is, in fact, talk of "becoming male" as a metaphorical expression of an inner development and of the attainment of spiritual perfection.[4] As we shall see, similar imagery can be found among prominent Christian authors of the early period as well.

170

In other words, the sex-change metaphor was in widespread use and indications are that this metaphor can be regarded as part of the cultural *koine* of late Antiquity. On the basis of a common scale of values, the categories "male" and "female" are polarized, and the "becoming male" metaphor indicates in all contexts a development from a lower to a higher stage of moral and spiritual perfection. Used as a religious and literary metaphor, "becoming male" need not necessarily be given a more precise interpretation than this.

The first question under consideration is whether the sex-change metaphor has a specifically Gnostic meaning content so that it may be said to be an integral part of Gnostic anthropological thought.

Furthermore, no parallel between Gnostic and Christian use of the sex-change metaphor has so far been drawn, and a comparison between the use of the sex-change metaphor in the two religious systems is all the more interesting since these systems partly converged and partly diverged sharply during the first centuries C.E.

In this way we will be able to gain a better understanding of how this religio-literary metaphor might have its meaning determined by theological context, either Gnostic or Christian, and consequently might have a more precise and nuanced content than what is conveyed by the general idea of a development from a lower to a higher state.

In the present context the term "sex-change metaphor" will refer to metaphors that explicitly refer to a change from one sex to the other. It can be either "woman becomes man," which expresses a positive development, or "man becomes woman," which expresses moral degeneration and perdition. Consequently, no mention will be made of the phenomenon of a female state that is superseded by a qualitatively better male state, as described in the Ps. Clementine literature and in the *Gospel of the Egyptians*. In our context these are not regarded as sex-change metaphors in the strict sense.

In the Gnostic as well as in the Christian texts, the dominant metaphor of change is the "woman turned into man" variant, expressing spiritual progress and salvation. There are two main types of this metaphor: (a) in the *Gospel of Thomas* the process of change applies to women only; (b) in *Excerpta ex Theodoto*, the metaphor indicates a change which either sex can undergo.

The Sex-Change Metaphor in Gnostic Anthropology

In Gnostic myths crucial cosmic and anthropological events are described through the use of a plethora of images taken from human biology. Since these images often have sexual reference, the male-female categories are brought to the fore. Body symbolism, or what Mary Douglas calls "natural symbols," can be said to be typical of the period and the same time it is the Gnostic vehicle of expression par excellence. In Gnostic texts, therefore, we must regard the sex-change metaphor as part of a larger and more all-encompassing symbolic language, where the conflicting or complementary nature of the male-female categories is central.[5]

Current work on this topic will quite spontaneously refer to the sex-change metaphor as Gnostic (or alternatively as apocryphal Judaeo-Christian) and consequently regard it as extraneous to Christian orthodoxy. In the light of this fact it is surprising to discover the extremely small number of the explicit sex-change metaphors we can actually find in Gnostic literature.

In the Gospel of Mary, Mary Magdalene tells the apostles that Jesus made her as well as them into "human beings" or "into men" (*afaan nro*).[6] This statement has recently been interpreted in the light of the sex-change metaphor as we find it in Logion 114.[7] In the Nag Hammadi library Codex VII 2:65, we read that the chosen are warned against being "made woman" or to "become like women" (*mprsope nshime*).[8] Apart from these examples, the sex-change metaphor in its explicit form can only be found in the Church Fathers' comments on the Gnostic systems; and of these there are only three instances: (1) In Clement's *Excerpta ex Theodoto.* 21:3; 22:3; and 79, (2) in a *Fragment of Heraklion* quoted by Origen *In Johannem* VI, XX, 111, (3) and a somewhat vaguer reference in Hippolytos' *Refutationes* V, 8, 44 in connection with the Naassenes. And this is all. Both Theodotos and Heraklion represent the Valentinian Gnosis in the second half of the second century; the Oriental and the Italian branch respectively. In this paper we shall take a closer look at Clement's rendering of Theodotos. The *Fragment of Heraklion*, in the rendering given by Origen, is an exegesis of Joh. 1:23, and, in terms of ideas expressed, in line with the *Excerpts*. In the *Excerpts* we have the additional advantage that the sex-change metaphor is used with a good deal of contextual support.

"Woman Turned into Man" in *Excerpta ex Theodoto*

Exc. 21:2 is an exegesis of Gen. 1:27b, "male and female He created them" and of Cor. 1:15, 29, "What will those do who are baptized for the dead." According to Theodotos, Gen. 1:27 talks of Sophias' emission (*probole*): Sophia brought forth Christ and the angels, the chosen male, as well as the female element which is called upon to be saved and which stands for the Valentinians themselves. Throughout the text male stands for angels, perfection, the elect. Opposed to this there is female which stands for imperfection, yet an imperfection that is called upon to become perfect. In this context female is a positive category even if it manifests itself as being temporarily an imperfect state. This positive connotation linked to the female concept can be found in the description of the pleromatic world. Here we find a positive *conjunctio oppositorum:* the female is an integrated part, even though it is derived and secondary to male.

In Valentinian anthropological thinking this pleromatic *conjunctio* is lost and the human being in the material world is characterized by the separation between male and female. In the *Gospel of Philip* it is expressed in this way: "When Eve was still in Adam death did not exist. When she was separated from him death came into being."[9] When salvation is described in *Exc.* 21:3, it is said that "the female (pneumatic) elements, becoming men (*apandrothentha*), are united to the angels and pass into Pleroma."

The female constitution is, as we can see, common to men and women and both sexes are "made male." In the Gnostic context, however, all human beings do not stand the same chance of achieving salvation; only the chosen few can reach salvation aided by their pneumatic nature which is given at the outset, not acquired.

In 22:1-3 another aspect is brought forward: Cor. 1:15, 29, "Now if there is no resurrection, what will those do who are baptized for the dead?" Theodotos' interpretation of this is that the angels "among whose numbers we are" as he characteristically puts it, let themselves be baptized for the human beings, who are called "the dead." The angels are here called "the men" and "the living" because they are not part of the divided material existence. On this basis we get the following equations: (1) worldly existence = death = female; (2) angel-likeness and pleromatic existence = life = male. Equating female with death, and the negative terminology flowing from this equation is the main theme in *Exc.* 67, 68, and 79. In these passages a distinction is made between "woman's child," who is devoid of reason, power, and form, and "man's child," the manly, pneumatic element or "the manly fruit." Those who are brought forth by woman are destined to die, only those who are "formed" and transformed into men (*morfothen de metetethe eis andra*) will have life.[10]

Here the category called "female" differs from the male category by its double nature or ambiguity: female indicates first of all those who are chosen and may achieve salvation; and at the same time and within the same system, female stands for that which is evil and doomed to perdition and death. In the Gnostic system evil is linked to sexuality and procreation, and the sexuality-salvation polarity is paralleled by the female-male polarity.[11] In this sense salvation will always represent the final parting of the ways for male and female. A most salient expression of this is found in Nag Hammadi library's Codex VIII, *Zostrianos*, in a passage which reads, "Flee from the bondage of femininity, and choose for yourselves the salvation of masculinity." It should be noted that even this quotation is taken from a text where femaleness has obvious positive connotations when the pneumatic world is described.[12]

In the anthropological and soteriological context under discussion, female is thus a term that is inherently ambiguous on the one hand, it is positive even though it may be temporarily imperfect; on the other hand, it is negative, evil and linked to desire. In this respect it is in stark contrast to the concept of male, which does not have the same duality attached to it, but which unambiguously stands for reunion and unity: salvation is *conjunctio*, which could be called *becoming male*.

The quotation from the *Gospel of Philip* 68 shows how the separation of Adam and Eve was used as an image of the degenerate state of the cosmos. In the same text we also read, "If he (Adam) becomes complete and attains his former self, death will be no more." To be "made man" is thus primarily linked to the idea of regaining unity, and *Exc.* 22:3 uses a number of parallel expressions covering the same idea: "Therefore we are raised up 'equal to angels,' and restored as males, member for member in unity." Here we see how the metaphor "restored as males" duplicates other central Valentinian metaphors that all refer to the restoration, *apokatastasis*, of a lost unity: "to become equal to angels," the "members that are united"; similar, also, to metaphors in other texts like: "to be united with one's image" or "with oneself" or "to come together in the nuptial chamber." Metaphors like "woman changed into man" or "female made male" are central in soteriological imagery. It seems reasonable, therefore, to consider the sex-change metaphor an integral part of this imagery.

And even if the sex-change metaphor is seldom used in its explicit form in Gnostic texts, it would be wrong to consider it a foreign element in these texts.

The specific trait of the sex-change metaphor is that it focuses on sex differentiation *per se*. The passage in the *Gospel of Thomas*, Logion 114, where Mary is "made male" is often interpreted in light of Logion 22, which reads, ". . . so that the male not be male nor the female female." Variations on this theme are found also in Logion 106. In these cases we are obviously dealing with descriptions of a process of salvation where sex categories are used as spiritual categories, indicating an asexual or a metasexual state. This metasexual interpretation of the sex-change metaphor, which is reasonable for the quotations from the *Gospel of Thomas,* cannot rule out different interpretations in other contexts. In Hippolytos, among others we find, in connection with the Naassenes, that salvation involves the coming into existence of a new being who is neither man nor woman, but a man-woman, *arsenothelys.*[13] It seems reasonable to look upon this as a variation on another and related Gnostic motif, that of androgyny, of which there are also definite traces in early Christian texts.[14]

The "Becoming Male" Metaphor in Early Christian Texts

So far we have interpreted the Gnostic sex-change metaphor as a nonliteral, symbolic expression. Are there instances where "woman turned into man" has been given a more concrete and literal interpretation? A literal interpretation is, in fact, suggested in Augustine's *De Civitate Dei* 22:17 where the resurrection of the dead is discussed. Unfortunately, Augustine does not develop this point beyond stating that some, he does not say who, have interpreted Rom. 8:29, "to be even formed to the image of the Son" and Eph. 4:13, about "becoming the perfect man," to mean that women are supposed to be resurrected as men. Augustine rejects this interpretation as do other Christian authors of the period.[15] We are not here focusing on Augustine's interesting text *per se,* but we want to use it to draw attention to New Testament passages which may have served as scriptural foundation for the "woman turned into man" theme as it appears in a Christian context. Looking at the patristic material in order to check specifically the use of *teleios aner,* we find that Eph. 4:13 in particular has played an important role in giving the sex-change metaphor moorings in Christian thought.[16]

Clement of Alexandria is the first Christian author who makes use of Eph. 4:13 and whose work gives prominence to *teleios aner.* Clement describes the Christian Gnostic as *the perfect man;* and in an interesting but overlooked passage in *Strom.* VI, 100:3, we read of the Christian Gnostic wife who frees herself from the bondage of the flesh and reaches perfection in the same way as her husband; "souls are neither male nor female, when they no longer marry nor are given in marriage. And is not woman turned into man, (*gynaika eis andra metatithestai*), the woman who is no more female than he, the perfect, manly woman."

"Making women manly" is certainly not a central theme in Clement's writings. However, on the basis of this passage and his anthropology generally, where the relations between a common human soul and sex-differentiated nature are discussed in detail, there are good reasons for assuming that he includes women when, for instance, in a context where he quotes Eph. 4:13 *in extenso*, he exhorts the believers to become "male and perfect" (*Strom.* IV, 132:1). To become *teleios aner*, "male and perfect," is thus the aim for both sexes, and the metaphor "woman turned into man" shows women as *anthropos* and is used by Clement as an image of salvation.

To sum up, in the writings of Clement we see how the "becoming male" theme, coloured as it is by its time and cultural background, converge with certain New Testament texts where *teleios aner* can he regarded as a determining metaphor. We would, of course, need a more thorough analysis of this motif in Clement as Eph. 4:13 is not the only relevant text. However, our aim in the present paper is primarily to point to important themes and to achieve this objective some passages from Origen will serve to illustrate the Christian use of the "becoming male" metaphor.

In Origen's work the male and female polarity is strongly stressed. This has consequences for his ideas on anthropology and ethics; consequences which must be seen in the light of the fact that he links the categories male and female to his concept of the soul. The masculine part of *homo interior*, i.e. the spirit, is regarded as superior and qualitatively better than the female part, *anima*, whose domain is the senses. However, male and female categories constitute not only the inner hierarchy, but are also used metaphorically to indicate moral qualities.[17] "Woman" stands for weakness, sensuality, laziness, dependency and can also be linked directly to the sphere of sin. This is, of course, a well-known theme in patristic literature. The point we want to make here is that Origen at the same time spiritualizes the category of sex.

This means that he explicitly states that the individual human being's real sexual appartenance is of an inner nature. It is the moral and spiritual quality of *homo interior* which decides whether the individual should be named man or woman. In *Homilia in Josue* 9:9 we read, "Men and women are distinguished according to differences of heart. How many belong to the female sex who before God are strong men, and how many men must be counted weak and indolent women." This text, among several other possible texts, is of special interest because it expressly links the metaphor and the extra-metaphorical reality. A woman by virtue of her moral and spiritual qualities may be turned into a man, i.e. may be saved, while a man may "become a woman," i.e. may degenerate and be lost.

Just like Clement, Origen uses Eph. 4:13 as a text about the progress (*prokope*) of the soul, and the goal of human salvation is described as a transformation into "the perfect man." To get a clearer idea of the interrelationship between the "becoming male" metaphor and other soteriological metaphors in Origen, we must take a closer look at the concept of *homo interior.*

We find in a number of Christian writers of late Antiquity that *homo interior* is described as a man with all the ordinary limbs and sense organs.[18] This is a frequently used metaphor, not only in theological literature, but in hagiographic texts as well.[19] Two texts from Origen are well suited to shed some light on the early version of the imagery under consideration, namely *Homiliae in Genesim* and *Dialektos.*[20]

The most detailed and systematic description of *homo interior* in all of Origen's work is given in *Dialektos,* where the starting point is, characteristically, an exegesis of Gen. 1:27b. Here we read that "every member of the outward man has a name corresponding to what is true of the inward man."[21] The idea of growth and change of this inner man is central because it is only *homo interior* who is created in the image of God and this image must be renewed constantly. To achieve *homoiosis* and to "become like Christ" thus duplicates the metaphor of becoming "the perfect man." In accordance with this the aim of salvation is described as leaving the female state or cease to be a woman through a change of sex. The concept of a *homo interior* of either sex is thus clearly expressed in Origen's work and it is precisely the contrast between the inner and the outward man that is crucial: *homo interior* can be man or woman independently of observable, empirical sex. Moral quality and spiritual progress are the decisive factors when it comes to be called man or not.

Sex categorization in this spiritualized sense is in Origen's work part of a soteriological terminology. Whether an individual should be called woman or man is thus decided on the basis of the development and perfection of *homo interior.* It is worth noticing that when the term "female" or "woman" is used in a derogatory sense, then these terms are not primarily related to empirical, observable sex, but refer to *homo interior.*

In the centuries that followed, a number of Christian authors used the sex-change metaphor to point out harmony or disharmony between the "outward" and the "inner" man. Didymos the Blind of Alexandria expresses this idea clearly in his comments on Gen. 1:27, where he points out that human beings according to the ways of nature can neither choose nor change their sex; for the inner man, on the other hand, sex is an acquired quality.

It is not without interest to look more closely at Didymos's way of reasoning. It is well-known than Didymos has a lot in common with Origen, and in his commentary on Genesis he brings together and juxtaposes with great lucidity a number of themes found in Alexandrian anthropology. In this way the "becoming male" metaphor is used in a larger and more comprehensive context.

In his discussion of Gen. 1:27 Didymos concentrates on *homo interior*. The inner man is identical to the soul, which alone is created in the image of God. This *eikon* is the precondition for achieving likeness: through spiritual progress (*prokope*) the soul comes to partake in God and achieves "likeness" (*homoiosis*). Thus Didymos subscribes to the view that the relationship between *eikon* and *homoiosis* is a dynamic one: it is through spiritual progress that the human being can reach salvation and become like Christ.

At the same time Didymos links the progress of the soul to the idea of ruling (*arkein*) over the inner man as well as over the outward nature of man. Didymos specifies that the concept of ruling can be applied on two different levels: there is first of all the command over outward nature and then the command over the inner world, over "the wild beasts inside" and over "the fishes in the spiritual ocean." Certain people have achieved such command over the inner world that consequently they can command also in the outward world, i.e. have legitimate authority over others. It is not only the apostles and the "Just" in the Scriptures that come into this category; Didymos extends the category to take in "the holy" (*hagioi*) who have legitimate authority over other people based on their possibility of leading them "from the worst to the better through the Word."[22]

It is against this background that we must read Didymos' exegesis of Gen. 1:27b, "male and female He created them." Didymos points out that a literal interpretation of this passage implies that the two sexes are equal; the distinction between them is restricted to different roles in relation to procreation. In this way Didymos presents the Alexandrian point of view which is that woman too is created in God's image. The anagogical interpretation, however, differs slightly from Origen's exegesis of Genesis. Whereas Origen points out that male and female are two aspects of *homo interior*, Didymos restricts his discussion to the dissimilarity between male and female souls; i.e. "male" as superior and "female" as subordinate and inferior. This implies that the male soul is capable of leading and teaching; i.e. standing forth as an authority and as a leader of others, whereas the female soul is described as a passive receiver.

At this point in his discussion Didymos draws a clear line between the world of the senses on the one hand and the spiritual world on the other. In the former, God has decreed whether an individual is to be a man or a woman, and it is impossible to change nature (*fysis*). In the spiritual world, on the other hand, it is possible for an individual to choose to become a man.

The person who is a woman (*en taksei tylesos*) may through spiritual progress become a man (*ek prokopes aner*) and thereby also become a *didaskolos* with authority to lead and teach others; i.e. to be the possessor of legitimate authority. Only through being a spiritual man (*pneumatikos*) in constant progress can the soul reach its highest perfection. According to Didymos process involves a transformation into "the perfect man," a metaphor which in his work is interchangeable with "becoming like Christ."[23]

In continuation of this Didymos touches on another theme: the "becoming male" of the soul is linked to another set of metaphors which has received much more attention in patristic research, i.e. those metaphors giving expression to the idea that all souls are female before God. This goes to show how the very same author quite effortlessly can link up these two sets of metaphors which appear to be incompatible. And what ties them together is first of all the nuances of meaning that go with "woman" and "female." They may refer either directly to negative qualities or conditions, which the believers must put behind them, or, as particularly underlined by Didymos, to a temporary, worldly and secondary condition. When the soul's relationship to God is described with a bridal metaphor, this is precisely to underline its dependency and inferiority in relation to God. After having developed the theme of how the soul becomes male, Didymos adds, "If we apply this to the Word of God (*logos*), it is the whole rational nature (*logike fysis*) which in relation to Him has the female role.[24]

Social Context of the Sex-Change Metaphor

Our starting point for the discussion of the sex-change metaphor was the cultural frame in which it was set; a frame where male was considered superior and female inferior. However, in a social context the value system that goes with this frame of reference raises problems for Gnostics as well as for Christians. In a Gnostic context we see this when those who are chosen may be said to be equal not only in relation to salvation but also in terms of religious authority. As E. Pagels has already pointed out, in several Gnostic texts there is a possible connection between: (1) *mythical and precosmic reality;* where the female is integrated both in teachings about the syzygies, and in female saviours; (2) *mythic history;* where an esoteric message of salvation is also entrusted to women, e.g. Mary Magdalene, and where women can function as carriers of messages of revelation; (3) *socially;* where it is most likely that in several Gnostic communities women have been priests as well as teachers and prophets.[25]

How did this work in the Christian community? Is it possible to point to concrete application of the sex-change metaphor?

To answer these questions a passage from Hieronimus' commentary on the Epistle of Ephesians will serve as a starting.point: "So long as woman is subject to childbirth and the care of children, she is different from man, like the body is different from the soul. If she chooses to serve Christ and not the world, however, she ceases to be a woman and can be called a man, as we all crave to become perfect man." (*Mulier esse cessabit, et dictur vir, quia omnes in perfectum virum copimus occurrere*).[26] In other words, if a woman chooses to live an ascetic life, she ceases to be a woman and can be called *vir*. And this is a prominent metaphor in the ascetic-monastic literature in the 4th and 5th centuries where holy women can be referred to as having become manly, *gynaikes andreiai*.

A case in point: In Palladios' *Life of Chrysostome*, we find the following dialogue between a deacon and a bishop where the person referred to is the deaconess Olympias. The deacon asks, "Where does this woman come from?" The bishop: "Do not say 'woman' (*gyne*), but 'man' (*he anthropos*) for this is a man (*aner*) in spite of the outer appearance of the body (*skema*)."[27]

Early hagiographic literature thus emphasizes the holiness of woman by polarizing "male" and "female," and by describing holiness as something that transcends femaleness.

For a woman to be called a man is clearly a term of praise. However, other shades of meaning seem more important. In a letter from Hieronimus to Lucinus, a woman, his continent wife Theodora, is described in this way: "she has become your sister, has changed from woman to man, from subject to equal" (*de femina virum de subjecta parem*). After the death of Lucinus, he writes to Theodora, "even on earth he saw you as a sister, or better, as a brother." Other sources too will confirm that social contact, friendship or cooperation between the sexes is explained and legitimized through metaphors where sex is either neutralized or radically changed.

One concrete example, chosen among several, of such a legitimizing metaphor can be found in Melanias' *Vita* where the heroine visits the monks in Kellia. The brothers receive her "as if she were a man." And her biographer adds that she had "transcended femaleness" and acquired a "manly" and "heavenly" frame of mind.[29]

When the sex-change metaphor is used in this literature, it gives expression to the idea of a redefined human relationship. Even if the ascetic life in principle presupposes absolute segregation between man and woman, this segregation could in certain circumstances be considered unnecessary and irrelevant.

And this is exactly how monastic literature of late Antiquity describes the future paradisiacal condition, namely, a condition where segregation of the sexes is no longer necessary. As an image of human transformation after resurrection, Ps. Makarios points to Gal. 3:28 and writes, "without offence to decency the brother directs words of peace to the sister, as they are both one in Christ. Enjoying peace in the same light, they will be looking at each other."[30] This paradisiacal state comes true for the holy even in this world.

Nuances in this legitimizing use of the "becoming male" metaphor are further specified in the *Apophthegmata*-collections. Here it is applied in a context where *women's* authority is highlighted and justified In this context we could say that Hieronymus' expression *de subjecta parem* comes into its own. The fact is that the *Sayings* of the Desert Fathers (*Apophthegmata Patrum*) also contains the *logoi* of the *ammas*. The activities of the "mothers" and their authority can be seen in the light of two *logoi* attributed to *amma* Sarra. The first text, Sarra 4, tells of two great anchorites who come to see her. On their way, they conspire to humiliate her, and they say to her, "Be careful not to become conceited thinking to yourself: 'Look how anchorites are coming to see me, a mere woman. But *amma* Sarra said to them, 'According to nature I am a woman, but not according to my thoughts.'"[31] Here a contrast is set up between nature (*fysis*) and thought (*logismos*), thus driving home the point that the "outward being," which in this case is a woman according to nature (*fysin*), does not reveal anything about the inner being and its qualities. In this way the text manages to convey the discrepancy between femaleness and perfection as well as pointing out the basis of true authority. In Sarra 9 this point is again elaborated and the message made even clearer, "She said to the brothers: 'I am a man, and you, you are women.'"[32] *Amma* Sarra's statement *"ego eimi aner"* reveals a hidden hierarchy: charismatic authority belongs to those whose inner life is the most advanced and this authority is independent of both sex and official position.[33]

In the monastic literature of late Antiquity, ascetic life is pictured as the restoration of paradise and as an anticipation of heavenly life. To express this, a symbolic language, prolific in images, was developed. "Woman turned into man" emerges, then, as one of the metaphorical elements representing paradise regained and also the link that binds doctrine, symbolic language and social reality together. Under certain conditions some women achieved "the rank of man." This implies that saints of both sexes were accorded the same charismatic authority.

Conclusion

Sex-change metaphors are found as part of the shared imagery in the Graeco-Roman cultural sphere of late Antiquity. It would also have been of interest to trace the use of such a metaphor over time and in diverse cultural contexts. The fact is that we find a great spread in the use of the sex-change metaphor: from *Papyrus Louvre* 3079 where Isis "makes herself male even if she is a woman"[34] to the Chinese Buddhist *Lingpao* scriptures from the 5th century C.E. where the bodhisattva says, "When I am made a Buddha, I vow to bring it about that, within my land, there will be no women or maidens. Those who desire to be born in my land will first become male."[35] The transformation of woman into man is moreover a frequent theme in Indian Buddhist *Mahayana* literature.[36] And in an Islamic hagiographic text, *Tadhkirat al-Auliya*, Farid al-Din Attar says, concerning the female mystic Rabe'a al-Adawiya: "When a woman becomes a 'man' in the path of God, she is a man and one cannot anymore call her a woman."[37]

It is thus not difficult to find apparently parallel metaphors in other cultures. It will be sufficient here to point this out without elaborating further. One result of this investigation into Gnostic and Christian sex-change metaphors is, in fact, that their content can only be understood in an historical and doctrinal context. We have also established that the male-female polarity and sex-change metaphors are found both in Gnostic and Christian texts as part of soteriological symbolic language. The sex-change metaphor is found much more often in Christian than in Gnostic texts. This *may* be because the Gnostic material is, after all, fragmentary, but there is no basis for characterizing the sex-change metaphor as a Gnostic or apocryphal-Christian phenomenon.

These sex-change metaphors were to have a long history, not only in orthodox Christian hagiography, but among marginal religious groups in Europe in the Middle Ages as well.

When court documents from the Inquisition show that a certain Guillaume Belibasta in 1321 maintained that women in order to reach salvation had to be changed into men after death (*converti in viros, in homines masculos*),[38] this does not necessarily mean, as H. Ch. Puech suggests, that the French Cathari knew the *Gospel of Thomas*.[39] It seems more reasonable to assume that marginal religious groups were drawing on a tradition of symbolic language which was well-known and often used by prominent Christian writers of an earlier period. Convincing documentation of such a connection, which has so far escaped notice, can, in our opinion, be found in the Cathari's use of Eph. 4:13 as a basis for claiming that women are transformed into men.[40]

There are two aspects of Christian authors' use of the sex-change metaphor that deserve special attention. Firstly, this metaphor duplicates well-known New Testament metaphors. "Becoming male" is interchangeable with such metaphors as Rom. 8:29, "to be conformed to the image of the Son" and with Eph. 4:13 "to become perfect man" (*aner*). These are linked to Pauline metaphors which describe "the inner man" (*anthropos*) in relation to *eikon* and *homoiosis*. The manner in which the "becoming male" metaphor is used in Christian texts shows that it is well integrated in the theological anthropology of the period.

"Becoming male" or becoming "perfect man" involves both sexes and refers to a metasexual sphere; "man" and "male" can therefore describe human nature (in what is common to the sexes) and relate to a state in which sex is transcended. "Woman" and "female" on the other hand always refer in such contexts to the inferior beings in this world. All this literature redefines and spiritualizes the category "sex": belonging to one or the other sex is not something given; it has to be achieved by the inner man. In this context, "sex" depends on spiritual progress, and it has a decisive role in the attainment of salvation.

Secondly, in the Christian texts, the "becoming male" metaphor also appears in a *social context*. Didymos' comments on Genesis 1:27 show clearly *how* the sex-change metaphor could be linked up with the idea of legitimate authority. When "maleness" is acquired by the "inner man," which is described as either male or female, then empirical, observable sex as a criterion for becoming *didaskalos*, teacher, becomes irrelevant.

In monastic-hagiographic literature we find variations on this theme. The metaphor "woman turned into man" is used as part of a richly developed symbolism describing paradise, and sex-change anticipates the attainment of salvation. In continuation of this paradise motif, we can also observe how the metaphor often is used (1) to legitimize interaction and cooperation between the sexes, and (2) to justify charismatic authority and thereby also *women's* charismatic authority.

(1987)

Notes

1. In this article the term *metaphor* is used as defined in the classical rhetorical tradition by Du Marsais: 'La métaphore est une figure par laquelle on transporte, pour ainsi dire, la signification propre d'un mot à une autre signification qui ne lui convient qu'en vertu d'une comparaison qui est dans l'esprit,' cf. Le Guern

(1973), p. 11. Whether a metaphor is used as part of symbolic language or not, is determined by context, cf. Le Guern *Métaphore et symbole*, p. 39.

2. Puech, p. 51.
3. Quispel, p. 104-105, Puech, p. 280, Tardieu, p. 231, where the 'becoming male' motif in logion 114 is mentioned as 'thèse judéochrétienne.'
4. Porphyrios, *Epistula ad Marcellam*, 33. Philo, *Quast in Exodum*, I,8; *Quast in Gen.* II,49. Philon, cf. Baer, p. 45-49.
5. This subject is discussed by Sælid Gilhus (1984).
6. Till, p. 66.
7. Tardieu, p. 231.
8. Robinson, p. 336.
9. Robinson, p. 141.
10. *Exc.* 79, SC 23, p. 203, cf. Sagnard, *Lexique*, p. 647.
11. Similar ideas in *Apocryphon Johannis*, cf. Sælid Gilhus (1983), p. 42.
12. *Zostrianos*, 131, S–8. Robinson, p. 392.
13. Hippolytos, *Ref.* V, 7, 15.
14. van den Broek, 357 ff.
15. Hieronimus, Ep. CVIII, Bourdet, t. V, p. 190.
16. The use of Eph. 4.13 by Clemens of Alexandria, cf. Vogt (1985), p. 97-99.
17. *Homiliae in Genesim I*, 12-14, PG 12, p. 146ff.
18. Cf. *Orientalia Christiana Analecta*, t. 117, p. 5-8, ed. F. Diekamp, Roma 1938.
19. Cf. *Vita Syncleticae*, PG 28, chap. 99, p. 1548-49. Palladius, *Historia Lausiaca*, chap. 12,2.
20. *Homiliae in Genesim*, 1, 13 and 15; PG 12, cf. note 17. *Entretien*, SC 67, pp. 89-103.
21. *Entretien*, SC 67, p. 89.
22. *Sur la Genèse*, I, SC 233, p. 156.
23. *Sur la Genèse*, I, SC 233, p. 163.
24. *Sur la Genèse*, I, SC 233, p. 161.
25. Pagels, p. 25.
26. Hieronimus, PL 26, p. 567.
27. Palladius, *De Vita S. Johannis Chrysostomi*, chap. XVI, PG 47/48, p. 56.
28. Ep. 71,3; Ep. 75,2. Labourt, t. VI, p. 10; p. 34.
29. *Vie de Sainte Mélanie*, SC 90, p. 200.
30. Ps. Makarios, p. 261.
31. Sarra 4, PG 65, p. 420.
32. Sarra 9, Guy, *Recherches*, p. 34.
33. For similar ideas on charismatic authority in early hagiographic literature, cf. Vogt (1987).
34. *Lexicon der Ägyptologie*, bd. 3, p. 198.
35. Both quotations in Strickelman, p. 473.
36. The need for women to change their sex to reach higher Bodhisattva-stages is a frequent theme in Mahayana literature. A women has either to wait until she is

reborn as a man before she can enter the career of the Bodhisattva, or, as in certain texts, women are granted the right to become lowerstage Bodhisattvas, but their sex is transformed as they reach the levels immediately preceding the Buddhahood. D. Paul maintains that in certain texts the change of sex is described as both a physiological and a mental process, cf. D. Paul, pp. 171-174.

37. Alberry, p. 40.
38. von Döllinger, p. 177.
39. 'Les cathares faisaient-ils usage des plus anciens de nos Évangiles apocryphes?', Puech, p. 51.
40. Duvernoy, pp. 98-99.

Works Consulted

Arberry, A. J., (ed.) (1976): *Muslim Saints and Mystics. Episodes from the Tadhkirat al-Aulya' by Farid al-Din 'Aṭṭār.* London.

Baer, R. A., (1970): *Philo's Use of the Categories Male and Female,* Leiden.

Broeck, van den, R. (1972): *The Myth of the Phoenix,* Leiden.

Buckley, J. Jacobsen (1986): *Female Fault and Fulfilment in Gnosticism.* Chapel Hill, NC.

Clement d'Alexandrie (1970): *Extraits de Théodote,* Sources Chrétiennes 23, Paris.

Deseille, P. (1984): *Les homélies spirituelles de Saint Macaire,* Spiritualité Orientale 40, Abbaye Bellefontaine.

Didyme l'Aveugle (1976): *Sur la Genèse I,* Sources Chrétiennes 233, Paris.

Duvernoy, J. (1986)[2]: *La Religion des Cathares. Le Catharisme.* Toulouse.

Dollinger, von, Ign. (1890): *Beiträge zur Sektengeschichte des Mittelalters,* t. II, München.

Dorries, H., Klostermann, E., Koeger, M. (1964): *Die 50 Geistliche Homilien des Makarios,* Patristische Texte und Studien, Band 4, Berlin.

Guillaumont, A. et al. (1959): *L'Évangile selon Thomas,* Paris.

Gilhus, I. Sælid (1983): "Male and Female Symbolism in the Apocryphon of John," *Temenos* 19, 33-43.

—— (1984): "Gnosticism – A Study in liminal Symbolism." *Numen* XXXI, 106-128.

Guy, J-C. (1962): *Recherches sur la tradition grecque des Apophthegmata Patrum,* Bruxelles.

Labourt, J. (1955; 1958): *Saint Jerôme, Lettres,* V-VI, Paris.

Le Guern, M. (1973): *Sémantique de la métaphore et de la métonymie,* Paris.

Makarios, Ps. (1964): *Patristische Texte und Studien,* Band 4, Berlin.

Origène (1960): *Entretien d'Origène avec Héraclide.* Sources Chrétiennes 67, Paris.

Origène (1970): *Commentaire sur S. Jean,* II, Sources Chrétiennes, 157, Paris.

Pagels, E. (1982): *The Gnostic Gospels,* Penguin Books, Harmondsworth.

Puech, H.-Ch. (1978): *En quête de la Gnose, II, Sur L'Evangile selon Thomas,* Paris.

Paul, D. M. (1979): *Women in Buddhism: Images of the Feminine in the Mahayana Tradition.* Asian Humanity Press. Berkeley, CA.

Quispel, G. (1967): *Makarios, das Thomaslied und das Lied von der Perle.* Leiden.

Robinson, J. M. (1977): *The Nag Hammadi Library in English.* Leiden.

Sagnard, F. M. (1947): *La Gnose valentinienne,* Paris.

Strickelmann, M. (ed.) (1983): *Tantric and Taoist Studies in Honor of R. A. Stein,* Mélanges Chinois et bouddhiques, XXI, Bruxelles.

Tardieu, M. (1984): *Écrit gnostiques. Codex de Berlin.* Paris.

Till, W. C. (1955): *Die gnostischen Schriften des koptischen Papyrus Berolinensis 8502,* Berlin.

Vogt, K. (1985): "'Devenir mâle': Aspect d'une anthropologie chrétienne primitive," *Concilium* 202, Paris, 95-107.

Vogt, K. (1987): "La moniale folle du monastère des Tabennésiotes. Une interpretation du chap. 34 de l'Historia Lausiaca de Pallade, *Symbolae Osloensis* LXII, Oslo, 95-108.

7

GOD'S IMAGE, MAN'S IMAGE? PATRISTIC INTERPRETATION OF GEN. 1,27 AND I COR. 11,7

∽ Kari Elisabeth Børresen

Patristic "Feminism"

Christian doctrine of humanity's creation in God's image is based on interacting anthropology and theology, i.e. definition of the human being and concept of the divine, as displayed both in biblical texts and subsequent exegesis. Patristic interpretation of human God-likeness, *imago Dei*, presupposes andromorphic or metasexual God-imagery. In consequence, creational image of God is attributed to human males or man-like, asexual souls. As a patriarchally inculturated, monotheistic religion, Christianity excludes femaleness at the divine level. It follows that women cannot be God-like *qua* females, with corresponding lack of fully human status, i.e. full religious capacity, *qua* women.

Traditional Christian anthropology starts with two contrasting tenets: 1. Androcentric gender hierarchy or female subordination is established by God's creative order. 2. Human equivalence in the sense of women's parity with men is realised through Christ in redemption. The ensuing asymmetry between women's creational inferiority and their salvational equality is affronted by "feminist" church Fathers, in order to include women in human God-likeness *already* from creation, *in spite* of their God-alien femaleness. The classical stratagem, initiated by Clement of Alexandria (d. before 215) and elaborated by Augustine (d. 430), defines God's image, *imago Dei*, as an incorporeal and consequently sexless quality, linked to human capacity of virtue and intellect. This genderfree privilege in man-like disguise permits *backdating* women's redemptive Christ-likeness to the creational level, without affecting their God-given subservience *qua* females, a split which has been upheld in theological anthropology until this century.

The present accommodation to post-patriarchal culture supersedes andro-centric duality by updated definition of God's image: both women and men are created God-like *qua* male and female human beings. It is important to note that this *aggiornamento* builds upon the church Fathers' efforts to insert women as God-like and therefore fully human, their *sub-male* female-ness notwithstanding. In fact, contemporary biblical interpretation utilises three equality strategies, all of which are inherited from patristic exegesis: 1. The sexual differentiation expressed in Gen. 1,27b, "male and female he created them," is *disconnected* from the consecutive blessing of fertility in Gen. 1,28 and *linked* to the preceding image text of Gen. 1,26-27a: "Let us make Adam (collective male) in our image, according to our likeness. . . . And God created Adam in his image, in the image of God he created him." 2. Paul's argument for men's exclusive God-likeness in I Cor.11,7: "For man should not cover his head, since he is the image and glory of God, but woman is the glory of man," is *veiled.* In context, Gen. 1,26-27a is here combined with God's for-mation of Adam from clods in the soil and blowing into his nostrils the breath of life, according to Gen. 2,7. In I Cor. 11,8-9, Paul asserts man's theomor-phic precedence in terms of woman's derivative formation from Adam's rib, as "an aid fit for him," according to Gen. 2,18,21-23. 3. The *negating* citation of Gen. 1,27b in Gal. 3,28: "there is not male and female, for you are all one (col-lective male) in Christ," is interpreted as *including* women instead of *abolish-ing* femaleness.

Androcentric Christ-likeness

Christianity starts from what I call "redemptional democracy," where both men *and* women are saved in Christ through baptism, in order to be restored by resurrection. Since Christ is incarnated in perfect humanity and conse-quently in male God-likeness, women's salvational equality is realised by achieving Christ-like maleness, as expressed in Eph. 4,13: "until we all arrive at the unity of the faith and of the full knowledge of the Son of God, unto a perfect man, unto the measure of the stature of the fulness of Christ." This early Christian theme of "becoming male" as a prerequisite to, and conse-quence of, redemptive conformity with the new Adam, Christ, is succinctly verbalised in the last *logion*, 114, of the Gospel of Thomas (ca. 150 or earlier): "Simon Peter said to them, 'Let Mary (Magdalene) leave us, for women are not worthy of Life.' Jesus said, 'I myself shall lead her in order to make her male, so that she too may become a living spirit (cf. Gen. 2,7) resembling you males. For every woman who makes herself male will enter the Kingdom of Heaven.'"

A striking example of female internalisation of such Christ-like maleness is provided by the Egyptian desert Mother, Amma Sarra (4th century). Talking to some great visiting anchorites, she refers to her God-given charismatic authority in these terms: "I am a man (*ego eimi aner*), and you, you are women."[1]

Christocentric Typology

Early Christian anthropology defines the first human male as God-like prototype by combining Gen. 1,26–27a and Gen. 2,7. The creation of Eve, according to Gen. 2,18,21–23, is regularly linked to the fertility blessing of Gen. 1,28 and *not* to theomorphic privilege. The fundamental Adam-Christ typology starts from Rom. 5,14: "Adam, who is a type (*typos*) of the coming (Christ)." The correlated nuptial symbolism of Christ-church in Eph. 5,32, cf. II Cor. 11,2, is from the 2nd through the 4th century amplified in the sense of a salvational couple: new Adam–new Eve. In this extended typology, creational gender hierarchy is transposed to the order of redemption, as man-like Christ and woman-like church. Theomorphic maleness is here a self-evident premise, with corollary exclusion of femaleness at the divine level. It is essential to note that this symbolism aggravates the patriarchal subordination of Eve, made *from*, *after* and *for* Adam. The first pair consists of one autonomous and one derived partner, but both are created beings. In contrast, the salvational couple features a divinely supreme Lord and humanity as his submissive bride. When Eve's inferior femaleness serves as model for human dependency of divine omnipotence, women's sub-male status is in fact reenforced.

Nevertheless, by opposing Mary's instrumental obedience in Christ's conception to Eve's disobedience as instrumental in Adam's fall, Justin (d. ca. 165) and Irenaeus (d. ca. 200) display what I call "androcentric innocence." A reenactment (*recapitulatio*) of subordinate Eve is realised by Mary, as complement to the Adam-Christ typology. Eve's inverted helpmate performance, leading to Adam's fall, is here counteracted by Mary's ancillary role in the incarnation of God's Son.[2] Eve's lack of God-likeness is an axiomatic premise of this argumentation, where Christ-like Adam is counterbalanced by God-like Christ, incarnated in perfect male humanity.

Less innocent, Tertullian (d. ca. 220) refers to women's punishment, according to Gen. 3,16, as resulting from the devil's use of Eve to obtain the fall of theomorphic Adam. Addressing them directly, he states: "You are the one who opened the door to the Devil, you are the one who first plucked the fruit of the forbidden tree, you are the first who deserted the divine law; you are the one who persuaded him whom the Devil was not strong enough to attack. All too easily you destroyed the image of God, man. Because of your fault punished by death, even the Son of God had to die."[3] In the same work against female adornment, Tertullian attributes to resurrected women a mixed angelic and male transformation: "The same angelic nature is promised to you, women, the selfsame sex is promised to you as to men, and the self-same dignity of being a judge."[4]

Tertullian continues Christocentric typology by transposing gender roles from creation, through the first sin and into the order of redemption. Like Adam shaped from virgin earth, Christ is incarnated in the virginal womb of Mary, thereby restoring man's God-likeness. "It is because God by a contrary operation has regained possession of his own image and similitude taken captive by the devil." Into Eve, while still a virgin, had crept the word, constructive of death: into a virgin was likewise to be introduced the Word of God, constructive of life, so that which by the female sex had gone astray into perdition should through the same sex be led back again into salvation. Eve had believed the serpent (Gen. 3,6), Mary believed Gabriel (Luke 1,38).[5]

Tertullian also identifies the church as new Eve, by comparing the first woman's formation from Adam's rib during his sleep, according to Gen. 2,21–22, with the church as emerging from Christ's pierced side after his death on the cross: "that from the wound inflicted on his side, in like manner be typified the church, the true mother of the living."[6] This interpretation of John 19,34, where blood and water signify *ecclesia* as Christ's new Eve, that is mother of the living by dispensing baptism and eucharist, was to become standard in patristic ecclesiology. From Ambrose (d. 397) onwards, Mary and the church are fused as new Eve through their shared virginal motherhood, in relation to Christ as incarnated Son and redeeming husband.[7]

In this androcentric perspective, it is significant that the Roman aristocratic matron, Faltonia Betitia Proba, in her biblical paraphrase (Virgilian *Cento* composed ca. 360) connects Gen. 1,26–27a and Gen. 2,7 in a decidedly mancentred way. Adam, termed man, *uir*, is created God-like: "He pulled plump clay and gave it shape by kneading on the spot the fertile ground, its soil quickened from the year's first months. And now, so suddenly, the image of such holiness! Man's new shape went forth, handsome at first beyond comparison, resembling God in countenance and shoulders. Man, whose mind and intellect a greater God influences, and so sends forth to greater tasks."

Eve's formation from Adam's rib is interpreted in the traditional sense of her subordinate sex role: "And now in the middle course of a shady night, the almighty Sire laid the ribs and entrails bare. One of these ribs he plucked apart from the well-knit joints of the youthful Adam's side, and suddenly arose a wondrous gift – imposing proof – and shone in brilliant light: Woman, a virgin she, unparalleled in figure and in comely breasts, now ready for a husband, ready now for wedlock. For him, a boundless quaking breaks his sleep; he calls his bones and limbs his wedded wife. Dazed by the will divine he took and clasped her hand in his, folded his arms around her."[8]

Male God-likeness

The so-called Ambrosiaster, an unidentified commentator of the Pauline corpus who was active in Rome shortly after Proba (ca. 370–380), probably disliked dominating matrons. It is noteworthy that the contemporary pope Damasus (d. 384) was otherwise scorned as adulating influential female aristocrats: "whom the matrons loved to such an extent that he was called their 'earscratcher.'"[9] Eventually reacting against this "feminist" challenge, Ambrosiaster underlines women's lack of creational God-likeness by invoking I Cor. 11,7, in order to corroborate their God-willed subjection. Later attributed to Ambrose and Augustine, this exegesis survived in medieval canon law, thereby prescribing women's inferior status in church and society.[10]

In *Liber quaestionum ueteris et noui testamenti* Ambrosiaster defines men's exclusive God-likeness and firmly negates that women are created in God's image. Combining Gen. 1,26–27a and Gen. 2,7, Adam's *imago Dei* is stressed by comparing monotheism and monogenism: "Man is the image of God because one God made one man, so that just as all things are from the one God, so the entire human race comes from the one man." This juxtaposition of theocentrism and androcentrism, where one man-like God creates one God-like man, states that Adam transmits his image quality to all human males, whereas all human females inherit Eve's God-alien subservience. Her derivation from Adam's rib, according to Gen. 2,21–22, establishes his preeminence, *auctoritas*, as origin of mankind. Adam's God-resemblance, *similitudo*, is described by a startling parallel between the Father's ineffable generation of the Son and the Creator's corporeal formation of Eve from Adam. Combining Gen. 1,26–27a and I Cor. 11,7a, theomorphic man, *homo*, is then identified with Paul's God-like man, *uir*. Without citing I Cor. 11,7b, Ambrosiaster concludes that Paul's woman, *mulier*, must be veiled "because she is not God-like, *non est imago Dei*." Her lack of image privilege is finally stressed by citation of I Tim. 2,12: "I do not permit woman to teach, nor to domineer over man."[11]

Further analysing the concept *imago Dei,* Ambrosiaster repeats the parallel of one andromorphic God and one theomorphic man. The image quality is again defined in terms of uniqueness, since Adam as carnal origin of humanity imitates God as origin of the spiritual universe: "Man is God's image in the sense that, just as there is one God in heaven from whom all spiritual things derive their existence, so there was to be one man on earth from whom the others would have their origin in the flesh." Ambrosiaster observes that according to Gen. 1,28 the male-female pair is given power, *dominatio,* over the animals *together:* "they are perceived to be subject not only to man, but also to woman, who it is clear does not possess the image of God." Since women are not God-like, it would be absurd to define *imago Dei* in the sense of a dominance which is *shared* by both sexes. Ambrosiaster ends his argument by invoking men's God-given rule, *dominium,* over women as proof of their lacking image quality: "If man's God-likeness consists in having dominion, it would be absurd to attribute this to woman, who is not created in God's image. For how can it be said of woman that she is the image of God, she who has been constituted as subject to the mastery of man and as having no authority? She cannot teach, nor be a witness in court, cannot take an oath nor pass judgment. Still less can she govern!"[12] This uneasy distinction between inclusive human *dominatio* and exclusive male *dominium* survived as key-text in *Corpus Iuris Canonici,* in order to legitimate women's theological and sociological inferiority.[13] In another exegesis of Gen. 1,26-27a and I Cor. 11,7, Ambrosiaster invokes female subservience and privation of *imago Dei,* thereby defining Adam's God-likeness as representative of God's unique and regal lordship: "This image of God is in man so that one alone might be made the lord from whom the others would originate, possessing regal power as God's vicar, since every king possesses the image of God, and this is why woman is not made in God's image."[14] Also this text had good fortune in medieval canon law, but with politically significant omission of royal God-likeness.[15]

Ambrosiaster's commentary on I Cor. 11,7 stresses women's inferiority as being subject to men's power, *imperium:* "Therefore woman is inferior to man by being a portion of him, since man is the origin of woman; for she comes from him. Thus it can be seen that woman is subordinate to man, since she is subject to his rule." The parallel of monotheism and monogenism is repeated: "And this is the image of God in man, because the one God made one man so that just as all things come from one God so all human beings might come from one man, and the image of one invisible God might be possessed on earth by the one visible man." Since women are not God-like, they are to be veiled: "this is why woman ought to veil her head, because she is not the image of God and must be displayed as subject to man."[16] Women's lack of God's image is equally invoked in commenting I Cor. 14,34, in order to justify female submission in the church: "For if the image of God is man, not woman, and if she is subject to man by the law of nature, how much more should females be subject in church, out of reverence for him who is the legate of Him who is the head of man."[17]

It is important to note that Ambrosiaster's focus on Adam's uniqueness in terms of monogenism differs from the argumentation for male God-likeness in Antiochene exegesis, but both have the same conclusion: men's dominion over the rest of creation, women included, is divinely ordained. Diodor of Tarsus (d. before 394) invokes I Cor. 11,7 in order to stress that only men are God-like, since they have power over women. When both sexes dominate the animals according to Gen. 1,28, women do not reign over men and female human beings are consequently not theomorphic.[18] John Chrysostom (d. 407) equally uses I Cor. 11,7 as proof-text for subordinate women's lack of God-likeness, defined as men's imitation of divine hegemony. Rather illogically, he affirms creational gender hierarchy with reference to Gen. 3,16, where female subjection is a punishment for Eve's sin. With more sophistication, Chrysostom underlines that theomorphic privilege cannot consist in human form as such, *morphe*, which is shared by both sexes. The consequence would be to describe God as andromorphic, and even more absurd, gynecomorphic.[19]

It is noteworthy that Ambrosiaster's exegesis of Gal. 3,28 does not refer to the abolition of sexual difference, but underlines moral differentiation in the same faith: "There is no discrimination among persons with God, except in the realm of morals and life, so that human beings are distinguished by the merits of their faith alone, not by their persons."[20] Ambrosiaster's exegesis of Col. 3,11 emphasises women's salvational God-likeness obtained through Christocentric faith, *in contrast* to their lack of creational *imago Dei* according to Gen. 1,26–27a and I Cor. 11,7: "This image, which is said to be created by the recognition of the saviour, is different from the image of God in which the first man was made. For the former image is present in woman too, when she recognizes the one God who created her and obeys his will by refraining from a sordid life and perverse conduct, but the latter image is present only in man."[21] This exegetical displacement of genderfree equivalence corresponds to an interesting "feminist falsification" attested in versions of the Latin Bible, *Vetus Latina*, like the 5th-century *Codex Claromontanus*, where the formula from Gal. 3,28: "there is not male and female, *non est masculus et femina*," is *added* to the beginning of Col. 3,11: "where there is not male and female, *ubi non est masculus et femina."*

Asexual God-likeness

Clement of Alexandria is the *first* author I have found who connects the sexual differentiation of Gen. 1,27b to the theomorphic male prototype in Gen. 1,26–27a, using the Christomorphic asexuality of Gal. 3,28 as proof-text. By this ingenious "feminist" device, Clement manages to anticipate women's salvational God-likeness *already* at creation. Given the fundamental incompatibility of Godhead and femaleness, theomorphic privilege is here linked to asexual moral and intellectual capacity, shared by men and women alike, since all are human beings and termed *anthropos*. In his work on divine pedagogy towards humankind, Clement insists that Christ is *Logos Paidagogos* for both men and women, leading humans of both sexes to salvation. Citing Luke 20,34–35 on the absence of marriage in the resurrection, Clement affirms that the female differs from the male only in *this* world.[22]

In his conglomerate *Stromata*, Clement invokes Gen. 1,26, to define human God-likeness as incorporeal, fulfilled through spiritual immortality.[23] Its dynamic character, starting with creational image to be achieved in salvational resemblance with God, is illustrated by a citation from Plato's *Theaitetos* 176b: "That is why we should make all speed to take flight from this world to the other; and that means becoming like the divine as far as we can, and that again is to become righteous with the help of wisdom."[24] Clement's inclusive argumentation combines the Stoic concept of humanity, as attributable even to women and slaves, with Neoplatonic restriction of male and female characteristics to the *bodily* level. With combined reference to Col. 3,11 and Gal. 3,28, Clement underlines that all humankind is capable of attaining wisdom in Christ. The same human nature and virtuous power are to be found in barbarians, Greeks, slaves, children and women. Following Stoic acquiescence of sociological inequality, this moral equivalence does not affect bio-social gender hierarchy. From an androcentric perspective, woman shares man's spiritual and moral nature by being God-like human being, *anthropos*, in her rational soul, although she differs from exemplary maleness in her female corporality and sexual function, as *gyne*. Citing I Cor. 11,3,8, Clement states the hierarchical relationship between Christ/man and man/woman, as displayed in Adam's priority and Eve's derived origin. Nevertheless, invoking I Cor. 11,11 and Gal. 5,16–17, Clement underlines that women can imitate men's moral headship by dominating inferior bodily appetites.[25] Male precedence notwithstanding, even women shall devote themselves to *philosophia*, i.e. love of wisdom. Female subservience is further illustrated by citations of Greek classical texts, together with I Cor. 11,3 and 7a.[26] The omission of I Cor. 11,7b is here significant; since Clement defines theomorphic privilege as sexless, he does not need affirmation of exclusively male God-likeness in order to legitimate creational gender hierarchy.

In spite of this genderfree concept of God's image, Clement regularly describes moral and intellectual perfection with reference to Eph. 4,13, in the sense of virile prowess. Salvational Christ-likeness in perfect manhood, is thus achieved by conquering womanish lust through Stoic insensibility to passion, *apatheia*.[27] Enlightened knowledge is equally qualified as andromorphic excellence, invoking Eph. 4,13.[28] Consequently, Clement's praise of asexual virtue and intellect in man-like disguise enhances theomorphic women by classifying them as honorary men.

It is important to remember that this combined androcentric and gender-less validation is significantly changed in Clement's anti-gnostic defence of human fertility. Connecting not only Gen. 1,27b, but also Gen. 1,28 to the preceding image text of Gen. 1,26–27a, Clement defines human God-likeness as actualised by procreating offspring in collaboration with divine creativity: "The human being, *anthropos*, is God's image, because he cooperates through his humanity in the birth of another human."[29] The term *anthropos* is here deliberately inclusive, since Clement underlines that both male and female generative functions participate in divine creativity. In fact, both men's sowing of seed and women's nourishing formation of the embryo take part in God's creative action.[30]

Symbolic God-likeness

The commentary on Genesis 1 by Didymus of Alexandria (d. 398) was found in 1941. Like Clement he defines human God-likeness as a purely spiritual quality. Interpreting Gen. 1,26–27a, Didymus states that only the interior human being, *anthropos*, or the intellect is created in God's image. Like the Antiochenes he defines theomorphic privilege as dominion, but in the symbolic sense of intellectual and moral hegemony over the exterior *anthropos*, i.e. not God-like corporality. In this perspective, Didymus cites I Cor. 11,7a and 3 in order to affirm the rational soul's Christomorphic headship.[31] Reference to I Cor. 11,7b, "but woman is the glory of man," is omitted just like in Clement. Didymus proceeds to interpret the reign over animals according to

Gen. 1,26 in terms of rational control, with Christocentric progress from creational image to salvational resemblance.[32] Following Clement, Didymus connects the sexual differentiation in Gen. 1,27b to the preceding image text in
Gen. 1,26–27a, with explicit definition of women as God-like. He starts by literal exegesis, explaining that woman, *gyne*, is a human being, *anthropos*, just
like man, *aner*. The terms male and female, *"arsen kai thelu,"* designate sexual difference which is restricted to the body and ordained to procreation of
offspring. On the spiritual level, both man and woman have the same capacity
to imitate God through the Holy Spirit and thereby achieving virtue. In his
symbolic exegesis of Gen. 1,27b, Didymus interprets the male-female couple
as signifying generating intelligence and conceiving soul, *nous* and *psyche*.
The leading male teacher is sowing his verbal seed in the docile and receptive
female disciple. This androcentric bio-sociology is further transposed to the
salvational order, where human rational souls are woman-like in relation to
God as husband. Didymus' nuptial symbolism corresponds to Christocentric
typology, featuring the divine *Logos* with his church as human bride. This
symbolic gender hierarchy is supplemented by a reference to Eph. 4,13, in the
sense of attaining perfect manhood through divine virtue.[33]

Didymus' allegorical exegesis of Gen. 1,27b is inspired by Origen (d. ca.
254), who defined God-likeness as incorporeal and residing in interior humanity, *homo interior*, according to Gen. 1,26–27a. In order to insert the bodily
terms male and female in this context of spiritual creation, Origen interprets
the terms male and female in Gen. 1,27b, *masculus et femina*, as signifying
spirit and soul, *spiritus et anima*.[34]

Didymus' literal inclusion of God-like women by connecting Gen. 1,27b to
Gen. 1,26–27a has an interesting echo in Basil of Caesarea (d. 379). His "feminist" exegesis uses the literary fiction of an androcentric lady who has certainly read I Cor. 11,7, but without directly referring to Paul. Commenting on
Gen. 1,27a, this woman, *gyne*, affirms that the term *anthropos* as grammatically masculine only concerns man, *aner*. Basil retorts that Gen. 1,27b is
added in the scriptural text to emphasise the inclusion of *gyne* in God-like
humanity: "Also woman possesses, like man, the privilege of being created in
God's image. Equally honorable in their two natures, sharing equal virtuous-
ness, they are equal in reward and like in condemnation. Woman should not
say: I am feeble. Feebleness is of the body, in the soul is power." Basil under-
scores that pious women can even surpass men in virtue, arduous prayer and
good works. In spite of female feebleness, the virtuous *gyne* achieves resemblance with God through generous charity and subjection of passions, thus
attaining theomorphic dominion.[35] A similar "feminist" approach is found in

Basil's commentary of Psalm 112,1, where he interprets the blessed man, *makarios aner,* as equally designating virtuous woman. His exegesis explicitly invokes Gen. 1,26-27b in terms of inclusive God-likeness.[36]

Presexual God-likeness

The leading Father of Greek theology, Basil's younger brother Gregory of Nyssa (d. ca. 395), includes women in God-like humanity by defining creational image of God as presexual privilege. Gregory's interpretation is a mitigated variant of encratite protology, where the original perfection of humankind is understood as either all-male, presexual or asexual. In consequence, gender differentiation, or more precisely, femaleness, is explained as a *cause* or *consequence* of primeval sin. In this perspective, sexual abstinence, *enkrateia,* is indispensable for restoring humanity to initial, God-willed wholeness. The corollary double creation reappears in Gregory's two-stage theory. According to Gen. 1,26-27a, the first creation in God's image is purely spiritual. This original, presexual and perfect humanity will be restored in the order of redemption, a typical encratite theme. The second phase, creation of sexually differentiated bodies according to Gen. 1,27b-28, is by Gregory connected to the formation of Adam and his woman, expressed in Gen. 2,7,18, 21-23. This introduction of animal physicality, which assimilates humanity with beasts, is motivated by God's *foreknowledge* of the first sin. Sub-human mortality as consequence of the fall is to be counteracted by equally *sub-human* fertility.[37]

Gregory's twofold anthropology is "feminist" in the sense that by placing Adam's formation in Gen. 2,7 on the *same* secondary level as derived woman in Gen. 2,18,21-23, he severs the traditional link between theomorphic humanity and exemplary maleness. The androcentric combination of Gen. 1,26-27a and Gen. 2,7, as expressed in I Cor. 11,7, is therefore entirely alien to Gregory's thought. In contrast, he regularly invokes Gal. 3,28 in favour of presexual God-likeness, to be restored in Christ by reverting to the initial perfection, as *before* the creation of bodies in Gen. 1,27b-28. Gregory's definition of fully God-like humanity therefore excludes both male and female gender. This, what I call "castrational equality," is succinctly expressed in Gregory's treatise on the resurrection, where his older sister Makrina (d. 379/380) is teacher of doctrine.[38] Nevertheless, in his biography of this exemplary virgin, Gregory stresses Makrina's manly courage, *andreia,* whereby she distances herself from lowly and womanish behaviour.[39] The same androcentric evaluation is present in Gregory's praise of encratite virginity, where desexualised virtue is achieved through virile subjugation of carnal passions. On the other hand, Gregory applies nuptial symbolism to define the relationship between incorporeal Godhead and virgins of both sexes. Combining Gal. 3,28 and Col. 3,11, Gregory describes the spiritual marriage of Christ as husband to male and female virgins alike.[40] These lapses into gendered imagery notwithstanding, Gregory's God-language is firmly metasexual. Commenting on the Song of Songs 3,11, he interprets Salomo's mother in the sense of a conjectural female metaphor for God. Alluding to Gal. 3,28, Gregory underlines that there is no sexual distinction in divine nature, with corresponding presexual God-likeness. In this context of divine ineffability, he points to the equal inadequacy of both male and female names for God, who remains untarnished by human discourse. In fact, the terms father and mother are equivalent as equally unfit to verbalise divine reality.[41]

Gregory's theology can be labelled "feminist" in the sense of defining maleness and femaleness as equally alien to divinity, and thereby correcting andromorphic God-language. Nevertheless, Gregory's correlated anthropology is particularly inapplicable from a modern feminist standpoint, since his definition of perfect humanity excludes both male and female gender. In fact, Gregory's double Adam and Eve are not properly human beings, but *hybrid* creatures, with angel-like, spiritual image quality and beast-like, sexually differentiated corporality. It is important to remember that this variant of encratite double creation was upheld by major theologians, like Maximus Confessor (d. 662) and John of Damascus (d. ca. 749). In consequence, Gregory's divisive scheme survived in Greek Orthodoxy throughout the Middle Ages.

God-like Women

In comparison with Clement of Alexandria's inclusion of genderfree women in creational God-likeness and Gregory of Nyssa's exclusion of gender from theomorphic humanity, Augustine's *holistic* definition of both maleness and femaleness as properly human marks a culmination of patristic "feminism." Confronting Manichaean dualism and encratite duality, this leading Father of Latin theology affirms the *unity* of creation. In his *De Genesi ad litteram* Augustine strives to combine the two creation accounts, an arduous task, since the hypothesis of two biblical sources here was first proposed in 1711 by Henning Bernhard Witter. Augustine distinguishes between two modes of God's *unique* creation act: the instant, seminal *informatio* expressed in Gen. 1, and the successive *conformatio* described in Gen. 2.[42] By this exegetical device, Augustine is able to connect the sexual differentiation according to Gen. 1,27b–28 with the preceding image text of Gen. 1,26–27a. It follows that the formation of Adam *and* his woman in Gen. 2,7,18,21–32 is linked to the creation of theomorphic humanity. This protological leap from Gregory's duality is "feminist" in the sense of including the female human being, *femina/mulier,* in the God-like human prototype, *homo.* Nevertheless, it is important to note that Augustine's holistic effort is hampered by his Neoplatonic spiritualism, in that he endorses Gregory's genderless definition of the image quality, *in spite* of rejecting its presupposed dual creation. The ensuing logical *incoherence* of Augustine's anthropology becomes particularly visible through his "feminist" striving to incorporate female human beings in andromorphic or asexual God-likeness.

Augustine is the *first* church Father I have found who directly affronts I Cor. 11,7 by stating that women *too* are created in God's image. It is important to note that all patristic exegesis understands this text as literally affirming men's *exclusive* God-likeness. Augustine's scriptural dilemma results from his inclusive interpretation of theomorphic humanity, by connecting Gen. 1,26–27a and Gen. 1,27b. Refusing to accept Paul's denial of women's God-likeness, *imago Dei,* Augustine resorts to allegorical exegesis. In contrast to Didymus of Alexandria, he does not apply the higher and lower parts of interior humanity, *homo interior,* to the male-female distinction, *masculus et femina,* in Gen. 1,27b, but to the couple man/woman, *vir/mulier,* in I Cor. 11,7. Consequently, Augustine neutralises Paul by explaining that God-like man signifies the superior element of the human soul, which is dedicated to contemplation of eternal truth; in contradistinction to non-God-like woman, who represents the soul's inferior element and is charged with earthly matters. Nevertheless, by invoking Col. 3,11 and Gal. 3,28, Augustine succeeds to backdate women's salvational God-likeness to the order of creation, since also *femina* is a theomorphic human being, *homo,* in her rational, God-like soul. This argumentation is clearly expressed in *De Genesi ad litteram:* "Although the physical and external differences of man and woman symbolize the double role which the mind is understood to have in one human being, nevertheless a woman, who is female in her body, is also renewed in the spirit of her mind in the knowledge of God according to the image of her Creator, where there is no male and female. Therefore, women are not excluded from this grace of renewal and this reformation of the image of God, although otherwise figured by their bodily sex, since man alone is said to be the image and glory of God. In the original creation of mankind, inasmuch as woman was a human being, she also had a rational mind according to which even she was made to the image of God."[43]

Creational gender hierarchy is a self-evident premise of this reasoning, with corollary disparity between femaleness and God-likeness. It follows that human female beings are theomorphic *in spite* of their bodily sex, whereas men's spiritual God-likeness, *imago Dei,* corresponds to their exemplary maleness. Exclusion of femaleness at the divine level remains basic in Augustine's God-language. The resulting split between women's God-like mind, *homo interior* and their sub-male corporeality, *homo exterior,* is further exposed in *De Trinitate.* Citing Gen. 1,27a–b, Augustine affirms that women are not excluded from creational *imago Dei:* "For he (the Genesis text) says that human nature itself, which is complete in both sexes, has been made to the image of God, so that he does not exclude woman from being understood as God's image." Augustine proceeds to explain the affirmation of man's exclusive God-likeness in I Cor. 11,7: "In what sense, therefore, are we to understand the Apostle, who says that man is the image of God, and consequently is forbidden to cover his head, but that woman is not, and therefore is ordered to do so? The solution lies, I think, in what I already said concerning the nature of the human mind: woman together with her husband is the image of God, so that the whole substance is one image. When she is assigned as a helpmate, a function which pertains to her alone, then she is not God's image. But man is by himself alone the image of God, just as fully and completely as when he and the woman are joined together into one. Therefore, we said that the nature of the human mind as a whole is the image of God when it contemplates the truth. But when its functions are divided so that something is diverted to the handling of temporal things, the superior part which consults the truth is nevertheless God's image, although the inferior part is not in the image of God."[44] Referring to the higher and lower elements of the same human mind, Augustine's androcentric identification of theomorphic *homo* and male *vir* emphasises man's God-like autonomy. As exemplary human being, man is *imago Dei* in himself alone, whereas woman is not God-like *qua* inferior female being, *mulier.* It is significant that Augustine's preference for sexual abstention hinders any definition of God-likeness in terms of human bonding as such. Consequently, *vir* cannot be theomorphic through his relation with *mulier.* Woman's attainment of God-likeness despite her subordinate place in the human couple is therefore an exceptional, "feminist" stratagem, but firmly anchored in Augustine's self-evident identification of superiority and maleness.

It follows that Augustine cites Gal. 3,28, Col. 3,10 and Eph. 4,23 together with I Cor. 11,7, in order to attribute spiritual autonomy in male disguise also to women, in spite of their sub-male femaleness: "Have the believing women, therefore, lost their bodily sex? But because they are renewed to the image of God where there is no sex, man is made in God's image where there is no sex, namely in the spirit of the mind. Why then is the man not bound to cover his head because he is the image and glory of God, but the woman must cover her head because she is the glory of man; as if she were not renewed in the spirit of her mind, which is renewed unto the knowledge of God who created him? Since she differs from man in her female sex, that part of reason which is diverted to regulate temporal things, could be properly symbolised by her corporeal veil; so that the image of God does not remain except in that part of the human mind which clings to the contemplation and consideration of eternal reasons, which, as is evident, not only men but also women possess. Therefore, in their minds a common nature is recognised, but in their bodies the division of this one mind is symbolised."[45]

Androcentric bio-sociology and Neoplatonic anthropology are here exegetically twisted in order to insert deviant femaleness as fully human in terms of religious capacity, thereby dismantling male God-likeness through asexual device. Nevertheless, women's *imago Dei* persists in man-like disguise, thus sharpening the conflict between rational privilege and subordinate female humanity. In fact, Augustine's holistic combination of *informatio* and *conformatio* as describing God's unique creative act, strengthens the mancentered identification of patriarchal sex roles and God-willed gender hierarchy.

In a commentary on Gal. 3,28 which was regularly cited in medieval exegesis, Augustine emphasises that salvational equivalence of gentiles, slaves and women, obtained through faith in Christ, does not modify racial, social and sexual inequality in *this* world: "Such difference of race or social rank or sex has already been removed by the unity of faith, but it remains in the mortal condition and is prescribed by the apostles as normative for the path of this life. They also transmit most salutary rules, by which Jews and Greeks should live among themselves on account of their different race, masters and slaves on account of their unequal social rank, and men and wives on account of their sexual disparity. Similar rules apply to parallel circumstances. The Lord himself was the first to order this, when he said: 'Give to Caesar what belongs to Caesar, and to God what belongs to God.'"[46] Thus referring to political obedience in Matth. 22,21, Augustine compares gender hierarchy with ethnic and economic stratification. On the other hand, he defines female subordination as ordained by God's creative order, whereas slavery is understood as resulting from the first sin.[47] Man's domination over woman is part of the natural order, justified by female inferiority; man's domination over another man is caused by injustice: "Iniquity or adversity has made a man slave of another man. . . . For the natural order among human beings requires that women should serve men and children their parents, because here it is just that the weaker reason should serve the stronger. In consequence, evident justice claims that those who excel through reason should also excel in domination."[48]

Significantly, Augustine underlines that God's only purpose for creating woman, *femina/mulier*, as man's helpmate, *adiutorium*, according to Gen. 2,18, is woman's subordinate and receptive role in procreation: "Now, if woman was not made for man to be his helper in begetting children, in what was she to help him? She was not to till the earth with him, for there was not yet any toil to make help necessary. If there were any such need, a male helper would be better, and the same could to be said of the comfort of another's presence if Adam were perhaps weary of solitude. How much more congenially could two male friends, rather than a man and a woman, live together in companionship and conversation. . . . Therefore, I do not see in what sense the woman was made a helper for the man if not for the sake of begetting children."[49]

Female Resurrection

Nevertheless, when Augustine in *De civitate Dei* describes God's final restoring of perfect humanity through Christ-like resurrection, he introduces a "feminist" exegesis of Eph. 4,13. With explicit reference to creational wholeness, Augustine interprets perfect manhood, *uir perfectus*, in terms of human fulfilment, according to inclusive *homo* in Gen. 1,26–27b and holistic *conformatio* as expressed in Gen. 2,7,18,21–23. Since femaleness is part of God's unique creation, women will not be restored to Christ-like humanity by resurrecting as males. Women shall consequently resurrect as female human beings, although their procreative finality will be superseded: "A woman's sex is natural and no vice, but in the resurrection her nature will be immune from coition and child-bearing. Her female members will subsist with the former purpose transformed to a new beauty, so that no concupiscence will be aroused. Femaleness shall praise the wisdom of God, who first made a woman, and who liberated her from the corruption into which she fell." Augustine's viewpoint is here decidedly androcentric, since he argues that the recreated beauty of female bodies will no longer divert resurrected human males, henceforth liberated from their sinful concupiscence. Augustine continues this argument for female resurrection by invoking Christocentric typology, with reference to Gen. 2,21–22, Eph. 5,32 and John 19,34. The formation of Eve from Adam prefigures the union of Christ and his church, and is consequently validating both created and recreated femaleness: "Woman is as much the creation of God as man is. If she was made from the man, this was to show her oneness with him; and if she was made in the way she was, this was to prefigure the oneness of Christ and the church, as it is said." Finally, Augustine cites Matth. 22,30: "For in the resurrection they will neither be married nor take wives, but they are like angels in heaven." He firmly rejects any encratite interpretation of such sexless bliss in terms of all-male perfection. Augustine stresses that in the resurrection marriage, not women, will be eliminated: "So the Lord said that there shall be no marriage in the resurrection, not that there shall be no women."[50]

Returning to Eph. 4,13, Augustine connects inclusive Christ-like manhood to the *beatus vir* of Psalm 112,1, which he interprets in conformity with Basil. He states that: "Even if referring to the shape each one will have in the resurrection, nothing prevents us from understanding woman also when man is named; taking *uir* to mean *homo* as in the text: "Blessed is the man who fears the Lord," which likewise includes women who fear the Lord."[51]

Inclusive Typology

It is important to note that Augustine's application of the new Adam/new Eve typology has an aspect of what I call "androcentric feminism." Although Adam's sole responsibility for humanity's collective guilt is counteracted through Christ's redemption, according to Augustine's exegesis of Rom. 5,12, Eve's instrumental role in the first sin is repaired by the subordinate function of Mary/church as Christ's mother/bride. Christ takes human nature in the form of a *man*, but this incarnation is realised through the intermediary of a *woman*. Augustine emphasises that a female element in the redemptive order thus guarantees the salvation of *both* sexes: "Our Lord Jesus Christ, who came to deliver the human race, in which both men and women are called to salvation, did not disdain men, since he became man, nor women, since he was born by a woman. Here is a great mystery; just as death came to us through a woman, life was born to us through a woman. And so, by both natures, that is female and male, the devil was vanquished and put to torture, he who had rejoiced in their downfall. It would have contributed little to his punishment if those two natures had been delivered in us without our being liberated by both of them."[52] The parallel of Eve and Mary is here invoked in order to embrace both variants of human nature, female and male. In Augustine's androcentric context, this application of redemptive typology serves to enhance creationally inferior femaleness, with corresponding inclusive definition of the term *homo:* "It was necessary that human liberation should be manifest in both sexes. Therefore, since it was fitting that he (Christ) became man, taking the more honourable sex, it followed that deliverance of the female sex should be shown by the fact that this man was born by a woman."[53]

Conclusion

Augustine's main doctrinal achievement is the defence of protological unity, thereby discarding the dual creation and divisive anthropology of Gregory of Nyssa. Augustine's holistic concept of humanity is clearly expressed in *De natura et origine animae*, where he succinctly declares that to strip human nature of the body is to be crazy: "The whole human nature includes spirit, soul and body; anyone who tries to alienate the body from human nature is out of his mind."[54] In contrast, Augustine follows Gregory by restricting human God-likeness to the incorporeal soul. The resulting incoherence between embodied humanity and bodiless *imago Dei* is manifest in Augustine's juxtaposition of two logically *irreconcilable* themes: androcentric typology and asexual God-likeness. Nevertheless, Augustine's theomorphic woman in man-like disguise, where *femina/mulier* is God-like *homo* through her defeminised higher reason, symbolised by *masculus/vir*, marks the final performance of patristic "feminism." It is important to remember that the fundamental conflict between divinity and femaleness remains unaltered, since women's salvational God-likeness is backdated to the order of creation despite their deviance from exemplary male humanity.

In consequence, Augustine's doctrinal sexology becomes perfectly inapplicable when gender hierarchy is no longer defined as divinely ordained. It is essential to note that Christocentric typology, even in Augustine's "feminist" version, presupposes God-like Adam served by non-God-like Eve. Christ as new Adam is incarnated in perfect manhood, whereas the new Eve, Mary/church, reenacts the first woman's ancillary role. A nuptial symbolism which transposes creational androcentrism to the order of redemption, appears particularly anachronistic in post-patriarchal culture. In spite of this, Christocentric typology still persists as fundamental in both Latin and Greek God-language, christology and ecclesiology. On the contrary, asexual God-likeness as introduced by Clement of Alexandria and enforced through Augustine, is in modern theological anthropology dismissed by a combined inclusive and holistic definition of God's image, where both women and men are fully God-like in their male or female humanity. It follows that sexless *imago Dei* in andromorphic disguise is now superseded. This new inculturation makes the survival of early patristic typology, based on exclusively male God-likeness, even more contradictory. When invoked to legitimate ecclesiastical power structures, the obsolete new Eve becomes perfectly noxious. Augustine's "feminist" intent can inspire the necessary reformation of Christian God-language, in order to reconstruct a sustainable doctrine, *sana doctrina.*[55]

Notes

1. Sarra 9. In Guy, Jean-Claude: *Les Apophtègmes des Pères du Désert,* 1966, 229.
2. Justin: Dialogus 100,5. In Goodspeed, Edgar J.: *Die ältesten Apologeten,* 1914, 215. Irenaeus: *Adversus Haereses* 5,19,1. SC 153, 248-250. *Demonstratio* 33. SC 62,83-86.
3. *De cultu feminarum* 1,1,2. CCSL 1,343: "Tu es diaboli ianua; tu es arboris illius resignatrix; tu es diuinae legis prima desertrix; tu es quae eum suasisti, quem diabolus aggredi non ualuit; tu imaginem dei, hominem, tam facile elisisti; propter tuum meritum, id est mortem, etiam filius Dei mori habuit; et adornari tibi in mente est pelliceas tuas tunicas?"
4. *De cultu feminarum* 1,2,5. CCSL 1,346: "Nam et uobis eadem tunc substantia angelica repromissa, idem sexus qui et uiris, eamdem iudicandi dignationem pollicetur."
5. *De carne Christi* 17,3-5. CCSL 2,904-905: "quod deus imaginem et similitudinem suam a diabolo captam aemula operatione recuperauit."
6. *De anima* 43,10. CCSL 2,847: "ut de inuiria perinde lateris eius uera mater uiuentium figuraretur ecclesia."
7. *Liber de institutione virginis* 14,88-89. PL 16,341. *Expositio evangelii secundum Lucam* 2,7. CCSL 14,33.
8. *Cento Probae* 116-135. CSEL 16,1,576-577: "felicem trahit limum fingitque premendo pingue solum primis extemplo a mensibus anni. iamque inprouiso tantae pietatis imago procedit noua forma uiri pulcherrima primum, os umerosque deo similis, cui mentem animumque maior agit deus atque opera ad maiora remittit . . . atque illi medio in spatio iam noctis opacae omnipotens genitor costas et uiscera nudat. harum unam inueni laterum conpagibus artis eripuit subitoque oritur mirabile donum – argumentum ingens – claraque in luce refulsit insignis facie et pulchro pectore uirgo, iam matura uiro, iam plenis nubilis annis. olli somnum ingens rumpit pauor: ossaque et artus coniugium uocat ac stupefactus numine pressit excepitque manu dextramque amplexus inhaesit." Translated in Clark, Elizabeth A., Hatch, Diane F.: *The Golden Bough, the Oaken Cross.* Chico, CA 1981, 27-29.

9. *Collectio Avellana, Epistula* 1,9. CSEL 35,1,4: "quem in tantum matronae diligebant, ut matronarum auriscalpius diceretur."

10. Børresen, Kari Elisabeth: "Imago Dei, privilège masculin? Interprétation augustinienne et pseudo-augustinienne de Gen. 1,27 et I Cor. 11,7." *Augustinianum* 25 (1985): 213-234.

11. *Liber quaestionum ueteris et noui testamenti* 21. CSEL 50,47-48: "Hoc est ad imaginem dei factum esse hominem, quia unus unum fecit, ut sicut ab uno deo sunt omnia, ita et ab uno homine omne genus humanum . . . igitur uir imago dei est. sic etenim scriptum est: et fecit deus hominem, ad imaginem dei fecit eum. unde et apostolus: uir quidem, inquit, non debet uelare caput, cum sit imago et gloria dei; 'mulier autem,' inquit, 'uelet caput.' quare? quia non est imago dei."

12. *Liber quaestionum ueteris et noui testamenti* 45,2-3. CSEL 50,82-83: "in eo autem imago dei est homo, ut, sicut unus est deus in caelis, ex quo omnia subsistunt spiritalia, ita unus esset in terris homo, ex quo ceteri haberent carnalem originem . . . cum non solum uiro, sed et mulieri ista cernantur subiecta, quam constat dei imaginem non habere . . . si imaginem dei homo in dominatione habet, et mulieri datur, ut et ipsa imago dei sit, quod absurdum est. quo modo enim potest de muliere dici, quia imago dei est, quam constat dominio uiri subiectam et nullam auctoritatem habere? nec docere enim potest nec testis esse neque fidem dicere nec iudicare; quanto magis imperare!"

13. *Decreti secunda pars, causa* 33,5,17. CIC 1,1255.

14. *Liber quaestionum ueteris et noui testamenti* 106,17. CSEL 50,243: "haec ergo imago dei est in homine, ut unus factus sit quasi dominus, ex quo ceteri orirentur, habens imperium dei quasi uicarius eius, quia omnis rex dei habet imaginem. ideoque mulier non est facta ad dei imaginem."

15. *Decreti secunda pars, causa* 33,5,13. CIC 1,1254.

16. *Ad Corinthios prima* 11,7-10. CSEL 81,2,121-123: "inferior ergo mulier viro est, portio enim eius est, quia origo mulieris vir est; ex eo enim est ac per hoc obnoxia videtur mulier viro, ut imperio eius subiecta sit. . . . haec est autem imago dei in viro, quia unus deus unum fecit hominem, ut sicut ab uno deo sunt omnia, ita essent et ab uno homine omnes homines, ut unius dei invisibilis unus homo visibilis imaginem haberet in terris, . . . mulier ergo idcirco debet velare caput, quia non est imago dei, sed ut ostendatur subiecta."

17. *Ad Corinthios prima* 14,34. CSEL 81,2,163: "si enim imago dei vir est, non femina, et viro subiecta est lege naturae, quanto magis in ecclesia debent esse subiectae propter reverentiam eius, qui illius legatus est, qui etiam viri caput est."

18. *Fragmenta in Genesim* 1, 26. PG 33,1564-1566.

19. *In Genesim homilia* 8,3-4. PG 53,72-73. *In Genesim sermo* 2,2. PG 54,589.

20. *Ad Galatas* 3,28. CSEL 81,3,42: "apud deum enim nulla discretio personarum est, nisi morum ac vitae, ut homines unius fidei meritis distinguantur, non personis."

21. *Ad Colosenses* 3,11. CSEL 81,3,195-197: "alia est tamen imago haec, quam de agnitione salvatoris dicit creari, et alia imago, ad quam factus est primus homo.

ista enim imago est et in femina, cum agnoscit eum, qui se creavit, et obtempe-
rans voluntati eius abstinet a vita turpi et actu perverso. illa autem imago in solo
viro est."
22. *Paidagogos* 1,4,10,1-11,1. SC 70,128.
23. *Stromata* 2,19,102,6-7. SC 38,113.
24. *Stromata* 2,22,131,5-133,3. SC 38,133-134.
25. *Stromata* 4,8,58,2-60,4. GCS 15,275-276.
26. *Stromata* 4,8,62,4-63,5. GCS 15, 277.
27. *Stromata* 7,14,84,2. GCS 17,60.
28. *Stromata* 7,2,10,1. GCS 17,8-9.
29. *Paidagogos* 2,10,83,2. SC 108,164.
30. *Paidagogos* 2,10,91,2,93,1. SC 108,176,178.
31. *In Genesim* 1,26-28,56-57. SC 233,142-146.
32. *In Genesim* 1,26-28,58-61. SC 233,146-156.
33. *In Genesim* 1,26-28,62-64. SC 233,156-162.
34. *In Genesim homilia* 1,13,15. GCS 29,15,19.
35. *De creatione hominis sermo* 1,18. SC 160,212-216.
36. *Homilia in psalmum* 1,3. PG 29,216-217.
37. *De hominis opificio* 16-18,22. PG 44,177-196,204-205.
38. *De anima et resurrectione.* PG 46,145-149.
39. *Vita Macrinae* 10. SC 178,172-174.
40. *De virginitate* 20,4. SC 119,498-502.
41. *Commentarius in canticum canticorum oratio* 7. *Opera* 6,12-213.
42. Børresen,Kari Elisabeth: *Subordination and Equivalence. The Nature and Role of Woman in Augustine and Thomas Aquinas.* Washington, DC 1981,15-17.
43. *De Genesi ad litteram* 3,22. CSEL 28,1,88-90: "itaque quamuis hoc in duobus hominibus diuersi sexus exterius secundum corpus figuratum sit, quod etiam in una hominis interius mente intellegitur, tamen et femina, quia corpore femina est, renouatur etiam ipsa in spiritu mentis suae in agnitionem dei secundum imaginem eius, qui creauit, ubi non est masculus et femina. sicut etiam ab hac gratia renouationis et reformationis imaginis dei non separantur feminae, quam-uis in sexu corporis earum aliud figuratum sit, secundum quod uir solus dicitur esse imago et gloria dei, sic et in ipsa prima conditione hominis secundum id, quod et femina homo erat, habebat utique mentem suam eandemque rationalem, secundum quam ipsa facta est ad imaginem dei."
44. *De Trinitate* 12,7,10. CCSL 50, 364-365: "Ad imaginem quippe dei naturam ipsam humanam factum dicit quae sexu utroque completur, nec ab intelligenda imagine dei separat feminam. . . . Quomodo ergo per apostolum audiuimus uirum esse imaginem dei unde caput uelare prohibetur, mulierum autem non et ideo ipsa hoc facere iubetur nisi, credo, illud esse quod iam dixi cum de natura humanae mentis agerem, mulierem cum uiro suo esse imaginem dei ut una imago sit tota illa substantia; cum autem ad adiutorium distribuitur, quod ad eam ipsam solam attinet non est imago dei; quod autem ad virum solum attinet imago

dei est tam plena atque integra quam in unum coniuncta muliere. Sicut de natura humanae mentis diximus quia etsi tota contempletur ueritatem, imago dei est, et cum ex ea distribuitur aliquid et quadam intentione deriuatur ad actionem rerum temporalium, nihilominus ex qua parte conspectam consulit ueritatem imago dei est; ex qua uero intenditur in agenda inferiora non est imago dei."

45. *De Trinitate* 12,7,12–13. CCSL 50,366–367: "Numquidnam igitur fideles feminae sexum corporis amiserunt? Sed quia ibi renouantur ad imaginem dei ubi sexus nullus est, ibi factus est homo ad imaginem dei ubi sexus nullus est, hoc est in spiritu mentis suae. Cur ergo uir propterea non debet caput uelare quia imago est et gloria dei, mulier autem debet quia gloria uiro est, quasi mulier non renouetur spiritu mentis suae, qui renouatur in agnitionem dei secundum imaginem eius qui creauit eum? Sed quia corporis distat a uiro, rite potuit in eius corporali uelamento figurari pars illa rationis quae ad temporalia gubernanda deflectitur ut non maneat imago dei nisi ex qua parte mens hominis aeternis rationibus conspiciendis uel consulendis adheaerescit, quam non solum masculos sed etiam feminas habere manifestum est. Ergo in eorum mentibus communis natura cognoscitur; in eorum uero corporibus ipsius unius mentis distributio figuratur."

46. *Expositio ad Galatas* 28. CSEL 84, 92–93: "differentia ista vel gentium vel conditionis vel sexus iam quidem ablata est ab unitate fidei, sed manet in conversatione mortali eiusque ordinem in huius vitae itinere servandum esse et apostoli praecipiunt, qui etiam regulas saluberrimas tradunt, quemadmodum secum vivant pro differentia gentis Iudaei et Graeci et pro differentia conditionis domini et servi et pro differentia sexus viri et uxores, vel si qua talia cetera occurunt, et ipse prior dominus, qui ait: Reddite Caesari, quae Caesaris sunt, et deo, quae dei sunt."

47. *De ciuitate Dei* 19,15. CCSL 48,682–683.

48. *Quaestiones Genesis* 153. CCSL 33,59: "Seruum autem hominem homini uel iniquitas uel aduersitas fecit. . . . Est enim ordo naturalis in hominibus, ut seruiant feminae uiris et filii parentibus, quia et illic haec iustitia est, ut infirmior ratio seruiat fortiori. Haec igitur in dominationibus et seruitutibus clara iustitia est, ut qui excellent ratione, excellant dominatione."

49. *De Genesi ad litteram* 9,5. CSEL 28,1,273: "Aut si ad hoc adiutorium gignendi filios non est facta mulier uiro, ad quod ergo adiutorium facta est? si, quae simul operaretur terram, nondum erat labor, ut adiumento indigeret, et, si opus esset, melius adiutorim masculus fieret, hoc et de solacio dici potest, si solitudinis fortasse taedebat. quanto enim congruentius ad conuiuendum et conloquendum duo amici pariter quam uir et mulier habitarent?. . . quapropter non inuenio, ad quod adiutorium facta sit mulier uiro, si pariendi causa subtrahitur."

50. *De ciuitate Dei* 22,17. CCSL 48,835–836: "Non est autem uitium sexus femineus, sed natura, quae tunc quidem et a concubitu et a partu immunis erit; erunt tamen membra feminea, non adcommodata usui ueteri, sed decori nouo, quo non alliciatur aspicientis concupiscentia, quae nulla erit, sed dei laudetur sapientia atque clementia, qui et quod non erat fecit et liberauit a corruptione quod fecit.

... Creatura est ergo Dei femina sicut uir; sed ut de uiro fieret, unitas commendata; ut autem illo modo fieret, Christus, ut dictum est, et ecclesia figurata est. Qui ergo utrumque sexum instituit, utrumque restituet. ... Nuptias ergo Dominus futuras esse negauit in resurrectione, non feminas."

51. *De ciuitate Dei* 22,18. CCSL 48,836–837: "Verum si hoc ad resurrectionis formam, in qua erit unusquisque, referendum esset, quid nos impediret nominato uiro intellegere et feminam, ut uirum pro homine positum acciperemus? sicut in eo quod dictum est: Beatus uir qui timet Dominum, utique ibisunt et feminae quae timent Dominum."

52. *De agone christiano* 22,24. CSEL 41,124–125: "dominus autem Iesus Christus, qui uenerat ad homines liberandos, in quibus et mares et feminae pertinent ad salutem, nec mares fastidiuit, quia marem suscepit, nec feminas, quia de femina natus est. huc accedit magnum sacramentum, ut, quoniam per feminam nobis mors acciderat, uita nobis per feminam nasceretur: ut de utraque natura, id est feminina et masculina, uictus diabolus cruciaretur, quoniam de ambarum subuersione laetabatur; cui parum fuerat ad poenam, si ambae naturae in nobis liberarentur, nisi etiam per ambas liberaremur."

53. *De diuersis qaestionibus* 11. CCSL 44A,18: "Hominis autem liberatio in utroque sexu debuit apparere. Ergo quia uirum oportebat suscipere, qui sexus honorabilior est, consequens erat ut feminei sexus liberatio hinc appareret, quod ille uir de femina natus est."

54. *De natura et origine animae* 2,3. CSEL 60,383: "natura certe tota hominis est spiritus, anima et corpus; quisquis ergo a natura humana corpus alienare uult, desipit."

55. Børresen, Kari Elisabeth: "In defence of Augustine: how *femina* is *homo.*" In Bruning, B., Lamberigts, M., Van Houtem, J., eds.: *Collectanea Augustiniana Mélanges T. J. van Bavel.* Louvain 1990, 411–428. "Patristic 'Feminism,' the Case of Augustine." *Augustinian Studies* 25 (1994): 137–152.

8

GOD'S IMAGE. IS WOMAN EXCLUDED? MEDIEVAL INTERPRETATION OF GEN. 1,27 AND I COR. 11,7

∞ Kari Elisabeth Børresen

Augustine and Pseudo-Augustine

In 585 a bishop attending the provincial synod in Mâcon denied that woman, *mulier*, could be called man, *homo*. The incident is reported by the bishop Gregory of Tours (d. 594) in his *Historia Francorum*, but it is not preserved in the synodal Acts. Apparently told to illustrate the proponent's lack of sophistication, Gregory underlines that he complied when his fellow bishops invoked Gen. 1,27ab: "There came forward at this council a certain bishop who maintained that woman could not be included in the term 'man.' However, he accepted the reasoning of the other bishops and did not press his case: for the holy book of the Old Testament tells us that in the beginning, when God created man, 'Male and female created he them,' and called their name Adam, which means earthly man; even so He called the woman Eve, yet of both He used the word 'man.' Similarly our Lord Jesus Christ is called the Son of man, although he was the son of the Virgin, that is to say of a woman. When He was about to change the water into wine, He said to her: 'Woman, what have I to do with thee?' and so on. They supported their argument with many other references, and he said no more."[1] The episcopal majority's argumentation is clearly Augustinian: *mulier* is defined as *homo* because she is created to God's image, according to Gen. 1,26–27b. However, the bishops' immediate concern seems to have been more christological than "feminist." Since Christ is Son of man, *filius hominis*, (cf. Matt. 16,27–28) through his mother Mary, who is called woman, *mulier*, in John 2,4 and Gal. 4,4, the two terms will have to be interchangeable.

Between the 8th and the 12th centuries, monastic exegesis and legal texts either presume or deny women's creational God-likeness. Ambrosiaster's definition of God's image, *imago Dei* as exclusively male privilege, survives in texts attributed to Ambrose or Augustine, especially in canon law. Monastic authors regularly refer to Augustine's asexual God-likeness in man-like disguise, although they often combine his inclusive exegesis with Ambrosiaster, preserved as pseudo-Augustine.[2] Consequently, Ambrosiaster's God-like man is invoked to corroborate female subordination in church and society, whereas Augustine's creationally theomorphic woman, *femina*, is veiled by redemptive equivalence. In scholastic exegesis, Augustine's genderfree backdating of women's salvational God-likeness is more coherently followed, and henceforth endorsed in Western theological anthropology. In contrast, Ambrosiaster's refusal of women's creational *imago Dei* is recorded by Yves of Chartres (d. 1116) and repeated in *Decretum Gratiani* (ca. 1146), to be incorporated in *Corpus Iuris Canonici* under Gregory XIII in 1582.[3] This legal collection functioned until 1917, when it was replaced by the *Codex Iuris Canonici.*

Monastic Exegesis

In his commentary *In Genesim*, the Benedictine Bede the Venerable (d. 735) defines *femina* as God-like human being, *homo*, repeating Augustine's exegesis to connect Gen. 1,27b and Gen. 1,26–27a: "And God created man, to God's image created He him, with immediate addition: 'He created them male and female,' but Scripture did not wish to add: 'to God's image He created them.' For the woman too was created to God's image because she too had a rational mind, so that Scripture did not think it necessary to add this about her. Woman's God-likeness is understood from her intimate conjunction with man."[4] It is significant that Bede rehearses Augustine's inclusive interpretation without reference to his neutralising of I Cor. 11,7. Women's creational God-likeness is here accepted as uncontroversial.

Another Benedictine, Haimo of Auxerre (d. 855), interprets I Cor. 11,7 in terms of Ambrosiaster's parallel between monotheism and monogenism. According to Gen. 1,26–27a and Gen. 2,7, one God creates one Adam as God-like male prototype: "Man is the image of God because just as all things took their origin from one God, so the entire human race issued from the one man Adam. He is the glory of God because God is glorified by the fact that he made a rational man. This is why man ought not to veil his head in order to show that he is not subject to woman, but has power over her. And woman is the glory of man, because she was made from him. Or said differently, man has glory in the fact that woman is subject to him."[5] This identification of

God-like *homo* and Paul's theomorphic *vir* is not directly pursued by negating women's creational *imago Dei*, Haimo concentrates on their derived subordinate condition. In his exegesis of Col. 3,11, apparently with the addition from Gal. 3,28 attested in versions of the Latin Bible, *Vetus Latina*, Haimo insists on Augustinian God-likeness of the asexual mind, *homo interior:* "In the mind of man, where God's image is found, there is no discrimination with God according to sex, social condition, race or province. Consequently, there is no distance between persons with God, because there is no sex in the human soul. All that is required is good conduct in right faith."[6] Haimo's commentary on Eph. 4,13 includes resurrected women in the perfect manhood of Christomorphic *vir perfectus*, by achieving Christ's fullgrown age as members of his body, the church. Following Augustine, resurrected fulness is not restricted to male perfection, but Haimo leaves out Augustine's explicit inclusion of femaleness in restored humanity.[7]

The Benedictine abbot and archbishop Hraban Maur (d. 856) copies Bede's commentary on Gen. 1,26–27b, thereby repeating Augustine's exegesis of *femina* as theomorphic *homo*.[8] Referring to the image variant in Gen. 5,1-2, Hraban Maur defines the term man, *homo*, by echoing the bishops of Mâcon: "And Scripture says that He called their name Adam, that is human being. Therefore, the term '*homo*' applies equally to man and to woman."[9] In contrast, Hraban Maur's interpretation of I Cor. 11,7 cites Ambrosiaster's explicit refusal of women's creational *imago Dei*, comparing monotheism and monogenism. Quite incoherently, he proceeds with a citation from Augustine's combined exegesis of Gal. 3,28 and I Cor. 11,7, thereby affirming women's asexual God-likeness already from creation.[10] In his commentary on Gal. 3,28, Hraban Maur insists on women's salvational equality in the redemptive order, where they often can lead man towards salvation, thus preceding them in spite of bodily feebleness: "The male and the female are likewise distinguished by their respective bodily strength and weakness, but otherwise their faith is accounted according to the devotion of their minds. It often happens that a woman is the cause of salvation for a man, and that a man has greater religious zeal than a woman." This genderfree inclusion is further displayed by a short citation of Augustine, significantly omitting his treatment of I Cor. 11,7. Finally, Augustine's commentary on Gal. 3,28 is cited, where salvational equivalence does not redress sociological disparity in this world.[11] Hraban Maur's commentary on Col. 3,11 inserts Gal. 3,28 by citing Augustine's interpretation of renovated and sexless *imago Dei*, but without his exegesis of I Cor. 11,7.[12]

The Benedictine Angelomus of Luxueil (d. ca. 895), combines Gen. 1,26–

27b and I Cor. 11,7 in Augustinian manner. The God-like higher reason, sym-bolised by Paul's *vir*, is here confronted with the soul's lower part, Paul's *mulier*. Angelomus underlines that when God-like *homo interior* turns to worldly sinfulness, he becomes woman-like and must be veiled: "For when a man strives towards heavenly things and contemplates the divine, he ought not to cover his head, that is obstructing his mind with sin. In contrast, if he neglects to meditate on divine things and carelessly turns to mundane affairs, he can no longer be called a man, but a female. Then let him veil his head like a woman, that is impeding justice. Unless he starts to think about lawful things, he will persist in lawless behaviour, squandering himself on external affairs and thereby offending God."[13]

The canonist and bishop Atto of Vercelli (d. ca. 960) interprets I Cor. 11,7 by echoing Ambrosiaster's parallel between monotheism and monogenism. Interestingly, Atto concentrates on the distinction: God's glory/man's glory, *gloria Dei/gloria viri*, thereby avoiding an explicit denial of women's cre-ational God-likeness. Atto proceeds to invoke Augustinian exegesis of Eph. 4,23-24, Col. 3,10-11 and Gal. 3,28, pointing to women's share in sexless and renovated *imago Dei:* "If the human being is renovated in the spirit of his mind, then this *homo* is clearly made to God's image where there is obviously no sex. (Scripture describes) the spirit of the mind, likewise the carnal body or the bodily flesh. Therefore, if man is renovated in the spirit, woman is not excluded from this renewal." It follows that *mulier* is *homo* by possessing genderfree God-likeness, although her femaleness represents the lower human soul, *anima*, in contradistinction to the higher human mind, *spiritus*, identified with Paul's man, *vir*.[14] Atto's commentary on Gal. 3,28 follows Hra-ban Maur, but with more focus on the reciprocity between women and men in the order of salvation: "We know that the male is distinguished from the female because of her sex and weakness, nevertheless they are not divided in faith, since faith belongs to interior humanity where there is no sex. There-fore, men are often led to salvation through women, and inversely women through men."[15] Atto's commentary on Col. 3,11 is also referring to Gal. 3,28, with citation of Augustine like in Hraban Maur. Atto's conclusion is similar to Haimo's formula: "There is no discrimination with God according to sex, social condition, race or province, only good conduct in the right faith is required. "[16]

The Benedictine abbot and archbishop Lanfranc of Canterbury (d. 1089) commented the whole *corpus Paulinum*, his text is preserved with ample citations from Augustine and Ambrosiaster. Concerning I Cor. 11,7, Lanfranc invokes the Augustinian device of interpreting *vir* and *mulier* as higher and lower reason. Affirming that man is primarily created in God's image, Lanfranc avoids direct denial of creational God-likeness for dependent woman. It is important to note that Lanfranc also attributes man's privilege of being *gloria Dei* to woman, since she too is created to glorify God, but secondarily: "Man is primarily created to God's image and woman is formed secondarily from man's rib, so that man ought to have his head uncovered. Even woman is the glory of God, by whom she is created to glorify, but in a secondary sense since man has priority." Lanfranc proceeds to cite Ambrosiaster's exegesis, but with the significant omission of: "because she is not God's image, *quia non est imago dei.*" In this rendering, female subordination is caused by Eve's role in the fall and not by her lack of initial God-likeness.[17] Lanfranc's commentary on Gal. 3,28 cites a part of Augustine's exegesis.[18] Concerning Col. 3,11, Lanfranc repeats Augustine concerning asexual renovated *imago Dei*, but without accent on the inclusion of women: "Man is renovated to God's image through knowledge of God, for this is God's image to which man was created, that he should be rational and always love heavenly things."[19]

In conclusion, early medieval interpretation of Gen. 1,27 and I Cor. 11,7 regularly invokes Ambrosiaster's exegesis. Nevertheless, his explicit negation of women's creational God-likeness is veiled. Being transmitted as written by Ambrose or Augustine, Ambrosiaster's texts are combined with genuine Augustinian exegesis, mainly from *De trinitate* and *Expositio ad Galatas.* To ease the incoherence of this mixture, the commentators focus on redemptive inclusiveness. Augustine's symbolical gender roles, played by the human soul's higher and lower reason, are consequently repeated without his contextual neutralisation of Paul's non-theomorphic *mulier.* Augustine's "feminist" intention is thereby obscured, although his resulting definition of woman, *femina* as God-like human being, *homo*, is preserved.

Early Scholastic Variants

This interlacing of Augustinian and pseudo-Augustinian sources persists in the early scholastic period. Nevertheless, Augustine's stratagem is refused by a vigorous opponent of women's creational *imago Dei*, Peter Abelard (d. 1143). In *Expositio in Hexaemeron*, addressed to his wife, the abbess Héloïse and her nuns, Abelard elaborates Ambrosiaster's argument of monotheism and monogenism. Combining Gen. 1,27 and I Cor. 11,7, he makes an original distinction between Adam's image, *imago*, and Eve's resemblance, *similitudo*. Since man is more similar to God than woman, *vir* is created both in God's image and resemblance. On the other hand, also *fem-*

ina has human rationality and immortal soul, woman is therefore created in God's resemblance, but not in his image: "Because man has a greater dignity than woman and thereby is more similar to God, he is called God's image. Woman is called God's resemblance because even she, just as man, imitates God through reason and immortality of the soul. But man excels in similarity to God, since just like all things derive their existence from God, so woman herself and the entire human race have their origin from one man according to bodily transmission." Abelard proceeds to invoke the *similitudo* in Gen. 5,1-2, defined as *vir* being more similar to triune Godhead than *femina,* and therefore exclusively God-like: "Since both man and woman have resemblance to the divine persons, as said above, man is created to God's image in terms of his greater similarity." This trinitarian argument is further explored with reference to Gen. 1,26-27b, stating the resemblance between God's Son and Adam, respectively generated and created: "Man is created in God's image because he has this excellent likeness to the Son of God. Just as He is said to be begotten by the Father alone, so man is said to be created by God alone, and not assumed from any animal in the way that woman is taken from man and formed of his rib."[20] The same theocentric androcentrism is found in Abelard's *Theologia "Scholarium,"* where Gen. 1,26 and I Cor. 11,7 are combined by defining woman as God's resemblance and man's image, *imago uiri:* "man is created to God's image, but woman is in His likeness. For the Apostle says that man, not woman, is God's image; but just as man is *imago dei,* so woman is man's image."[21]

The Benedictine Hervé of Bourg-Dieu (d. 1149/50) resumes the earlier monastic concoction of Ambrosiaster and Augustine. His commentary on I Cor. 11,7 starts with reference to Augustine's lower reason, represented by Paul's veiled *mulier.* Hervé continues by citing Ambrosiaster, but contrary to Hraban Maur he leaves out the explicit refusal of women's creational *imago Dei.* Hervé concentrates on the definition of man's glory, *gloria viri,* in terms of female subordination. When interpreting Gen. 1,26-27b, Hervé insists on inclusive God-likeness: "Genesis teaches that man and woman are made in God's image." I Cor. 11,7 is consequently neutralised by citing Augustine, but Hervé provides an interlude echoing Lanfranc and focusing on women's minor rationality: "For man is primarily created to the image of God, since reason is naturally stronger in man, as if he himself is reason, that is God's glory. But woman is sensuality, which prevails naturally in the female, and this must be subject to rationality in order to be the glory of reason."[22] The ensuing conflict between sensual femaleness and rational God-likeness is resolved through salvational equivalence, as Hervé underlines in his paraphrase of Gal. 3,28: "There you are not different, because you are all, whether Jews, Greeks, slaves, free, males or females, one in Christ Jesus through the unity of faith and charity."[23] Like in Haimo, Hraban Maur and Atto, Col. 3,11 is interpreted with addition of Gal. 3,28, in the sense of Christocentric abolishment of socio-sexual inequality: "Thus neither nation, nor rite pertaining to the flesh, nor sex makes any difference there, but is invalid and without effect. In this new man Christ is all, so that there is nothing except Christian piety and Christian devotion."[24]

The incoherent blending of Augustine and pseudo-Augustine culminates with Peter Lombard (d. 1160). It is important to note that this leading theologian and later bishop does not directly discuss women's God-likeness in his *Libri Sententiarum*, which were amply commented upon by subsequent scholastic authors. Lombard's treatment of the topic is presented in his Pauline exegesis. Interpreting I Cor. 11,7, Lombard opens with a citation of Ambrosiaster, where women's creational image of God is explicitly excluded. The parallel of monotheism and monogenism is summed up: "Man is the image of God because just as all things come from God, so all human beings come from Adam." Male theomorphic priority is then expressed by following Lanfranc and Hervé: "Man is the glory of God because he exists from Him, and therefore glorifies God principally. But woman is the glory of man, because she derives from him and is subservient to man. Also, man is said to be *imago Dei* because he is primarily created to God's image, so that reason is naturally more vigorous in man than in woman, as if he himself were reason." This hierarchisation of God's image, where women have an inferior share, is followed by a confrontation of I Cor. 11,7 and Gen. 1,26–27b, citing Eph. 4,24 and Col. 3,10. Lombard paraphrases the allegorical exegesis of Augustine's *De Trinitate*, precising the spiritual definition of God's image by a citation from *De Genesi ad litteram*. Like in Bede and Hraban Maur, the exegetical problem is how to include derived *femina/mulier* in God-like *homo*, which is solved by woman's possession of genderfree *spiritus:* "God made the whole man in his own image, i.e. according to the spirit."[25] Interpreting Gal. 3,28, Lombard rehearses the traditional equivalence in spite of ethnic and socio-sexual differences: "these do not give anyone a greater dignity according to the faith in Christ."[26] Lombard's exegesis of Col. 3,10–11 resumes his application of the contradictory sources invoked. He starts with a citation from *De Genesi ad litteram*, insisting on the incorporeal character of *imago Dei*. This is followed by citing Hraban Maur on the renovated sexless image. In contrast, Lombard continues with a paraphrase of Ambrosiaster's sharp distinction between exclusively male God-likeness in the order of creation and the salvational inclusion of women. The resulting incoherence is eased by a citation of Lanfranc's exegesis, in the sense of continuity between creational and redemptive God-likeness. Lombard concludes his interlaced exposition by affirming Christocentric equivalence: "In renovated man there is no discrimination from exterior diversity, such as sex, nation, observance or social rank. Christ is all, so that the wholeness of renovated humanity is Christ's work, and Christ is in all the faithful who are restored by Him."[27] Commenting on Eph. 4,13, Lombard repeats Haimo's interpretation of perfect man, *vir perfectus*, as including resurrected women, but without Augustine's emphasis on recreated femaleness.[28]

The strictly eschatological character of this redemptive God-likeness makes it perfectly compatible with human stratification in this world. It is essential to note that in all these reassuring formulas, the normative difference between creationally ordained gender hierarchy on one side and female subjection or slavery as resulting from the first sin on the other, is obscured. Nevertheless, sexual differentiation is regularly defined as restricted to the corporeal sphere, especially when femaleness is concerned. In contrast, man as exemplary human being remains bodily proportioned to the excellence of his spiritual *imago Dei*. The fundamental incoherence between Godhead and female humanity persists unchallenged.

Scholastic Typology

The Franciscan Bonaventura (d. 1274) treats women's God-likeness in his commentary to Peter Lombard's exposition of human creation, in the second book of *Libri Sententiarum*. This topic is not discussed in Lombard's text, Bonaventura's contribution is therefore enlarging the issue. It is significant that women's creational *imago Dei* is not contested as such, the problem is how to explain man's precedence according to I Cor. 11,7. This scriptural source is now so efficiently veiled by Augustine's inclusive neutralisation that it can no longer be interpreted *ad litteram*, as literally excluding women's God-likeness. Bonaventura formulates the heading of his *quaestio* in terms akin to Lanfranc, Hervé and Lombard, where man is God-like in the first place, *principaliter*, but not exclusively: "Whether God's image is more principally in the male than in the female, *Utrum imago principalius sit in masculo quam in femina.*" The objections listed concern I Cor. 11,7 and Ambrosiaster's literal exegesis: Man is made in God's image, whereas woman is not, *Ad imaginem Dei factus est vir, non mulier.*" Christ's incarnation in the exemplary sex affirms man's God-likeness and Gen. 1,26 is interpreted in the Antiochene sense of male dominion over all creation, women included. The counter-arguments define Gen. 1,27ab in terms of Augustinian gender-free creational and redemptive *imago Dei*. Bonaventura concludes that human God-likeness, as to its essence, is equal in man and woman, although accidentally greater in man because of his exemplary maleness: "The image quality as such is not more present in man than in woman, only as an accidental property." Bonaventura then defines *imago Dei* in its essence, *quantum ad suum esse:* "The image's essence consists primarily in the human soul and its faculties, and chiefly in the fact that they must be directed to God. In this sense, there is no distinction between male and female, slave and free. Therefore the image, in terms of its fulfilment and essence, is not greater in man than in woman." This backdating of salvational equality, as affirmed in Gal. 3,28, to the order of creation is followed by a definition of God's image in its essential goodness, *quantum ad bene esse:* "The image's essential goodness or clear expression consists more in the soul, with its ordered habitude. Sexual differentiation concerns the body, where maleness represents rational authority and rule, since (I Cor. 11,3,9) 'man is the head of woman, and man does not exist for the sake of woman, but woman for the sake of man.'" Only in this sense is God's image found more excellently in the male sex than in the female, not according to the essence of the image itself, but according to contingent sexual diversity. Bonaventura underlines that the objections all refer to gender hierarchy according to bodily difference, defined as accidental quality: "It is obvious that the reason why God's image is not greater in man than in woman results from the image in its essence. Opposite arguments result from the image's accidental properties or its relation with the body." It is significant that man's exclusive God-likeness according to I Cor. 11,7 is here relegated to the corporeal sphere, and consequently without impact on the *imago Dei* as such. Bonaventura concludes his *quaestio* by returning to Paul's non-theomorphic *mulier* and Ambrosiaster's literal exegesis. Invoking Augustine's allegorical neutralisation, he rejects I Cor. 11,7 as interpreted literally: "And if you object that the Apostle speaks of man and woman *ad litteram*, the answer is that he is not speaking about their essential equality, but about their diverse signification. Since man is strong and rules over woman, he signifies the superior part of human reason, whereas she signifies the inferior part. Therefore, in marriage the husband signifies God and the wife signifies the church or the Christian soul. Male strength on the one hand and female weakness or frailness on the other do not refer to the image as such, but to contingent bodily properties, thus not essentially but accidentally."[29]

In consequence, Bonaventura's variant of Augustine's strategy, mixed with pseudo-Augustinian male God-likeness disguised as privilege *principaliter,* curtails Augustinian "feminism." Bonaventura's combination of sexless *imago Dei* and androcentric typology serves to reduce women's God-like equivalence.

This becomes quite clear in his argument against priestly ordination of women, where female inability to represent Christ, is the main feature. The question is not discussed in Lombard's *Libri Sententiarum,* Bonaventura provides here a new theological elaboration under the heading: "Whether the male sex is required to receive ordination, *Utrum ad susceptionem ordinis requiratur sexus virilis.*" Bonaventura argues that the requirement of maleness for ordination to the priesthood, both *de iure* and *de facto,* follows from men's creational precedence because exemplary maleness reflects the excellence of asexual *imago Dei.* Bonaventura starts by a reference to women's veiling in I Cor. 11,4–5. He then invokes 11,7 in the sense of men's exclusive God-likeness *qua* human males. Consequently, women cannot be ordained because they do not possess God's image *qua* human females: "It is impossible to be ordained without possessing God's image, because this sacrament makes man somehow divine by sharing divine power. Only man is the image of God by virtue of his sex, according to I Cor. 11,7. In consequence, woman can in no manner be ordained." This priestly sharing of divine power in the sense of an exclusively male prerogative is affirmed by citing I Tim. 2,12: "I do not permit a woman to teach, nor to domineer over man." Bonaventura also states that *mulier* is unable to receive priestly ordination, since this would qualify her for promotion to episcopal dignity. A typological argument, where the bishop is bridegroom of his church, excludes female ordinands. The objections listed invoke women's equivalence exemplified through Deborah (Judges 4,4), ruling abbesses, asexual God-likeness and female martyrs. Bonaventura responds by defining Deborah's function as temporal power, which also women can exercise, in contrast to spiritual power, *potestas spiritualis:* "Women are permitted to perform secular control, but not spiritual dominion, where the person in power represents Christ's headship. Therefore, since woman cannot be the head of man, she is unable to receive priestly ordination." Abbesses receive delegated power over nuns in order to avoid the danger of cohabitation with ruling abbots. Consequently, abbesses do not possess ordinary jurisdiction, *praelatio ordinaria.* "The sacrament of ordination does not concern the soul alone, but the soul as joined to the body, in terms of signification involved in the visible sign, and therefore including the body. The exercise and use of priesthood is consequently related both to soul and body. This is why a woman is unable to be ordained, since she can neither

signify nor actualise the sacrament of order." Because the eminence of sacerdotal authority pertains both to the spiritual and the bodily sphere, only male
human beings can signify the power of Christ-like priesthood. In consequence, conformity of excellence between the priest's office and the priest's
Christomorphic maleness is necessary. In contrast, the spiritual perfection of
martyrdom results from redemptive grace, and is bestowed independently of
the receiver's sex.

Bonaventura's conclusive response starts with references to current canon
law, prohibiting women to touch sacred vessels. The deaconess, *diaconissa*, is
defined as a mature woman who reads the homily, like a deacon. *Presbytera*
denotes an older widow or matron, not a woman priest. Bonaventura's main
argumentation is based on Christocentric typology. Women are excluded
from priestly ordination not only by ecclesiastical law, but because their
femaleness is an obstacle to receive the sacrament as such. Subordinate
females are unable to signify Christ the mediator, who was incarnated in the
primary male sex: "The reason for this is not so much the church's decision as
the non-congruity of priesthood with the female sex. In this sacrament the
person who is ordained signifies Christ as mediator. Because this mediator
existed only in the male sex, He can be signified only through the male sex. In
consequence, only men have the possibility of receiving priestly ordination,
since they alone can naturally represent and actually carry the sign of the
mediator by receiving the sacramental character." It is to be noted that
Bonaventura qualifies his conclusion as the most probable, *probabilior*, supported by tradition.[30]

Women's incapacity of being cultic mediators between God and humankind
results from their lack of God-likeness *qua* females. Creationally theomorphic
in spite of their derived sex, women are incapable of representing Christ's perfect maleness as priests. The traditional disparity between Godhead and
femaleness remains fundamental, most obviously demonstrated by women's
combined corporeal and symbolic deficiency, *impedimentum sexus*, resulting
from their secondary and subordinate womanhood. In patristic doctrine,
androcentric typology corresponds to the early theme of Christomorphic
maleness, where women become salvationally Christ-like by gender reversal.
Asexual definition of *imago Dei* emerges later and is used to insert women as
God-like already from creation, despite their non-theomorphic femaleness.
These two motifs continued to coexist in traditional theological anthropology, but without explicit connection. Bonaventura's new synthesis is especially important because he so clearly combines the two, logically incoherent
themes, when he argues both *for* women's sexless *imago Dei* and *against*

female priests. Christocentric typology is here applied as a restrictive device, making women unable to represent Christ's incarnated humanity and redeeming divinity. Cultic incapacity is thus explained in terms parallel to women's lacking representation *qua* females of their Godgiven, asexual image quality. Correspondingly, men's primary sex symbolises both their sexless *imago Dei* in male disguise and Christ's perfect manhood, making them capable of sharing divine power as priests.

Scholastic Sexology

The Dominican Thomas Aquinas (d. 1274) elaborates his doctrine on women's nature and role in terms of Aristotelian socio-biology, rather uneasily combined with Augustinian anthropology.[31] In *Summa Theologica* Thomas discusses women's Godlikeness under the heading: "Whether the image of God is found in every human being, *Utrum imago Dei inveniatur in quolibet homine.*" Unlike Bonaventura, he does not give this topic a separate treatment, it occurs only as one of the listed objections. Following Augustine's definition of *mulier* in terms of *homo*, Thomas affirms women's creational *imago Dei*, but with pseudo-Augustinian emphasis on male priority. In his main response to the question whether all human beings possess God's image, Thomas defines God-likeness as threefold. The first degree is a natural capacity for understanding and loving God: "and this aptitude consists in the very nature of the mind and is common to all human beings." The second degree is actually knowing and loving God, but still imperfectly. This image by conformity of grace, *imago per conformitatem gratiae*, is found only in the just of this world. The final stage is actually knowing and loving God perfectly. This image by likeness of glory, *imago secundum similitudinem gloriae*, is found only among the blessed in heaven. Thomas' creational *imago Dei* is consequently given to all, whereas the salvational image is actualised in the just and fulfilled through redemption, regardless of sexual difference. The first objection invokes exclusively male God-likeness according to I Cor. 11,7, cited as: "man is God's image, but woman is man's image, *vir est imago Dei, mulier autem est imago viri.*" Since Paul's non-theomorphic woman is an individual member of the human race, *individuum humanae speciei*, it follows that not all human beings are God-like. Thomas' answer repeats Augustine's connection of Gen. 1,27b and Gen. 1,26–27a, but omits his allegorical stratagem to include sub-male women in human *imago Dei.* Instead, Thomas refers to Augustine's rejection of initial androgyny in *De Genesi ad litteram*, where he links the God-like prototype to sexual differentiation ordained to fertility. In fact, Thomas' definition of creational *imago Dei*, in terms of intellectual nature common to all human beings, does not need symbolic exegesis in order to include women in rational humanity: "God's image is found both in man and in woman, as consisting principally in intelligent nature." I Cor. 11,7, accurately cited as: "man is God's image and glory, but woman is man's glory, *vir imago et gloria est Dei, mulier autem est gloria viri*," is then interpreted as regarding a secondary point. Nevertheless, Paul's male priority is explained by a sharpened variant of the pseudo-Augustinian parallel of monogenism and monotheism: "But in a secondary manner God's image is found in man and not in woman, for man is the beginning and end of woman, just as God is the beginning and end of all creation."[32] The standard Augustinian finality of woman as man's helpmate, illustrated by I Cor. 11,8–9, is here forced into complete juxtaposition of androcentrism and theocentrism.

In Thomas' commentary on I Cor. 11,7 (reported by his student Reginald of Piperno), man's special God-likeness is exposed echoing Lombard. With reference to Col. 3,10–11 in the sense of Gal. 3,28, Thomas affirms that spiritual *imago Dei* is not greater in man than in woman: "Because God's image in the human being is understood to exist according to the spirit, where there is no difference between male and female, as said in Col. III. Therefore, it ought not to be said that man is more God's image than woman." Nevertheless, because of his exemplary sex, man is especially God-like *qua* human male. Thomas applies here the pseudo-Augustinian comparison of monogenism and monotheism together with patristic Christ-church typology, thereby firmly establishing male priority: "But it must be said that man is God's image in a special way through certain external characteristics, i.e. because man is the origin of his entire human race just as God is the origin of the entire universe. Equally because the sacraments of blood and water, by which the church was fashioned, flood from the side of Christ as he slept on the cross." This exterior God-likeness is complemented with man's interior precedence, defined as stronger rational capacity: "With reference to interior qualities, it can also be said that man is more especially God's image according to the mind, since his reason is stronger." The interaction between women's mental and bodily imperfection as compared to the male human norm is well attested in Aristotelian socio-biology. This androcentric sexology is adopted by Thomas when he defines the female human being as a deficient male, *mas occasionatus*. In contrast, it is important to note that Thomas endorses the Augustinian definition of *imago Dei* as incorporeal and consequently asexual privilege when he argues for women's creational God-likeness, in spite of inferior femaleness. Thomas therefore concludes his discussion by stating that both *vir* and *mulier* possess *imago Dei*, although man alone is God's glory, *gloria Dei:* "It is better to say that the Apostle is speaking symbolically. For he says about man that he is the image and glory of God, but he does not say about woman that she is the image and glory of man, only that she is the glory of man. This means that the image of God is common to both man and woman, whereas to be God's glory applies only to man."[33] Thomas' "feminist" transformation of Paul *ad litteram* shows how Augustine's inclusiveness has become normative in scholastic anthropology, but loosened from his allegorical exegesis and rather ingeniously coupled with surviving Ambrosiaster.

Thomas' treatment of the resurrection in the *Supplementum* of *Summa Theologica* is taken from his commentary to Peter Lombard's fourth book of *Libri Sententiarum.* Unlike Lombard and Bonaventura, Thomas explicitly debates the topic of resurrected females, under the heading: "Whether all will be resurrected in the male sex, *Utrum omnes resurrecturi sint in sexu virili.*" The objections in favour of exclusively male resurrection invoke Eph. 4,13, creational gender hierarchy and female inferiority as defective male. The counter-argument refers to Augustine's inclusive interpretation of Eph. 4,13 in *De civitate Dei,* where women will be raised in their sex through God's restoration of human wholeness: "In the resurrection, God will restore the human being as it was first made. But He made woman from man's rib, as shown in Gen. 2. Consequently, He will restore the female sex in the resurrection." Thomas' main response follows Lombard in stating that all human beings will rise in youthful maturity, i.e. at the age of risen Christ, and each with its fullgrown shape. In addition, Thomas underlines that this individual wholeness will include bodily sex, which belongs to the perfection of the human species. With Augustine, he emphasises that sinful concupiscence, attached to sexual activity after the fall, will be superseded in recreated fulness: "I answer that concerning the nature of individuals, different quantity is due to different persons. Thus, with regard to individual nature, different sex is due to different human beings. This diversity pertains to the perfection of the human species, whose differing grades are completed by such sexual or quantitative diversity. Therefore, just as human beings will rise in different shape, they will rise in different sex. Although sexual diversity will exist, there will be no mutual confusion caused by libidinous glare, inciting to and resulting from obscene activity." It is to be noted that Thomas' prognostication of the two sexes untroubled mutual sight corrects male-centered Augustine, who stressed that perfect men would no longer be aroused by resurrected female beauty. In answer to the first objection, Thomas interprets Eph. 4,13 not in terms of perfect maleness, but as the soul's perfect virtue, which will be found in all, both men and women: "When it is said that all will become 'perfect man,' this does not refer to the male sex but to the virtuous soul, which will be present in all, both men and women. Concerning the second objection, Thomas defines creational female subordination as resulting from women's combined mental and physical feebleness. Nevertheless, after the resurrection this sexually determined inequality will be abolished; individual diversity will correspond to different degrees of virtue, regardless of bodily sex: "Woman is subject to man because of her natural weakness, having less vigour of the soul and less bodily strength. But after the resurrection there will be no diversity according to sex, only according to merit. It follows that female feebleness is irrelevant." Thomas' answer to the third objection explains that the female human being is imperfect in the sense of not having reached exemplary, i.e. male humanity, which the paternal seed should by nature produce. On the other hand, femaleness is necessary for the perfection of the human species as a whole, since both sexes are needed for propagation. Women will therefore rise again, but without the defects connected with their sex: "Although the procreation of a female is beyond the intention of individual nature, it is in conformity with the intention of universal nature, which requires both sexes for perfection of the human species. Nor will there be any deficiency in connection with sex, as already stated."[34]

In fact, Thomas' Aristotelian anthropology, where the soul is substantial form of the body, implies a close interaction between mental and physical qualities. It follows that women's rational capacity is weaker than men's, in proportion to their corporeal inferiority. Interpreting woman's creation in *Summa Theologica*, Thomas cites Augustine's exegesis of Gen. 2,18 in order to emphasize her finality as subordinate helpmate in procreation. This receptive function is further explained according to Aristotelian biology, where the male generative power is active and the female is passive. Although a deviated and thus not fully developed result of male generation, which is primarily intended to produce another perfect male human being, imperfect female humanity is aimed at by nature since it is indispensable for conception, pregnancy and birthing. In consequence, God created not only the male but also the female: "It is to say that as regards individual nature, the female is something deficient and incomplete. For the active power of the male seed seeks to produce something like itself, with perfect male sex. But the procreation of a female results from debility of the male seed, insuitability of the material or some exterior negative influence, like the south wind which is humid (cf. Italian (*girocco*), as referred to in (Aristotle's) *De generatione animalium* (737a,

766b, 767a,b, 775a). With reference to universal nature, the female is not a misfit but intended by nature for the procreation of children. The finality of universal nature is ordered by God, who is the maker of universal nature. Therefore, when God established nature He produced not only the male but also the female." This exclusively reproductive purpose of female existence makes women creationally subjected to men, who have stronger rational equipment. Against the invocation of Gen. 3,16, where female subservience is established as punishment for Eve's sin, Thomas defines gender hierarchy as part of creationally given domestic or civil inequality, which operates to the advantage of the subjects ruled. In contrast, slavery, in which the subject is used for the ruler's advantage, is established after the first sin: "Subjection is of two kinds; one is that of slavery, in which the ruler manages the subject for his own advantage, and this sort of subjection was introduced after sin. But the other sort of subjection is domestic or civil, in which the ruler manages his subjects for their advantage and benefit. And this sort of subjection would have existed even before sin. For the human multitude would have lacked the benefit of order had some of its members not been governed by others who were wiser. Such is the subjection in which woman is by nature subordinate to man, because rational discernment is by nature stronger in man."[35]

The same Aristotelian socio-biology is applied in Thomas' discussion of femaleness as obstacle to priestly ordination, found in the *Supplementum* of *Summa Theologica*. Here womanhood excludes both the validity and the lawfulness of sacramental priesthood. In contrast, canonical deficiencies such as lacking the use of reason, like in boys, or being a serf, having committed murder, being of illegitimate birth or having a grave bodily defect make ordination unlawful, but not invalid. In order to explain how a serf can be validly but not lawfully ordained, Thomas distinguishes between femaleness as Godgiven inferior condition and slavery as not divinely sanctioned. One of the listed objections refers to serfdom as excluding sacramental priestly power itself, not only impeding the exercise of ordained priesthood, since a less subjugated woman cannot receive this sacrament at all: "It seems that serfdom is an impediment resulting with necessity from the sacrament as such. For a woman cannot receive the sacrament because of her subjection. But there is greater subjection in a serf, because woman is not given to man as a servant, since she is not taken from his feet. Therefore, also a serf cannot receive the sacrament." Thomas' solution defines woman as subject to man by nature, and consequently incapable of representing the excellence of priesthood. Femaleness is therefore an obstacle to the sacramental sign, whereas economically established serfdom is not: "It must be said that sacramental signs represent by natural likeness. Woman has subjection from nature, the serf has not. Therefore the case is not similar."[36] Thomas' main treatment of women's inability to receive priestly ordination is presented under the heading: "Whether the female sex impedes priestly ordination, *Utrum sexus femineus impediat ordinis susceptionem.*" The listed objections cover female prophets and martyrs, the judge Deborah, ruling abbesses and sexless spiritual equivalence. The biblical text invoked against women's authority is I Tim. 2,12. In his response, Thomas argues that maleness is necessary both for the validity of the sacrament as such and for its lawfulness, i.e. imposed both *de necessitate sacramenti* and *de necessitate praecepti.* "I answer that the nature of the sacrament requires certain properties in a person who receives it, the lack of which impedes the reception, both of the sacrament as such (*sacramentum*) and its effects (*res sacramenti*). Other properties are required, not by the nature of the sacrament, but by law in conformity with the excellence of the sacrament. He who does not satisfy these conditions may receive the sacrament, but not its effects. Consequently, the male sex is indispensable not only to fulfill the second group of requirements, but also the first. Therefore, even if a woman were to go through all the ceremonies connected with ordination, she would not thereby receive the sacrament of priesthood. Since a sacrament is a sign, the execution of a sacrament requires not only the thing (*res*), but the signification of the thing (*significatio rei*). This is exemplified by the necessity of a sick person to signify the need of healing in the sacrament of extreme unction. Because woman is in a state of subjection, it is impossible to signify eminence of rank through the female sex. Consequently, a woman cannot receive the sacrament of priesthood." Finally, Thomas underlines that canonical references to the ordaining of deaconesses do not imply that womanhood is only an obstacle to the lawfulness of priestly ordination. Like Bonaventura, he explains that *diaconissa* denotes a woman who shares in some act of a deacon, like reading the homily in church. *Presbytera* means a widow, not priestess, for the word *presbyter* means elder. The objection invoking female prophets is answered by defining prophecy as a spiritual charisma. It follows that *significatio* is not necessary, only Godgiven *res:* "Prophecy is not a sacrament, but a gift of God. Therefore it does not need any symbolism, but only charismatic actualisation. Because woman does not differ from man in the reality of the soul, and sometimes a woman is better in her soul than many men are, she may well receive the gift of prophecy and other like gifts, but she cannot receive priestly ordination." Following Bonaventura, Thomas replies to the other objections by stating that abbesses rule with delegated power and Deborah had temporal dominion only.[37]

Thomas' argumentation against women priests is firmly based on his new inculturation of Aristotelian socio-biology. This empirical reasoning, in Thomas' time very up to date, makes his sexology particularly conjectural and therefore completely superseded. Unlike Bonaventura, Thomas does not invoke Christocentric typology as excluding priestly ordination of women. The obstacle of femaleness is explained in purely bio-social terms; women's cultic incapacity is determined by their female inferiority and ensuing subjection. Women are consequently unable both to function as priests and to signify Christ-like eminence. This coherent androcentrism is contradicted by Thomas' adoption of Augustine's asexual *imago Dei* in order to include women in creational God-likeness. The early medieval mixture of Augustinian genderfree equality attributed to women already from creation and Ambrosiaster's creational God-likeness reserved for men only, is by Thomas and by Bonaventura reproduced as Christomorphic priority of the exemplary male sex. It follows that human spiritual equivalence in the order of salvation makes women capable of receiving all sacraments, except ordination to the priesthood. Male excellence is here a necessary prerequisite for signifying priestly eminence. Thomas' exposition is especially useful because of its manifest male-centered logic, which in Bonaventura's typological argument is less clearcut. Nevertheless, while Thomas' *impedimentum sexus* is no longer invoked, Bonaventura's Christocentric variant is vigorously surviving. It is important to note that not only scholastic sexology, but also scholastic typology mark a significant regression in comparison with Augustine's "feminist" application of the redemptive couple new Adam-new Eve, and his strenuous inclusion of woman, *femina/mulier,* as God-like human being, *homo.*

Typological Gender Models

In this perspective of androcentric "feminism," the widely learned Benedictine abbess Hildegard of Bingen (d. 1179) provides a poignant rejection of women priests. In her visionary *Scivias,* Hildegard ingenuously combines male-centered gynecology and Christ-centered typology, with an innovative "feminist" conclusion. Women's feebleness and receptive role in procreation make them incapable of performing sacramental consecration of bread and wine. Priestly activity is interpreted as a male sex role, with Christ as exemplary high priest. Hildegard proceeds by a nuptial imagery where the virgin or widow as bride of Christ assimilates his priestly eminence, just like the loving woman encloses her husband's body in sexual intercourse: "So too those of female sex should not approach the office of My altar; for they are an infirm and weak habitation, appointed to bear children and diligently nurture them. A woman conceives a child not by herself but through a man, as the ground is plowed not by itself but by a farmer. Therefore, just as the earth cannot plow itself, a woman must not be a priest and do the work of consecrating the body and blood of My Son; though she can sing the praise of her creator, as the earth can receive rain to water its fruits. And as the earth brings forth all fruits, so in Woman the fruit of all good works is perfected. How? A virgin betrothed to My Son will receive Him as Bridegroom, for she has shut her body away from a physical husband; and in her Bridegroom she has the priesthood and all the Ministry of my Altar, and with Him possesses all its riches. And a widow too can be called a bride of My Son when she rejects a physical husband and flees beneath the wings of my Son's protection. And as a bridegroom loves his bride with exceeding love, so does My Son sweetly embrace His brides, who for love of chastity eagerly run to Him."

Hildegard ends this symbolic incorporation of Christocentric priestly power and excellence with a contrasting reference to unnatural crossdressing. Except to protect a man's life or a woman's chastity in case of danger, such deviation from the creational order is comparable to abusive women priests: "But as a woman should not wear a man's clothes, she should also not approach the office of My altar, for she should not take on a masculine role either in her hair or in her attire."[38]

Hildegard's typological "feminism" is no longer applicable, due to her encratite validation of sexual abstinence in androcentric disguise.[39] Nevertheless, the present refusal to ordain women, both in Roman Catholic and Greek Orthodox Christianity, can be overcome by clarifying the strong connection between women's lacking God-likeness *qua* females and their cultic incapacity. The influence of canon law is well documented.[40] I find the impact of Christocentric typology to be of equally great importance. In fact, the modern redefinition of human God-likeness as including both women and men *qua* male or female, is logically incompatible with typological doctrine and symbolism.[41] Medieval mixture of pseudo-Augustinian male *imago Dei* and Augustinian asexual God-likeness in male disguise ensured the survival of androcentric new Adam. Scholastic sexology is finally discarded because of its superseded presuppositions. In contrast, the ensuing male-centered conclusions are still operative in traditional christology and ecclesiology, where scholastic typology continues to be applied.

Notes

1. *Historiarum* 8,20. MGH, *Scriptores rerum merovingicarum* 1,1,386–387: "Extetit enim in hac synodo quidam ex episcopis, qui dicebat, mulierem hominem non posse vocitare. Sed tamen ab episcopis ratione accepta quievit, eo quod sacer Veteris Testamenti liber edoceat, quod in principio, Deo hominem creante, ait: Masculum et feminam creavit eos, vocavitque nomen eorum Adam, quod est homo terrenus, sic utique vocans mulierum ceu virum; utrumque enim hominem dixit. Sed et dominus Iesus Christus ob hoc vocitatur filius hominis, quod sit filius virginis, id est mulieris. Ad quam, cum aquas in vina transferre pararet, ait: Quid mihi et tibi est, mulier? et reliqua. Multisque et aliis testimoniis haec causa convicta quievit."

2. Børresen, Kari Elisabeth: "Imago Dei, privilège masculin? Interprétation augustinienne et pseudo-augustinienne de Gen. 1,27 et I Cor. 11,7." *Augustinianum* 25 (1985): 213–234.

3. *Decreti secunda pars, causa* 33,5,13, CIC 1,1254 cites *Liber quaestionum ueteris et noui testamenti* 106,17 as of Augustine. *Decreti secunda pars, causa* 33,5,17, CIC 1, 1255 cites *Liber Quaestionum ueteris et noui testamenti* 45,3 as of Ambrose. *Decreti secunda pars, causa* 33,5,19, CIC 1, 1255–1256 cites *Ad Corinthios prima* 11,10 as of Ambrose.

4. *In Genesim* 1,27. CCSL 118A,28: "Et creauit Deus hominem, ad imaginem Dei creauit illum, statimque subiungeret, Masculum et feminam creauit eos, noluit addere 'ad imaginem Dei creauit eos.' Et femina enim ad imaginem Dei creata est secundum id quod et ipsa habebat mentem rationalem; sed addendum hoc de illa non putauit scriptura propter unitatem coniunctionis etiam in illa intelligendum reliquit." cf. *De Genesi ad litteram* 3,22.

5. *Expositio in epistolam I ad Corinthios* 11. PL 117, 567–568: "Homo imago est Dei, quia sicut ab uno Deo omnia originem sumpserunt, et ab illo facta sunt, ita ab uno homine Adam omne genus humanum profluxit: gloria quoque Dei est, quia glorificatur Deus per hoc quod hominem rationabilem fecit. Ideoque non debet velare caput, ut ostendat non esse subditum mulieri, sed potestatem habere super eam. Mulier autem gloria viri est, quia ex ipsa facta est: vel quia subjecta est ei, et in hoc gloriam habet vir."

6. *Expositio in epistolam ad Colossenses* 3. PL 117,760–761: "Ubi, id est in mente hominis ubi est imago Dei, non praejudicatur apud Deum sexus vel conditio, aut genus, aut provincia, id est nulla distantia est hominum apud Deum, quia in anima non est sexus, nisi tantummodo sola bona conversatio cum fide recta requiritur."

7. *Expositio in epistolam ad Ephesios* 4. PL 117,720–721.

8. *Commentaria in Genesim* 1,7. PL 107,461.

9. *Commentaria in Genesim* 2,3. PL 107,509: "Et vocavit, inquit, nomen eorum Adam, id est homo. Hominis autem nomen tam viro quam feminae convenit."

10. *Enarratio in epistolam I ad Corinthios* 11. PL 112,100–101. cf. *Ad Corinthios*

prima 11,7. *De Trinitate* 12,7,12–13.

11. *Enarratio in epistolam ad Galatas* 3. PL 112,307–309: "Masculus similiter et femina, fortitudine et imbecillitate corporum separantur: caeterum fides pro mentis devotione censetur, et saepe evenit, ut et mulier viro salutis causa fiat, et mulierem vir in religione praecedat." cf. *De Trinitate* 12,7,12. *Expositio ad Galatas* 28.

12. *Enarratio in epistolam ad Colossenses* 3. PL 112,536. cf. *De Trinitate* 12,7,12; 14,16,22.

13. *Commentarius in Genesin* 1,26–27. PL 115,121–123: "In quantum enim homo ad coelestia tendit et divina contemplatur, non debet velare caput, id est, obstaculum peccati mentem opponere. Si autem omiserit divina meditari, et converterit ad terrena superflue, non jam vir, sed femina dicitur, et ideo velet caput ut mulier, id est ponat obstaculum justititae, ne dum licita cogitare coeperit, ad illicita prorumpat, et totum se ad exteriora diffundat, unde Deum offendat."

14. *Expositio in epistolam I ad Corinthios* 11. PL 134, 376–377: "si in spiritu mentis homo renovatur, ibi ipse homo ad imaginem Dei factus monstraretur, ubi nullus sexus ostenditur. Spiritus mentis dicitur, velut corpus carnis, aut caro corporis; si enim in spiritu renovatur homo mulier ab hac renovatione non separatur."

15. *Expositio in epistolam ad Galatas* 3. PL 134,523: "Sciendum quia masculus et femina discernuntur sexu atque fragilitate; verumtamen non dividuntur in fide, quia fides interioris hominis est, ubi nullus est sexus. Hinc est quod saepe viri trahuntur ad salutem per mulieres, et econtra mulieres per viros."

16. *Expositio in epistolam ad Colossenses* 3. PL 134,633: "Apud Deum non praejudicat sexus, vel conditio, aut genus, vel provincia, sed sola conversatio cum fide recta requiritur." cf. *De Trinitate* 12,7,12.

17. *Commentarius in epistola I ad Corinthios* 11. PL 150, 191–192: "Vir principaliter ad imaginem Dei creatus est. Mulier e costa viri postea formata est; atque vir discoopertum caput debet habere. Est et mulier gloria Dei, a quo et ad quem glorificandum creata est, sed et secundo loco, principaliter enim vir." cf. *De Trinitate* 12,7,10. *Ad Corinthios prima* 11,10.

18. *Commentarius in epistolam ad Galatas* 3. PL 150,274. cf. *Expositio ad Galatas* 28.

19. *Commentarius in epistolam ad Colossenses* 3. PL 150,328: "In agnitione Dei renovatur homo ad imaginem Dei: haec est enim imago Dei, ad quem creavit hominem, ut videlicet rationalis esset, et caelestia semper diligeret." cf. *De Trinitate* 14,16,22.

20. *Expositio in Hexaemeron. De sexta die.* PL 178,760–764: "Quia ergo vir dignior quam femina est et per hoc Deo similior, imago eius dicitur; femina vero similitudo, cum ipsa etiam sicut vir per rationem et immortalitatem animae Deum imitetur. Vir autem hoc insuper habet quo deo similior fiat, quod sicut omnia ex Deo habent esse, ita ex uno viro secundum traducem corporis tam femina ipsa quam totum genus humanum initium habet. . . . Cum itaque ambo juxta prae-

dicta similitudinem cum divinis personis habeant, vir tamen quo majorem cum eis similitudinem, verum etiam ad imaginem creari dicitur. . . . Vir itaque ad imaginem Dei creatus est, quia in hoc praecipuam habet cum Filio Dei similitudinem, quod sicut ille ex solo Patre tanquam genitus, ita iste ex solo Deo habet esse tanquam creatus, non de aliquo animali assumptus, sicut mulier de viro sumpta est et de costa ejus formata."

21. *Theologia "Scholarium"* I,38-39. CCCM 13, 333-334: "uirum quidem ad imaginem, mulierum uero ad similitudinem. Vir quippe, iuxta apostolum, imago est dei, non mulier; sed sicut uir est imago dei, ita et mulier imago dicitur uiri." cf. *Theologia "Scholarium," Rescensiores breviores* 45. CCCM 12,418.

22. *Commentarium in epistolam I ad Corinthios* 11. PL 181, 924-928: "Genesis docet virum et mulierem factos ad imaginem Dei. . . . Vir enim principaliter creatus est ad imaginem Dei, in quo naturaliter amplius viget ratio, quae est gloria Dei. Mulier autem est ipsa sensualitas, quae subserviendo gloria est rationis, quia haec in femina naturaliter praevalet." cf. *Ad Corinthios prima* 11,7. *De Trinitate* 12,7,10.

23. *Commentarium in epistolam ad Galatas* 3. PL 181,1162: "Non estis ibi differentes, quia omnes vos, sive Judaei, sive Graeci, sive servi, sive liberi, sive mares, sive feminae, unum estis in Christo Jesu per unitatem fidei et charitate."

24. *Commentarium in epistolam ad Colossenses* 3. PL 181, 1344-1345: "Itaque nec natio, nec ritus carnalis, nec sexus ullam differentiam facit, aut valet sive operatur ibi aliquid; sed omnia in homine hoc novo Christus, id est nihil in eo nisi Christiana pietas et Christiana religio."

25. *In epistolam I ad Corinthios* 11. PL 191,1630-1633: "Unde igitur vir est imago Dei sicut ex Deo sunt omnia, sic ex Adam omnes homines. . . . Et gloria Dei est vir quia ex eo est, et quia Deum principaliter glorificat. Mulier autem gloria est viri. Ex quo ipsa est, et cui subservit. Vel vir dicitur esse imago Dei, quia principaliter creatus est ad imaginem Dei in quo naturaliter amplius quam in muliere viget ratio, quasi ipse sit ratio. . . . Fecit ergo Deus hominem totum ad imaginem suam, hoc utique secundum spiritum." cf. *Ad Corinthios prima* 11,7. *De Trinitate* 12,7,12-13. *De Genesi ad litteram* 3,22.

26. *In epistolam ad Galatas* 3. PL 192,133: "id est propter nihil horum aliquis dignior est in fide Christi."

27. *In epistolam ad Colossenses* 3. PL 192,281-283: "novo homine nulla exterior diversitas alicui praejudicat, scilicet nec sexum, nec nationum, nec observationum, nec conditionum; sed Christus est omnia, id est omnes partes novi hominis, sunt opera Christi, et ipse Christus in omnibus fidelibus qui per eum novi sunt." cf. *De Genesi ad litteram* 3,20. *Ad Colossenses* 3,11.

28. *In epistolam ad Ephesios* 4. PL 192,201. Same argument in *Libri Sententiarum* 4,44,1,1.

29. *Sententiarum* 4,16,2,2: "Ratio imaginis non est magis in viro quam in muliere quoad primum esse, sed tantum quoad accidentalem proprietatem . . . imago quantum ad suum esse principaliter consistit in anima et eius potentiis, et in his

232 *Kari Elisabeth Børresen*

potissime, prout habent ad Deum converti; et quantum ad hoc non est distinctio masculi et feminae, servi et liberi: ideo imago, quantum ad id quod est de complemento eius et de eius esse, non magis reperitur in viro quam in muliere. Quantum autem ad bene esse sive ad clariorem expressionem, consistit magis in anima, secundum quod habet ordinem et habitudinem. Et quoniam ex parte corporis est sexuum distinctio, et secundum sexuum distinctionem maior est repraesentatio sive quantum ad rationem praesidendi, sive quantum ad rationem principandi, quia vir est caput mulieris, et non vir propter mulierem, sed mulier propter virum: quantum ad hunc unique modum excellentiori modo reperitur imago in sexu masculino quam feminino, non ratione eius quod est de esse ipsius imaginis, sed ratione ipsius quod adiacet. . . . Rationes enim ostendentes, quod non magis est imago vir quam mulier, procedunt de imagine quantum ad suum primum esse, sicut intuenti patet. Rationes vero ad oppositum procedunt de imagine quantum ad aliquam accidentalem proprietatem sive per relationem ad corpus. . . . Etsi tu obiicias, quod Apostolus loquitur de viro et de muliere ad litteram; dicendum, quod loquitur de eis non secundum se, sed secundum significationem. Vir enim, quia fortis est et praesidet mulieri, superiorem portionem rationis significat, mulier vero inferiorem. Unde etiam est in matrimonio, quod vir significat Deum, et mulier significat ecclesiam sive animam. Hoc autem est virilitatis ex parte una, et infirmitatis sive fragilitatis ex altera, quae non respiciunt imaginem secundum se, sed ratione corporis annexi, et ita non essentialiter, sed accidentaliter." cf. *Ad Corinthios prima* 11,7.

30. *Sententiarum* 4,25,2,1: "Item, nullus est possibilis ad ordines suscipiendos nisi qui Dei gerit imaginem, quia in hoc Sacramento homo quodam modo fit Deus sive divinus, dum potestatis divinae fit particeps; sed vir ratione sexus est imago Dei, sicut dicitur primae ad Corinthios undecimo: ergo nullo modo mulier potest ordinari. . . . Mulieribus autem bene licet temporaliter dominari, sed non spirituali dominio, quod est signum, quod ille qui dominatur, gerit typum capitis Christi; quoniam ergo mulier non potest esse caput viri, ideo ordinari non potest . . . dicendum, quod non respicit animam tantum, sed animam, ut est carni coniuncta et hoc ratione significationis, quae consistit circa signum visibile, ac per hoc etiam circa corpus; et exsecutio et usus ordinis coniunctum respicit. Quoniam nec ordinis significatio nec etiam dispensatio sic competit mulieri, sicut superius probatum est; ideo patet illud. . . . Et si quaeratur ratio hujus, dicendum, quod hoc non venit tam ex institutione Ecclesiae quam ex hoc, quod eis non competit ordinis Sacramentum. In hoc enim Sacramento persona, quae ordinatur, significat Christum mediatorem; et quoniam mediator solum in virili sexu fuit et per virilem sexum potest significari: ideo possibilitas suscipiendi ordines solum viris competit, qui soli possunt naturaliter repraesentare et secundum characteris susceptionem actu signum huius ferre."

31. Børresen Kari Elisabeth: *Subordination and Equivalence. The Nature and Role of Woman in Augustine and Thomas Aquinas*. Washington, DC 1981, 174–178, 195–196.

32. *Summa Theologica* 1,93,4: "et haec aptitudo consistit in ipsa natura mentis, quae est communis omnibus hominibus. . . . Dicendum quod tam in viro quam in muliere invenitur Dei imago quantum ad id in quo principaliter ratio imaginis consistit, scilicet quantum ad intellectualem naturam. . . . Sed quantum ad aliquid secundarium imago Dei invenitur in viro quod non invenitur in muliere; nam vir est principium mulieris et finis, sicut Deus est principium et finis totius creaturae." cf. *De Genesi ad litteram* 3,22.

33. *Super primam epistolam Pauli Apostoli ad Corinthios* 11, lectio 2: "quia imago Dei attenditur in homine secundum spiritum, in quo non est differentia maris et feminae, ut dicitur Col. III. Non ergo magis debet dici, quod vir dicitur imago Dei, quam mulier. Dicendum est autem, quod vir dicitur hic specialiter imago Dei secundum quaedam exteriora, sc. quia vir est principium totius sui generis, sicut Deus est principium totius universi, et quia de latere Christi dormientis in cruce fluxerunt sacramenta sanguinis et aquae, a quibus fabricata est Ecclesia. Potest etiam quantum ad interiora dici, quod vir specialius dicitur imago Dei secundum mentem, inquantum in eo magis ratio viget. Sed melius dicendum quod Apostolus signanter loquitur. Nam de viro dixit, quod vir imago et gloria Dei est: de muliere autem non dixit, quod esset imago et gloria viri, sed solum quod est gloria viri, ut detur intelligi quod esse imaginem Dei, commune est viro et mulieri: esse autem gloriam Dei immediate proprium est viri.

34. *Supplementum* 81,3: "Deus reparabit in resurrectione quod in homine fecit in prima conditione. Sed ipse fecit mulierem de costa viri, ut patet Genes. 2. Ergo ipse sexum femineum in resurrectione reparabit. . . . Respondeo dicendum quod sicut considerata natura individui, debetur diversa quantitas diversis hominibus; ita considerata natura individui, debetur diversus sexus diversis hominibus. Et haec etiam diversitas competit perfectionem speciei, cujus diversi gradus implentur per dictam diversitatem sexus, vel quantitatis. Et ideo sicut resurgent homines in diversis staturis, ita in diversis sexibus. Et quamvis sit differentia sexuum, deerit tamen confusio mutuae visionis, quia aberit libido incitans ad turpes actus, ex quibus confusio causatur. Ad primum ergo dicendum quod cum dicitur omnes Christo occurrere 'in virum perfectum,' non propter sexum virilem, sed propter virtutem animi, quae erit in omnibus et viris et mulieribus. Ad secundum dicendum, quod mulier subditur viro propter imbecillitatem naturae, et quantum ad vigorem animi, et quantum ad robur corporis. Sed post resurrectionem non erit differentia in his secundum diversitatem sexuum, sed magis secundum diversitatem meritorum. Et ideo ratio non patet. Ad tertium dicendum, quod, quamvis feminae generatio sit praeter intentionem naturae particularis, est tamen de intentione naturae universalis, quae ad perfectionem humanae speciei utrumque sexum requirit. Nec ex sexu erit ibi aliquis defectus, ut ex dictis patet." cf. *De ciuitate Dei* 22,17.

35. *Summa Theologica* 1,92,1: "Dicendum quod per respectum ad naturam particularem femina est aliquid deficiens et occasionatum. Quia virtus activa quae est in semine maris, intendit producere sibi simile perfectum secundum masculinum

sexum; sed quod femina generetur, hoc est per virtutis activae debilitatem, vel propter aliquam materiae indispositionem, vel etiam propter aliquam transmutationem ab extrinseco, puta a ventis australibus, qui sunt humidi, ut dicitur in libro De generatione animalium. Sed per comparationem ad naturam universalem femina non est aliquid occasionatum, sed est de intentione naturae ad opus generationis ordinata. Intentio autem naturae universalis dependet ex Deo, qui est universalis auctor naturae. Et ideo instituendo naturam non solum marem sed etiam feminam produxit. Dicendum quod duplex est subiectio. Una servilis, secundum quam praesidens utitur subiecto ad sui ipsius utilitatem; et talis subiectio introducta est post peccatum. Est autem alia subiectio oeconomica vel civilis, secundum quam praesidens utitur subiectis ad eorum utilitatem et bonum. Et ista subiectio fuisset etiam ante peccatum; defuissent enim bonum ordinis in humana multitudine, si quidam per alios sapientiores gubernati non fuissent. Et sic ex tali subiectione naturaliter femina subiecta est viro, quia naturaliter in vir magis abundat discretio rationis." cf. *De Genesi ad litteram* 9,5.

36. *Supplementum* 39,3: "Sed contra, videtur quod impediat quantum ad necessitatem sacramenti. Quia mulier non potest suscipere sacramentum ratione subiectionis. Sed maior subiectio est in servo, quia mulier non datur viro in ancillam, propter quod non est de pedibus sumpta. Ergo et servus sacramentum non suscipit. . . . Ad quartum dicendum quod signa sacramentalia ex naturali similitudine repraesentant. Mulier autem habet subiectionem a natura, sed non servus. Et ideo non est simile."

37. *Supplementum* 39,1: "Respondeo dicendum quod quaedam requiruntur in recipiente sacramentum quasi de necessitate sacramenti, quae si desint, non potest aliquis suscipere neque sacramentum, neque rem sacramenti. Quaedam vero requiruntur non de necessitate sacramenti, sed de necessitate praecepti, propter congruitatem ad sacramentum. Et sine talibus aliquis suscipit sacramentum, sed non rem sacramenti. Dicendum ergo quod sexus virilis requiritur ad susceptionem ordinum non solum secundo modo, sed etiam primo. Unde etsi mulieri exhibeantur omnia quae in ordinibus fiunt, ordinem tamen non suscipit. Quia cum sacramentum sit signum, in his quae in sacramento aguntur requiritur non solum res, sed significatio rei; sicut dictum est quod in extrema unctione exigitur quod sit infirmus ut significatur curatione indigens. Cum igitur in sexu femineo non possit significari aliqua eminentia gradus, quia mulier statum subiectionis habet, ideo non potest ordinis sacramentum suscipere. . . . Ad primum dicendum quod prophetia non est sacramentum, sed Dei donum. Unde ibi non exigitur significatio, sed solum res. Et quia secundum rem in his quae sunt animae, mulier non differt a viro, cum quandoque mulier inveniatur melior quantum ad animam viris multis; ideo donum prophetiae, et alia huiusmodi potest recipere, sed non ordinis sacramentum."

38. *Scivias* 2,6,76–77. CCCM 43,290–291: "Sic etiam nec feminae ad idem officium altaris mei debent accidere, quoniam ipsae infirmum et debile habitaculum sunt, ad hoc positae ut filios pariant et eos parientes diligenter enutriant. Sed femina

non per semetipsam, sed de uiro infantem concipit, sicut nec terra semetipsam arare non potest, ita nec feminae in officio censecrationis corporis et sanguinis Filii mei sacerdoti comparanda est, quamuis in laude creatoris sui sonare possit, ut et terra ad irrigationem fructum pluuiam suscepit. Et ut terra omnem fructum profert, ita etiam et in femina omnis fructus boni operis perficitur. Quomodo? Quia summum sacerdotum sponsum accipere potest. Quomodo? Virgo desponsata Filio meo sponsum eum accipit, quoniam corpus suum carnali uiro conclusit, et ideo in sponso suo sacerdotium et omne ministerium altaris mei habet atque omnes diuitias ipsius cum eo possidet. Sed et uidua eiusdem Filii mei sponsa potest appellari, quae carnalem uirum renuens sub alas protectionis eius fugit. Et ut sponsus sponsam suam ualde diligit, sic etiam Filius meus sponsas suas dulcissime amplectitur quae ad eum in amore castitatis sollicite currunt. . . . Et quoniam femina uirili habitu uestiri non debet, ideo etiam ad officium altaris mei non accedet, quia uirili personam nec in capillis nec in uestitu suo demonstrabit." Translated in Hart, Columba, Bishop, Jane: *Hildegard of Bingen. Scivias.* New York, Mahwah NJ 1990, 278.

39. Concerning Hildegard's innovative use of female metaphors describing God, see Newman, Barbara: *Sister of Wisdom. St. Hildegard's Theology of the Feminine.* Berkeley, CA 1989. Placing Hildegard in the context of medieval matristics, see Børresen, Kari Elisabeth: "Ancient and Medieval Church Mothers." In Børresen, Kari Elisabeth, Vogt, Kari: *Women's Studies of the Christian and Islamic Traditions. Ancient, Medieval and Renaissance Foremothers.* Dordrecht, Boston, London 1993, 245–275.

40. Raming, Ida: *The Exclusion of Women from the Priesthood. Divine Law or Sex Discrimination?* Metuchen, NJ 1976.

41. Børresen, Kari Elisabeth: "The Ordination of Women: to Nurture Tradition by Continuing Inculturation." *Studia Theologica* 46 (1992): 3–13. "Women's Ordination: Tradition and Inculturation." *Theology Digest* 40 (1993): 15–19.

9

THE IMAGE OF GOD IN WOMEN
AS SEEN BY LUTHER AND CALVIN

∞ Jane Dempsey Douglass

In view of the many significant shifts in theology which took place within the various Reformations of the sixteenth century, both Catholic and Protestant, it is important to ask whether the doctrine of the image of God, particularly as it relates to distinctions between men and women, was among those doctrines disputed or reformulated. Because a broad literature is not yet available on this topic, we will focus on two influential reforming theologians, Martin Luther and John Calvin.[1]

As we examine the writings of Luther and Calvin, it appears that this doctrine was not singled out by them as one in need of such major reformulation as were, for example, the doctrines of justification and the sacraments. Both Reformers take up the traditional question of the nature of the image of God, with heavy dependence on the Fathers of the ancient church, especially Augustine, and desire to show their continuity with that tradition. On the other hand, questions had arisen in the Renaissance which shape the discussions of Luther and Calvin somewhat differently than had been the case in the ancient and medieval church. Calvin, more deeply steeped in the Renaissance tradition than Luther, shows this influence more clearly.

Physicians of the Renaissance had taken up again the issue of the physical nature of women, putting the writings of Galen (somewhat imperfectly understood) against the views of Aristotle which had dominated the Middle Ages. By the late sixteenth-century the physicians generally had given up Aristotle's view that women were misbegotten males in favor of a view that the female sex is normal in itself, just as the male sex is. As important as this scientific shift may have been for the dignity of women, one must note that the physicians continued to believe, nonetheless, that women are weaker and more frail than men, needing to remain under the protection of the home.[2] Another biological question under discussion was whether women as well as men contributed "seed" in the procreative process. Increasingly the older view that women merely nurtured the male seed was being replaced by the opinion that women, too, contributed seed to the fetus.[3]

The question of the possibility and the propriety of women holding public office was alive in the sixteenth century. At stake were several questions closely related to the nature of the image of God: whether women have the inherent capacity to govern, whether God wills for them to hold public office, and more generally, what their relationship should be to men. Though a very few queens and other noblewomen in the fifteenth and sixteenth centuries did in fact exercise considerable political and social influence, many more women discovered the extent of their vulnerability in the hysteria of the witch trials, which extended even beyond the Reformation period.

Deeply contradictory assumptions about women are also evident in intellectual circles from the end of the fourteenth century into the sixteenth in the Renaissance *querelle des femmes*, the literary debate by both men and women about women's nature. During 1404-5 in France Christine de Pizan in her *Book of the City of Ladies* described her difficulty reconciling her own experience and that of other women with the vilifying portrait of women drawn by the male authors she read. Yet she so respected their authority above that of her own experience that she came to detest herself and the whole female sex as monstrosities in nature.[4] A visit from three ladies, Reason, Rectitude, and Justice, freed her from these false assumptions by teaching her about women's true nature and place in history. Reason countered male views of the shameful imperfection of the female body, among other arguments, retelling the Genesis story of Eve's creation in Paradise and asserting that the Supreme Craftsman was not ashamed to create a female body.

> . . . she was created in the image of God. How can any mouth dare to slander the vessel which bears such a noble imprint? But some men are foolish enough to think, when they hear that God made man in his image, that this refers to the material body. This was not the case, for God had not yet taken a human body. The soul is meant, the intellectual spirit which lasts eternally just like the Deity. God created the soul and placed wholly similar souls, equally good and noble in the feminine and in the masculine bodies.[5]

As the debate continued, women were alternately viciously deprecated and extravagantly lauded. One common question discussed was whether women's weaknesses are the result of nature or nurture – poor education and limited experience outside the home.[6] Women's defenders often made the point that the Scriptures as a whole and especially the writings of Paul are read one-sidedly emphasizing all negative statements about women and suppressing those that favor women's equality and freedom.[7] They often attacked the assumption of Paul that Adam's creation prior to Eve guarantees his natural superiority.[8] Finally in 1598 came a treatise entitled "A New Disputation against Women, in which it is proved that they are not human beings." Usually attributed to Valens Acidalius, and certainly satirical, it was seriously debated by theologians, doctors, and lawyers. The last academic trial on the question was held in Wittenberg in 1688; Lutheran theologians refuted the treatise. But the text and its refutations were republished into the late eighteenth century.[9]

Since the question of the nature of women was a lively question, particularly in Renaissance culture, at the end of the Middle Ages and through the Reformation period, one should be alert for evidence of Luther's and Calvin's awareness of it as they discuss the image of God. For twentieth-century readers to explore the issue of gender in relation to the image of God in the Reformation period is by no means anachronistic.

Reformation theologians like Luther and Calvin, committed to the authority of "Scripture alone," worked differently than most of the medieval theologians. Though they knew and valued the theological tradition, were more deeply shaped by it than they acknowledged, and often explicitly dialogued with it, they tried to start freshly with the biblical text, accepting the theological tradition only where they believed it was in accordance with Scripture. Since the Renaissance, biblical scholarship had been able to profit from the new knowledge of Hebrew and Greek and from textual criticism, was much more restrained in its use of the allegorical method than the medieval tradition had been, and was more interested in the historical context out of which the biblical passages arose. Because earlier theologians had depended heavily on allegory at many points in their discussions of men and women in the image of God,[10] the nature of that discussion changed. Emphasis on "Scripture alone" reinforced the warnings against rash speculation beyond revelation which the Reformers inherited from late medieval scholasticism.[11]

I. Luther

Since Luther did not leave us a systematic theological work with a discussion of the image of God, the most useful focus for study seems to be his extensive commentary on Genesis from 1535, a product of his mature thought.[12] Some comparisons will be made with commentaries on such key texts as I Timothy 2 from 1528 and Galatians 3:28 from 1535. Unfortunately no sermon or commentary from Luther is available for I Cor. 11, containing the much-discussed verses 7 and 8: "man is the image and glory of God; but woman is the glory of man. For man was not made from woman, but woman from man." We will see that this text is in his consciousness, and so we wonder about the significance of its omission.

In Luther's 1535 commentary on Genesis, he takes the first three chapters of Genesis as a single narrative of creation, imagining that both God's instruction about the forbidden fruit and the fall take place on the sabbath, though he acknowledges that he cannot be certain of the dating.[13] Critical of Hilary and Augustine, as propounded by Nicholas of Lyra, Luther believes that Moses' six days of creation should be taken literally rather than allegorically. Moses "wants to teach us, not about allegorical creatures and an allegorical world, but about real creatures and a visible world apprehended by the senses."[14] If the nature of the days is not clear to us, it is preferable to admit that one does not understand rather than to resort to distortion with a "foreign meaning."[15] Luther often presents glimpses of "the philosophers'" opinions about creation, frequently from Lyra, but he regards Moses as the better and safer teacher in these matters.[16]

Luther's most explicit discussion of the nature of the image of God in humanity follows Augustine, referring to his book on the Trinity. But Luther believes this is common teaching:

> Moreover, the remaining doctors closely follow Augustine, who retains Aristotle's classification: that the image of God is the powers of the soul: memory, mind or intellect, and will. These three, they say, comprise the image of God which is in all human beings. . . . Moreover they say that the similitude [likeness] lies in the gifts of grace. For just as a similitude is a certain perfection of an image, so, they say, nature is perfected through grace. And so the similitude of God consists in this, that the memory is adorned with hope, the intellect with faith, and the will with love.[17]

Notice that Luther does not reject the distinction traditionally made between the "likeness" and the "image" of God.

Luther is aware that Augustine and others following him have gone on to make further distinctions to "devise diverse trinities in a human being."[18] Although Luther expresses a certain intellectual admiration for these "not unpleasing speculations," he doubts that they are useful for understanding the image of God; and he fears that some people may be led by them into error, as when an understanding of human freedom is too easily derived from the freedom of God.[19] Luther's deep suspicion of the use of philosophy in theology[20] certainly surfaces here and distances him from much of the patristic discussion of the image of God.

An important function of the image of God in humanity, Luther believes, is to show that human beings, though sharing many similarities with animals in their physical lives, were created "by a special plan and providence of God" for a better, spiritual life in the future. Even if Adam had not sinned, when the determined number of saints had been reached, "Adam and his descendants would have been translated to an eternal and spiritual life" without eating, drinking, and procreating.[21] So special was the act of creation of humanity that Moses even uses a different phrase than he had used earlier: "Let us make," which expresses God's "obvious deliberation and plan."[22]

The image of God in Paradise was far more excellent than modern people can imagine, Luther explains. Adam's "inner and outer senses were all exceedingly pure. His intellect was the most faultless, his memory was the best, and his will was the most sincere – all in the most beautiful composure, without any fear of death and without any anxiety."[23] Added to this was a superb body, strong, with acute senses. Still another description of the image of God includes Adam's possessing it in his own being, not only his knowledge of God as good, but also his godly life, his fearlessness, and his contentment with God's favor, and also Eve's fearlessness in speaking to the serpent.[24] Or Luther will list Adam's enlightened reason, his true knowledge of God, his will to love God and his neighbor so that he immediately embraced Eve as his own flesh, and also his remarkable knowledge of other living things.[25]

The reason this image is so unknown to modern people, Luther thinks, is that God's declaration proved true: when Adam and Eve sinned, disobeyed God, they lost the image of God. The remaining powers of the image have become "leprous and unclean," impaired and weakened.[26] But in Luther's day the Gospel, he thought, was bringing about a restoration of the image of God in humanity, with the hope of eternal life. Though that image was still unfinished in the godly, when the kingdom comes all the powers of the image will be renewed, there will be freedom from fear, and all the creatures will be even more completely under human rule than in Paradise. Until then there can be no truly adequate knowledge of the lost image of God, except that it included eternal life, freedom from fear, and all that is good. Humankind hardly knows what it has lost.[27] But God takes pleasure in this work of restoration through Christ just as God rejoiced in the creation of humanity.[28]

Already Luther has alluded to the dominion of humanity over all creatures in his discussion of the image of God. When he reaches the section of Gen. 1:26 where God commands humanity to have dominion over all the animals, it seems evident that ruling, dominion, is part of the image of God. Luther seems not so much to identify ruling as a separate aspect of the image as to connect it with the intellect, knowledge: Adam and Eve had insight into all aspects of the natural world. Because they knew so deeply all the creatures and all the plants and herbs, they were able to obey God's explicit command to rule over all the animals even though they were naked, "without weapons or walls." Indeed Luther introduces his discussion of ruling with a description of Adam and Eve which mentions their knowledge of God, their enlightened reason, justice, and wisdom. They become models of an outstanding philosopher with their most perfect knowledge of God, whose similitude they feel within themselves. Luther thinks people in his own day retained as a mere vestige of the image of God the capacity to rule some creatures through industry and skill, but not through the intimate knowledge of nature which Adam and Eve had.[29] A little farther along, on Gen. 1:28, Luther will suggest that people in his own day can hardly even imagine what the nature of "dominion" was in Paradise, but creatures were surely used with less greed and more admiration of God and holy joy than among his contemporaries.[30]

So far Luther in discussing humanity in Paradise has sometimes spoken simply of "Adam," as though he were alone, or as though "Adam" means humankind of both sexes, sometimes of "Adam and Eve." Perhaps this is because Luther in dealing with the first three chapters of Genesis as a single narrative is faced with the problem of creation of humanity in both sexes in chapter one, then the creation of Eve in chapter two. Whatever the explanation for this language, Luther has not appeared to make distinctions between male and female with regard to the image of God or their non-reproductive capacities.

Here, however, after speaking of the remarkable knowledge of nature and capacity for dominion which Adam and Eve possessed, Luther feels it necessary to emphasize that "Eve had these abilities equally with Adam. . . ." Luther is certainly aware of the practice of most patristic writers to identify dominion with the male, and he must be consciously refuting that tradition. Eve knew the purpose of her creation and the source of her knowledge of it. "Therefore she not only heard these things from Adam, but her own nature was pure and full of the knowledge of God, so that by herself she understood and reflected on the word of God."[31]

But already in the following verse, where the text declares that God created both male and female in the image of God, Luther introduces gender distinctions. On the one hand Luther understands that Moses includes mention of women in order to be clear that they, too, share the image and the likeness of God, as well as the rule over all things. They will share eternal life and are joint heirs of the same grace, and they may not be excluded from any glory of human nature.[32] He rejects Talmudic tales of a bisexual creature split apart into male and female and also such pejorative and ridiculing terms for women as Aristotle's "damaged male" or "monster." Luther clearly rejects Aristotle's view of women as botched or imperfectly formed men. He insists that woman as well as man was expressly made by God's special counsel as a most excellent work in which God took delight.[33] Women seem here to share fully in all human dignity.

On the other hand, still commenting on this same biblical verse which makes no distinction between men and women, Luther observes that:

> . . . woman seems to be a somewhat different sort of being from man, because she has both dissimilar members [of her body] and a nature [*ingenium*] which is far weaker. And although Eve was a most extraordinary creature, similar to Adam with respect to the image of God, that is in justice, wisdom, and soundness, still she was a woman. For just as the sun is more extraordinary than the moon (although the moon is also a most extraordinary body), so even though the woman is a most beautiful work of God, still she does not equal the glory and worthiness [*dignitatem*] of the male.[34]

Luther draws the parallel to a household where "the wife is a partner in managing the household affairs and has common possession of the children and property, yet still there is a great difference between the sexes."[35]

This ambivalence between Eve as fully equal to Adam in Paradise before sin and Eve as inherently inferior to Adam because she is female continues through the discussion of the first three chapters of Genesis. Since often there is nothing in the immediate biblical text to explain Luther's inconsistency, one must assume that he feels the tension between biblical texts like Gen. 1:27 where there seems clearly to be an equality in the creation of man and woman on the one hand, and on the other hand the weight of his cultural and theological tradition, which had usually read these texts through the perspective of other biblical texts which assume the subordination of woman.

Once again Eve is portrayed as the equal of Adam in what Luther believes to be the institution of marriage and the family, already in Paradise. Luther sees Gen. 2:18, where God determines to make a help for Adam, as Moses' way of emphasizing that woman as well as man was created according to a unique counsel of God, suitable for the life planned for Adam and useful for procreation. "Had the woman not been deceived by the serpent and sinned, she would have been in all things the equal of Adam . . . [before sin] she was in no respect inferior to Adam, whether you count the qualities of the body or of the mind."[36] This point is repeated twice in the discussion of Gen. 3:16 about Eve's punishment after sin. Eve is placed "under the power of her husband, she who previously was very free and, as the sharer of all the gifts of God, was in no respect inferior to her husband. . . . If Eve had persisted in the truth, she would not only not have been subjected to the rule of her husband, but she herself would also have been a partner in the rule which now entirely belongs to males."[37]

These themes come together in a somewhat different way in Luther's commentary on Gen. 2:23: "This one will be called woman, because she has been taken from the man." Though he thinks the Hebrew cannot be fully imitated in Latin, he proposes as an equivalent for the Hebrew "Ischa": "virago" or "vira," "she-man," "a heroic woman who does manly deeds.[38] Luther sees this term for Eve as revealing marriage to be a partnership in which the wife possesses in entirety all that the husband has: money, children, home. "For whatever the man in the home has and is, that the woman has and is, differing only in sex. Then also there is what Paul notes in I Tim. 2: she is woman, "virago," by origin, because the woman descends from man, not man from woman."[39] Eve and – by extension in Christ's teaching in Mt. 19:5 – all wives can be said to be of one flesh with their husbands. This point that woman differs only in sex from man is repeated three times in two paragraphs: once the point is made very explicitly that, apart from her difference in sex, she is "clearly man" [*vir*].[40] Here again Luther argues that had sin not intervened, Eve would not have been subject to her husband but would have shared "equal governance" [*gubernatio aequalis*] with Adam.[41]

Luther's ambivalence about the nature of Eve in Paradise can be seen also in the discussion about her temptation by the serpent. He acknowledges that at first Eve resisted the serpent admirably, because she was still led by Spirit, having been created perfect in the likeness of God, but then she allowed herself to be persuaded.[42] In what did her sin consist? Although she was not aware at the time that she was sinning, she fell into doubting God's Word, unbelief, "inquisitive discussion" beyond God's Word, desire to eat the forbidden fruit, disobedient action, lying.[43] ". . . Eve, created a most wise woman, longs for another wisdom beyond the Word and on account of this wisdom thus sins in many ways with all her senses by seeing, thinking, desiring, and acting."[44] Why did the serpent approach Eve rather than Adam? Because just as in all of nature, the male is stronger than the female, so even in Paradise, though Adam and Eve were created "equally righteous," still Adam surpassed

Eve. Therefore the serpent approached "the weak part of human nature," Eve, "for he sees that she trusts so confidently in her husband that she does not believe that she is able to sin."[45] Luther believes that if the serpent had tempted Adam, Adam would have triumphed by stomping upon the serpent and ordering him to be quiet, for "the Lord commands otherwise."[46]

This assumption by Luther that the serpent chose the weaker person to tempt stands strangely in the context of an argument for the cleverness of the serpent; Luther has just argued for the serpent's cleverness because he assails precisely the greatest strength of the human being, the very likeness of God, the will properly disposed toward God.[47] One might assume such a clever tempter would challenge the strongest, not the weakest human being. So Luther must be drawing uncritically on the tradition of Eve's weakness. Yet in this commentary he is noticeably freer of the carping about women's frailties and vices which is so common in medieval and Renaissance popular literature than in his first commentary on Genesis.[48]

On the other hand, Luther criticizes the whole exegetical tradition for its unsatisfactory dealing with Gen. 3:1-6, especially because Augustine has influenced Gregory and even Nicholas of Lyra to see here an allegory where the woman refers to the "lower reason." Luther believes the story should rather be read according to the "historical and literal meaning" as dealing with a real man, woman, and a serpent dominated by Satan. But he also regards it as absurd to see Eve as the lower part of reason because "she was in no respect, either in body or in mind, inferior to her husband Adam."[49]

How does Luther share the blame between Adam and Eve for original sin? We have seen that he devotes considerable comment to Eve's encounter with the serpent and her yielding to his temptation. But Luther notes that in Gen. 3:9, it is specifically Adam who is at first called to trial by God. This seems appropriate to Luther because it was Adam alone on the sixth day to whom the command about the forbidden tree was addressed. But because Eve also sinned, she also hears God's judgment and shares the punishment.[50] Luther seems somewhat concerned about the fact that the Genesis text does not indicate that Eve was present when the command not to eat of the tree of knowledge was given. However the church was established even before Eve's creation, before the creation of the home, when God preached to Adam, commanding what he could lawfully eat.[51] So he explains that though Adam alone heard God's sermon, he later informed Eve of God's Word.[52] In fact he suggests that early on the sabbath day Adam preached to Eve about God's will, perhaps even taking her to see the forbidden tree.[53] At the trial which God conducts, both Adam and Eve try to pass along the blame: Adam to Eve, whom God created, Eve to the serpent, whom God created. Yet finally Eve admits her sinful deed, while Adam tries to hide it.[54]

When the question arises why God allowed Satan to tempt Eve, Luther cautions strongly against attempting to investigate such questions. Job teaches us that God cannot be called to account. Luther thinks only one answer ought to be given: "it pleased the Lord that Adam [!] should be put to the test and should exercise his powers."[55]

Luther reflects on Paul's statement in I Tim. 2:13-14: "For Adam was formed first, then Eve; and Adam was not deceived, but the woman was deceived and became a transgressor." Luther believes nearly everyone understands this to mean that Adam was not seduced by the Devil but sinned willingly. He wanted to please his wife and placed his love of his wife ahead of his love to God. This common view, he says, presumes the serpent was afraid to approach Adam, the master, but thought Eve, though holy, was weaker and could more easily be seduced. Either Adam was seduced by the woman, who gave him the apple, or he seduced himself by noticing that she did not immediately die, therefore thinking they might escape punishment. Luther "does not disapprove" of this interpretation.[56]

Indeed this material is traditional. Much of it can be found in Augustine, for example: the view that Adam's personal sin was in obeying his wife out of affection for her; that the serpent approached Eve as the weaker of the two; that Adam and Eve each pass the blame to another.[57] But there are differences from Augustine. Whereas Augustine stresses pride as the essence of original sin,[58] Luther begins with unbelief. There is no indication in this material that he agrees with Augustine's view that Eve fell into sin because she was weaker intellectually than Adam, since he was created first.[59]

A few years earlier, 1527-28, Luther had prepared a commentary on I Timothy, which treats the text in greater detail. Whereas Luther in his two references to this text in the Genesis commentary[60] has shown little interest in the point about the order of creation, in the earlier commentary on I Timothy Luther took this context very seriously. Here he argues that because Adam was first, man has greater authority than woman. This is God's intent, demonstrated also from the story of Adam and Eve. He understands verse 14 to function as evidence for Paul's view that man is to be dominant over woman. God chose to create Adam first, making him superior to Eve because of "primogeniture." Furthermore Adam was wiser and more courageous than Eve. "Thus it has been proved by divine and human law that Adam is the master of the woman. That is, Adam did not err. Therefore there was greater wisdom in Adam than in the woman, and thus greater dominion."[61] Then Luther goes on to make some of the same arguments he had made in the Genesis commentary from "common interpretation": Adam was not deceived quite simply because the serpent did not approach him but rather Eve, the weaker one. Adam sinned knowingly to please his wife. He states here, in contrast to the Genesis commentary, that we do not know whether Adam would have sinned had he listened to the serpent. He also clarifies that Adam received God's command directly from God, Eve indirectly through Adam. Adam was deceived by the woman, believing that disobedience was not a very important matter. The woman became the transgressor and therefore was punished by becoming subject to her husband and bearing children in pain.[62]

Though much of the content of the argument is similar to the discussion on Genesis, the later Genesis commentary lacks the self-conscious focus on the order of creation, the rights of primogeniture so conspicuous in the commentary on I Timothy, Adam's superiority just because God created him first. Even where Luther in the later Genesis commentary cites the I Tim. text on Eve's coming from Adam, it is to stress their solidarity as one flesh. The Genesis commentary also lacks the single-minded focus on Eve as the transgressor which Paul's letter to Timothy exhibits. It is not clear how much of the difference should be attributed simply to the different nature of the biblical text on which Luther is commenting and how much to change in Luther's thought over time.

One further point should be made concerning Luther's view of woman in Paradise: even there, though he usually portrays Eve as possessing equally all the gifts Adam had, he focuses on Eve's role in home and family. According to Moses God does not "form" or "create" her like other creatures but "builds" her; Luther claims that Scripture commonly refers to a wife as a household building because of her role in bearing and rearing children.[63] The vision of affectionate couples moving away from their parents to their own homes, raising their own families, but visiting their parents and praising God together is part of Luther's picture of Paradise. Fertility would have been even greater than now because of the absence of illness and other impediments. In the absence of lust, children would be conceived chastely and without shame.[64] Sexual union would be as honorable as eating or talking at the table with one's wife. Bearing and rearing children would be very easy, without any difficulty, and full of joy.[65] Luther realizes, however, that as he believes the fall took place on the first sabbath, the day after Eve was created, none of this idyllic family life which he envisions ever in fact took place in Paradise.

In Luther's discussions of the wonders of God's plan for procreation, it is interesting that although he has repudiated Aristotle's view of the formation of the female sex, he continues to assume that women are without "seed," merely nurturing the child which comes from a drop of the father's blood or semen.[66]

Since the fall of Adam and Eve, Luther believes, the whole human situation has changed. As we have seen, Luther thought people after the fall can scarcely imagine what original humanity was like, and they can only picture what humanity is intended to be through the Gospel of Jesus Christ. The powers of the intellect and of the body are seriously weakened, and human dominion over the creatures is only a vestige of its former effectiveness. Eve has lost her freedom and become subject to her husband, and she must bear children in pain. Luther regards this punishment as a very serious one. In fact, he claims that Eve has received a far more severe punishment than Adam.[67] Not only must she suffer many physical ills in conjunction with pregnancy and childbirth,[68] she must stay at home, caring for the household, "like a nail driven into the wall," deprived of any share in the governance of public matters outside the home.[69] But Adam, too, has been punished, Luther believes. He must contend with raging lust. His duty to support and govern his family as well as to rule over the world beyond is a very great burden. The earth is cursed with decreased fertility, weeds and harmful plants, disease, natural disasters, and the air is less pure.[70] He must see his wife's misery in childbearing.[71]

In short, one cannot discover the true nature of humanity as God created it by looking at the present inhabitants of the world. The very existence of "damage" such as lust, ignorance, the difficulties of the "work of procreation," and the loss of the righteous will leads Luther to disagree with those scholastics who claimed that "natural endowments" remain unimpaired after the fall.[72]

Human relationships are disrupted still further because of sin, Luther observes. Women are impatient of the burden of subjection to their husbands' rule and seek to regain what they lost through sin. At least they grumble about their situation.[73] The papists force people into celibacy, ignoring the blessings and promises relating to God's gift of sexuality, pretending wrongly that they are neither male nor female, despising marriage.[74] The heathen who do not know God see the great sufferings of women in pregnancy and childbirth and discourage marriage.[75] Many people [apparently among Christians], especially the nobility, also refrain from marriage in order not to have children. Luther finds this aversion to parenthood a "more than barbaric savageness and inhumanity."[76] The lack of respect for procreation, aggravated by celibacy, leads to insult or abuse against the female sex. "However it is a great favor that God has preserved woman for us almost against our will for generation and also as a medicine against the sin of fornication . . . we are hardly able to speak of her without shame, and we are certainly not able to use her without shame."[77] Sexual union, such a noble delight in Paradise, created and blessed by God, is now, "alas, such a shameful and dreadful pleasure that it is compared by the doctors with epilepsy. . . ."[78] ". . . we are begotten and also born in sin because our parents do not come together only for the sake of duty but also for the sake of remedy or avoiding sin."[79] Like the earlier theological tradition, Luther regards sexual union even within marriage as at least somewhat sinful if it is the result of sexual desire rather than simply the intent to have children.

Still marriage remains for Luther a very significant vestige of the life of original humanity. We have seen that Luther regards marriage as essential for most people to avoid sin and loneliness, and we have seen that there remains some vestige of partnership between the sexes in the management of the family. Procreation remains a blessing, though marred by sin.[80]

Especially for women, Luther sees marriage and childbearing, despite its suffering, as revealing something of God's intention for humanity and as a source of hope. He tries to help women to think positively about their situation, emphasizing the hope of immortality and eternal life, the virtue of suffering in teaching humility, and the remaining outstanding glory – even since the fall – of motherhood and the blessing of the womb. The marvels of mothers' care for infants before and after birth are other gifts which remain even in fallen humanity. Luther seems quite sincere in his eloquent admiration for women's skill, even as young girls, in caring for children. He contrasts women's deftness in handling a fussy baby with men's clumsiness, like a camel dancing! Since the fall "women cannot administer manly offices, like teaching and ruling. But they are mistresses [*magistrae*] of bearing, feeding, and nurturing children."[81] Luther's personal warmth here about motherly skills suggests that he is drawing on his own family experience of a decade with Katie. He believes Eve would have had a joyful heart even in her sorrow at God's punishment:

> . . . Eve hears that she is not rejected by God . . . that she is not being deprived in this punishment of the blessing of procreation promised and given before the fall. She sees that she retains her own sex and is a woman . . . that she is not separated from Adam . . . that the glory of motherhood is left to her. . . .[82]

When one adds to all this that she has the hope of eternal life and the promise of bearing the Seed who will crush the head of Satan, Luther believes that Eve must have been very greatly encouraged, even joyful.[83]

This same mingling of punishment and promise is present in the story of Adam's naming of Eve, Luther thinks. He emphasizes that Adam's right to name Eve is part of the power over her given as punishment for sin. He relates this story to the custom of his own day that a wife takes her husband's name when she marries, losing her own family name. It would be monstrous for a husband to wish to take his wife's name, Luther declares. Wives in Luther's day were also compelled to follow their husbands if they moved, another evidence for Luther of the husband's power over his wife.[84] But Adam gives Eve a delightful name, Eve, Mother of all living. Luther attributes this wisdom to Adam's having been enlightened by the Holy Spirit to understand the promise of the coming Seed who will crush the tempter, the promise of the forgiveness of sins. The name was a very beautiful witness to Adam's faith and his recreated spirit, and it comforted him and strengthened his faith.[85] Nothing at all is said by Luther here concerning Eve's feelings about her name.

We have seen several examples of Luther's forbidding women to hold public authority since the fall, to speak outside the home. Frequently he refers to I Tim. 2:11 as justification. In his commentary on this text from 1528, he does indeed emphasize that this text has to do with public affairs. In public assemblies, including the church, the woman must be a hearer, subject to men. She must not teach or pray in public gatherings – at least where men are present, because God's good order and the peacefulness of the assembly would be broken. Luther thinks Paul believes women are clever, but he is concerned that they would argue against men in public. Yet in an awkward insert into the argument, Luther raises the opposing point that women are spoken of in Scripture as having authority: Queen Candace, Huldah, Deborah, Jael, for example. Luther responds that these women, like Philip's daughters who prophesied, were unmarried; "woman" in the text means "wife," and wives should not have authority over their husbands. Yet Luther nowhere in this discussion offers hope to unmarried women that they could hold public office. Indeed the basic concern seems to be the problem of uppity women like Miriam who upset the proper order of male dominance.[86] After the discussion we have detailed above on Adam and Eve from I Tim 2:14, Luther moves to verse 15 where women can be saved through childbearing, if they are faithful. He repeats his familiar theme that the penalties of sin: pain in childbearing and subjection to husbands, must be borne till judgment. The guilt of sin is taken away, but the penalty remains. But suddenly at the very end of the chapter Luther interjects: "And if the Lord should raise up a woman so that we should hear her, we would allow her to rule like Hulda."[87]

One wonders how Luther would recognize that she had been raised up by God!

Finally we should see how Luther deals with Gal. 3:28: ". . . there is neither male nor female; for you are all one in Christ Jesus." Here Paul is dealing with the restoration of fallen human nature through the Gospel. Luther says in 1535 that one could add: "There is neither magistrate nor subject, neither professor nor listener, neither teacher nor pupil, neither lady nor servant, etc. Because in Christ Jesus all social stations, even those that were divinely ordained, are nothing."[88] In salvation, the Law which makes such distinctions has been abolished, and all are saved by putting on Christ. Still,

> In the world and according to the flesh there is a very great difference and inequality among persons, and this must be observed very carefully. For if a woman wanted to be a man, if a son wanted to be a father, if a pupil wanted to be a teacher, if a servant wanted to be a master, if a subject wanted to be a magistrate there would be a disturbance and confusion of all social stations and of everything. In Christ, on the other hand, where there is no Law, there is no distinction among persons at all.[89]

Luther makes no mention here of any consequences at all for the sixteenth-century hierarchical social structure – indeed in Luther's Germany still feudal – of this spiritual oneness in Christ.

What conclusions can we draw from an examination of these selections from Luther's commentaries written during his mature years? Perhaps that Luther is a theologian in transition between two worlds. Educated a scholastic, he has so deeply imbibed the older tradition of understanding the image of God and the different relation of men and women to it that he simply cannot consciously lay aside that tradition, though he tries very hard to do so. He has abandoned allegorical interpretation like that of Augustine as a way to deal with the image of God in woman,[90] along with the double-creation schemes of several of the Fathers.[91] The connection of "male and female" in Genesis 1:27 to the image of God is taken for granted by Luther, though it has not always been so.[92] Luther's intent is to substitute a biblically-derived picture of humanity as created in God's image for the traditional one he regards as too much derived from Greek philosophy. In fact he regards the mixing of Aristotle with theology as a serious mistake. He perceives his own view from Genesis to be a much more positive picture of humankind and especially of woman's nature than the scholastic one, giving her greater dignity. He also believes he offers a much more positive picture of the home and child-rearing, woman's special sphere, than that of the Fathers.

For the most part in the 1535 Genesis commentary Luther argues that before the fall Eve was equal in endowments to Adam, despite her different body, and shared equally in governance over the other creatures. Female subjection to men is punishment for the fall. But at times the older view of Eve's subjection to Adam from creation itself creeps back into the discussion, and what is different from the male becomes necessarily inferior. The theology of women's subordination in passages like I Cor. 11:7 and I Tim. 2:14, both of which he attributes to Paul, influences his reading of Genesis[93] and perhaps also of another key Pauline text, Gal. 3:28. There is no evidence that he sees any real tension between the Galatians text and those clearly teaching women's subordination to men.

Insofar as Luther places the beginning of women's subordination after the fall, as the result of sin, he contributes to genuine reform in theology, stressing a full equality between women and men as intended by God at creation. This teaching has come to dominate modern theology. But Luther does not see women's subordination as simply an unfortunate disordering of human relationships as a consequence of sin; rather he sees it as God's express punishment of women which must endure till the end of time.[94] By giving women's inferior place in society the full weight of God's command, Luther effectively eliminates any possible practical consequences flowing from the creational equality of women with men for the earthly lives of real women.

II. Calvin

Calvin is really a second-generation Reformer, able to profit from the exegetical and theological work of Luther and other older Reformers. His education was also more humanistically oriented than Luther's. As Calvin was writing, Erasmus had published many works from the early church Fathers not available when Luther began his work, widening Calvin's range of first-hand knowledge of writers in the ancient church. Calvin shared Luther's determination to work directly from the biblical material in the original languages, rejecting the heavy dependence of medieval theology on classical philosophy. His humanistic training in languages and attention to historical context permitted him often to bring greater critical analysis to the biblical text. We will see, for example, that he struggled repeatedly with the tension he perceived between Genesis 1 and I Cor. 11 on the image of God and resolved it in a surprisingly modern way.

Because he realized how difficult a task it was for students to understand the Bible, he prepared a handbook to assist them, *The Institutes of the Christian Religion.* Here he organized biblical insights around traditional topics in

theology. Calvin urged his readers to look first at the *Institutes* for a comprehensive view of biblical theology, and only then at his biblical commentaries
for complementary material, since he wished to avoid boring his students
with constant repetition.[1] This advice of Calvin suggests that we should famil-
iarize ourselves first with his discussions of the image of God in the *Institutes*
as a framework, then turn to the commentaries. Because the sheer quantity
of discussion of the image of God is so vast and its interpretation so disputed,[2] we can only sketch the broad outlines of his approach and then select
those passages which most usefully bear on the question of women's relation
to the image of God and help to set Calvin in the trajectory of tradition
described in earlier chapters of this volume.

The first edition of the *Institutes* appeared in 1536, the year the young
scholar Calvin went to Geneva and was persuaded to remain as a teacher for
the newly reformed city. At the opening of his discussion of the law, Calvin
argues that "Nearly the whole of sacred doctrine consists in these two parts:
knowledge of God and of ourselves."[3] What do we need to know about God?
. . . that he is infinite wisdom, righteousness, goodness, mercy, truth, power,
and life. And all of these things, wherever seen, come from him . . . that all
things in heaven and on earth have been created for his glory."[4] Therefore we
are obliged to serve God. We also need to know that God is a just judge who
will take "harsh vengeance" on the disobedient and will also be merciful and
gentle to those who trust God's mercy.[5] What do we need to know about ourselves? "Adam, parent [*parens*] of us all, was created in the image and likeness
of God. That is, he was endowed with wisdom, righteousness, holiness or
sanctity and was clinging by these gifts of grace to God in such a way that he
could have lived forever in Him, if he had stood fast in this integrity of nature
which he had received from God."[6]

Though Calvin speaks of human "endowments," in fact the striking part of
this description is that Adam mirrors or reflects God's nature in the state of
creation. But when Adam sinned, "this image and likeness of God was can-
celled and effaced," and he became a "complete stranger." He was stripped of
"all wisdom, righteousness, power, life, which — as has already been said —
could be held only in God. As a consequence, nothing was left to him except
ignorance, iniquity, impotence, death, and judgment."[7] It is only in relationship with God that humanity can share in God's life-giving qualities; sinners
cut off from God are left only with death-dealing qualities.

Christ put on human flesh, paid the debt to God's justice, and redeemed
humanity from God's judgment; Christ's work renews believers and leads
them into eternal life.[8] Indeed it is in Christ that the image of God can be

seen most clearly. Even before the incarnation ". . . holy men knew God only by beholding him in his Son as in a mirror . . . God has never manifested himself to humanity in any other way than through the Son, that is, his sole wisdom, light, and truth. . . . When it was at length revealed in the flesh, it declared loudly and clearly to us whatsoever can be comprehended and ought to be pondered concerning God by the human mind."[9]

This sketch of Calvin's 1536 discussion of the image of God leaves us wondering what happened to Eve; only Adam as human "parent," certainly understood as corporate humanity, takes part in the drama. On the one hand this use of the male as representative of humanity is typical of the patriarchal tradition, making women invisible. On the other hand, Eve's absence represents a new silence in place of the traditional focus of popular religion on Eve's culpability for the human fall into sin; here the point is simply that all humanity sinned. There is also new silence on any differences between men and women with regard to the image of God. Throughout this edition of the *Institutes* Calvin seems uninterested in the differences between men and women; again and again he stresses the corporateness of humanity, the relationship of all human beings to one another. There is a strong implicit suggestion that the image of God has weighty ethical implications, requiring human justice and mercy.[10] This implicit point will become very explicit in later revision.[11]

Only once in this work is there mention of women's subordination. In a discussion of the difficulty of seeing the image of God in wicked rulers, Calvin makes clear that rulers are accountable to God; nonetheless he urges the duty of obedience to all in authority, even if they do not perform their offices uprightly as God intends. Among his examples is an admonition to wives to be obedient to their husbands, even if the husbands are "wicked and undutiful."[12] One suspects that there is implicit behind this discussion the view of Chrysostom and others that dominion or ruling as God's vice-regent in governing the world is part of the image of God.[13] And here dominion seems to be a male property.

Calvin continued to revise his *Institutes* over the years. We should look now at the final edition of 1559 to see how the discussion of the image of God has changed. Because the section dealing with the knowledge of God has been expanded considerably, the concise and neatly parallel structure of what we need to know about God and about ourselves from 1536 has disappeared, and with it the very explicit description of humanity's reflection of God's nature. Now Calvin takes up many of the more traditional points associated with the image of God.

Calvin is clear that the image of God is spiritual, and the "proper seat of

God's image is in the soul."[14] Yet he does not object to saying that the image "glows" in outward marks like the human face uplifted to the stars, a mark of human superiority to other creatures. In fact, ". . . the likeness of God extends to the whole excellence by which human nature towers over all the kinds of living creatures."[15] The image of God is the perfection of humanity which could be seen in Adam before the fall.[16] The two faculties of the human soul are understanding and will; humanity before the fall was so magnificently endowed and possessed such integrity that these faculties not only were sufficient for proper earthly life but even for attaining eternal life.[17]

Though the discussion of the faculties of the soul sounds much more scholastic than Calvin's view of the image of God in 1536, Calvin constantly distances himself from particular traditional views. For example, he regards the subtle discussions over the difference between "image" and "likeness" of God as ridiculous, since the two terms simply represent Hebrew parallelism.[18] He rejects Augustine's vision of the soul as the reflection of the Trinity as "by no means sound"; and he regards as improbable the view that the image of God consists in dominion given to humanity over the world, since the image is to be found within the soul, not outside the person.[19] The last point suggests that Calvin may have changed his mind since 1536 on the relation of the image of God to rulers.

More sharply and explicitly than in 1536 Calvin explains that since the fall it is very difficult to see the image of God in corrupted human nature. Therefore we must see it in Christ, the Second Adam, who restores the integrity of humanity and renews the image of God. Insofar as humanity is conformed to Christ's image, the most perfect image of God, it bears again God's image "with true piety, righteousness, purity, and intelligence."[20]

At this point for the first time in the whole discussion Calvin alludes to the image of God with relation to women. He has been arguing with Osiander about the relation of the image to soul and body, finding Osiander's view too bodily, and he suggests that he has disposed of the erroneous view. But then there follows a puzzling, abrupt insertion, new in 1559: "But the statement in which man alone is called by Paul 'the image and glory of God' and woman excluded from this place of honor is clearly to be restricted, as the context shows, to the political order."[21] The reference is surely to I Cor. 11:7: "For a man ought not to cover his head, since he is the image and glory of God; but woman is the glory of man." Calvin's basic point seems clearly to be that women's different bodies do not exclude them from bearing the image of God, which is spiritual.

Still there are three aspects of this insert worth noting: 1) Calvin shows by his paraphrase of the biblical text that he understands the obvious sense or perhaps the traditional reading to be that women are excluded from the image of God, borne only by men; 2) he is uncomfortable with that reading of the text and eager to reinterpret it; 3) having been trained to search for the proper historical context in which to interpret a biblical text, he believes that context restricts the force of Paul's words to the "political order," the realm of human governance, the realm of human law rather than divine law.[22] Calvin understands the context of I Cor. 11 to be Paul's views about liturgical order; Paul is handing down traditions which concern order and polity rather than salvation. He offers apostolic advice for the ordering of worship in matters where Christ has given no definitive law. "We know that each church is free to set the form of polity that suits its circumstances, and is to its advantage, since the Lord has not given any specific directions about this."[23]

Though this view of the context of I Cor. 11 is certainly not traditional, Calvin himself is quite consistent in his treatment of the issues involved. From the first edition of the *Institutes* till the last, Calvin argues that women's silence in church, along with the covering of their heads, matters addressed by Paul in the context of worship, are matters of decorum and order to be decided by human law, along with such things as burial customs, kneeling in worship, days and hours and structures for worship, and the psalms to be sung on a particular day. "Is religion located in a woman's shawl, so that it is sinful for her to go out with a bare head? Is that decree of Paul's concerning silence so holy that it cannot be violated without the greatest offense? . . . Not at all . . . let the established custom of the region, finally, humanity itself and the rule of modesty, dictate what is to be done or avoided in these matters."[24] It is not uncommon in the Reformation to find women's headcovering treated as an "indifferent" matter, a matter of human judgment,[25] but Calvin seems to stand alone in treating Paul's advice for women to be silent in church in precisely the same category.

Calvin explicitly asks whether there is a contradiction between Paul's argument in I Cor. 11:7 and Gal. 3:28. He decides that the difference is the context. The Galatians text with its insistence that there is no male nor female has to do with the spiritual kingdom of God. There no differences of class or sex or nationality will exist.[26] But he says about I Cor. 11:7 ". . . both sexes were created according to the image of God, and Paul urges women, as much as men, to be re-formed according to that image. But when he [Paul] is speaking about image here, he is referring to the conjugal order. Accordingly it has to do with this present life, and on the other hand, has nothing to do with conscience."[27] The issue is not of sanctity or innocence, affecting both sexes.

But rather Paul is talking of a certain superior degree of dignity given to the man, relating to his preeminence or dominion.[28] Like Luther, Calvin sees no immediate social relevance in Gal. 3:28. He probably fears social revolution as much as Luther. Though he rarely alludes to women's subordination in the *Institutes* and certainly does not make any point of teaching about it there, those allusions remind us that he presupposes a social order in which men rule over women. In the biblical commentaries where the text requires it, he strenuously upholds male dominance as the social order of the day. Where the text requires it, he can even claim that God has ordained women's subordination to men forever.[29] But clearly Calvin's method of interpreting those texts is far more complex than Luther's simple assumption that God punished women with submission to men as the penalty for original sin and ordains their submission till the end of time.[30]

One other relevant point from the 1559 *Institutes* should be mentioned. Calvin sides with the Renaissance physicians in rejecting Aristotle's view of female physiology. Unlike Luther, Calvin accepts the position that women, too, have "seed" which they contribute to their offspring. He scoffs at bad theologians who use bad biology to bolster their case that Christ took his body out of nothing since women have no "seed."[31]

Ephesians 4:13, with its now famous and troublesome phrase, "the perfect male" as the goal of Christian life,[32] is not interpreted by Calvin as though it posed any problems for women. Calvin understands this text christologically. He suggests in the commentary that the verse can be read as: "What is the ultimate perfection of Christians?" It is the fulness of life in Christ. The perfect male is Christ himself.[33] In the sermon on the same text, the message is one of continual growth in Christian faith throughout life. Jesus Christ is the goal or the target towards which Christians direct themselves.[34]

Calvin's comments on I Tim. 2:11-15[35] reveal some contrasts with Luther's approach to that text. The basic teaching Calvin derives from the text, that women, who have the right to speak and to instruct the family at home, do not have the authority to hold teaching office in the public realm of the church assembly, is in agreement with Luther. But Calvin at the outset refers the reader to his explanation of this matter in his commentary on I Cor.[36] As we have pointed out above, Calvin understands the I Cor. discussion of women's silence in church to fall in the category of decorum and order, subject to change as culture and circumstances require. Therefore the systematic context of Calvin's discussion of I Tim. 2 is different from that of Luther.

Calvin then briefly refers to the objection that could be made that Deborah and other women are said by Scripture to have been placed in authority to rule over the people "by the command of God." His response is "easy": "the common polity [governance] to which God wishes us to be bound is not to be overturned by the extraordinary acts of God."[37] Calvin admits that women have held offices of prophesying and teaching, and that they were called to them by the Spirit of God who is "free from all law. But because this action is extraordinary, it is not in opposition to continuing and customary polity [governance]."[38] Calvin also considers the fact that subjection does not necessarily preclude authority to teach, since prophets and teachers are subject to kings and other magistrates. But he thinks woman's situation is different because "by nature (that is, by the ordinary law of God) she is born to obey. For all prudent people always have repudiated women's ruling as monstrous."[39] Therefore it would be like a mixing of heaven and earth if women were to seize for themselves the right to teach. Paul commands them to be silent, to confine themselves to their own rank.[40] We notice here the strong emphasis on what is customary and accepted in society, appropriate to his view of the context of the apostolic advice given, and the objection to women "seizing for themselves" a right to teach if neither God nor society has conferred it upon them. There is also a notable emphasis on the freedom of God and the relation between the customary and the extraordinary order of God's ruling which is important to Calvin's broader theology.[41]

Paul's two arguments for women's subjection: that unlike Eve, Adam was created first and was not deceived, were easily accepted by Luther but seem to Calvin to require discussion. The argument that woman was second in the order of creation, Calvin says, is admittedly not strong enough [*parum valida*], since John the Baptist precedes Christ but is inferior in dignity.[42] One suspects that Calvin remembers the defenders of women in the *querelle des femmes*, sometimes satirical, who ridiculed Paul's argument, describing Eve rather as the culmination of creation, the most perfect of the creatures.[43] The argument that Adam was not deceived also causes Calvin some difficulty. He admits that even Adam was caught in the diabolical deception, but explains Paul by saying that Eve was the cause or source of the transgression in giving fatal advice to Adam. But he thinks Paul's view is not based simply on the cause of the transgression but also on God's judgment and the order of creation itself. This leads him to argue that Eve must have been subject to Adam in some sense even before the fall. To deal with the possible contradictions involved, he thinks Eve could have been given a natural condition of obedience which was made less befitting of a free person [*liberalis*] after the fall.[44]

The Genesis commentary was written after Calvin had commented on the epistles. On Gen. 1:26 Calvin goes over many of the points we have made from the *Institutes:* he rejects a distinction between likeness and image, Augustine's "trinity" in the soul, the image of God in the body, and Chrysostom's dominion. He does admit, however, that dominion is "some portion, though very small, of the image of God."[45] He repeats that we must know the image from its restoration in Christ, and that it has to do with the perfection of our whole nature, as it was seen in Adam in Paradise.[46]

Calvin raises the "difficulty . . . why Paul should deny the woman to be the image of God, when Moses honors both, indiscriminately, with this title. Again he has a "brief" solution: Paul is speaking there only about the "domestic relation (*oeconomicum statum*). He therefore restricts the image of God to dominion or ruling (*principatum*), in which the man has superiority over the wife, and certainly he means nothing more than that man is superior in the degree of honor."[47] In the Genesis text the point is different, Calvin thinks, dealing with the glory of God shining forth in human nature.[48] One can see here that Calvin has worked so long with Paul that he is now self-consciously reading Genesis through the eyes of Paul, and he is somewhat critical of the traditional way of doing so. He feels the tension between the Paul of Galatians 3:28 and the Paul of I Cor. 11:7 or of I Tim. 2:16 (which he believes to be Pauline). Calvin's own sense of the Genesis text is that no distinction is made between male and female concerning the image of God. But he feels obliged to reconcile this text with Paul. Calvin may be arguing that Chrysostom's view of dominion as the image of God is applicable only in the realm of human governing, and that Paul refers to this in I Cor. 11. But Calvin wishes to emphasize that this is a very small part of the image of God. Dominion is given to humankind [*homo*] in Gen. 1:26 with no comment from Calvin about gender distinction.[49] God's creation of male and female is said by Calvin to be a commendation of marriage; the man alone is understood to be less than a whole human being, so the woman is added as a companion in order that they might both be one.[50]

The second creation story in Gen. 2:18 describes God's intention to make Adam a "helper." Calvin rejects an interpretation that God's speaking in the first person singular here rather than in the plural as before is an indication of lower rank for woman than man. Rather he prefers a not entirely contrary view that the whole human race had previously been honored in the creation of Adam by the plural speaking of God, and the woman was nothing else but an accession to the man. "Certainly it cannot be denied, that the woman also, though in the second degree [*secundo gradu*], was created in the image of God; whence it follows that what was said in the creation of the man belongs to the female sex."[51] The woman is a helper, but of a companionable sort, not a "necessary evil." Man, her head and leader, has responsibility to the woman; their obligations are mutual.[52] In this context the woman is clearly derivative of the man and subordinate, and in this sense created secondarily in the image of God.[53] Calvin echoes here the view he had suggested on I Tim. 2 that Eve must have been already subject to Adam before the fall by her very nature as one who obeys, though her obedience before the fall was more befitting a free person than the servitude which became her lot after the fall. This point is made more clearly on Gen. 3:16.[54]

Strangely enough, the very next section has a quite different tone. Commenting on the phrase, "fit for him," Calvin explains that the phrase connotes some equality; the woman is a counterpart, opposite to or over against the man. This for Calvin is an indication that those who claim she was made only for propagation are wrong; she is to be a companion in all of life. He rejects another explanation, "Let her be ready to obedience," as "cold; for Moses intended to express more. . . ."[55] As in the previous story Calvin stresses that in the creation of the couple God wishes human nature to have a common origin; but here it is the origin in one person rather than two sexes, an even more intimate unity. Adam is "to recognize himself in his wife, as in a mirror; and Eve, in her turn, to submit herself willingly to her husband, as being taken out of him.[56] Here again is subordination from the moment of creation despite Calvin's linguistic sense that something more like equality is intended by some of the language of God.

A comparison with Luther's interpretations of the Hebrew may be useful. On Gen. 2:21 Calvin is also interested in the use of the term "to build" in relation to the creation of woman. He mentions the view of others that relate this term to "the domestic economy," suggesting that a legitimate family order has been instituted. He does not object to this view, which is closely related to Luther's. But he prefers the interpretation that Moses used the term to teach that with the creation of woman the human race was brought to completion.[57] Less emphasis is here placed on Eve's domestic role.

One has the impression that Calvin in the Genesis commentary is caught between his knowledge of a tradition which read the Old Testament through Paul's eyes and his growing awareness of different voices in the Hebrew text itself. Here he insists that woman is made in the image of God, but he accepts traditional qualifications, that she is derived from the man and possesses the image in this derivative sense.

Therefore it is interesting that when Calvin prepared his final edition of the *Institutes* near the end of his life, summarizing what it is important to know about biblical theology, there is no teaching of woman's possession of the image of God in a secondary degree, no teaching of women's inherently sub-ordinate nature. The qualifications he accepts in relation to a particular bibli-cal text are not carried over into his systematic theology. Rather the insertion interpreting I Cor. 11:7 which he makes into the last edition of the *Institutes* (as well as other writings) seems to function to allow him to reject qualifica-tions of the image of God based on gender while remaining faithful, he believes, to Pauline theology, distinguishing different senses of the image of God. Such an interpretation also has the function, however, of protecting his belief that women's subordination in the society of his own day was not only customary and proper but also biblically sanctioned. Insofar as he under-stands the custom of his day to require women's subordination to men in church and society, his theology provides no liberation for women from that inferior position. His insistence that polity must be changed as culture and circumstances change, for the edification of the church, does, however, leave the door open to change, though he may not have foreseen how wide the door eventually would swing. In the name of Christian freedom he argues against oppression in matters of order and decorum: ". . . establishing here no perpetual law for ourselves, we should refer the entire use and purpose of observances to the upbuilding of the church. If the church requires it, we may not only without any offense allow something to be changed but permit any observances previously in use among us to be abandoned."[58]

To the degree that Calvin struggles with the question of women's equality in the image of God more self-consciously than Luther, he is probably indebted to the French Renaissance culture where the *querelle des femmes* was a significant issue and where women rulers – in several cases sympa-thetic to the calvinistic Reformation – were a fact of life. Calvin does concede, without enthusiasm but much more readily than Luther, the legitimacy of women succeeding to the throne where the culture accepts that possibility. This seems to suggest that his discussions placing subordination in the con-text of polity, of human governance and changing customs, are to be taken seriously.[59] Calvin's indebtedness to the Renaissance preoccupation with women's questions can perhaps be seen also in the sorts of questions he poses when he deals with classic texts teaching women's subordination, even when his final practical advice is not much different from Luther's.

Like Luther, Calvin remains deeply influenced by a tradition which sees men as more fully made in the image of God than women, partly because of biblical assumptions that ruling is a male prerogative. But his exegetical and systematic struggles to deal with the tension he recognizes between I Cor. 11:7 and Gen. 1:26-7 represent a new step in critical exegesis of the Scriptures and continued progress towards a teaching of the full equality of men and women in the image of God from the time of their creation.

(*1989*)

Notes

I. Luther

1. Early versions of this discussion were included in broader presentations given in 1989 as the Scott Lecturer at Brite Divinity School of Texas Christian University and the Schaff Lecturer at Pittsburgh Theological Seminary. Those opportunities for engagement with these issues are most appreciated.
2. See Ian Maclean, *The Renaissance Notion of Woman: A Study in the Fortunes of Scholasticism and Medical Science in European Intellectual Life* (Cambridge: Cambridge University Press, 1980), pp. 28-46.
3. Maclean, pp. 35-37.
4. Christine de Pizan, *The Book of the City of Ladies*, transl. Earl Jeffrey Richards (New York: Persea Books, 1982), pp. 3-5.
5. de Pizan, p. 23.
6. See Joan Kelly, "Early Feminist Theory and the *Querelle des Femmes*, 1400-1789," *Signs* 8 (1982), pp. 4-28. Cf. Jane Dempsey Douglass, *Women, Freedom, and Calvin* (Philadelphia, PA: Westminster Press, 1985), pp. 66-73.
7. For examples from Marguerite of Navarre, Henricus Cornelius Agrippa of Nettesheim, and Marie Dentière in Geneva, see Douglass, pp. 68-71, 103-4.
8. See Douglass, p. 68.
9. Maclean, pp. 12-13; Manfred P. Fleisher, "'Are Women Human?' – The Debate of 1595 Between Valens Acidalius and Simon Gediccus," *Sixteenth Century Journal* 12 (1981), pp. 107-120.
10. See for example, Kari Elisabeth Børresen, *Subordination and Equivalence: The Nature and Role of Woman in Augustine and Thomas Aquinas*, transl. Charles H. Talbot (Washington, D.C.: University Press of America, 1981), pp. 26-29.
11. Heiko A. Oberman, *The Harvest of Medieval Theology: Gabriel Biel and Late Medieval Nominalism* (Cambridge, MA: Harvard University Press, 1963), pp. 50-55. Gerhard Ebeling, *Luther: An Introduction to His Thought* (Philadelphia, PA: Fortress Press, 1964, chaps. 5,14. William J. Bouwsma, *John Calvin: A Sixteenth Century Portrait* (New York: Oxford University Press, 1988), pp. 106-127, 157.
12. "Vorlesungen über 1. Mose von 1535-45," ed. G. Koffmane and D. Reichert, *D. Martin Luthers Werke; Kritische Gesamtausgabe* (Weimar, 1911), vol. 42. Hereafter cited as WA 42. Though there has undoubtedly been more extensive editing of this Luther text than in the case of some other writings of Luther, it should serve our purpose adequately. For a discussion by Jaroslav Pelikan of the questions of authenticity raised by Peter Meinhold, see Pelikan, "Introduction to Vol-

ume 1," *Luther's Works 1: Lectures on Genesis Chapters 1-5* (St. Louis, MO: Concordia Publishing House, 1958) pp. ix-xii.

13. Gen. 2:3, WA 42, 61-2; cf. Gen. 2:16-17, WA 42, 80 where God's sermon is on the sixth day, before Eve's creation.
14. Gen. 1, preface, WA 42,4.
15. Gen. 1, preface WA 42,5; cf. Gen. 1:6, WA 42,20 and 22.
16. Gen. 1, preface, WA 42,5.
17. Gen. 1:26, WA 42,45. Cf. Augustine, *De Trinitate* IX-XI.
18. Gen. 1:26, WA 42,45.
19. Gen. 1:26, WA 42,45.
20. See for example Paul Althaus, *The Theology of Martin Luther* (Philadelphia, PA: Fortress Press, 1966), chaps. 2, 3, 8.
21. Gen. 1:26, WA 42,42.
22. Gen. 1:26, WA 42,41-2.
23. Gen. 1:26, WA 42,46.
24. Gen. 1:26, WA 42,47.
25. Gen. 1:26, WA 42,47.
26. Gen. 1:26, WA 42,46-7.
27. Gen. 1:26, WA 42,48-9.
28. Gen. 1:27, WA 42,51.
29. Gen. 1:26, WA 42,49-51.
30. Gen. 1:28, WA 42,54.
31. Gen. 1:26, WA 42,50.
32. Gen. 1:27, WA 42,51-52.
33. Gen. 1:27, WA 42,53.
34. Gen. 1:27, WA 42,51-2. See parallel WA 42,52 l. 18-21.
35. Gen. 1:27, WA 42,52.
36. Gen. 2:18, WA 42,87.
37. Gen. 3:16, WA 42,151.
38. Gen. 2:23, WA 42,103.
39. Gen. 2:23, WA 42,103.
40. For discussion of the traditional theme of woman as *vir* (a male person) rather than *homo* (a human being), see chapter 6 of this volume by Kari Vogt. Despite Luther's protestations about women's likeness to men, his use of the term *vir* suggests that at least to some degree he assumes the woman's humanity to be secondary to that of men.
41. Gen. 2:23, WA 42,103.
42. Gen. 3:1, WA 42,113.
43. Gen. 3:3-6, WA 42,116-22.
44. Gen. 3:6, WA 42,121.
45. Gen. 3:1, WA 42,114.
46. Gen. 3:1, WA 42,114.
47. Gen. 3:1, WA 42,113.

48. Compare for example Luther's sermons on Genesis from 1519-21: WA 9,332-334.
49. Gen. 3:14, WA 42,138.
50. Gen. 3:9, WA 42,129.
51. Gen. 2:16-17, WA 42,79.
52. Gen. 2:16-17, WA 42,80.
53. Gen. 3:1, WA 42,108.
54. Gen. 3:13, WA 42,135.
55. Gen. 3:1, WA 42,109.
56. Gen. 3:13, WA 42,136.
57. See Børresen, pp. 53-56.
58. Børresen, pp. 54-55.
59. Børresen, p. 53.
60. Gen. 2:23, WA 42,103; Gen. 3:13, WA 42,136.
61. I Tim. 2:14, WA 26,47.
62. I Tim. 2:13-15, WA 26,47-8.
63. Gen. 2:22, WA 42,98-9.
64. Gen. 2:18, WA 42,87-90; Gen. 2:22-3, WA 42,98-103.
65. Gen. 3:16, WA 42,151.
66. Gen. 2:7, WA 42,64; Gen. 2:21, WA 42,94-8; Gen. 3:15, WA 42,145.
67. Gen. 3:16, WA 42,150.
68. Gen. 3:16, WA 42,149-50.
69. Gen. 3:16, WA 42,151; cf. on Eccl. 7:28, WA 20,148-9.
70. Gen. 3:17-19, WA 42,152-63.
71. Gen. 3:16, WA 42,150.
72. Gen. 3:1, WA 42,106; Gen. 3:14, WA 42,139-40.
73. Gen. 3:16, WA 42,151.
74. Gen. 4:1, WA 42,177.
75. Gen. 3:16, WA 42,150.
76. Gen. 2:18, WA 42,89.
77. Gen. 2:18, WA 42,89.
78. Gen. 2:18, WA 42,89.
79. Gen. 2:18, WA 42,88.
80. Gen. 1:28, WA 42,54.
81. Gen. 3:16, WA 42,150-1.
82. Gen. 3:16, WA 42,148.
83. Gen. 3:16, WA 42,148.
84. Gen. 3:20, WA 42,163-4.
85. Gen. 3:20, WA 42,164-5.
86. I Tim. 2:11-12, WA 26,46-7.
87. I Tim. 2:14-15, WA 26,48-9.
88. Gal. 3:28, WA 40,1,542.
89. Gal. 3 :28, WA 40,1,544-45.
90. Børresen, pp. 26-30.

91. Børresen, pp. 16-21, 153-63. See also her chapters 7 and 8 in this volume.
92. See chapter 2 of this volume by Phyllis Bird.
93. See in Luther's sermons on Genesis from 1519-21 the *catena* of New Testament passages, including those mentioned here, which he adduces to explain Gen. 3:16. WA 9,336, cf. 333.
94. In Luther's sermons on Genesis from 1519-21, he seems to suggest that whereas Adam's punishment is remedial, Eve's is merely punitive. WA 9,334.

II. Calvin

1. "John Calvin to the Reader," Preface to the *Institutes of the Christian Religion, Johannis Calvini Opera selecta*, ed. P. Barth and G. Niesel (München, 1967), III,6. This edition is hereafter cited as O.S.
2. For an overview of the scholarly discussion of Calvin's view of the image of God, see Mary Potter Engel, *John Calvin's Perspectival Anthropology* (Atlanta, GA: Scholars Press, 1988), chapter 2. Gender is not considered in this chapter.
3. O.S. I,37.
4. O.S. I,37.
5. O.S. I,37.
6. O.S. I,38.
7. O.S. I,38.
8. O.S. 40-41.
9. O.S. I, 236.
10. For a fuller discussion and further documentation, see my article, "The Image of God in Humanity: A Comparison of Calvin's Teaching in 1536 and 1559," *In Honor of John Calvin, 1509-64: Papers from the 1886 International Calvin Symposium, McGill University*, ed. E. J. Furcha (Montreal: McGill University, 1987), pp. 175-203.
11. Inst. III, vi, 6.
12. O.S. I, 277-8. This example is an addition to my list of the very rare references to women's subordination in the *Institutes*. See Douglass, *Women, Freedom, and Calvin*, pp. 46, 62.
13. See chapter 7 in this volume by Kari Elisabeth Børresen.
14. Inst. I, xv, 3.
15. Inst. I, xv, 3.
16. Inst. I, xv, 4.
17. Inst. I, xv, 7-8.
18. Inst. I, xv, 3.
19. Inst. I, xv, 4.
20. Inst. I, xv, 4.
21. Inst. I, xv, 4. "Quod autem vir solus imago et gloria Dei vocatur apud Paulum, et mulier excluditur ab hoc honoris gradu ad ordinem politicum restringi ex contextu patet."

22. For discussion of the meaning of the "political order," see *Women, Freedom, and Calvin*, chapter 2.

23. Com. I Cor., *Calvini opera quae supersunt omnia*, ed. G. Baum, E. Cunitz, E. Reuss, in *Corpus reformatorum*, 49,473. This edition hereafter will be cited as C.O.

24. "Prioris generis exempla sunt apud Paulum, ne mulieres in ecclesia doceant, ut velatae procedant (I Cor. 11 et 14), et in perpetuo vitae usu spectari possunt: ut flexis genibus, nudoque capite publice oremus, ne nuda hominum cadavera in foveam proiiciantur, ne Domini sacramenta profane et sordide administrentur, et quae alia eodem pertinent. Quid, an in mulieris carbaso sita religio est, ut nudo capite egredi sit nefas, an sanctum de eius silentio decretum, quod violari sine summo scelere non possit, an aliquod in genuflexione aut tegendo cadavere mysterium, quod praeteriri sine piaculo non possit? Minime. . . . et est ubi loqui non minus opportunum illi sit, quam alibi tacere. . . . Sed est nihilominus in istis rebus, quod agendum aut cavendum mos regionis, instituta, ipsa denique humanitas et modestiae regula dictet." 1536 Inst. 6,33, O.S. I, 256-7; 1559 Inst. IV, x, 29,31. See *Women, Freedom, and Calvin*, pp. 29-34.

25. For example, Augsburg Confession II, vii (art. xxviii); see *Women, Freedom, and Calvin*, pp. 105-6 for other examples.

26. Com. I Cor., C.O. 49,474. Cf. Serm. Gal., C.O. 50,567-8.

27. "Creatus enim est uterque sexus ad imaginem Dei: neque minus feminas quam masculos ad illam imaginem reformari iubet Paulus. Sed imago, de qua nunc loquitur, ad ordinem coniugalem refertur; ideoque pertinet ad praesentem vitam, non autem in conscientia sita est. Haec est simplex solutio . . ." Com. I Cor., C.O. 49,476.

28. "In hoc superiore dignitatis gradu conspicitur Dei gloria, sicuti relucet in omni principatu." Com. I Cor., C.O. 49,476.

29. Serm. I Cor., C.O. 49,727-9; Com. I Pet., C.O. 55,247-8; Com. I Cor., C.O. 49,546-7.

30. The complexity of Calvin's view of women is clearly seen by Mary Potter in "Gender Equality and Gender Hierarchy in Calvin's Theology," *Signs* 11 (1986), 725-39. She documents vigorously both Calvin's concern for equality of men and women and also his teaching of women's subordination to men. Her solution, that Calvin looks at women from two perspectives: the *cognitio dei* and the *cognitio hominis*, corresponds generally with what Calvin describes as the equality of men and women in the spiritual kingdom of God and in the possession of the spiritual image of God over against the gender hierarchy of the realm of human governance in this world. It is not clear, however, what additional help is given by use of her terms rather than Calvin's own interpretative categories.

31. Inst. II, xiii, 3. See Ian Maclean, *The Renaissance Notion of Woman*, pp. 28-46; for the debate within Protestantism, see Joyce Irwin, *Womanhood in Radical Protestantism: 1525-1675* (New York: Edwin Mellen Press, 1979), pp. 12-20.

32. See in this volume chapter 6 by Kari Vogt and chapter 7 by Kari Elisabeth Børresen.
33. Com. Eph. 4:13, C.O. 51, 200.
34. Serm. Eph. 4:13, C.O. 51, 570-4.
35. For further discussion of the commentary and also the sermons on this text, see *Women, Freedom, and Calvin*, pp. 55-8.
36. Com. I Tim. 2:11, C.O. 52,276.
37. Com. I Tim. 2:11, C.O. 52,276.
38. "Ergo si aliquando prophetandi et docendi locum tenuerunt mulieres, idque Dei spiritu excitatae: potuit hoc qui ab omni lege immunis est. Sed quia hoc singulare est, non pugnat cum perpetua et usitata politia." Com. I Tim. 2:11, C.O. 52,276.
39. Com. I Tim. 2:11, C.O. 52,276.
40. Com. I Tim. 2:11, C.O. 52,276.
41. *Women, Freedom, and Calvin*, chapter 2.
42. Com. I Tim. 2:13, C.O. 52,276-7.
43. *Women, Freedom, and Calvin*, pp. 68ff.
44. Com. I Tim. 2:14, C.O. 52,277.
45. Com. Gen. 1:26, C.O. 23,26.
46. Com. Gen. 1:26, C.O. 23,26-7.
47. Com. Gen. 1:26, C.O. 23,27.
48. Com. Gen. 1:26, C.O. 23,27.
49. Com. Gen. 1:26, C.O. 23,27.
50. Com. Gen. 1:27, C.O. 23,27-8.
51. Com. Gen. 2:18, C.O. 23,46.
52. Com. Gen. 2:18, C.O. 23,47.
53. The article by John L. Thompson, "Creata ad imaginem dei, licet secundo gradu: Woman as the Image of God according to John Calvin," *Harvard Theological Review* 81:2 (1988), 125-43, has many useful insights concerning the sense in which the image of God for Calvin continues to carry with it authority and dominion and therefore excludes women, despite Calvin's claim that dominion is not part of or at least not a very large part of the image of God. Though heavily dependent on *Women, Freedom, and Calvin*, he apparently disagrees with the weight given there to Calvin's systematic formulations in the *Institutes* as a context in which to read the commentaries.
54. Com. Gen. 3:16, C.O. 23,72.
55. Com. Gen. 2:18, C.O. 23,47-8.
56. Com. Gen. 2:21, C.O. 23,48-9.
57. Com. Gen. 2:21, C.O. 23,49.
58. Inst. IV, x, 32.
59. For further discussion of the issue of women rulers, see *Women, Freedom, and Calvin*, pp. 94-8.

10

IMAGO DEI, CHRISTIAN TRADITION AND FEMINIST HERMENEUTICS

∞ Rosemary Radford Ruether

The Genesis 1:27 text that describes God as creating Adam in the "image of God," "male and female he created them," continues today to be a key reference point for Christian theological discussion of anthropology and gender. Contrary to classical Christian tradition, as that development has been described in the essays in this volume, contemporary Christian theologians generally take this text to be an egalitarian one. Women are assumed to be equally included in the divine image. It is assumed that this is the original and "true" meaning of this text.

1. The *Imago* in Contemporary Catholic Documents

Most contemporary theologians are unaware of the history of asymmetrical reading of the text. They assume that women have 'always' been included in the image of God in Christian theological tradition. Yet, despite the egalitarian reading of the text, ecclesiastical authorities still find theological bases for assigning different and unequal roles to women, in the church and in society. This is particularly true of recent statements released by the Roman Catholic Magisterium, such as the American Catholic bishops' pastoral letter on women,[1] and the statement of Pope John Paul II on "The Dignity and Vocation of Women."[2]

The American bishops, in their pastoral letter, take as their theological starting point the Genesis 1:27 text. They take for granted that this text means, and has always meant, the full equality of women and men in the image of God. They see this text as establishing both an equal relation with God and also a relationship of egalitarian mutuality or partnership between

267

men and women. They organize their letter around this theme of partnership, seeking to reflect upon and promote this partnership relationship between men and women in the three spheres of home, paid work and the church.

Despite this bold beginning, the bishops are unable to carry through their partnership model in any of these three areas. Their presuppositions remain those of patriarchal clericalism. In speaking of the partnership of men and women as spouses and parents, the bishops are curtailed by their anti-contraceptive views. Their frequent affirmations of the value of motherhood are unmatched by any corresponding affirmation of fatherhood. Motherhood is described as women's essential 'vocation,' while fatherhood is not defined as a male vocation. What this means in practice is that parenting is not a partnership of men and women, but a female job with auxiliary help from fathers.

In the realm of paid work, the bishops accept women's right to work and also endorse their right to equal pay. They are concerned about issues such as impoverishment of female-headed households, and suggest that the church might help with day care. But they continue to refuse to support the Equal Rights Amendment. Most importantly, however, women are described as working only out of economic necessity, as primary or secondary breadwinners for their families. Women are never said to have a vocation to work in society.

A study of these sections of the document shows that the asymmetrical gender model of family and work remains basically unchanged in their thinking. Women's essential vocation lies in motherhood. Men's essential vocation lies outside the family in work. The commitment to partnership of men and women in the family and in society has not been accompanied by any genuine paradigm shift in social roles. But the bishops' failure to carry through their egalitarian partnership model becomes most obvious when one turns to the question of ministry in the church. Here all the bishops are able to offer is partnership of women with men in the ministry of the laity. The ordained priesthood remains an all-male preserve.

The bishops endorse the position of the 1976 Vatican Declaration against the ordination of women which said that women are ontologically incapable of being ordained because women cannot image Christ.[3] This claim brings their Christology into contradiction with their theological anthropology. What does it mean to say that women are images of God equally with men, but they cannot image Christ? This contradiction is based on an unexamined disjunction, found also in the 1976 Vatican Declaration, between anthropology and Christology, or between the natural, created order and the sacrament-priest-Christ relationship.

Contrary to traditional Catholic teaching, recent Catholicism of this type affirms women's equality with men on the level of nature and secular society. It also claims, quite unhistorically, that it has "always" taught this equality in society. But eucharistic and priestly matters are removed to a second, supernatural sphere unconnected with gender equality in creation. The ability to 'image Christ' is seen as reserved only for males, even though, in Scripture, Christ as 'image of God' is intended to parallel 'Adam' as 'image of God' which the bishops are reading as including women.[4] Although women are now said to 'image' God, they are still denied the capacity to 'image' Christ.

The same contradictions, although in even more convoluted form, are found in the September 30, 1988 Papal statement on the "Dignity and Vocation of Women." The Pope also begins by affirming the full equality of men and women in the image of God. Both sexes are said to possess rationality and to share dominion over the rest of creation. God's original intention for humanity is one of egalitarian mutuality between man and woman.

The Pope follows certain lines of modern theology[5] in seeing this partnership mirrored in the Trinity. He boldly claims that God also can be said to have both male and female qualities, and that the mutuality between men and women in the image of God mirrors the mutual love within the Persons of the trinitarian God. (Has one of the three Persons changed gender?) Human procreation is also said to reflect divine generativity in such a way that God can be said to be both father and mother.

Sin distorted this intended relationship of mutuality between the sexes and created a wrongful domination of men over women. But redemption in Christ is said to overcome this sinful domination of men over women and to restore women to full dignity. Christ in his ministry displayed full acceptance of women's humanity, contrary to his culture. Women are also said to have been included in the prophetic gifts poured out at Pentecost and in the general priesthood of the church by which the whole church expresses the redemptive ministry of loving service of people to one another.

The Pope's meditation on gender and theology is a confused mixture of egalitarian and complementarian models of relationship of men and women. He also is unable to sort out the difference between 'masculinity' and 'femininity' as symbols and real human men and women. The Pope seems to feel that the qualities of 'femininity' better express the redemptive mystery of Christ than 'masculinity'. 'Femininity' essentially means, for him, selfless self-giving. Christ is the ultimate exemplar of this self-giving, but women are said to be naturally better at it than men, and they need to teach men how to do it.[6]

One might conclude from this that it is women, rather than men, who are the 'natural' symbolic representatives of Christ. But when the Pope gets to the Last Supper, and Jesus' presumed establishment of the Eucharist and the priesthood at that meal, we are told that women were excluded by Christ's deliberate intention. This, the Pope opines, is because Christ represents the 'bridegroom' in relation to the church as bride. Since this relationship is presumed to be essentially one of masculinity over feminity, women cannot play the role of representing Christ in the eucharistic ministry. Only males can represent Christ as priest.[7]

Thus the Pope, too, ends up with a contradiction between anthropology and Christology. Women image God but cannot image Christ. The bridegroom-bride analogy for Christ and the church of Ephesians 5,32, incorrectly read as analogous to priest and laity,[8] might suggest that men cannot represent the laity. The Pope has no difficulty claiming, however, that men, especially celibates, are, symbolically, 'brides of Christ.' If men can be 'brides,' symbolically, why can't women be symbolic 'bridegrooms'?

The traditional answer to this is to assert that women's status of subjugation means that they can only represent the subjected, creaturely, and not the dominant, divine side of the relationship, while men can represent either side.[9] But the Pope has undercut this argument by reading both masculinity and femininity into God and rejecting domination as sinful. Thus his effort to use patriarchal, hierarchical symbolism to exclude women from priesthood hangs in the air, with all its traditional supports in anthropology and theology having been removed.

2. The *Imago:* Ancient Roots of an Analogy

The concept of the human as image of God or analogous to God is based on cosmological presuppositions about the relationship of divinity to visible reality. Christian theology, in the New Testament and subsequent tradition, is rooted in two different readings of cosmology, Hebraic (and ancient Near Eastern) and Greek. Although Genesis was the canonical Christian text for understanding the relationship of God, creation and humanity, Plato's *Timaeus* was often in the back of the minds of early Christian writers in interpreting Genesis. These disparate sources provided fundamentally different possibilities for reading the Genesis 1:27 text.

The priestly story of creation of Genesis 1 was itself shaped by partial appropriation and partial repudiation of the classical Babylonian story of creation, the *Enuma Elish*, which was solemnly recited yearly as part of the New

Year's Festival that assured the renewal and orderly functioning of the cosmos. In this story Marduk, the champion of the Gods and Goddesses of the divine assembly, defeats Tiamat, the leader of the powers of chaos that threaten the cosmic and human order. He slays her and then splits her body "like a shellfish into two parts, half of her he set up and ceiled it as sky."[10] In language that is echoed in the Genesis account, Marduk separates the waters above the firmament from the waters below and arranges the stars and planetary system.

Having completed the shaping of the cosmos, Marduk then turns to the creation of human beings. Marduk takes the blood of the slain consort of Tiamat, Kingu, and from it fashions humans. Humanity is charged with "service to the Gods that they might be at ease."[11] This statement reflects the basic analogy between Gods and humans in Sumero-Babylonian thought. Humans are to Gods as slaves to masters.[12] The Gods are like a ruling leisure class to a subjugated working class. Like the aristocracy, the Gods do not work. They are freed from labor by an inferior servant class.

In Babylonian myth there can be no question of exclusion of women as representatives of the divine, since the deities come in both male and female forms. Moreover the creation myth suggests an older, female primacy among the Gods that is being contested by a younger generation of Gods. These Gods also are both male and female, but a male warrior God is their champion. Patriarchal social patterns were in place in Babylonian society in this period,[13] so this lingering concept of earlier female primacy should be seen as reflecting an assumed primacy of the female in generativity; i.e. the mother as primary source of life for both males and females.

However, as women become subjugated in society, this earlier mythic concept of female ontological primacy will be gradually erased, to be finally replaced by the concept of a single male deity transcendent to generation. The *Enuma Elish* can be seen as an early transitional stage of this process of deposition of the female from the heavens. Hebrew thought represents the end process of this religious revolution against female primacy and, finally, against female presence at all in the heavens. Patriarchal social patterns have reshaped the images of divinity. Henceforth the female will appear as representative either of the creaturely in relation to transcendent male divinity, or, at most, as an immanent 'side' of God in relation to divine male transcendency.[14]

Hebrew thought continues the Near Eastern analogy of God to human as Lord to servant. But this analogy is transformed from a demeaned to a lordly role in Genesis 1. Adam is God's servant as a king is God's servant. But this relationship is understood, first of all, as representative of God's sovereign rule over creation. Most interpretations of Genesis 1:27 from contemporary scholars of Hebrew Scripture concur in the view that dominion over creation is the essential meaning of the term 'image' in this text.[15] Like the royal image that represents the absent king, Adam, as God's image, is the living representative of God, exercising God's rule over the world of plants and animals.

As Phyllis Bird has shown in her study of this text, gender relations are not addressed in relation to the image of God. The phrase 'male and female created he them' does not refer to the divine image, but rather to the bisexuality which humans share with animals, but not with God. The religious sociology of the author of the text almost surely meant that he took for granted that this sovereignty over creation was exercised by the male head of family. If Adam represented collective humanity, it was the male head of family who represented this corporate humanity in practice. The androcentric character of Hebrew religion is dramatically reaffirmed in Anders Hultgård's account of early Jewish religion. Here we learn that even female animals are excluded as sacrificial victims from the heart of the temple cult.

The text appears to us today to make male and female equal as images of God only because this patriarchal assumption is not spelled out. But to read it this way is to read into the text both egalitarian and also individualistic assumptions of modern democratic societies, foreign to the social context of the ancient author.

Plato's creation story, the *Timaeus,* starts with a different set of cosmological assumptions. Reality is not held together by a sovereign God and his creative will, but by a basic division of reality into opposed substances; eternal, invisible, intellectual Being and mutable, visible Becoming. What exists eternally is the invisible realm of Ideas. Over against it is mutable matter, composed of the four primal elements. The Creator or Artisan shaped the primal matter into a spherical cosmos by looking up to the realm of eternal Ideas as the archetypal pattern.[16]

The Artisan then mixed together the primal principles of unchangeability and changeability into an intermediate being. He fashioned this intermediate substance by mathematical proportions and infused it into the cosmic body as the world soul. In this way the cosmos became a living thing, a moving 'image of eternity.' The term 'image', for Plato, is a term drawn from art. It means picture or statue which imitates, but in an inferior medium, a higher reality, as a statue imitates in stone a living person. So the endless circular motion of the planetary spheres imitates, on an inferior level, eternal, unchanging being.

Human beings are created by first fashioning their souls out of the dregs of the world soul. This establishes a basic identity between human souls and the cosmic soul. Human souls are 'bits' of the same life-force that moves the cosmos. These souls are first placed in the stars, so they can contemplate the eternal world of Ideas. This preexistent state allows the souls to become imbued with knowledge of the eternal truths which is, for them, the source of blessed and immortal life. After this preexistent 'education,' the souls were sown in bodies made by the inferior planetary Gods, this being too lowly a task to be undertaken directly by the Artisan Himself.

For human beings, embodied life is an encasement in an alien, sensual and mortal type of existence that drags down and obscures the powers of the soul. A period of embodied life is thought of as a kind of trial or testing period. Those who are able to conquer and subdue the passions that arise from the sensual body will return after death to their "native star" and there enjoy a "blessed and congenial existence." But those who fail to attain this will be reincarnated in lower bodily forms, first that of a woman, and then that of brutes "who resemble the evil nature he had acquired"[17]

Plato's creation story reveals fundamentally different assumptions from that of the Hebrew Genesis. For Plato, embodied life is secondary and alien to the true life of humans as disembodied souls. This dualism of spirit and matter is not found in the Torah. For the ancient Hebrews the soul is the life breath of the body. Life does not exist apart from bodily form. Plato sees the soul as the essential life of man, the body as discardable. Moreover he identifies the lower principle of bodily life with lower forms of beings beneath the male ruling class: women and animals.

The soul is seen as sharing the same life principle of the cosmos, itself derivative in part from the eternal or divine substance of the Ideas. Later Greek philosophy will identify the eternal Ideas of Plato with the governing divine Mind of Aristotle's *Metaphysics,* and the cosmic *Logos* of Stoicism. So the life principle of the soul becomes more explicitly a sharing in the life principle of God.[18] The eternal and rational powers of the soul will continue to be seen as normatively represented by (ruling class) males. Female embodiment represents a fall of the soul under the control of the sensual principle of the body. This hierarchy of soul and body as analogous to male and female will shape the patristic reading of the Genesis 1:27 text.

3. The *Imago* and Gender in Christian Tradition

Christianity, from its beginning, included women equally with men in its rite of initiation of baptism. Women equally with men were redeemed. They too died to their sinful state of existence and rose with Christ as heirs of heaven. Moreover Christians took as axiomatic that in heaven there would be no marriage or giving in marriage. In the immortalized state of the risen body, death and hence procreation would no longer be necessary (Mark 12:25; Matt. 22:30; Luke 20:35).

Early Christians also lived in a state of imminent eschatological expectation. They assumed that the present form of this world was passing away, and the eschatological age was at hand. For some this suggested that the baptized could or should anticipate the heavenly state by renouncing marriage and procreation now. This raised the urgent question of how baptism transformed women's spiritual and social status in the church. Had male domination over women, which belonged to the married state, been overcome between the baptized? This question applied particularly to those Christians who anticipated the heavenly order by renouncing marriage. Did celibacy give women equal spiritual authority with men?

In sorting out the changed status of the baptized women, both in its ultimate eschatological reference point and its present anticipation in celibate women, early Christians drew on contemporary Jewish and Hellenistic interpretations of the creation myths of the two traditions, Genesis 1-2 and Plato's *Timaeus*. These two myths had already been combined in Hellenistic Judaism. In the early first century Philo had put the two stories together to describe a two-stage creation of 'man,' first a heavenly state of asexual spiritual life; and, secondly, an embodied state as a male androgyne. Female existence came about only through a fall from this androgynous state, and the separation of the lower female from the higher male part of the original Adam.

For Philo, gender hierarchy was fundamental both to divine-human relations and to the superiority of mind over body. Gender hierarchy was the basic model for all relations of dominion and subjugation. Thus the soul was 'masculine' in relation to the body, but was 'feminine' in relation to God.[19]

This Hellenistic Jewish mixture of Genesis 1-2 and the Timaeus allowed early Christians several ways of thinking about how woman's subjugated status as sexual, procreative wife might have been transformed by her baptized and anticipated eschatological status. The question of her changed eschatological status also raised questions about her protological status. Was her new humanity in Christ a restoration of her prelapsarian status?

The presupposition among all groups of Christians of this period was the subjugated status of the married woman. Woman in the present order of nature was under the domination of her husband. The male (head of household) was the image of God, for he was the one who exercised domination, both over his non-human property and over the other members of his household: his wife, children and slaves. Since male slaves and male children could be emancipated or grow up and become heads of households, it was only women who, 'by nature,' were seen as excluded from exercising domination and hence from the divine image.

However, in the light of the coming eschatological order, this married state was evaluated as a fallen state, or at least a temporal state, belonging to historical creation, but not to the heavenly order to come. This heavenly order, in turn, could be seen as restoring a pretemporal, prelapsarian state. What was the relation of gender to that pretemporal and prelapsarian state?

One option was to split an asexual soul from gendered bodies. The soul could be seen as existing in an original, asexual, disembodied state. Only with the Fall was the soul incarnated into either a male or a female body. The fall into the body brought death and hence the necessity of procreation. The image of God referred to the soul, not to the body. Souls were essentially equal as images of God. So, in their spiritual nature, women and men are equal. This spiritual equality has been restored in Christ, anticipating a future time when souls returned to their disembodied, prelapsarian state in the heavens.

However, this simple split between asexual, disembodied, original and future souls and gendered bodies in the fallen, incarnate state was complicated by two further ideas. Christians were committed to the Jewish concept of the resurrection of the body as the final eschatological state. Was gender retained for the resurrected body? Also the soul was seen as spiritually masculine in relation to the body. This further suggested that souls be normatively manifest in male bodies. The female body came about as a later degeneration.

Paul's letters represented the first partial effort to wrestle with these contradictions between woman's present status in temporal creation and her eschatological status 'in Christ.' As head of the eschatological humanity, Christ is seen as restoring 'man' to 'his' prelapsarian state. This was assumed to be a male androgynous state prior to sexual differentiation. In Christ the baptized are taken up into this male-identified non-sexual state. As Lone Fatum has shown in her very careful study of Pauline theological anthropology, women, seen as non-sexual persons, can be included in this presexual Christlikeness (Gal. 3:28). But, considered as woman in relation to men in social relations, women were not included in the image of God, but stood under male domination, as men, in turn, stood under the domination of Christ and Christ under the dominion of God (I Cor. 11:3).

Paul's writings left ambiguous and undecided whether the celibate woman was freed from male social domination here and now in the church and could exercise male authority. This was to be the source of a conflict in deutero-Pauline churches between those who insisted that marriage and patriarchal relations remained normative for Christian leadership now, and those who thought that Christians could anticipate the heavenly order by renouncing marriage here and now. Some who took the second view also thought that Christian virgins were freed from male domination and could exercise male authority as teachers and leaders. This conflict is reflected in the opposed deutero-Pauline writings of I Timothy and the *Acts of Paul and Thecla.*[20]

As Giulia Sfameni Gasparro and Kari Vogt have shown, in their essays in this volume, this conflict over the spiritual authority of celibate women continued to be intense in second and third century Christianity. Those committed to the superiority of the celibate over the married life tended to believe that the virginal woman had been freed from male domination at least in ecclesial roles of teaching and prophecy. In Christ she had become spiritually 'male' and could exercise male roles of leadership in the church.

Some Christians followed the tripartite concept of the self as divided into *sarx, psyche* and *pneuma*. The *psyche* was the intermediate, sensual part of the soul, and thus was analogous to the femaleness of the body in relation to the masculinity of the mind. Since both men and women were composed of all three components, masculinity and femininity became symbols for spiritual maturity versus degenerate sensuality. Men who catered to their lower selves were 'effeminate,' while women who crushed their sensual selves and rose to spiritual maturity became 'masculine.' Such celibate women were freed from subjugation and could exercise male spiritual authority.

The feminist question of patristic and early medieval Christianity was over the issue of the liberation and autonomy of the celibate woman. The continued subjugation of the married woman was never doubted. As Kari Elisabeth Børresen has shown, male church leaders attempted to resolve the question of how women's spiritual and social status were related by splitting women's spiritual inclusion in redemption in Christ from her social status, both in society and in the church. Spiritually, woman was included in an androcentric spiritual life, symbolized by the *imago*-Christ. But socially, both as married woman and as celibate woman, she remained under male authority in the created order of the family and in the church as a temporal society.

The married woman was under the authority of her husband. The celibate woman was freed from the authority of her husband, but continued to be under the authority of her bishop. Her spiritual status was higher than the married woman, but she too could not exercise public authority. Yet the subjugation of the celibate woman remained incomplete for most of the Middle Ages. Celibate women continued to think that redemption in Christ freed them from male domination in some respects. The struggle to silence and rule over the celibate woman was renewed in the counter-Reformation and continues on today in the conflict between the Vatican and women religious.[21]

Medieval mystics added further nuances to this transference of patriarchal relations of male over female to soul-body and divine-human hierarchies. The soul of the celibate spiritual woman could be seen as advancing to 'male' status, particularly as one who had subdued her own body. But the souls of all Christians, especially those dedicated to the spiritual life, were passive and receptive and hence 'feminine,' in the positive sense, in relation to Christ. In this sense, all Christian mystics were 'brides of Christ' in their relation to their bridegroom, Christ.

Since vulnerability, passivity and suffering were spiritually 'feminine' qualities, Christ also could be seen as symbolically 'feminine,' as the one who suffers for us. This lent itself to feminine imagery for Christ, both as human sufferer and also as second person of the Trinity. Since, officially, Christians were committed to the equality in being of the Persons of the Trinity, this introduction of feminine gender into God might raise questions about how relations between Persons in the Trinity related to maleness and femaleness.

If God is both father and mother, does this mean that both are on an equal plane? Or, could it be seen as reactivating a never quite overcome tendency in Christian trinitarian thought to set up a hierarchy of being between the Father-Godhead and the *Logos* and Spirit of God? In either case, however, female Christian mystics did not touch the fundamental split between spiritual equality and social inequality. The right of men to dominate women, both in the church and in society, was not questioned. The celibate woman simply tried to carve out a sphere of spiritual autonomy within her interior life, at most exercised covertly within the walls of the convent.[22]

Reformation theology did not fundamentally change the terms of this discussion of women's subjugated social status vis-à-vis her equality in a male-identified *imago*-Christ. The most important shift in the Reformation was the abolition of celibacy as a superior religious option for women and as a requirement for ordination for men. Since all Protestant women and men were to be married, this theoretically ended the discussion about the possible liberation of the celibate woman from male control.

Protestantism inherited from its medieval forebears the belief that woman was included in the divine image and in redemption in Christ. Luther entertains a distinction between woman's prelapsarian and lapsarian condition. In unfallen Eden woman was not under male domination, but was equal in status and shared with Adam domination over the lower creatures. The fall, however, in which woman had a greater fault, was a degeneration of this original equality. Women were placed under male domination in the family and excluded from public leadership.

This male domination in the fall cannot be construed, for Luther, as male sin, to be changed by Christian society. It now expresses God's ordained will as punisher of sin. Like the state, it is a permanent feature of the temporal world as it is now. Luther leaves no room for a radical social interpretation of women's prelapsarian equality. Moreover, Luther is inconsistent even in his views of prelapsarian equality. As Jane Dempsey Douglass shows in her essay, he also construes women as unequal in nature and confined to the domestic realm even in Paradise.

Calvin is a cleaner and more logical thinker, as always, than Luther. For him women's spiritual equality as image of God, as well as their equal depravity before God in sin, is differentiated from their social status as subjects of male authority in the family, society and the church. Before God, women stand in exactly the same spiritual status as men, created in the image of God, deserving of damnation as sinners and gratuitously elected by God's grace. Women's subjugated status in family, society and church does not reflect any spiritual inferiority, but rather reflects God's ordained will for the social order. Women's eternal destiny does not free her, but rather directs her all the more diligently to accept her obedient subjugation to male authority in the temporal order as God's will.

But this differentiation between equality before God in the covenant of grace and the hierarchy of the social order does not prevent Calvin and Calvinists from slipping into language that suggests female 'natural' inequality. Nor did it prevent radical Calvinists, such as antinomian Anne Hutchinson or the men and women of the Society of Friends, from suggesting that equality in Christ overcomes subjugation of women in the church. These radical Puritans believed that converted women have been restored to spiritual equality and can exercise authority in the church as preachers and prophets.

Now, however, these spiritually liberated women usually were also married women. Thus the struggle over the liberating social consequences of restored spiritual status is renewed in the conflict between patriarchal and radical Puritans in seventeenth century England and New England. Yet, even these radical Puritans did not touch the basic assumption that the married woman was subject to her husband in the family. They only sought to allow a sphere of equality for her in the church as teacher and guide of souls.[23]

The Image and Gender in Modern Protestantism

Modern Protestantism inherited these Reformation developments, but it also incorporated major shifts in social philosophy that developed from the Enlightenment. The Protestant insistence on the historical sense of Scripture made metaphysical ideas about a disincarnate pre-existent state of the soul unacceptable. It was assumed that the prelapsarian state was an actual historical period with two bodily primal parents.

This set the stage for a further naturalization of the Christian idea of the image of God as the possession of reason and sovereignty. In the Enlightenment and liberalism (influenced also by classical thought[24]) there develops the idea of an original State of Nature, prior to organized human society. All human persons were seen as equal in this original State of Nature. Later societies have departed from this original State of Nature and introduced unjust privilege and servility into relations between 'men.'

Revolutionary liberalism sought to reform or overthrow feudal systems of society based on aristocratic privilege and to create new civil societies modeled after original equality in the State of Nature. Redemption, as the restoration of the 'image,' has now become a social project that can be undertaken within history by human beings. It is no longer limited to a divine grace beyond natural human capacities that points to a post-historical, eschatological state, anticipated only in a spiritual way in the church. Liberalism laid the basis for modern social theologies of liberation.

However, most male liberals of the period did not consider women to be included in the 'rights of men' that are to be restored in the new democratic civil society. They continued to assume that reason and sovereignty were capacities restricted to males. They also did not include slaves, children and propertyless men. They continued the patriarchal assumption that the male head of family was the corporate representative of human personhood, for himself and his family.

However, liberalism would lay the basis for the feminist demand for women to be included in civil rights as autonomous persons. Movements for the abolition of slavery and for universal manhood suffrage promoted the extension of civil rights to all adult males. These civil rights movements expressed an increasing individualism of modern social thought. Those traditionally classed as dependents under the male head of family emerged to claim autonomous personhood and civil standing.

Nineteenth century romanticism represents diverse forms of reactions against the threats to traditional corporate society posed by liberal rationalism and democratic individualism. In contrast to the androcentric, unitary model of human nature, defined as reason and moral will, posed by liberalism, romanticism revived belief in diverse human types; by race, social class and gender. Nineteenth century Western thought began to stress the different and 'opposite' natures of men and women. Men were rational and active; women were emotional and passive. With the secularization of public society and the privatization of religion, increasingly women were assigned primacy in religious piety and morality. Men were thought of as more naturally 'secular,' needing to be 'uplifted' by the piety and moral suasion of women.

These shifts in gender image and role renewed, in naturalized form, the Western Christian patterns of Mariology and the feminization of Christ. Women come to be seen as the more naturally 'Christlike' gender, suited by nature to moral purity (asexuality), patient suffering and altruistic service to others. This suggested that women were, in Christian religious terms, the superior sex. But their moral and spiritual superiority unfitted them for the rough tasks of power. Women's virtue was transcendent, to be exercised in a sphere outside of history. These notions of woman's 'sacred' nature, too pure and delicate for the male secular world, became a stock argument against allowing women rights in public society.[25]

The German Protestant theologians who began to write in the period after the First World War reflected a deep sense of betrayal by the progressive movements of the immediate past. They sought to revive the strict doctrines of Reformation anthropology, with its stress on human depravity, over against optimistic faith in human goodness found in the Enlightenment, liberalism and romanticism. Yet they were also influenced by new social philosophies of their time, especially by Martin Buber's concept of I-Thou relationship.

Buber's philosophy sharply distinguished between subject-subject and subject-object relations. The latter were dehumanizing, while the former expressed mutual affirmation between persons. Buber's I-Thou concept overcame the division between individualism and society that deeply troubled European thinkers. It provided a model for the affirmation of both autonomy and community together. This would have a major effect on these theologians' interpretation of the image of God.

Neo-orthodox Protestant theologians approached the text of Genesis 1:27 with several anthropological presuppositions. They wished to deny the

Roman Catholic view that the image of God was only distorted by the Fall, not completely lost.[26] They insisted that fallen 'man' has lost entirely the capacity to know and to please God by 'his' natural capacities. He was dependent on God alone for salvation. This grace came to him by God's sovereign act, unrelated to human merit.

Protestant theologians also wanted to make a radical distinction between created and divine natures and to deny any shared 'being' between God and creatures. They made a sharp distinction between nature and history and between lower creatures and human beings. Buber's I-Thou gave them a model for interpreting the distinctive nature of humans within these anthropological presuppositions. What was distinctive about humans, separating them from animals and making them 'like God,' was their capacity for subject-subject relationships. The God-likeness of humans was defined as the *analogia relationis*, to be distinguished from Catholic ideas of *analogia entis*, or similarity of spiritual substance between humans and God.

Buber's concept of I-Thou relationship was one of equivalency of status between subjects. Patriarchal concepts of male and female as mind-body, ruler-ruled, were basically subject-object relations. Although Buber could assume that the Thou could be different from the I in nature (he imagined I-Thou relations between humans and trees and humans and God[27]), but as I and Thou there was an equivalency of inter-subjectivity. How was this equivalency of intersubjectivity to be understood in terms of human-God relations and in terms of inter-human male-female relations? (Protestants eliminated inter-subjectivity between human and non-human creatures as 'pagan' and un-Biblical).

Dietrich Bonhoeffer developed this idea of the image as *analogia relationis* in his treatise *Creation and Fall* in 1933. What is essential about human nature is that it is created and exists in relationship. God created humans free from servitude to nature and free for relationship to one another. This freedom has been lost in sin, but restored in Christ. Although the basis of this concept of the image as relationship comes from connecting the concept of 'image' with the primal human pair, Bonhoeffer never explores this freedom for others in terms of gender relations. Instead he habitually refers to this freedom for others as the relationship to the 'brother.' When he discusses the fall, it is clear that he thinks that women are essentially 'weaker' than men, and, for this reason, the serpent approached woman first.[28]

Emil Brunner, in his many writings on theological anthropology, creation and redemption, also develops this concept of the image as *analogia relationis*. Humans stand over against nature as the transcendent I against the world of objects. They image God as Subject who is capable of response to the divine Self. Humans also exist essentially as community. The primal pair of man and woman reflects this essential analogy between I-Thou relations with God and with one another as persons who can only exist in community. The two parts of Genesis 1:27, the image of God and male and female, are essentially interconnected. They are not two separate ideas, but aspects of the same idea.

Unlike Bonhoeffer, Brunner is more aware, and is troubled by, the equivalency of subjects suggested by the I-Thou concept. When speaking of humanity as community he too tends to substitute the term 'brother' as the essential 'other.' His concept of male-female relations is shaped by the accepted models of masculine-feminine complimentarity. Although he wishes to concede that women have greater rights to autonomy and personal development than traditionally granted to them by patriarchal society, he also wants women to stay in their traditionally feminine roles in relation to men. He fervently hopes that 'real women,' who understand their true feminine nature, will voluntarily submit to these roles, aiding men thereby to be their true masculine selves.[29]

It is Karl Barth who most clearly develops the interpretation of the image of God as *analogia relationis* in such a way as to make the God-creature hierarchy the essential analogue for male-female relations. Barth understands the relationship of God as the one who addresses 'man' and man as the one who responds to God's word (through Christ) as hierarchical. For Barth there can be no confusion between God as transcendent Subject and man as transcendent subject. God as the one who addresses man is wholly other. Man cannot respond out of his present fallen nature, but only in Christ, who responds to God for us.[30]

Barth constructs a series of hierarchically ordered I-Thou relationships: the relation of the Father to the Son in the Trinity; the relation of God the Father to Christ as incarnate Son; the relation of God and creatures. The male-female dyad becomes an analogue of each of these relationships. I Corinthians 11:3 is key for Barth's understanding of these analogical relationships of 'headship.' This means that Barth does not shrink from introducing an element of hierarchy into the Trinity, in the relationship of the Father to the Son.[31]

The Father is related to Christ as his 'head,' Christ, in turn, represents the headship of God over the church. The male-female analogy of Christ and church establishes, for Barth, gender relations as the basic image of the relation of God to redeemed creation. Woman images the creature in relation to its Creator and Redeemer. The relation of male and female as the human pair is thus ordered through this God-creature analogy. Given Barth's belief in the absolute gulf between the divine and the human, this establishes the most hierarchical model imaginable as analogue for male-female relations.

This suggests that women by themselves do not image God. For Barth, of course, this is a false way of putting the matter, since neither man nor woman can exist by themselves, but only as the inseparable human dyad. But, within this dyad, the male images God in relation to the creature, and the woman images the creature in relation to the Creator. Barth has here reestablished the patriarchal concept of corporate personality in which the male possesses the image of God for himself and for woman. She, in turn, images the creaturely in relation to God for the whole human dyad. Together the human pair images the God-man and the man-God relationship.

Against potential feminist critique, Barth attempts to insist that this is in no way an expression of female inferiority. As human woman is fully man's equal. She stands before God in exactly the same position as the man, as sinner redeemed by grace. The hierarchical ordering of male and female, in the family and in society, says nothing about male intrinsic superiority or female inferiority. It is a purely positive decree of God to manifest and express the covenant of creation between God and creatures. Man and woman are each to accept their place and roles in this ordering, not as personal merit or dismerit, but as submission to the divine will.[32]

More recent Protestant theologians, influenced by the feminist movement, have sought to save the concept of the image of God as *analogia relationis*, while overcoming Barth's hierarchical ordering of male and female as 'A' and 'B.' The evangelical theologian Paul Jewett, in his 1975 study, *Man as Male and Female*, sets up an analogy between the relationship of the Persons within the Trinity and the relations of man and woman in the basic human community. Both of these are seen as relations of egalitarian mutuality. There can be no hierarchy in God. The Persons in God share equally in divine being.

Jewett argues that, once it is acknowledged that woman is in no way inferior to man as a human being, then one can no longer argue on the basis of the analogy to God that the male-female relation is a hierarchical one.[33] However Jewett has failed to notice that the concept of *analogia relationis* essentially links the image of God with male and female in a way that makes the male-female relation analogous to the God-human relation. This God-human relation, for Jewett, is surely not a relationship of egalitarian mutuality.

Jürgen Moltmann, in his 1984–85 Gifford lectures, *God in Creation: A New Theology of Creation and the Spirit of God,* also seeks to reinterpret the interconnection of the image of God and male and female as *analogia relationis*. He also insists that the relation of the divine Persons in the Trinity is one of egalitarian mutuality and that this is the model for partnership between male and female in the human dyad. He goes beyond Jewett in attempting to make the God-creation relationship also one of mutuality and dynamic interaction.[34]

Yet, however much Moltmann might wish to make the God-creature relation interactive, rather than a one-sided, active-passive relationship, the divine and the human hardly stand on an equal footing for him. Thus he too has failed to deal fully with the basic problem of the *analogia relationis*, which is that it makes the male-female pair an analogue of the divine-human relationship. Unless one is to remove entirely any idea that the divine is superior to the human and the dominant side of the partnership, one cannot make the God-human relation analogous to the male-female relationship without making the male-female relationship hierarchical.

Thus the modern Protestant concept of the image of God as *analogia relationis* has not succeeded in including women in the image of God, despite its belief that it has done this. Instead it has reaffirmed the basic tendency of the Christian tradition to make the male 'like God' vis-à-vis the woman who represents the creaturely in relation to God.

5. Gender and Human Nature in Feminist Anthropology

Christian feminist anthropology has taken for granted the claims of recent Christian theology that Genesis 1:27 is an egalitarian text in which woman, equally with man, is the image of God. It has also assumed that Gal. 3:28 parallels this modern individualistic reading of Gen. 1:27. However, these claims are, as it were, props for what is essentially a belief in woman's full and autonomous humanness that derives from modern feminism. To paraphrase Mary Daly's famous statement about the authority of Jesus, "even if the Bible doesn't believe that women are equal with men, feminists do."[35]

The primary issue in feminist anthropology, secular as well as theological, is the question of how gender is related to humanness. Is there one essential human nature, and do women and men equally possess this generic humanness? Or does gender differentiation mean that each gender possesses a distinct and different kind of human nature? This feminist discussion has been shaped by the modern ambiguities between the rationalist unitary view and the romantic dualist view of human nature.

Anne Carr, in her 1988 book, *Transforming Grace: Christian Tradition and Women's Experience,* has done a helpful summary of the various options in feminist anthropology.[36] I have done a similar survey, in a broader historical context, in *Sexism and God-Talk: Toward a Feminist Theology.*[37] The rationalist and the romantic dualist anthropologies both pose a dilemma for women's claims to full, autonomous humanness. Thus feminism has basically sought to move beyond these two alternatives to a dialectical synthesis of the two.

The liberal tradition claims that all humans possess the same human nature. This human nature is defined by the possession of reason and moral conscience. The roots of this definition of humanness lie in the classical Christian tradition. Yet this tradition basically assigned reason, together with dominion over lower nature, to males. Women were thought of as having an inferior capacity for reason and moral will, at best, and to be incapable of exercising dominion.

The liberal tradition revealed its patriarchal origins when it denied civil rights to women on the grounds that the male head of family corporately represented this 'human nature' for those dependent on him. But, even when a further individualizing of civil personhood allowed women to be included in these 'rights of man,' this continued to be based on the patriarchal split of home and public society. Women's legal equality as a civil person in public society concealed her continued economic dependency in the home-work relation, exacerbated in industrialized societies. Thus liberal egalitarianism has been based on female assimilation into a male model humanness. It fails to provide the social basis for the real exercise of equality by women in practice, either in the family or in the work place.

Romantic complementarity surfaces the repressed side of the rationalist anthropology, the non-rational, sensual and intuitive psychic capacities. These have traditionally been assigned to women in a dependent and auxiliary relation to male rationality. Dualistic theories of anthropology see men as masculine and women as feminine as though they had entirely different and opposite natures. The feminine qualities became associated with a privatized piety and altruistic morality in a way that suggested that women were more naturally 'Christian' than men, but which also relegated these Christians to an otherworldly powerlessness.

Victorian and contemporary feminisms have sought to appropriate the dualist anthropology in two ways, in a reformist and in a separatist way. The reformist way assumes the claims of woman's superior morality, associated with her maternal role. It sees the male, public world as a fallen world of violence, injustice and moral corruption. Hence woman's maternal morality is seen as a base for a crusade into the public realm of government, business and war to reform it and uplift it to the higher morality of womanly love and care.[38]

Separatist feminism, by contrast, regards male violence and injustice as irreformable. In effect, men come to be regarded as an inferior species, lacking the full human capacities for love, care and mutuality. Males, by nature, tend to brutality, unfeeling egoism and violence. Women should withdraw into an all-female world and cease to relate to and compensate for this male inhumanity.[39]

Most contemporary feminists are not attracted to these traditions of female moral superiority in their cruder forms, although such ideas continue in more subtle forms. Basically, however, feminism has taken its stand on an expanded unitary view of human nature, possessed fully and equally by both men and women. The expanded unitary view brings into the definition of humanness the qualities of sensual and intuitive feeling, altruism and care, along with the capacities for reason and moral will. It seeks to synthesize the two sides of the complementary model in one androgynous humanness, possessed equally by women and men.

Many more subtle versions of this androgynous synthesis have been proposed. Some would argue that we need to stop labeling psychic qualities as masculine and feminine. The expanded Jungian concept of androgyny has been based on the tendency to make the masculine set dominant and the feminine set recessive in men, and *vice versa* in women. Many feminists see this Jungian view as preserving too much the gender dichotomies of the romantic complementarian tradition. They argue that we need to speak of the capacities for both activity and passivity, reason and feeling in both men and women, without labeling one side masculine and the other feminine.[40]

Recent brain study has suggested that both men and women possess the full range of human capacities. But brain development makes men dichotomize the two sides of their brain more, while women integrate these capacities in a more wholistic way.[41] It is not the purpose of this essay to advocate one of these views. My purpose is simply to indicate that most feminism today favors some version of an expanded unitary view of human nature, rejecting both a male-identified unitary anthropology and a dichotomous complementarity.

6. The Image of God and Feminist Hermeneutics.

Feminist theology starts with anthropology, rather than deducing male-female relations from an *a priori* definition of God. The definition of God as patriarchal male is presumed to be a projection by patriarchal males of their own self-image and roles, in relation to women and lower nature, upon God. Thus it is not 'man' who is made in God's image, but God who has been made in man's image. This ideological critique of the image of God idea in Scripture and Christian tradition changes fundamentally the nature of the discussion.

A feminist reconstruction of the images of God thus starts by seeking a just and truthful anthropology. It then constructs images of God that will better manifest and promote the full realization of human potential for women and men. It assumes that all of our images of God are human projections. God in Godself is beyond human words and images, only partly and metaphorically expressed in any images.[42] The question is: what are worse projections that promote injustice and diminished humanness, and what are better projections that promote fuller humanness?

How does such a feminist view, that starts with human experience and then constructs morally appropriate understandings of God, relate to Biblical authority? What is the authority of the Bible for feminist hermeneutics? I believe that the studies in this volume have basically indicated that the modern claim that the image of God is an egalitarian concept cannot be substantiated as an accurate account of the meaning of this text in Hebrew Scripture or in its New Testament interpretation.

The Christian tradition included women in the image of God only in an androcentric way. The androcentric character of the concept of the image of God continues to bias even contemporary Protestant theologians who have attempted to use this idea to vindicate gender equality. Thus feminism has two options. Either we must discard the authority of the Bible altogether, or else we must claim the right to reinterpret Biblical ideas in a way that appropriates, not only changes in past tradition, but also new insights today as well.

The feminist view of hermeneutics cannot correspond either to classical Catholic or classic Protestant views of the relation of Scripture and tradition. The Catholic view believed that one must take into account both Scripture and the development of interpretation in tradition in deciding what a text means. But *de facto* this meant accepting an interpretation by the contemporary *Magisterium* that suited its purposes regardless of its historical accuracy to either Scripture or past tradition. This is the way Scripture is used in the Catholic magisterial documents with which we opened this essay.

Protestantism arose along with new methods of textual study of the Renaissance. It sought to undercut what it saw as bad traditions of the recent past by returning to the 'original' meaning of Scripture. It was assumed that Scripture in its original meaning was infallible, while tradition was fallible.

This theory was contradictory from its beginning, since the Christian tradition had originally developed by putting aside parts of Hebrew Scripture as no longer normative. Thus there has never been any way Christians can claim the whole Bible as equally normative without falling into unacknowledged contradictions.[43]

The historical-critical method, which was developed by Protestant scholars to discover and vindicate the 'original' meaning of the text, as the normative basis of its meaning, has, in fact, undermined the foundational thesis of the infallibility of the text. It has forced us to see the text in its original context, as part of assumptions and world views that we no longer share. Thus there has developed a largely unacknowledged split between Protestant Scriptural exegesis and Protestant theology.

As we have seen in this study, Protestant exegesis of the Gen. 1:27 text has made clear that the text did not connect the term 'image' with 'male and female.' The key idea of the term image is that of 'man' as representative of divine dominion, with this dominion exercised in practice by the male head of family. Yet modern Protestant theology has ignored these findings of historical exegesis and has pursued lines of interpretation that are the unacknowledged product of a long classical and modern Christian tradition of interpretation and reinterpretation.

Feminist hermeneutics cannot be controlled by either a Protestant concept of *sola Scriptura*, which has proved impossible to carry out in practice, or by a developmentalist idea of infallible Scripture and tradition. Rather we should be clear that all human constructs of thought are relative and fallible. We should attempt to gain clear and non-apologetic understanding of what ideas meant in their Scriptural context and in their various contexts in different periods of tradition. But we must also claim the authority to be new tradition-makers. This will not make our constructs infallible. But it will free us from false apologetics toward the past.

In our own reconstruction of key symbols, we must be rigorously truthful about the defects of the past. We must also be especially open to critique from those whose humanness has been most often diminished and denied. Our criterion for what is truthful is, finally, what is most ethically redemptive. We too will fail to express this vision fully, as all past traditions have failed to express it fully. But we must do for our times what they did for theirs; to seek our best understanding, open to that divine Spirit who is as much now as in the past.

(1989)

Christian Tradition and Feminist Hermeneutics   289

Notes

1. "Partners in the Mystery of Redemption: A Pastoral Response to Women's Concerns for Church and Society," The U.S. National Conference of Catholic Bishops, Washington, D.C., April, 1988.
2. Pope John Paul II. "The Dignity and Vocation of Women" (*Mulieris dignitatem*), Vatican, September 31, 1988.
3. "Declaration on the Question of the Admission of Women to the Ministerial Priesthood" (*Inter insigniores*), Vatican, October 15, 1976 (37).
4. Col. 1:15; also II Cor. 4:4.
5. The Pope's thought here seems similar to that found in Protestant theology, influenced by Buber's I-Thou philosophy. See below, pp. 280–282.
6. Op. cit., note 2.
7. Ibid., section 26.
8. Ephesians 5:32 refers to Christ as head of the church as model for husband-wife relations, but this analogy is never used for priest-laity relations in the New Testament. The term priest is not present in the New Testament as a term for a separate sacerdotal class.
9. This argument that men could symbolically represent either God or creatures, but women could only represent the creaturely side was expounded by Professor Peter Amiet, theologian of the Old Catholic Church, in an ecumenical consultation on the ordination of women, sponsored by the unit of "Men and Women in the Church" of the World Council of Churches, August 28–September 1, 1979, at Klingenthal, France (unpublished personal notes from the consultation).
10. "The Creation Epic," in *Religion in the Ancient Near East: Sumero-Akkadian Religious Texts and Ugaritic Epics*, Isaac Mendelsohn, ed. (New York: Liberal Arts Press, 1955), p. 35 (Tablet 4,137).
11. Ibid., p. 37 (Tablet 6,34).
12. See Samuel Noah Kramer, *History Begins at Sumer* (Garden City, NY: Doubleday, 1956), p. 104.
13. Raphael Patai, *Sex and Family in the Bible and the Middle East* (Garden City, NY: Doubleday, 1959).
14. This is the argument developed in the study comparing Ancient Near East and Hebrew views of divinity and gender by Judith Ochschorn, *Female Experience and the Nature of the Divine* (Bloomington, IN: Indiana University Press, 1981).
15. Gunnlaugur Jónsson, *The Image of God: Gen. 1:26–28 in a Century of Old Testament Research* (Stockholm: Almqvist and Wiksell, 1988).
16. Plato, *Timaeus, Dialogues of Plato*, vol. 2, B. Jewett, ed. (New York: Random House, 1937), p. 13 (29).
17. Ibid., p. 23 (42).
18. Philip Merlan, *From Plato to Neoplatonism* (The Hague: M. Nijhoff, 1960), 2nd ed.
19. Philo, "On the Creation of the World," *The Essential Philo*, Nahum Glatzer, ed.

(New York: Schocken, 1971); also Richard Baer, *Philo's Use of the Categories of Male and Female* (Leiden: Brill, 1970).

20. See Dennis MacDonald, *The Legend and the Apostle: The Battle for Paul in Story and Legend* (Philadelphia, PA: Westminster, 1983).

21. Ruth R. Liebowitz, "Women in the Service of Christ: The Dispute over an Active Apostolate for Women during the Counter-Reformation" in Rosemary R. Ruether and Eleanor McLaughlin, *Women of Spirit: Female Leadership in the Jewish and Christian Traditions* (New York: Simon and Schuster, 1979), pp. 131–152; also the study on the recent conflicts between the Sisters of Mercy of the Union and the Vatican: Madonna Kolbenschlag, *Authority, Community and Conflict* (Kansas City, MO: Sheed and Ward, 1986).

22. For a study of the ambiguities of this struggle for female autonomy within the monastic community vis-à-vis ecclesiastical authority, see Alison Weber, *Teresa of Avila and the Rhetoric of Femininity* (Princeton, NJ: Princeton University Press, 1990).

23. See Rosemary S. Keller, "New England Women: Ideology and Experience in First Generation Puritanism, 1630–1650," and Rosemary R. Ruether, "Women in Sectarian and Utopian Groups: Seventeenth Century Quakers" in Ruether and Keller, *Women and Religion in America: The Colonial and Revolutionary War Periods* (San Francisco, CA: Harper and Row, 1983), pp. 132–192, 260–262, 278–288.

24. Classical thought had its own concept of an original Golden Age, i.e. Hesiod's *Work and Days.* For the Enlightenment concept of the State of Nature, see Carl L. Becker, *The Heavenly City of the Eighteenth Century Philosophers* (New Haven, CT: Yale University Press, 1932), pp. 33–70.

25. See, for example, Ann Douglas, *The Feminization of American Culture* (New York: Avon, 1977).

26. Thomas Aquinas, *Summa Theologica,* Question 85, arts. 1–6.

27. Martin Buber, *I and Thou* (New York: Scribners, 1958) p. 6.

28. Dietrich Bonhoeffer, *Creation and Fall: A Theological Interpretation of Gen. 1–3* (1937) (London: SCM Press, 1959), pp. 33–38, 76.

29. Emil Brunner, *The Christian Doctrine of Creation and Redemption* (Philadelphia, PA: Westminster, 1952), pp. 55–68; see also *The Divine Imperative* (Philadelphia, PA: Westminster, 1957), pp. 373–380.

30. Karl Barth, *Christ and Adam: Man and Humanity in Romans 5* (New York: Macmillan, 1956).

31. Karl Barth, *Church Dogmatics,* III/1 (Edinburgh: T. & T. Clark, 1939), pp. 194–196, 472–473.

32. Ibid., III/4, pp. 169–171; see also Joann Ford, "Toward an Anthropology of Mutuality: A Critique of Karl Barth's Doctrine of Male-Female Order as A and B," Ph.D. dissertation, Northwestern University, June, 1984.

33. Paul K. Jewett, *Man as Male and Female: A Study in Sexual Relations from a*

Theological Point of View (Grand Rapids, MI: William B. Eerdmans Publishing Company, 1975), pp. 33–43.

34. Jürgen Moltmann, *God in Creation* (San Francisco, CA: Harper and Row, 1985), chapter 9.
35. Mary Daly, *Beyond God the Father: Toward a Philosophy of Women's Liberation* (Boston, MA: Beacon, 1973), p. 73.
36. San Francisco, CA: Harper and Row, 1988, pp. 117–133.
37. Boston, MA: Beacon, 1983, pp. 102–115.
38. See Carolyn Gifford, "Women in Social Reform Movements" in Rosemary R. Ruether and Rosemary S. Keller, *Women and Religion in America: The Nineteenth Century* (San Francisco, CA: Harper and Row, 1981), pp. 294–340.
39. This dualistic anthropology of separatist feminism is represented by Mary Daly's more recent books, such as *Pure Lust: Elemental Feminist Philosophy* (Boston, MA: Beacon, 1984).
40. See Ruether, *Sexism and God-talk*, pp. 109–115.
41. Unpublished article by James B. Ashbrook, "In the Image and Likeness of God: Male and Female"; also Beryl Lieff Benderly, *The Myth of Two Minds: What Gender Does and Doesn't Mean* (Garden City, NY: Doubleday, 1987).
42. Sallie McFague, *Metaphorical Theology: Models of God in Religious Language* (Philadelphia, PA: Fortress, 1982); also *Models of God: Theology for an Ecological, Nuclear Age* (Philadelphia, PA: Fortress, 1987).
43. New Testament and patristic Christianity, shaped by the Pauline dualism of Law and Gospel, relegated the Levitical codes to non-normative status. These have never been observed by any branch of historical Christianity. Since the observance of these codes would contradict the Pauline rejection of them, it is impossible for Christians to take the whole Bible, Old and New Testament, as equally normative.